THE ADIRONDACK READER

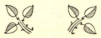

To St. Lawrence University, Candle in the Wilderness,
in recognition of its excellences and benefits,
not least of which is its fortunate proximity to Sunday Rock

THE
ADIRONDACK READER

Edited and with Introductions by
Paul Jamieson

THE ADIRONDACK MOUNTAIN CLUB, INC.
GLENS FALLS, NEW YORK

Second Edition

The Adirondack Mountain Club, Inc., Glens Falls, N.Y.

Library of Congress Cataloging in Publication Data

Main entry under title:

The Adirondack reader.

Includes index.

1. Adirondack Mountains (N.Y.)—Addresses, essays, lectures. I. Jamieson, Paul.

F127.A2A274 1983 974.7'53 82-20625

ISBN 0-935272-21-6 (cloth)

ISBN 0-935272-22-4 (paper)

Produced by Publishing Center for Cultural Resources, NYC
Manufactured in the United States of America

ACKNOWLEDGMENTS

Permission to use the following material is gratefully acknowledged:

Excerpts from unpublished letters of Kenneth Durant by permission of Mrs. Kenneth Durant. Lines from "All Men Are Pioneers" from *The Land of Unloving* by Lionel Wiggam, copyright © 1936, 1961, 1964 by Lionel Wiggam. Reprinted by permission of Macmillan Publishing Co., Inc. RICHES FOR THE ENTERPRISING From *The Story of Adirondac*, by Arthur H. Masten, 1923. Reprinted by permission of Arthur M. Crocker, executor. SCHOLAR'S UNWINDING and PHILOSOPHER'S HOLIDAY From *The Letters of William James*, copyright © 1920 by Atlantic Monthly Press. Reprinted by permission of Alexander R. James, executor. APPROACH TO THE MOUNTAINS From *Ad-i-ron-dac*, Mar.-Apr., 1955. Reprinted by permission of the Adirondack Mountain Club., Inc., and of the author. OLYMPIC VILLAGE From *Adirondack Life Magazine*, Jan.-Feb., 1980, copyright 1980 by *Adirondack Life*. All rights reserved. Reprinted by permission of *Adirondack Life* and of the author, George Christian Ortloff, and with acknowledgment also to Stephen C. Ortloff, co-author of *Lake Placid: The Olympic Years 1932-1980*, published by Macromedia, Inc., in 1976. CONFLICT OF INTERESTS From *Adirondack Life* Magazine, Jan.-Feb. 1981 copyright 1981 by *Adirondack Life*. All rights reserved. Reprinted by permission of *Adirondack Life* and of the author, Mason Smith. THE GOYD From the New York State *Conservationist*, Vol. 4, No. 2, October-November 1949. Reprinted by permission. SOURING OF THE DREAM From *Buttes Landing*, copyright 1961 by Jean Rikhoff.

Reprinted by permission of Barthold Fles, literary agent. THE STEVENSONS IN SARANAC Excerpt from Lloyd Osborne, *An Intimate Portrait of R. L. S.* Copyright 1923, 1924 by Charles Scribner's Sons; copyrights renewed. Reprinted with the permission of Charles Scribner's Sons. THE WAY OF THE LAKE From *An American Tragedy* by Theodore Dreiser. Copyright © 1925 by Horace Liveright, Inc. Copyright © 1926 by Theodore Dreiser. Copyright © 1953 by Helen Dreiser. Reprinted by arrangement with The New American Library, Inc., New York, New York. DEER IN THE STORM and THE YELLOW LADY-SLIPPERS From *One Man's Pleasure*, by Hugh Fosburgh, copyright © 1960 by Hugh Fosburgh. Reprinted by permission of the Estate of Hugh Fosburgh. THE VANISHED POND From *Bellefleur* by Joyce Carol Oates. Copyright © 1980 by Joyce Carol Oates, Inc. Reprinted by permission of the publisher, E. P. Dutton, Inc. A VISUAL HAPPENING From *Freedom in the Wilds* by Harold Weston. Copyright © 1971 by Harold Weston. Reprinted by permission of the Adirondack Trail Improvement Society, Inc. THE DISCOVERY OF LAKE TEAR From *Peaks and People of the Adirondacks* by Russell M. L. Carson. Copyright 1927; copyright renewed 1954 by the Adirondack Mountain Club, Inc. Reprinted by permission of the Adirondack Mountain Club, Inc. DISCOVERY From "Adirondack Trails" by Paul Schaefer, *The Living Wilderness*, Volume 29/Number 90 Autumn 1965. © 1966 by The Wilderness Society. Reprinted by permission. WHITEOUT From an article by Laura Viscome in the Lake Placid *News*, January 8, 1981. Reprinted by permission of the author. WILLIAM WEST DURANT AND THE LUXURY CAMP From *Township 34*, by Harold K. Hochschild. Copyright 1952 by Harold K. Hochschild. Reprinted by permission of The Adirondack Museum. THE FINEST TRIO From *Durant*, by Craig Gilborn, copyright © 1981 by The Adirondack Museum. Reprinted by permission of the author and of North Country Books, Sylvan Beach, N.Y. CAMP CHRONICLES From *Camp Chronicles*, by Mildred P. Stokes Hooker. Reprinted by permission of the executor of the Estate of Mildred P. S. Hooker. LOON LAKE From *Loon Lake*, by E. L. Doctorow. Copyright © 1980 by E. L. Doctorow. Reprinted by permission of Random House, Inc. MRS. CHASE From *The Heydays of the Adirondacks* by Maitland C. DeSormo. Copyright © 1974 by Maitland C. DeSormo. Reprinted by permission of the author and of Adirondack Yesteryears, Inc. THE HERMIT OF COLD RIVER From *The Adirondack High Peaks and the Forty-Sixers*, edited by Grace L. Hudowalski. Copyright 1970 by The Adirondack Forty-Sixers. Reprinted by permission of A. G. Dittmar and Grace Hudowalski. MERRY CHRISTMAS From *Just About Everything*, by William Chapman White, originally in the New York *Herald Tribune*, December 25, 1952, © I. H. T. Corporation. Used with permission. VIBRATIONS From *Vibrations* by George A. Woods. Copyright © 1970 by George A. Woods. Reprinted by permission of Harper & Row, Publishers, Inc. DECLARATION OF INDEPENDENCE, SPIRIT OF 1976 From *Small Town* by Sloan Wilson. © 1978 by Sloan Wilson. Reprinted by permission of the author and of Arbor House Publishing Co. THE LAND ETHIC From *Fifth Conference on the Adirondack Park*, copyright © St. Lawrence University 1980; with the permission of Allen P. Splete and Warder H. Cadbury. HERBERT CLARK, MOUNTAINEER From "Herbert Clark," by Robert Marshall, *High Spots*, October 1933. Reprinted by permission of George Marshall. FOURTEEN IN ONE From "Adirondack Peaks" by Robert Marshall, *High Spots*, October 1932. Reprinted by permission of George Marshall. THE WOODS Reprinted by permission from *Adirondack Life* Magazine, Mar.-Apr. 1981, and Thomas Kalinowski. Copyright © 1981 by *Adirondack Life*. All rights reserved. THE RIVER From *Old Hollywood* by Lewis L. Fisher. Copyright © 1980 by St. Lawrence County Historical Association. Reprinted by permission of the author. WHITE WATER DERBY From *Appalachia*, June 1968. Copyright © 1968 by the Appalachian Mountain Club. Reprinted by permission. SOME USES OF THE CANOE From *Adirondac* Mar-Apr 1969, copyright © 1969 by the Adirondack Mountain Club, Inc. Reprinted with permission. HEAVY WATER Reprinted by permission from *Adirondack Life* Magazine, May-June 1981, and Clyde H. Smith. Copyright © 1981 by *Adirondack Life*. All rights reserved. THE UPPER HUDSON From *Flow East* by John M. Kauffmann. Copyright © 1973 by John M. Kauffmann. Reprinted by permission of the publisher, McGraw-Hill Book Company. Epigraph by W. C. White from *Adirondack Country*, copyright © 1954 by William Chapman White, 1967 by Ruth M. White. Reprinted by permission of Alfred A. Knopf, Inc. PROSPECTS From *The High Peaks of the Adirondacks*, by Robert Marshall, published by the Adirondack Mountain Club, Inc. 1922. Reprinted by permission of George Marshall. EXPLORING INDIAN PASS From a letter by William Charles Macready. Reprinted by courtesy of The New-York Historical Society. WINSLOW HOMER IN THE ADIRONDACKS From "Homer in the Adirondacks" by James Fosburgh, copyright © ARTnews 1963 Portfolio. TO A WATERFOWL Abridged from *A Sharing of Joy*, © 1963 by Martha Reben. Reprinted by permission of Harcourt Brace Jovanovich, Inc. SCOTT POND From *Ad-i-ron-dac*, May-June 1960. Reprinted by permission of the Adirondack Mountain Club, Inc. CABIN VERSUS CITY From *Woodswoman* by Anne LaBastille. Copyright © 1976 by Anne LaBastille. Reprinted by permission of the publisher, E. P. Dutton.

Printed on Finch Opaque 50 lb. vellum finish cream white,
manufactured in Glens Falls, New York,
from trees grown in the Adirondack woodlands
of Finch, Pruyn & Company, Inc.

Preface

Here at the northwest corner of the Adirondacks the Raquette cascades into the St. Lawrence valley from its sources deep within the woods and mountains. Along the river runs a road which for generations has been "the way in" for people of the valley. At the base of the hills the road crosses rapids in the river and begins its winding ascent into South Woods.

The river crossing is not our only bounding mark between civilization and the woods. Beside the road is a tall rock with a plaque beside it reading:

SUNDAY ROCK
Preserved by
The Sunday Rock Association
1925

Well over a century ago, while geologists were explaining the big rock as a random glacial deposit, people of the valley found another meaning in it. Placed as it was, between farms and the wilderness, it must be Sunday Rock, for Sunday with its religious rites and moral restraints and imperatives stands for civilized man.

No one knows for sure who first called it Sunday Rock. Maybe it was the river-drivers from logging camps above. Maybe it was the circuit rider who held Sunday services in the little schoolhouse of Three Falls (now South Colton). Or maybe it was the merchant of the general store who went fishing on Sunday. But everyone knew the rock's effect on people. As you passed it, going south, primitive instincts of play and disorder arose. Deacon Sackrider, putting aside his go-to-meeting coat, said, "Stay there, Deacon, till I need you again." Hunters winked, drew out a bottle, and said, "No law beyond this rock, boys." A wagon load of college students on holiday launched into their repertoire of songs. Schoolchildren passing the rock wished that they lived on the other side where you didn't have to go to church on Sundays. And if you wonder at the number of clergymen and professors who are discovered roaming about in the woods in the following pages, is it not because they could unbend there?

With motor cars the trip into South Woods that had once taken a full day or more could be made in an hour or two, and the passing of the rock lost some of its leisurely ceremony. People grew a little vague about the shape, size, and color of the boulder. But no one forgot its meaning. In fact, the more civilization spread in the valley, the richer became the meaning of the rock. South of it was freedom, sport, sanctuary, exploration, health, exhilaration, or communion in a land where no day has any special significance, where the sun, the seasons, and the wayward will replace watch, calendar, and schedules. There is no Sunday beyond the rock. For that matter, there is no Monday, or any other workday, either. Days in the woods are days beyond time.

Public sentiment has twice thwarted designs on Sunday Rock by the state highway department. Originally the rock stood in the middle of the road, forcing traffic to one side. In 1925 road builders threatened to dynamite it for a concrete highway to replace the old dirt road. An avalanche of protest arose. Local weeklies and the Watertown *Daily Times* took up the cause. So did the Brooklyn *Eagle*. The Sunday Rock Association was formed, and dollars poured in from far and near—enough to pay for moving the rock to the east side of the road, embedding it in concrete, engraving a plaque, and publishing an eloquent booklet about its legend by Dr. Charles Leete, Potsdam town historian. South of Sunday Rock, he wrote, "The river, the brooks, the ponds, the mountains, and the trees, the fleet deer, the rushing trout, the wild cat and the bear reigned supreme. It was their land and there was no Sunday there."

Again, when the highway was widened in 1965, the rock was moved to a rest area designed for permanence on the west side of the road. So Sunday Rock can't be explained simply as the random dropping of a glacier. Solicitude, preservation, and immunity from the graffiti that disfigure other big rocks along state route 56 have firmly established it in the folk life of the North Country.

This is a book about the land on the other side of Sunday Rock, where some make their year-long homes and many more come as visitors or summer residents for release from the world of clocks and deadlines. A big land of six million acres, the Adirondack Park is the largest of all state and national parks save two in outsized Alaska. Larger than New Hampshire, it is about the size of Massachusetts and Rhode Island together. The Blue Line on state maps encircles an uplift of 2,300 lakes and ponds; over 30,000 miles of brooks, creeks, and rivers; and about 2,000 peaks prominent enough to figure among Easterners as "mountains," culminating, in the northeast sector, in over forty "high peaks" from 4,000 feet to a mile in elevation. Nearly two-fifths of the park is state-owned forest preserve. Another third consists of large corporate timberlands and preserves of the wealthy. The remainder is parceled out among small owners. Save for the hamlets and villages, the private land is devoted chiefly to forestry and open-space recreation. Mining and agriculture account for a small, diminishing fraction. The woods cover nearly all this land with a mantle of mystery.

Twice the woods have had to be saved by drastic measures. The first saving, against lumber barons and timber thieves, consisted of the creation of a forest preserve (1885) and of the Adirondack Park (1892); and an amendment to the state constitution (1894) reading: "The lands of the State, now owned or hereafter acquired, constituting the forest preserve as fixed by law, shall be forever kept as wild forest lands. They shall not be leased, sold, or exchanged, or be taken by any corporation, public or private, nor shall the timber thereon be sold, removed, or destroyed." Article XIV, Section 1, remains unchanged to this day.

The second saving began in 1970 and is still going on. This time the major threat came from developers of large-scale communities of second homes. But the 181 recommendations of the Temporary Study Commission on the Future of the Adirondack Park are far more comprehensive than a simple regulation of second-home development. Now being carried into effect by the State Department of Environmental Conservation and the Adirondack Park Agency, they amount to the most ambitious plan of stewardship ever applied to so large and diverse an area. State land is classified in five categories according to its characteristics and capacity to withstand use. Sixteen wilderness areas totaling over one million acres are designated for the highest degree of protection against the creeping tendency to domesticate the woods. The most bitterly contested part of the plan is the classification and zoning of the 3,700,000 acres of private land in the park in order to preserve open space while safeguarding the economy of the 125,000 permanent residents. Many natives are not convinced that the plan will achieve this fine-edged balance.

Adirondack literature is an unparalleled mirror of the relations of Americans to the woods. As William James entitled one of his books *The Varieties of Religious Experience*, so might the *Reader* be subtitled *The Varieties of Wilderness Experience* or *Wilderness as States of Mind*. I considered calling attention to this unifying theme by entering the latter phrase in the index but gave up the idea when I found myself paging almost every piece in the anthology. The diversity of attitude and experience is great partly because of the natural diversity of the human mind and soul and partly because of the cultural climate of the times: from Samuel de Champlain and Father Isaac Jogues in the first half of the seventeenth century to Joyce Carol Oates and Anne LaBastille in the closing decades of the twentieth.

No other wilderness area of the country has received so much attention from writers and the general public for so long a period of time. "By the 1880s," remarks Roderick Nash in *Wilderness and the American Mind*, "more had been written about the Adirondack country than any other wilderness area of the United States." Even as the opening of the West drew attention elsewhere, the flow of interest in the Adirondacks continued without interruption. The generation since World War II is particularly rich in the essay and the novel. In the last four years *Small Town*, *Bellefleur*, and *Loon Lake*, by three leading contemporary novelists, vindicate Longstreth's 1917 prediction that the Adirondack region would become of increasing value to American writers.

Much Adirondack writing concerns the timeless values of the woods; inasmuch as time is involved, it is the cyclical rhythms of day and night, growth and decay, revolution of the seasons. But the linear time of history also obtrudes in dramatic stories of conflict and in heated debate. First, Indian tribes fought over the region as a hunting ground; then the French and the British, with their Indian allies, seeking empire in America; next, the American colonies and the British. Once the question of nationhood and borders was settled, conflict shifted to ideas and values. Confreres of the Sunday Rock Association, who would preserve the woods for what they are in themselves, are opposed by those who would exploit them for gain. The latter can cite Christendom as justification. The Lord's injunction to Adam, to subdue the earth and have dominion over every living thing, was addressed to a primitive society; but Europe and America have embraced it eagerly, through all stages of development, as a warrant for exploitation. A land ethic persisting through two thousand years has yielded grudgingly to those who, as early as the 1840s in America, were feeling their way toward a new ethic best formulated in the present century by Aldo Leopold: the interdependence of all beings and man's role as steward of the land rather than as possessor and exploiter. There are spokesmen on both sides in Adirondack writing, and many shades of ambivalence are also voiced in the following pages.

This is a book about what Americans have sensed, felt, and thought about our unique heritage of wilderness. "Out of the woods we came, and to the woods we must return, at frequent intervals, if we are to redeem ourselves from the vanities of civilization."

Canton, New York
1982

Contents

x IMPERISHABLE FRESHNESS

Observations

[This] Country..., called by the Indians Couchsachrage, which signifies the Dismal Wilderness or Habitation of Winter, is a triangular, high mountainous Tract, very little known to the Europeans; and although a hunting Ground of the Indians, yet either not much known to them, or, if known, very wisely by them kept from the Knowledge of the Europeans. It is said to be a broken unpracticable Tract: I own I could never learn any Thing about it. *Thomas Pownall*, 1784

I have not forgotten that my business is with geology. But while this is true, I would remember that in a community like ours, many individuals require recreation during certain seasons; and while I am occupying time and space in details of this kind, I am also making known a new field for relaxation from business—one which has peculiar advantages and many resources for restoring health and spirits, such as are unknown at the more fashionable watering places. *Ebenezer Emmons, state geologist for the Adirondack region*, 1842

New York has her wilderness within her own borders; and though the sailors of Europe are familiar with the soundings of her Hudson, and Fulton long since invented the steamboat on its waters, an Indian is still necessary to guide her scientific men to its headwaters in the Adirondac country. *Henry David Thoreau*, 1848

[The Adirondack forest] should remain, as far as possible, in its primitive condition, at once a museum for the instruction of the student, a garden for the recreation of the lover of nature, and an asylum where indigenous tree, and humble plant that loves the shade, and fish and fowl and four-footed beast may dwell and perpetuate their kind, in the enjoyment of such imperfect protection as the laws of a people jealous of restraint can afford them.   *George Perkins Marsh*, 1864

Few fully understand what the Adirondack wilderness really is. It is a mystery even to those who have crossed and recrossed it by boats along its avenues—the lakes; and on foot through its vast and silent recesses. . . . Though the woodman may pass his lifetime in some section of the wilderness, it is still a mystery to him.   *Verplanck Colvin*, 1879

Judging by the effect already produced upon the water supply in our rivers by forest destruction in this State, we believe that there is no exaggeration in stating that the future prosperity and even the commercial existence of this State are bound up with these forests and that, unless we are prepared to abandon the natural advantages which made New York what it is, we must stop, and stop at once, any further destruction of the Adirondack forests. *Charles Sprague Sargent*, 1883

The Adirondack region is so full of beauty, so rich in historical association that it is easy to believe that as a fountainhead of literature it will be of increasing value to American writers.   *T. Morris Longstreth*, 1917

I am glad I shall never be young without wild country to be young in. Of what avail are forty freedoms without a blank spot on the map?   *Aldo Leopold*, 1945

None [other state and national parks] has the unique development that is Adirondack history. Few have thriving villages right next to the state woods and a permanent population that lives the year around with the woods at the back door, setting a pattern of life unique in America. It is that inseparable connection between the Adirondack woods, open on all sides, and the Adirondack people that makes the area what it is. *William Chapman White*, 1954

When an American looks for the meaning of his past, he seeks it not in ancient ruins, but more likely in mountains and forests, by a river, or at the edge of the sea. *Outdoor Recreation Resources Review Commission*, 1962

If the Adirondacks are to be saved, time is of the essence. *Harold K. Hochschild*, 1970, *in The Future of the Adirondack Park*

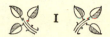

1

The Storied Path

This fair and most beautiful lake [Champlain] *is the bloodiest lake in the history of our land.*

Lincoln Barnett

BEFORE THE COMING of white men Indian tribes knew the Adirondacks as a hunting ground, but they left no written records. The story therefore begins with the discovery of Lake Champlain. In 1609 Samuel de Champlain voyaged up the St. Lawrence and Richelieu rivers into the lake now bearing his name and set foot on Adirondack soil near Ticonderoga. Confronting Iroquois warriors there, he fired the first shot in a series of conflicts that lasted for two centuries. While the wilderness to the west slumbered on, the Champlain valley and its Lake George extension resounded to war cries, screams of tortured victims, musketry, and cannonading.

It was a prize to contend for. With a few portages the long waterway made a relatively easy path between the St. Lawrence and the Hudson. The power that controlled it was in position to control much else. The Iroquois claimed it and, both before and after the coming of white men, used it for raids on enemy tribes in Canada. The Algonquins and Hurons in turn made forays southward in their birchbark canoes. By joining in one of these retaliatory raids, Champlain incurred for the French the enmity of the Iroquois. The conflict over the waterway intensified as the French entered it and as the Iroquois got firearms from Dutch settlers on the Hudson.

[5]

In 1690 the English began to dispute ownership with the French, and the colonial ambitions of two great powers turned the valley into a path of empire. For the next seventy years, as Hurons and Algonquins sided with the French and Iroquois with the English, both savage and chivalrous warfare raged through the valley.

In the final phase of the French and Indian War, New France lost her forts on Lake Champlain, and the English victory was completed in Canada in 1760. The valley had a short interval of peace. But the settlers lured to it then were soon uprooted by a new phase of the conflict, this time between rebel colonies and the Crown. After two more wars the issue of ownership was finally settled in 1814 by the American fleet, commanded by Thomas Macdonough, in the naval Battle of Plattsburg.

The beauty of the valley adds luster to the events of those two hundred years. History blends into romance. The names of the principal actors—Champlain, Father Jogues, General Johnson, Hendrick, Lord Howe, Duncan Campbell, Major Rogers, Montcalm, Ethan Allen, Benedict Arnold, and others—become half legendary. Flawed heroes though most of them were, they seem to have understood that their surroundings called for gestures out of the ordinary. Through "our dark unstoried woods" they made a storied path.

Storytellers worthy of the men and the events appeared in the historian Francis Parkman and the novelist James Fenimore Cooper. Both had the spatial imagination to make us see men in action on trail and lake. The spirit of place is strong in all they wrote about the Champlain-Lake George valley. Cooper preceded Parkman in discovering the literary possibilities of wilderness, but Parkman excelled him in vivid scene painting. Take, for instance, the historian's account of a French expedition in 1666 from Quebec against the Mohawk villages of central New York, by way of Lake George: "Amid this gorgeous euthanasia of the dying season, the three hundred boats and canoes trailed in long procession up the lake, threaded the labyrinth of the Narrows—that sylvan fairyland of tufted islets and quiet waters—and landed at length where Fort William Henry was afterward built."

Together with Father Jogues, Cooper and Parkman reflect three ways of interpreting the American forest. For the Jesuit missionary the forest is evil, breeding savagery and heathenism. For Cooper it is benign, favoring not only the strong but the well intentioned. Rugged, generous, self-reliant, the woodsman Leatherstocking owes much of his character to the forest, as well as his dignity and good fortune. His affairs prosper as long as he shuns the settlements. In *The Last of the Mohicans*, one of the five Leatherstocking tales, the scout Hawkeye is this hero in the full resourcefulness of maturity, the model by whom sportsmen of the nineteenth century measured their Adirondack guides.

The Lake George sections of Cooper's novel influenced the young Francis Parkman in the choice of his life work, "the history of the American forest" as he liked to call it. But Parkman's wilderness is more complex than Cooper's. It is a mixture of good and evil, beauty and savagery—a place where heroes are made and indifferently broken. Lord Howe, Parkman's ideal man, learns from the forest the discipline of the martial virtues. But it is the forest too that breaks him, at the moment when the fate of an army rests on his leadership.

Parkman is not only the unrivaled historian of wilderness warfare; he is a prose-poet of the forest itself. Ranging the wilds of northern New York and New Hampshire on vacation while a student at Harvard in the early 1840s, he became "haunted with wilderness images day and night." His description of the primeval forest is a good introduction to the storied path:

"Deep recesses where, veiled in foliage, some wild shy rivulet steals with timid music through breathless caves of verdure; gulfs where feathered crags rise like castle walls, where the noonday sun pierces with keen rays athwart the torrent, and the mossed arms of fallen pines cast wavering shadows on the illumined foam; pools of liquid crystal turned emerald in the reflected green of impending woods; rocks on whose rugged front the gleam of sunlit waters dances in quivering light; ancient trees hurled headlong by the storm, to dam the raging stream with their forlorn and savage ruin; or the stern depths of immemorial forests, dim and silent as a cavern, columned with innumerable trunks, each like an Atlas upholding its world of leaves, and sweating perpetual moisture down its dark and channelled rind—some strong in youth, some grisly with decrepit age, nightmares of strange distortion, gnarled and knotted with wens and goitres; roots intertwisted beneath like serpents petrified in an agony of contorted strife; green and glistening mosses carpeting the rough ground, mantling the rocks, turning pulpy stumps to mounds of verdure, and swathing fallen trunks as, bent in the impotence of rottenness, they lie outstretched over knoll and hollow, like mouldering reptiles of the primeval world, while around, and on and through them, springs the young growth that battens on their decay—the forest devouring its own dead; or, to turn from its funereal shade to the light and life of the open woodland, the sheen of sparkling lakes, and mountains basking in the glory of the summer noon, flecked by the shadows of passing clouds that sail on snowy wings across the transparent azure."

CHAMPLAIN
FRANCIS PARKMAN

The canoes advanced, the river widening as they went. Great islands appeared, leagues in extent—Isle à la Motte, Long Island, Grande Isle; channels where ships might float and broad reaches of water stretched between them, and Champlain entered the lake which preserves his name to posterity. Cumberland Head was passed, and from the opening of the great channel between Grande Isle and the main he could look forth on the wilderness sea. Edged with woods, the tranquil flood spread southward beyond the sight. Far on the left rose the forest ridges of the Green Mountains, and on the right the Adirondacks—haunts in these later years of amateur sportsmen from counting-rooms or college halls. Then the Iroquois made them their hunting-ground; and beyond, in the valleys of the Mohawk, the Onondaga, and the Genesee, stretched the long line of their five cantons and palisaded towns.

At night they encamped again. The scene is a familiar one to many a tourist; and perhaps, standing at sunset on the peaceful strand, Champlain saw what a roving student of this generation has seen on those same shores, at that same hour—the glow of the vanished sun behind the western mountains, darkly piled in mist and shadow along the sky; near at hand, the dead pine, mighty in decay, stretching its ragged arms athwart the burning heaven, the crow perched on its top like an image carved in jet; and aloft, the nighthawk, circling in his flight, and, with a strange whirring sound, diving through the air each moment for the insects he makes his prey.

The progress of the party was becoming dangerous. They changed their mode of advance and moved only in the night. All day they lay close in the depth of the forest, sleeping, lounging, smoking tobacco of their own raising, and beguiling the hours, no doubt, with the shallow banter and obscene jesting with which knots of Indians are wont to amuse their leisure. At twilight they embarked again, paddling their cautious way till the eastern sky began to redden. Their goal was the rocky promontory where Fort Ticonderoga was long afterward built. Thence, they would pass the outlet of Lake George and launch their canoes again on that Como of the wilderness, whose waters, limpid as a fountain-head, stretched far southward between their flanking mountains. Landing at the future site of Fort William Henry, they would carry their canoes through the forest to the river Hudson and, descending it, attack perhaps some outlying town of the Mohawks. In the next century this chain of lakes and rivers became the grand highway of savage and civilized war, linked to memories of momentous conflicts.

The allies were spared so long a progress. On the morning of the twenty-ninth of July, after paddling all night, they hid as usual in the forest on the western shore, apparently between Crown Point and Ticonderoga. The warriors stretched themselves to their slumbers, and Champlain, after walking till nine or ten o'clock through the surrounding woods, returned to take his repose on a pile of spruce boughs. Sleeping, he dreamed a dream wherein he beheld the Iroquois drowning in the lake; and, trying to rescue them, he was told by his Algonquin friends that they were good for nothing and had better be left to their fate. For some time past he had been beset every morning by his superstitious allies, eager to learn about his dreams; and, to this moment, his unbroken slumbers had failed to furnish the desired prognostics. The announcement of this auspicious vision filled the crowd with joy, and at nightfall they embarked, flushed with anticipated victories.

It was ten o'clock in the evening when, near a projecting point of land, which was probably Ticonderoga, they descried dark objects in motion on the lake before them. These were a flotilla of Iroquois canoes, heavier and slower than theirs, for they were made of oak bark [probably a mistake; the Iroquois canoes were usually of elm bark. The paper-birch was used wherever it could be had. Parkman's note]. Each party saw the other, and the mingled war-cries pealed over the darkened water. The Iroquois, who were near the shore, having no stomach for an aquatic battle, landed and, making night hideous with their clamors, began to barricade themselves. Champlain could see them in the woods, laboring like beavers, hacking down trees with iron axes taken from the Canadian tribes in war and with stone hatchets of their own making. The allies remained on the lake, a bowshot from the hostile barricade, their canoes made fast together by poles lashed across. All night they danced with as much vigor as the frailty of their vessels would permit, their throats making amends for the enforced restraint of their limbs. It was agreed on both sides that the fight should be deferred till daybreak; but meanwhile a commerce of abuse, sarcasm, menace, and boasting gave unceasing exercise to the lungs and fancy of the combatants—"much," says Champlain, "like the besiegers and besieged in a beleaguered town."

As day approached, he and his two followers put on the light armor of the time. Champlain wore the doublet and long hose then in vogue. Over the doublet he buckled on a breastplate and probably a back-piece, while his thighs were protected by cuisses of steel and his head by a plumed casque. Across his shoulder hung the strap of his bandoleer, or ammunition-box; at his side was his sword and in his hand his arquebuse. Such was the equipment of this ancient Indian-fighter, whose exploits date eleven years before the landing of the Puritans at Plymouth and sixty-six years before King Philip's War.

Each of the three Frenchmen was in a separate canoe, and, as it grew light, they kept themselves hidden, either by lying at the bottom or covering themselves with an Indian robe. The canoes approached the shore, and all landed without opposition at some distance from the Iroquois, whom they presently could see filing out of their barricade—tall, strong men, some two hundred in number, the boldest and fiercest warriors of North America. They advanced through the forest with a steadiness which excited the admiration of Champlain. Among them could be seen three chiefs, made conspicuous by their tall plumes. Some bore shields of wood and hide, and some were covered with a kind of armor made of tough twigs interlaced with a vegetable fibre supposed by Champlain to be cotton.

The allies, growing anxious, called with loud cries for their champion and opened their ranks that he might pass to the front. He did so and, advancing before his red companions in arms, stood revealed to the gaze of the Iroquois, who, beholding the warlike apparition in their path, stared in mute amazement. "I looked at them," says Champlain, "and they looked at me. When I saw them getting ready to shoot their arrows at us, I levelled my arquebuse, which I had loaded with four balls, and aimed straight at one of the three chiefs. The shot brought down two and wounded another. On this, our Indians set up such a yelling that one could not have heard a thunder-clap, and all the while the arrows flew thick on both sides. The Iroquois were greatly astonished and frightened to see two of their men killed so quickly, in spite of their arrow-proof armor. As I was reloading, one of my companions fired a shot from the woods, which so increased their astonishment that, seeing their chiefs dead, they abandoned the field and fled into the depth of the forest." The allies dashed after them. Some of the Iroquois were killed and more were taken. Camp, canoes, provisions, all were abandoned, and many weapons flung down in the panic flight. The victory was complete. . . .

Thus did New France rush into collision with the redoubted warriors of the Five Nations. Here was the beginning, and in some measure doubtless the cause, of a long suite of murderous conflicts, bearing havoc and flame to generations yet unborn. Champlain had invaded the tiger's den; and now, in smothered fury, the patient savage would lie biding his day of blood.

THE TORTURE TRAIL
Isaac Jogues

While voyaging in canoes up the St. Lawrence from Three Rivers to the Jesuit missions among the Hurons, Father Isaac Jogues (pronounced Saint Isaac by Pope Pius XI in 1930) and his party were captured on August 2, 1642, by Iroquois warriors of the Mohawk tribe. Along with Huron converts and two young French laymen serving with the missions, Jogues was conducted up the Richelieu River, Lake Champlain, and possibly Lake George (he was the first white man to visit Lake George, whether at this time or four years later, when he christened it "Lac St. Sacrement"), and then by forest trail to Ossernenon, first of the Mohawk villages, about thirty miles west of Albany.

We were twenty-two captives, without counting three Hurons killed on the spot. An old man, aged eighty years, having just received holy Baptism, said to the Hiroquois who were commanding him to embark: "It is no more for an old man like me to go and visit foreign countries; I can find death here, if you refuse me life." Hardly had he pronounced these words when they beat him to death.

So there we were, on the way to be led into a country truly foreign. Our Lord favored us with his Cross. It is true that, during thirteen days that we spent on that journey, I suffered in the body torments almost unendurable, and, in the soul, mortal anguish; hunger, the fiercely burning heat, the threats and hatred of those Leopards, the pain of our wounds—which, for not being dressed, became putrid even to the extent of breeding worms—caused us, in truth, much distress. But all these things seemed light to me in comparison with an inward sadness which I felt at the sight of our earliest and most ardent Christians of the Hurons. I had thought that they were to be the pillars of that rising Church, and I saw them become the victims of death. The ways closed for a long time to the salvation of so many peoples, who perish every day for want of being succored, made me die every hour, in the depth of my soul. It is a very hard thing, or rather very cruel, to see the triumph of the Demons over whole nations redeemed with so much love and paid for in the money of a blood so adorable.

Eight days after our departure from the shores of the great river of Saint Lawrence, we met two hundred Hiroquois who were coming in pursuit of the French and of the Savages our allies. At this encounter we were obliged to sustain a new shock. It is a belief among those Barbarians that those who go to war are the more fortunate in proportion as they are cruel toward their enemies; I assure you that they made us thoroughly feel the force of that wretched belief.

Accordingly, having perceived us, they first thanked the Sun for having caused us to fall into the hands of their fellow-countrymen; they next fired a salute with a volley of arquebus shots by way of congratulation for their victory. That done, they set up a stage on a hill; then, entering the woods, they seek sticks or thorns, according to their fancy. Being thus armed, they form in line—a hundred on one side, and a hundred on the other—and make us pass, all naked, along that way of fury and anguish; there is rivalry among them to discharge upon us the most and the heaviest blows; they made me march last, that I might be more exposed to their rage. I had not accomplished the half of this course when I fell to the earth under the weight of that hail and of those redoubled blows. I did not strive to rise again—partly because of my weakness, partly because I was accepting that place for my sepulchre. . . . Seeing me prostrate, they rush upon me; God alone knows for how long a time and how many were the blows that were dealt on my body; but the sufferings undertaken for his love and his glory are filled with joy and honor. Seeing, then, that I had not fallen by accident, and that I did not rise again for being too near death, they entered upon a cruel compassion; their rage was not yet glutted, and they wished to conduct me alive into their own country; accordingly, they embrace me and carry me all bleeding upon that stage they have prepared. When I am restored to my senses, they make me come down and offer me a thousand and one insults, making me the sport and object of their reviling; they begin their assaults over again, dealing upon my head and neck and all my body another hailstorm of blows. I would be too tedious if I should set down in writing all the rigor of my sufferings. They burned one of my fingers and crushed another with their teeth, and those which were already torn they squeezed and twisted with a rage of Demons; they scratched my wounds with their nails; and when strength failed me, they applied fire to my arm and thighs. My companions were treated very nearly as I was. One of those Barbarians, having advanced with a large knife in his right hand, took my nose in his left hand, wishing to cut it off; but he stopped suddenly, and as if astonished, withdrawing without doing aught to me. He returns a quarter of an hour later, as if indignant with himself for his cowardice; he again seizes me at the same place; you know, my God, what I said to you at that moment, in the depth of my heart. In fine, I know not what invisible force repulsed him for the second time. It was over with my life if he had proceeded; for they are not accustomed to leave long on the earth those who are notably mutilated. . . .

Those warriors, having made a sacrifice of our blood, pursued their course, and we ours. The tenth day after our capture we arrived at the place where it was necessary to cease navigation and to proceed by land; that road, which was about four days long, was extremely painful for us. The man to whose guard I was given, unable to carry all his booty, put a part of it on my back, which was all torn; we ate, in three days, only a few wild fruits, which we gathered by the way. The heat of the sun, at the warmest season of the summer, and our wounds greatly weakened us and caused us to walk behind the others. Seeing ourselves considerably separated from them and near the night, I told poor René that he should escape—indeed, we were able to do so; but, for myself, I would rather have suffered all sorts of torments than abandon to death those whom I could somewhat console and upon whom I could confer the blood of my Savior through the Sacraments of his Church. This good young man, seeing that I wished to follow my little flock, would never leave me: "I will die," he said, "with you; I cannot forsake you."

I had always thought, indeed, that the day on which the whole Church rejoices in the glory of the blessed Virgin—her glorious and triumphant Assumption—would be for us a day of pain. This made me render thanks to my Savior Jesus Christ, because, on that day of gladness and joy, he was making us share his sufferings and admitting us to participation in his crosses. We arrived on the eve of that sacred day at a little river, distant from the first village of the Hiroquois about a quarter of a league; we found on its banks, on both sides, many men and youths, armed with sticks which they let loose upon us with their accustomed rage. There remained to me now only two nails—those Barbarians tore them from me with their teeth, rending the flesh from beneath and cutting it clean to the bone with their nails, which they allow to grow very long. . . . After they had glutted their cruelty, they led us in triumph into that first village.

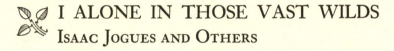

I ALONE IN THOSE VAST WILDS
Isaac Jogues and Others

During his captivity among the Mohawks Father Jogues served as slave in the fall hunt, after a march through the wilderness of about ninety miles to the hunting ground. According to one of his biographers, Francis Xavier Talbot (*Saint Among Savages*, New York, 1935), the direction of the journey was north into the mountains of the central Adirondacks. If so, Jogues may have been the first white man to penetrate into the interior of the region. The third-person parts of the following narrative are from Lalemant's Relation, the first-person part from Bressani's, in *The Jesuit Relations*.

They [the Mohawk captors] gave this poor Father to some families to serve them as a menial in their hunts. He follows them at the approach of winter and makes thirty leagues with them, serving them through two months, as a slave. All his clothes sheltered him no more than would a shirt and a sorry pair of drawers; his stockings and his shoes made like tennis slippers, and of a leather just as thin, without any soles—in a word, he was all in rags. The sharp reeds and briars, the stones and pebbles, the thickets through which he had to pass cut his legs and tore his feet. As they did not account him fit for hunting, they gave him a woman's occupation—that is, to cut and bring the wood to keep up the cabin fire. The chase beginning to furnish supplies, he could to some extent repair his strength—meat not being stinted to him; but when he saw that they were offering to the Demon of the chase all that they took, he told them plainly that he would never eat of flesh sacrificed to the devil. He therefore contented himself with a little very thin *sagamité*—that is to say, with a little Indian meal boiled in water; and even then he had it but seldom, because, gorged with meat, they despised their dry cornmeal.

He secretly confessed to one of our Fathers that God tried him exceedingly in that journey, and that he saw himself a long time without other support than Faith alone. . . .

"At the middle of October began the stag hunt, a time for them of sports and feasts, but for me, of outrages and persecutions, because when I began to announce to them a God, a Paradise, and a Hell, although indeed they listened to me at the start and admired, yet, weary with the continuation thereof, and because the chase was not successful, they began to accuse and persecute me. They have recourse in their necessities to a demon whom they call Aireskoi, to whom they offer, as it were, the first-fruits of everything. When, for instance, a stag has been taken, they call the eldest of the hut or of the village, to the end that he may bless it or sacrifice it. This man, standing opposite the one who holds some of the flesh, says with a loud voice: 'Oh, Demon Aireskoi, we offer thee this flesh and prepare for thee a feast with it, that thou mayest eat of it and show us where are the stags and send them into our snares—or at least, that we may see them again in the winter,' etc.; or, in sickness, 'to the end that we may recover health.' They do the same in fishing, war, etc.

"Having heard this ceremony, I was horrified, and I was always careful to abstain from this flesh offered to the Demon—toward whom they interpreted this action as manifest contempt and a cause of their lack of success in hunting. . . . Nor would they longer hear me speak of God, or answer me the questions that I put to them about the language, wherewith they saw that I was attacking their superstitions. I therefore went out every morning *de medio Babilonis*—that is, from a cabin where the Demon and the dreams were almost always adored—and escaped to a neighboring hill, where, in a large tree, I had made a great Cross; and there, now meditating, now reading, I conversed with my God, whom I alone in those vast wilds adored. The Barbarians did not perceive this till somewhat later, when they found me kneeling, as usual, before that Cross, which they hated, and said that it was hated by the Dutch; they began, on this account, to treat me worse than before—without, however, being able to hinder me from continuing elsewhere my prayers. . . .

"The snows having increased, the cold was added thereto, as I had only a rag for clothing and bed, and they would not allow me the use of any of those skins which they had in great abundance. . . . I suffered, besides the pain of my wounds, not yet perfectly healed, fears and inward pangs. . . . I thus passed two months 'in the school of the beech-trees'—as once said St. Bernard—until, being unable to endure me longer, they sent me away, carrying a load of meat, to the place whence I had started—there to be put to death, as was commonly said." . . .

Having learned that some old men wished to return to their village, this poor Father asked permission to accompany them; they send him without tinder, without shoes, and amid the snows of the month of December; and, after all that, they command him to carry on this march of thirty leagues a bundle of smoked meat, which would have served as burden to a stout porter. He had no answer to make; all the Savages are like carriers or packhorses. Steadfast charity and patience beget strength where there is none. There happened to be on this journey a pregnant woman, who also carried a heavy burden and a little child. As they came to cross a small stream, very deep and very swift, and which had no other bridge than a tree thrown across, this woman, swayed by her burden, fell into the torrent. The Father, who was following her—seeing that the rope about her bundle had slipped to her neck and that this burden was dragging her to the bottom—plunges into the water, overtakes her by swimming, disengages her from her burden, and takes her to the shore, saving her life and that of her little child, which he baptized at once, seeing it very ill; in fact, it took its flight, two days later, to Paradise. I leave you to think whether the cold made itself felt by that poor worn-out body. The fire which was made for that revived woman preserved their lives, which they would have lost without this help.

THE CHASE
JAMES FENIMORE COOPER

The action in these scenes from *The Last of the Mohicans* begins three days after Montcalm's capture (August 9, 1757) of Fort William Henry at the head of Lake George. The defeated British commander, Colonel Munro, his aide Duncan Heyward, and their guides find near the ruined fort evidence that the Colonel's daughters are captives of a Huron war party allied to the French. Two Mohican warriors, Chingachgook and his son Uncas, and the scout Hawkeye lead the pursuit. The latter is Cooper's hero Leatherstocking in full maturity.

The scout, after musing a moment, continued,—

"There is no woman in this wilderness could leave such a print as that but the dark-hair or her sister. We know that the first has been here, but where are the signs of the other? Let us push deeper on the trail, and if nothing offers, we must go back to the plain and strike another scent. Move on, Uncas, and keep your eyes on the dried leaves. I will watch the bushes, while your father shall run with a low nose to the ground. Move on, friends; the sun is getting behind the hills."

"Is there nothing that I can do?" demanded the anxious Heyward.

"You!" repeated the scout, who, with his red friends, was already advancing in the order he had prescribed; "yes, you can keep in our rear and be careful not to cross the trail."

Before they had proceeded many rods, the Indians stopped and appeared to gaze at some signs on the earth, with more than their usual keenness. Both father and son spoke quick and loud, now looking at the object of their mutual admiration, and now regarding each other with the most unequivocal pleasure.

"They have found the little foot!" exclaimed the scout, moving forward without attending further to his own portion of the duty. "What have we here? An ambushment has been planted in the spot? No, by the truest rifle on the frontiers, here have been them one-sided horses again! Now the whole secret is out, and all is plain as the north star at midnight. Yes, here they have mounted. There the beasts have been bound to a sapling, in waiting; and yonder runs the broad path away to the north, in full sweep for the Canadas."

"But still there are no signs of Alice—of the younger Miss Munro," said Duncan.

"Unless the shining bauble Uncas has just lifted from the ground should prove one. Pass it this way, lad, that we may look at it."

Heyward instantly knew it for a trinket that Alice was fond of wearing, and which he recollected, with the tenacious memory of a lover, to have seen, on the fatal morning of the massacre, dangling from the fair neck of his mistress. He seized the highly prized jewel; and as he proclaimed the fact, it vanished from the eyes of the wondering scout, who in vain looked for it on the ground, long after it was warmly pressed against the beating heart of Duncan.

"Pshaw!" said the disappointed Hawkeye, ceasing to rake the leaves with the breech of his rifle; " 'tis a certain sign of age when the sight begins to weaken. Such a glittering gewgaw, and not to be seen! Well, well, I can squint along a clouded barrel yet, and that is enough to settle all disputes between me and the Mingos. I should like to find the thing too, if it were only to carry it to the right owner, and that would be bringing the two ends of what I call a long trail together—for by this time the broad St. Lawrence, or, perhaps, the Great Lakes themselves, are atwixt us."

"So much the more reason why we should not delay our march," returned Heyward; "let us proceed."

"Young blood and hot blood, they say, are much the same thing. We are not about to start on a squirrel hunt, or to drive a deer into the Horican [Lake George], but to outlie for days and nights and to stretch across a wilderness where the feet of men seldom go, and where no bookish knowledge would carry you through harmless. An Indian never starts on such an expedition without smoking over his council-fire; and though a man of white blood, I honor their customs in this particular, seeing that they are deliberate and wise. We will, therefore, go back and light our fire tonight in the ruins of the old fort, and in the morning we shall be fresh and ready to undertake our work like men, and not like babbling women or eager boys." . . .

Just as the day dawned, they entered the narrows of the lake and stole swiftly and cautiously among their numberless little islands. It was by this road that Montcalm had retired with his army; and the adventurers knew not but he had left some of his Indians in ambush, to protect the rear of his forces and collect the stragglers. They, therefore, approached the passage with the customary silence of their guarded habits.

Chingachgook laid aside his paddle; while Uncas and the scout urged the light vessel through crooked and intricate channels, where every foot that they advanced exposed them to the danger of some sudden rising on their progress. The eyes of the Sagamore moved warily from islet to islet, and copse to copse, as the canoe proceeded; and when a clearer sheet of water permitted, his keen vision was bent along the bald rocks and impending forests that frowned upon the narrow strait.

Heyward, who was a doubly interested spectator, as well from the beauties of the place as from the apprehension natural to his situation, was just believing that he had permitted the latter to be excited without sufficient reason, when the paddle ceased moving, in obedience to a signal from Chingachgook.

"Hugh!" exclaimed Uncas, nearly at the moment that the light tap his father had made on the side of the canoe notified them of the vicinity of danger.

"What now?" asked the scout; "the lake is as smooth as if the winds had never blown, and I can see along its sheet for miles; there is not so much as the black head of a loon dotting the water."

The Indian gravely raised his paddle and pointed in the direction in which his own steady look was riveted. Duncan's eyes followed the motion. A few rods in their front lay another of the low wooded islets, but it appeared as calm and peaceful as if its solitude had never been disturbed by the foot of man.

"I see nothing," he said, "but land and water; and a lovely scene it is."

"Hist!" interrupted the scout. "Ay, Sagamore, there is always a reason for what you do. 'Tis but a shade, and yet it is not natural. You see the mist, major, that is rising above the island; you can't call it a fog, for it is more like a streak of thin cloud—"

"It is vapor from the water."

"That a child could tell. But what is the edging of blacker smoke that hangs along its lower side, and which you may trace down into the thicket of hazel? 'Tis from a fire; but one that, in my judgment, has been suffered to burn low."

"Let us then push for the place and relieve our doubts," said the impatient Duncan; "the party must be small that can lie on such a bit of land."

"If you judge of Indian cunning by the rules you find in books, or by white sagacity, they will lead you astray, if not to your death," returned Hawkeye, examining the signs of the place with that acuteness which distinguished him. "If I may be permitted to speak in this matter, it will be to say, that we have but two things to choose between: the one is, to return, and give up all thoughts of following the Hurons—"

"Never!" exclaimed Heyward, in a voice far too loud for their circumstances.

"Well, well," continued Hawkeye, making a hasty sign to repress his impatience; "I am much of your mind myself; though I thought it becoming my experience to tell the whole. We must then make a push, and if the Indians or Frenchers are in the narrows, run the gauntlet through these toppling mountains. Is there reason in my words, Sagamore?"

The Indian made no other answer than by dropping his paddle into the water, and urging forward the canoe. As he held the office of directing its course, his resolution was sufficiently indicated by the movement. The whole party now plied their paddles vigorously, and in a very few moments they had reached a point whence they might command an entire view of the northern shore of the island, the side that had hitherto been concealed.

"There they are, by all the truth of signs," whispered the scout; "two canoes and a smoke. The knaves haven't yet got their eyes out of the mist, or we should hear the accursed whoop. Together, friend! we are leaving them and are already nearly out of whistle of a bullet."

The well-known crack of a rifle, whose ball came skipping along the placid surface of the strait, and a shrill yell from the island, interrupted his speech and announced that their passage was discovered. In another instant several savages were seen rushing into the canoes, which were soon dancing over the water in pursuit. These fearful precursors of a coming struggle produced no change in the countenances and movements of his three guides, so far as Duncan could discover, except that the strokes of their paddles were longer and more in unison, and caused the little bark to spring forward like a creature possessing life and volition.

"Hold them there, Sagamore," said Hawkeye, looking coolly backward over his left shoulder, while he still plied his paddle; "keep them just there. Them Hurons have never a piece in their nation that will execute at this distance; but 'Killdeer' has a barrel on which a man may calculate."

The scout having ascertained that the Mohicans were sufficient of themselves to maintain the requisite distance, deliberately laid aside his paddle and raised the fatal rifle. Three several times he brought the piece to his shoulder, and when his companions were expecting its report, he as often lowered it to request the Indians would permit their enemies to approach a little nigher. At length his accurate and fastidious eye seemed satisfied, and throwing out his left arm on the barrel, he was slowly elevating the muzzle, when an exclamation from Uncas, who sat in the bow, once more caused him to suspend the shot.

"What now, lad?" demanded Hawkeye; "you saved a Huron from the death-shriek by that word; have you reason for what you do?"

Uncas pointed towards the rocky shore a little in their front, whence another war canoe was darting directly across their course. It was too obvious now that their situation was imminently perilous to need the aid of language to confirm it. The scout laid aside his rifle and resumed the paddle, while Chingachgook inclined the bows of the canoe a little towards the western shore, in order to increase the distance between them and this new enemy. In the meantime they were reminded of the presence of those who pressed upon their rear, by wild and exulting shouts. The stirring scene awakened even Munro from his apathy.

"Let us make for the rocks on the main," he said, with the mien of a tired soldier, "and give battle to the savages. God forbid that I, or those attached to me and mine, should ever trust again to the faith of any servant of the Louis's!"

"He who wishes to prosper in Indian warfare," returned the scout, "must not be too proud to learn from the wit of a native. Lay her more along the land, Sagamore; we are doubling on the varlets, and perhaps they may try to strike our trail on the long calculation."

Hawkeye was not mistaken; for when the Hurons found their course was likely to throw them behind their chase, they rendered it less direct until, by gradually bearing more and more obliquely, the two canoes were, ere long, gliding on parallel lines, within two hundred yards of each other. It now became entirely a trial of speed. So rapid was the progress of the light vessels that the lake curled in their front, in miniature waves, and their motion became undulating by its own velocity. It was, perhaps, owing to this circumstance, in addition to the necessity of keeping every hand employed at the paddles, that the Hurons had not immediate recourse to their fire-arms. The exertions of the fugitives were too severe to continue long, and the pursuers had the advantage of numbers. Duncan observed, with uneasiness, that the scout began to look anxiously about him, as if searching for some further means of assisting their flight.

"Edge her a little more from the sun, Sagamore," said the stubborn woodsman; "I see the knaves are sparing a man to the rifle. A single broken bone might lose us our scalps. Edge more from the sun and we will put the island between us."

The expedient was not without its use. A long, low island lay at a little distance before them, and as they closed with it, the chasing canoe was compelled to take a side opposite to that on which the pursued passed. The scout and his companions did not neglect this advantage, but the instant they were hid from observation by the bushes, they redoubled efforts that before had seemed prodigious. The two canoes came round the last low point, like two coursers at the top of their speed, the fugitives taking the lead. This change had brought them nigher to each other, however, while it altered their relative positions.

"You showed knowledge in the shaping of birchen bark, Uncas, when you chose this from among the Huron canoes," said the scout, smiling, apparently more in satisfaction at their superiority in the race than from that prospect of final escape which now began to open a little upon them. "The imps have put all their strength again at the paddles, and we are to struggle for our scalps with bits of flattened wood, instead of clouded barrels and true eyes. A long stroke, and together, friends."

"They are preparing for a shot," said Heyward; "and as we are in a line with them, it can scarcely fail."

"Get you then into the bottom of the canoe," returned the scout; "you and the colonel; it will be so much taken from the size of the mark."

Heyward smiled, as he answered,—

"It would be but an ill example for the highest in rank to dodge, while the warriors were under fire!"

"Lord! Lord! That is now a white man's courage!" exclaimed the scout; "and like too many of his notions, not to be maintained by reason. Do you think the Sagamore, or Uncas, or even I, who am a man without a cross, would deliberate about finding a cover in the skrimmage, when an open body would do no good? For what have the Frenchers reared up their Quebec, if fighting is always to be done in the clearings?"

"All that you say is very true, my friend," replied Heyward; "still, our customs must prevent us from doing as you wish."

A volley from the Hurons interrupted the discourse, and as the bullets whistled about them, Duncan saw the head of Uncas turned, looking back at himself and Munro. Notwithstanding the nearness of the enemy, and his own great personal danger, the countenance of the young warrior expressed no other emotion, as the former was compelled to think, than amazement at finding men willing to encounter so useless an exposure. Chingachgook was probably better acquainted with the notions of white men, for he did not even cast a glance aside from the riveted look his eye maintained on the object by which he governed their course. A ball soon struck the light and polished paddle from the hands of the chief, and drove it through the air, far in the advance. A shout arose from the Hurons, who seized the opportunity to fire another volley. Uncas described an arc in the water with his own blade, and as the canoe passed swiftly on, Chingachgook recovered his paddle, and flourishing it on high, he gave the war-whoop of the Mohicans, and then lent his strength and skill again to the important task.

The clamorous sounds of "Le Gros Serpent!" "La Longue Carabine!" "Le Cerf Agile!" burst at once from the canoes behind and seemed to give new zeal to the pursuers. The scout seized "Killdeer" in his left hand, and elevating it above his head, he shook it in triumph at his enemies. The savages answered the insult with a yell, and immediately another volley succeeded. The bullets pattered along the lake, and one even pierced the bark of their little vessel. No perceptible emotion could be discovered in the Mohicans during this critical moment, their rigid features expressing neither hope nor alarm; but the scout again turned his head, and laughing in his own silent manner, he said to Heyward,—

"The knaves love to hear the sounds of their pieces; but the eye is not to be found among the Mingos that can calculate a true range in a dancing canoe! You see the dumb devils have taken off a man to charge, and by the smallest measurement that can be allowed, we move three feet to their two!"

Duncan, who was not altogether as easy under this nice estimate of distances as his companions, was glad to find, however, that owing to their superior dexterity, and the diversion among their enemies, they were very sensibly obtaining the advantage. The Hurons soon fired again, and a bullet struck the blade of Hawkeye's paddle without injury.

"That will do," said the scout, examining the slight indentation with a curious eye; "it would not have cut the skin of an infant, much less of men, who, like us, have been blown upon by the heavens in their anger. Now, major, if you will try to use this piece of flattened wood, I'll let 'Killdeer' take a part in the conversation."

Heyward seized the paddle, and applied himself to the work with an eagerness that supplied the place of skill, while Hawkeye was engaged in inspecting the priming of his rifle. The latter then took a swift aim and fired. The Huron in the bows of the leading canoe had risen with a similar object, and he now fell backward, suffering his gun to escape from his hands into the water. In an instant, however, he recovered his feet, though his gestures were wild and bewildered. At the same moment his companions suspended their efforts, and the chasing canoes clustered together and became stationary. Chingachgook and Uncas profited by the interval to regain their wind, though Duncan continued to work with the most persevering industry. The father and son now cast calm but inquiring glances at each other, to learn if either had sustained any injury by the fire; for both well knew that no cry or exclamation would, in such a moment of necessity, have been permitted to betray the accident. A few large drops of blood were trickling down the shoulder of the Sagamore, who, when he perceived that the eyes of Uncas dwelt too long on the sight, raised some water in the hollow of his hand, and washing off the stain, was content to manifest, in this simple manner, the slightness of the injury.

"Softly, softly, major," said the scout, who by this time had reloaded his rifle; "we are a little too far already for a rifle to put forth its beauties, and you see yonder imps are holding a council. Let them come up within striking distance—my eye may well be trusted in such a matter—and I will trail the varlets the length of the Horican, guaranteeing that not a shot of theirs shall, at the worst, more than break the skin, while 'Killdeer' shall touch the life twice in three times."

"We forget our errand," returned the diligent Duncan. "For God's sake let us profit by this advantage and increase our distance from the enemy."

"Give me my children," said Munro hoarsely; "trifle no longer with a father's agony, but restore me my babes."

Long and habitual deference to the mandates of his superiors had taught the scout the virtue of obedience. Throwing a last and lingering glance at the distant canoes, he laid aside his rifle, and relieving the wearied Duncan, resumed the paddle, which he wielded with sinews that never tired. His efforts were seconded by those of the Mohicans, and a very few minutes served to place such a sheet of water between them and their enemies that Heyward once more breathed freely.

The lake now began to expand, and their route lay along a wide reach that was lined, as before, by high and ragged mountains. But the islands were few, and easily avoided. The strokes of the paddles grew more measured and regular, while they who plied them continued their labor, after the close and deadly chase from which they had just relieved themselves, with as much coolness as though their speed had been tried in sport, rather than under such pressing, nay, almost desperate circumstances.

Instead of following the western shore, whither their errand led them, the wary Mohican inclined his course more towards those hills behind which Montcalm was known to have led his army into the formidable fortress of Ticonderoga. As the Hurons, to every appearance, had abandoned the pursuit, there was no apparent reason for this excess of caution. It was, however, maintained for hours, until they had reached a bay, nigh the northern termination of the lake. Here the canoe was driven upon the beach, and the whole party landed. Hawkeye and Heyward ascended an adjacent bluff, where the former, after considering the expanse of water beneath him, pointed out to the latter a small black object, hovering under a headland, at the distance of several miles.

"Do you see it?" demanded the scout. "Now, what would you account that spot, were you left alone to white experience to find your way through this wilderness?"

"But for its distance and its magnitude, I should suppose it a bird. Can it be a living object?"

" 'Tis a canoe of good birchen bark and paddled by fierce and crafty Mingos. Though Providence has lent to those who inhabit the woods eyes that would be needless to men in the settlements, where there are inventions to assist the sight, yet no human organs can see all the dangers which at this moment circumvent us. These varlets pretend to be bent chiefly on their sun-down meal, but the moment it is dark they will be on our trail, as true as hounds on the scent. We must throw them off, or our pursuit of Le Renard Subtil may be given up. These lakes are useful at times, especially when the game takes the water," continued the scout, gazing about him with a countenance of concern; "but they give no cover, except it be to the fishes. God knows what the country would be if the settlements should ever spread far from the two rivers. Both hunting and war would lose their beauty."

"Let us not delay a moment without some good and obvious cause."

"I little like that smoke which you may see worming up along the rock above the canoe," interrupted the abstracted scout. "My life on it, other eyes than ours see it and know its meaning. Well, words will not mend the matter, and it is time that we were doing."

Hawkeye moved away from the lookout and descended, musing profoundly, to the shore. He communicated the result of his observations to his companions, in Delaware, and a short and earnest consultation succeeded. When it terminated, the three instantly set about executing their new resolutions.

The canoe was lifted from the water and borne on the shoulders of the party. They proceeded into the wood, making as broad and obvious a trail as possible. They soon reached a water-course, which they crossed, and continued onward until they came to an extensive and naked rock. At this point, where their footsteps might be expected to be no longer visible, they retraced their route to the brook, walking backwards, with the utmost care. They now followed the bed of the little stream to the lake, into which they immediately launched their canoe again. A low point concealed them from the headland, and the margin of the lake was fringed for some distance with dense and overhanging bushes. Under the cover of these natural advantages, they toiled their way, with patient industry, until the scout pronounced that he believed it would be safe once more to land.

The halt continued until evening rendered objects indistinct and uncertain to the eye. Then they resumed their route and, favored by the darkness, pushed silently and vigorously towards the western shore. Although the rugged outline of mountain to which they were steering presented no distinctive marks to the eyes of Duncan, the Mohican entered the little haven he had selected with the confidence and accuracy of an experienced pilot.

The boat was again lifted and borne into the woods, where it was carefully concealed under a pile of brush. The adventurers assumed their arms and packs, and the scout announced to Munro and Heyward that he and the Indians were at last in readiness to proceed. . . .

The party had landed on the border of a region that is, even to this day [1825], less known to the inhabitants of the States than the deserts of Arabia or the steppes of Tartary. It was the sterile and rugged district which separates the tributaries of Champlain from those of the Hudson, the Mohawk, and the St. Lawrence. Since the period of our tale, the active spirit of the country has surrounded it with a belt of rich and thriving settlements, though none but the hunter or the savage is ever known, even now, to penetrate its wild recesses.

As Hawkeye and the Mohicans had, however, often traversed the mountains and valleys of this vast wilderness, they did not hesitate to plunge into its depths, with the freedom of men accustomed to its privations and difficulties. For many hours the travellers toiled on their laborious way, guided by a star or following the direction of some watercourse, until the scout called a halt, and holding a short consultation with the Indians, they lighted their fire and made the usual preparations to pass the remainder of the night where they then were.

Imitating the example and emulating the confidence of their more experienced associates, Munro and Duncan slept without fear, if not without uneasiness. The dews were suffered to exhale, and the sun dispersed the mists and was shedding a strong and clear light in the forest, when the travellers resumed their journey.

After proceeding a few miles, the progress of Hawkeye, who led the advance, became more deliberate and watchful. He often stopped to examine the trees; nor did he cross a rivulet without attentively considering the quantity, the velocity, and the color of its waters. Distrusting his own judgment his appeals to the opinion of Chingachgook were frequent and earnest. During one of these conferences, Heyward observed that Uncas stood a patient and silent though, as he imagined, an interested listener. He was strongly tempted to address the young chief and demand his opinion of their progress; but the calm and dignified demeanor of the native induced him to believe that, like himself, the other was wholly dependent on the sagacity and intelligence of the seniors of the party. At last, the scout spoke in English and at once explained the embarrassment of their situation.

"When I found that the home path of the Hurons run north," he said, "it did not need the judgment of many long years to tell that they would follow the valleys and keep atween the waters of the Hudson and the Horican until they might strike the springs of the Canada streams, which would lead them into the heart of the country of the Frenchers. Yet here are we, within a short range of the Scaroon, and not a sign of a trail have we crossed! Human natur' is weak, and it is possible we may not have taken the proper scent."

"Heaven protect us from such an error!" exclaimed Duncan. "Let us retrace our steps and examine as we go, with keener eyes. Has Uncas no counsel to offer in such a strait?"

The young Mohican cast a glance at his father, but maintaining his quiet and reserved mien, he continued silent. Chingachgook had caught the look, and motioning with his hand, he bade him speak. The moment this permission was accorded, the countenance of Uncas changed from its grave composure to a gleam of intelligence and joy. Bounding forward like a deer, he sprang up the side of a little acclivity, a few rods in advance, and stood exultantly over a spot of fresh earth that looked as though it had been recently upturned by the passage of some heavy animal. The eyes of the whole party followed the unexpected movement and read their success in the air of triumph that the youth assumed.

" 'Tis the trail!" exclaimed the scout, advancing to the spot; "the lad is quick of sight and keen of wit for his years."

" 'Tis extraordinary that he should have withheld his knowledge so long," muttered Duncan, at his elbow.

"It would have been more wonderful had he spoken without a bidding. No, no; your young white, who gathers his learning from books and can measure what he knows by the page, may conceit that his knowledge, like his legs, outruns that of his father; but where experience is the master, the scholar is made to know the value of years and respects them accordingly."

"See!" said Uncas, pointing north and south at the evident marks of the broad trail on either side of him: "the dark-hair has gone towards the frost."

"Hound never ran on a more beautiful scent," responded the scout, dashing forward at once on the indicated route; "we are favored, greatly favored, and can follow with high noses. Ay, here are both your waddling beasts: this Huron travels like a white general. The fellow is stricken with a judgment, and is mad! Look sharp for wheels, Sagamore," he continued, looking back, and laughing in his newly awakened satisfaction; "we shall soon have the fool journeying in a coach, and that with three of the best pair of eyes on the borders, in his rear."

The spirits of the scout and the astonishing success of the chase, in which a circuitous distance of more than forty miles had been passed, did not fail to impart a portion of hope to the whole party. Their advance was rapid; and made with as much confidence as a traveller would proceed along a wide highway. If a rock, or a rivulet, or a bit of earth harder than common, severed the links of the clue they followed, the true eye of the scout recovered them at a distance and seldom rendered the delay of a single moment necessary. Their progress was much facilitated by the certainty that Magua had found it necessary to journey through the valleys; a circumstance which rendered the general direction of the route sure. Nor had the Huron entirely neglected the arts uniformly practised by the natives when retiring in front of an enemy. False trails and sudden turnings were frequent wherever a brook, or the formation of the ground, rendered them feasible; but his pursuers were rarely deceived and never failed to detect their error before they had lost either time or distance on the deceptive track.

By the middle of the afternoon they had passed the Scaroon and were following the route of the declining sun.

BATTLE IN THE FOREST
FRANCIS PARKMAN

It was nearly a month [July, 1758] since Abercrombie had begun his camp at the head of Lake George. Here, on the ground where Johnson had beaten Dieskau, where Montcalm had planted his batteries, and Monro vainly defended the wooden ramparts of Fort William Henry, were now assembled more than fifteen thousand men; and the shores, the foot of the mountains, and the broken plains between them were studded thick with tents. Of regulars there were six thousand three hundred and sixty-seven, officers and soldiers, and of provincials nine thousand and thirty-four. To the New England levies, or at least to their chaplains, the expedition seemed a crusade against the abomination of Babylon; and they discoursed in their sermons of Moses sending forth Joshua against Amalek. Abercrombie, raised to his place by political influence, was little but the nominal commander. "A heavy man," said Wolfe in a letter to his father; "an aged gentleman, infirm in body and mind," wrote William Parkman, a boy of seventeen, who carried a musket in a Massachusetts regiment and kept in his knapsack a dingy little notebook in which he jotted down what passed each day. The age of the aged gentleman was fifty-two.

Pitt meant that the actual command of the army should be in the hands of Brigadier Lord Howe, and he was in fact its real chief; "the noblest Englishman that has appeared in my time and the best soldier in the British army," says Wolfe. And he elsewhere speaks of him as "that great man." Abercrombie testifies to the universal respect and love with which officers and men regarded him, and Pitt calls him "a character of ancient times; a complete model of military virtue." High as this praise is, it seems to have been deserved. The young nobleman, who was then in his thirty-fourth year, had the qualities of a leader of men. The army felt him, from general to drummer-boy. He was its soul; and while breathing into it his own energy and ardor and bracing it by stringent discipline, he broke through the traditions of the service and gave it new shapes to suit the time and place. During the past year he had studied the art of forest warfare and joined Rogers and his rangers in their scouting-parties, sharing all their hardships and making himself one of them. Perhaps the reforms that he introduced were fruits of this rough self-imposed schooling. He made officers and men throw off all useless encumbrances, cut their hair close, wear leggings to protect them from briers, brown the barrels of their muskets, and carry in their knapsacks thirty pounds of meal, which they cooked for themselves; so that, according to an admiring Frenchman, they could live a month without their supply-trains. "You would laugh to see the droll figure we all make," writes an officer. "Regulars as well as provincials have cut their coats so as scarcely to reach their waists. No officer or private is allowed to carry more than one blanket and a bearskin. A small portmanteau is allowed each officer. No women follow the camp to wash our linen. Lord Howe has already shown an example by going to the brook and washing his own." . . .

On the evening of the fourth of July baggage, stores, and ammunition were all on board the boats, and the whole army embarked on the morning of the fifth. The arrangements were perfect. Each corps marched without confusion to its appointed station on the beach, and the sun was scarcely above the ridge of French Mountain when all were afloat. A spectator watching them from the shore says that when the fleet was three miles on its way, the surface of the lake at that distance was completely hidden from sight. There were nine hundred bateaux, a hundred and thirty-five whaleboats, and a large number of heavy flatboats carrying the artillery. The whole advanced in three divisions, the regulars in the centre, and the provincials on the flanks. Each corps had its flags and its music. The day was fair and men and officers were in the highest spirits.

Before ten o'clock they began to enter the Narrows; and the boats of the three divisions extended themselves into long files as the mountains closed on either hand upon the contracted lake. From front to rear the line was six miles long. The spectacle was superb: the brightness of the summer day; the romantic beauty of the scenery; the sheen and sparkle of those crystal waters; the countless islets, tufted with pine, birch, and fir; the bordering mountains with their green summits and sunny crags; the flash of oars and glitter of weapons; the banners, the varied uniforms, and the notes of bugle, trumpet, bagpipe, and drum, answered and prolonged by a hundred woodland echoes. "I never beheld so delightful a prospect," wrote a wounded officer at Albany a fortnight after.

Rogers with the rangers and Gage with the light infantry led the way in whaleboats, followed by Bradstreet with his corps of boatmen, armed and drilled as soldiers. Then came the main body. The central column of regulars was commanded by Lord Howe, his own regiment, the fifty-fifth, in the van, followed by the Royal Americans, the twenty-seventh, forty-fourth, forty-sixth, and eightieth infantry, and the Highlanders of the forty-second, with their major, Duncan Campbell of Inverawe, silent and gloomy amid the general cheer, for his soul was dark with foreshadowings of death. With this central column came what are described as two floating castles, which were no doubt batteries to cover the landing of the troops. On the right hand and the left were the provincials, uniformed in blue, regiment after regiment, from Massachusetts, Connecticut, New York, New Jersey, and Rhode Island. Behind them all came the bateaux, loaded with stores and baggage, and the heavy flatboats that carried the artillery, while a rear-guard of provincials and regulars closed the long procession.

At five in the afternoon they reached Sabbath-Day Point, twenty-five miles down the lake, where they stopped till late in the evening, waiting for the baggage and artillery, which had lagged behind; and here Lord Howe, lying on a bearskin by the side of the ranger, John Stark, questioned him as to the position of Ticonderoga and its best points of approach. At about eleven o'clock they set out again and at daybreak entered what was then called the Second Narrows; that is to say, the contraction of the lake where it approaches its outlet. Close on their left, ruddy in the warm sunrise, rose the vast bare face of Rogers Rock, whence a French advance party, under Langy and an officer named Trepezec, was watching their movements. Lord Howe, with Rogers and Bradstreet, went in whaleboats to reconnoitre the landing. At the place which the French called the Burned Camp, where Montcalm had embarked the summer before, they saw a detachment of the enemy too weak to oppose them. Their men landed and drove them off. At noon the whole army was on shore. Rogers, with a party of rangers, was ordered forward to reconnoitre, and the troops were formed for the march.

From this part of the shore a plain covered with forest stretched northwestward half a mile or more to the mountains behind which lay the valley of Trout Brook. On this plain the army began its march in four columns, with the intention of passing round the western bank of the river of the outlet, since the bridge over it had been destroyed. Rogers, with the provincial regiments of Fitch and Lyman, led the way, at some distance before the rest. The forest was extremely dense and heavy, and so obstructed with undergrowth that it was impossible to see more than a few yards in any direction, while the ground was encumbered with fallen trees in every stage of decay. The ranks were broken, and the men struggled on as they could in dampness and shade, under a canopy of boughs that the sun could scarcely pierce. The difficulty increased when, after advancing about a mile, they came upon undulating and broken ground. They were now not far from the upper rapids of the outlet. The guides became bewildered in the maze of trunks and boughs; the marching columns were confused and fell in one upon the other. They were in the strange situation of an army lost in the woods.

The advanced party of French under Langy and Trepezec, about three hundred and fifty in all, regulars and Canadians, had tried to retreat; but before they could do so, the whole English army had passed them, landed, and placed itself between them and their countrymen. They had no resource but to take to the woods. They seem to have climbed the steep gorge at the side of Rogers Rock and followed the Indian path that led to the valley of Trout Brook, thinking to descend it and, by circling along the outskirts of the valley of Ticonderoga, reach Montcalm's camp at the sawmill. Langy was used to bushranging; but he too became perplexed in the blind intricacies of the forest. Towards the close of the day he and his men had come out from the valley of Trout Brook, and were near the junction of that stream with the river of the outlet, in a state of some anxiety, for they could see nothing but brown trunks and green boughs. Could any of them have climbed one of the great pines that here and there reared their shaggy spires high above the surrounding forest, they would have discovered where they were, but would have gained not the faintest knowledge of the enemy. Out of the woods on the right they would have seen a smoke rising from the burning huts of the French camp at the head of the portage, which Bourlamaque had set on fire and abandoned. At a mile or more in front the sawmill at the Falls might perhaps have been descried and, by glimpses between the trees, the tents of the neighboring camp where Montcalm still lay with his main force. All the rest seemed lonely as the grave; mountain and valley lay wrapped in primeval woods, and none could have dreamed that, not far distant, an army was groping its way, buried in foliage; no rumbling of wagons and artillery trains, for none were there; all silent but the cawing of some crow flapping his black wings over the sea of treetops.

Lord Howe, with Major Israel Putnam and two hundred rangers, was at the head of the principal column, which was a little in advance of the three others. Suddenly the challenge, *Qui vive!* rang sharply from the thickets in front. *Français!* was the reply. Langy's men were not deceived: they fired out of the bushes. The shots were returned; a hot skirmish followed; and Lord Howe dropped dead, shot through the breast. All was confusion. The dull, vicious reports of musketry in thick woods, at first few and scattering, then in fierce and rapid volleys, reached the troops behind. They could hear, but see nothing. Already harassed and perplexed, they became perturbed. For all they knew, Montcalm's whole army was upon them. Nothing prevented a panic but the steadiness of the rangers, who maintained the fight alone till the rest came back to their senses. Rogers, with his reconnoitring party, and the regiments of Fitch and Lyman, were at no great distance in front. They all turned on hearing the musketry, and thus the French were caught between two fires. They fought with desperation. About fifty of them at length escaped; a hundred and forty-eight were captured, and the rest killed or drowned in trying to cross the rapids. The loss of the English was small in numbers, but immeasurable in the death of Howe. "The fall of this noble and brave officer," says Rogers, "seemed to produce an almost general languor and consternation through the whole army." "In Lord Howe," writes another contemporary, Major Thomas Mante, "the soul of General Abercrombie's army seemed to expire. From the unhappy moment the General was deprived of his advice, neither order nor discipline was observed, and a strange kind of infatuation usurped the place of resolution." The death of one man was the ruin of fifteen thousand. . . .

The peninsula of Ticonderoga consists of a rocky plateau, with low grounds on each side, bordering Lake Champlain on the one hand and the outlet of Lake George on the other. The fort stood near the end of the peninsula, which points towards the southeast. Thence, as one goes westward, the ground declines a little, and then slowly rises, till, about half a mile from the fort, it reaches its greatest elevation and begins still more gradually to decline again. Thus a ridge is formed across the plateau between the steep declivities that sink to the low grounds on right and left. Some weeks before, a French officer named Hugues had suggested the defence of this ridge by means of an abattis. Montcalm approved his plan; and now, at the eleventh hour, he resolved to make his stand here. . . . The whole French army fell to their task. The regimental colors were planted along the line, and the officers, stripped to the shirt, took axe in hand and labored with their men. The trees that covered the ground were hewn down by thousands, the tops lopped off, and the trunks piled one upon another to form a massive breast-work. The line followed the top of the ridge, along which it zig-zagged in such a manner that the whole front could be swept by flank-fires of musketry and grape. . . . Over this whole space to the distance of a musket-shot from the works, the forest was cut down, and the trees left lying where they fell among the stumps, with tops turned outwards, forming one vast abattis, which, as a Massachusetts officer says, looked like a forest laid flat by a hurricane. But the most formidable obstruction was immediately along the front of the breastwork, where the ground was covered with heavy boughs, overlapping and interlaced, with sharpened points bristling into the face of the assailant like the quills of a porcupine. . . .

Here then was a position which, if attacked in front with musketry alone, might be called impregnable. But would Abercrombie
so attack it? He had several alternatives. He might attempt the flank
and rear of his enemy by way of the low grounds on the right and
left of the plateau, a movement which the precautions of Montcalm
had made difficult but not impossible. Or, instead of leaving his
artillery idle on the strand of Lake George, he might bring it to
the front and batter the breastwork, which, though impervious to
musketry, was worthless against heavy cannon. Or he might do
what Burgoyne did with success a score of years later, and plant a
battery on the heights of Rattlesnake Hill, now called Mount Defiance, which commanded the position of the French and whence
the inside of their breastwork could be scoured with round-shot
from end to end. Or, while threatening the French front with a
part of his army, he could march the rest a short distance through
the woods on his left to the road which led from Ticonderoga to
Crown Point, and which would soon have brought him to the
place called Five-Mile Point, where Lake Champlain narrows to
the width of an easy rifle-shot, and where a battery of fieldpieces
would have cut off all Montcalm's supplies and closed his only way
of retreat. As the French were provisioned for but eight days, their
position would thus have been desperate. They plainly saw the
danger; and Doreil declares that had the movement been made,
their whole army must have surrendered. Montcalm had done what
he could; but the danger of his position was inevitable and extreme. His hope lay in Abercrombie; and it was a hope well
founded. The action of the English general answered the utmost
wishes of his enemy.

Abercrombie had been told by his prisoners that Montcalm had
six thousand men, and that three thousand more were expected
every hour. Therefore he was in haste to attack before these suc-
cors could arrive. As was the general, so was the army. "I believe,"
writes an officer, "we were one and all infatuated by a notion of
carrying every obstacle by a mere *coup de mousqueterie*." Leadership perished with Lord Howe, and nothing was left but blind,
headlong valor.

Clerk, chief engineer, was sent to reconnoitre the French works from Mount Defiance; and came back with the report that, to judge from what he could see, they might be carried by assault. Then, without waiting to bring up his cannon, Abercrombie prepared to storm the lines. . . .

Soon after nine o'clock a distant and harmless fire of small-arms began on the slopes of Mount Defiance. It came from a party of Indians who had just arrived with Sir William Johnson, and who, after amusing themselves in this manner for a time, remained for the rest of the day safe spectators of the fight. The soldiers worked undisturbed till noon, when volleys of musketry were heard from the forest in front. It was the English light troops driving in the French pickets. A cannon was fired as a signal to drop tools and form for battle. The white uniforms lined the breastwork in a triple row, with the grenadiers behind them as a reserve, and the second battalion of Berry watching the flanks and rear.

Meanwhile the English army had moved forward from its camp by the sawmill. First came the rangers, the light infantry, and Brad-street's armed boatmen, who, emerging into the open space, began a spattering fire. Some of the provincial troops followed, extending from left to right and opening fire in turn; then the regulars, who had formed in columns of attack under cover of the forest, advanced their solid red masses into the sunlight, and passing through the intervals between the provincial regiments, pushed forward to the assault. Across the rough ground, with its maze of fallen trees whose leaves hung withering in the July sun, they could see the top of the breastwork, but not the men behind it; when, in an instant, all the line was obscured by a gush of smoke, a crash of exploding firearms tore the air, and grapeshot and musket-balls swept the whole space like a tempest; "a damnable fire," says an officer who heard them screaming about his ears. The English had been ordered to carry the works with the bayonet; but their ranks were broken by the obstructions through which they struggled in vain to force their way, and they soon began to fire in turn. The storm raged in full fury for an hour. The assailants pushed close to the breastwork; but there they were stopped by the bristling mass of sharpened branches, which they could not pass under the murderous cross fires that swept them from front and flank. At length they fell back,

exclaiming that the works were impregnable. Abercrom[bie]
was at the sawmill, a mile and a half in the rear, sent orders t[o] [at]tack again, and again they came on as before.

The scene was frightful: masses of infuriated men who could not go forward and would not go back; straining for an enemy they could not reach and firing on an enemy they could not see; caught in the entanglement of fallen trees; tripped by briers, stumbling over logs, tearing through boughs; shouting, yelling, cursing, and pelted all the while with bullets that killed them by scores, stretched them on the ground, or hung them on jagged branches in strange attitudes of death. The provincials supported the regulars with spirit, and some of them forced their way to the foot of the wooden wall.

The French fought with the intrepid gayety of their nation, and shouts of *Vive le Roi!* and *Vive notre Général!* mingled with the din of musketry. Montcalm, with his coat off, for the day was hot, directed the defence of the centre and repaired to any part of the line where the danger for the time seemed greatest. He is warm in praise of his enemy and declares that between one and seven o'clock they attacked him six successive times. Early in the action Abercrombie tried to turn the French left by sending twenty bateaux, filled with troops, down the outlet of Lake George. They were met by the fire of the volunteers stationed to defend the low grounds on that side, and, still advancing, came within range of the cannon of the fort, which sank two of them and drove back the rest.

A curious incident happened during one of the attacks. De Bassignac, a captain in the battalion of Royal Roussillon, tied his handkerchief to the end of a musket and waved it over the breastwork in defiance. The English mistook it for a sign of surrender and came forward with all possible speed, holding their muskets crossed over their heads in both hands and crying *Quarter*. The French made the same mistake; and thinking that their enemies were giving themselves up as prisoners, ceased firing and mounted on the top of the breastwork to receive them. Captain Pouchot, astonished, as he says, to see them perched there, looked out to learn the cause and saw that the enemy meant anything but surrender. Whereupon he shouted with all his might: *"Tirez! Tirez! Ne voyez-vous pas que ces gens-là vont vous enlever?"* The soldiers, still standing on the breastwork, instantly gave the English a volley, which killed some of them and sent back the rest discomfited.

This was set to the account of Gallic treachery. "Another deceit the enemy put upon us," says a military letter-writer: "they raised their hats above the breastwork, which our people fired at; they, having loopholes to fire through and being covered by the sods, we did them little damage, except shooting their hats to pieces." In one of the last assaults a soldier of the Rhode Island regiment, William Smith, managed to get through all obstructions and ensconce himself close under the breastwork, where in the confusion he remained for a time unnoticed, improving his advantages meanwhile by shooting several Frenchmen. Being at length observed, a soldier fired vertically down upon him and wounded him severely, but not enough to prevent his springing up, striking at one of his enemies over the top of the wall, and braining him with his hatchet. A British officer who saw the feat and was struck by the reckless daring of the man ordered two regulars to bring him off; which, covered by a brisk fire of musketry, they succeeded in doing. A letter from the camp two or three weeks later reports him as in a fair way to recover, being, says the writer, much braced and invigorated by his anger against the French, on whom he was swearing to have his revenge.

Towards five o'clock two English columns joined in a most determined assault on the extreme right of the French, defended by the battalions of Guienne and Béarn. The danger for a time was imminent. Montcalm hastened to the spot with the reserves. The assailants hewed their way to the foot of the breastwork; and though again and again repulsed, they again and again renewed the attack. The Highlanders fought with stubborn and unconquerable fury. "Even those who were mortally wounded," writes one of their lieutenants, "cried to their companions not to lose a thought upon them, but to follow their officers and mind the honor of their country. Their ardor was such that it was difficult to bring them off." Their major, Campbell of Inverawe, found his foreboding true. He received a mortal shot, and his clansmen bore him from the field.

Twenty-five of their officers were killed or wounded, and ╲
men fell under the deadly fire that poured from the loopholes. C╲
tain John Campbell and a few followers tore their way through the
abattis, climbed the breastwork, leaped down among the French,
and were bayoneted there.

As the colony troops and Canadians on the low ground were
left undisturbed, Lévis sent them an order to make a sortie and attack the left flank of the charging columns. They accordingly
posted themselves among the trees along the declivity and fired upwards at the enemy, who presently shifted their position to the
right, out of the line of shot. The assault still continued, but in vain;
and at six there was another effort, equally fruitless. From this
time till half-past seven a lingering fight was kept up by the rangers and other provincials, firing from the edge of the woods and
from behind the stumps, bushes, and fallen trees in front of the lines.
Its only objects were to cover their comrades, who were collecting
and bringing off the wounded, and to protect the retreat of the
regulars, who fell back in disorder to the Falls. As twilight came on,
the last combatant withdrew, and none were left but the dead.
Abercrombie had lost in killed, wounded, and missing nineteen
hundred and forty-four officers and men. The loss of the French,
not counting that of Langy's detachment, was three hundred and
seventy-seven. Bourlamaque was dangerously wounded; Bougain-
ville slightly; and the hat of Lévis was twice shot through.

Montcalm, with a mighty load lifted from his soul, passed along
the lines and gave the tired soldiers the thanks they nobly deserved.
Beer, wine, and food were served out to them, and they bivouacked
for the night on the level ground between the breastwork and the
fort. The enemy had met a terrible rebuff; yet the danger was not
over. Abercrombie still had more than thirteen thousand men, and
he might renew the attack with cannon. But on the morning of the
ninth a band of volunteers who had gone out to watch him brought
back the report that he was in full retreat. The sawmill at the Falls
was on fire, and the last English soldier was gone. On the morning
of the tenth Lévis, with a strong detachment, followed the road to
the landing-place and found signs that a panic had overtaken the
defeated troops. They had left behind several hundred barrels of

provisions and a large quantity of baggage; while in a marshy place that they had crossed was found a considerable number of their shoes, which had stuck in the mud and which they had not stopped to recover. They had embarked on the morning after the battle and retreated to the head of the lake in a disorder and dejection woefully contrasted with the pomp of their advance. A gallant army was sacrificed by the blunders of its chief.

Montcalm announced his victory to his wife in a strain of exaggeration that marks the exaltation of his mind. "Without Indians, almost without Canadians or colony troops—I had only four hundred—, alone with Lévis and Bourlamaque and the troops of the line, thirty-one hundred fighting men, I have beaten an army of twenty-five thousand. They repassed the lake precipitately, with a loss of at least five thousand. This glorious day does infinite honor to the valor of our battalions. I have no time to write more. I am well, my dearest, and I embrace you." And he wrote to his friend Doreil: "The army, the too-small army of the King, has beaten the enemy. What a day for France! If I had had two hundred Indians to send out at the head of a thousand picked men under the Chevalier de Lévis, not many would have escaped. Ah, my dear Doreil, what soldiers are ours! I never saw the like. Why were they not at Louisbourg?"

On the morrow of his victory he caused a great cross to be planted on the battle-field, inscribed with these lines, composed by the soldier-scholar himself—

Quid dux? quid miles? quid strata ingentia ligna?
En signum! en victor! Deus hic, Deus ipse triumphat.

Soldier and chief and rampart's strength are nought;
Behold the conquering Cross! 'Tis God the triumph wrought.

THE GREEN MOUNTAIN BOYS TAKE TY Ethan Allen

Ever since I arrived to a state of manhood and acquainted myself with the general history of mankind, I have felt a sincere passion for liberty. The history of nations doomed to perpetual slavery, in consequence of yielding up to tyrants their natural born liberties, I read with a sort of philosophical horror; so that the first systematical and bloody attempt at Lexington, to enslave America, thoroughly electrified my mind, and fully determined me to take part with my country. And while I was wishing for an opportunity to signalize myself in its behalf, directions were privately sent to me from the then colony (now state) of Connecticut, to raise the Green Mountain Boys; (and if possible) with them to surprise and take the fortress Ticonderoga. This enterprise I cheerfully undertook; and, after first guarding all the several passes that led thither, to cut off all intelligence between the garrison and the country, made a forced march from Bennington and arrived at the lake opposite Ticonderoga on the evening of the ninth day of May, 1775, with two hundred and thirty valiant Green Mountain Boys; and it was with the utmost difficulty that I procured boats to cross the lake. However, I landed eighty-three men near the garrison and sent the boats back for the rear guard commanded by col. Seth Warner; but the day began to dawn, and I found myself under a necessity to attack the fort before the rear could cross the lake; and, as it was viewed hazardous, I harangued the officers and soldiers in the manner following: "Friends and fellow soldiers, you have, for a number of years past, been a scourge and terror to arbitrary power. Your valour has been famed abroad and acknowledged, as appears by the advice and orders to me (from the general assembly of Connecticut) to surprise and take the garrison now before us. I now propose to advance before you and in person conduct you through the wicket gate; for we must this morning either quit our pretensions to valour or possess ourselves of this fortress in a few minutes; and, in as much as it is a desperate attempt (which none but the bravest of men dare undertake), I do not urge it on any contrary to his will. You that will undertake voluntarily, poise your firelocks."

The men being (at this time) drawn up in three ranks, each poised his firelock. I ordered them to face to the right; and, at the head of the centre file, marched them immediately to the wicket gate aforesaid, where I found a centry posted, who instantly snapped his fusee at me; I ran immediately toward him, and he retreated through the covered way into the parade within the garrison, gave a halloo, and ran under a bomb-proof. My party who followed me into the fort, I formed on the parade in such a manner as to face the two barracks which faced each other. The garrison being asleep (except the centries) we gave three huzzas which greatly surprised them. One of the centries made a pass at one of my officers with a charged bayonet and slightly wounded him. My first thought was to kill him with my sword; but, in an instant, altered the design and fury of the blow to a slight cut on the side of the head; upon which he dropped his gun and asked quarter, which I readily granted him, and demanded of him the place where the commanding officer kept; he shewed me a pair of stairs in the front of a barrack, on the west part of the garrison, which led up to a second story in said barrack, to which I immediately repaired, and ordered the commander (capt. Delaplace) to come forth instantly, or I would sacrifice the whole garrison; at which the capt. came immediately to the door with his breeches in his hand, when I ordered him to deliver to me the fort instantly, who asked me by what authority I demanded it; I answered, "In the name of the great Jehovah, and the Continental Congress." (The authority of the Congress being very little known at that time) he began to speak again; but I interrupted him, and with my drawn sword over his head, again demanded an immediate surrender of the garrison; to which he then complied and ordered his men to be forthwith paraded without arms, as he had given up the garrison; in the mean time some of my officers had given orders and in consequence thereof sundry of the barrack doors were beat down and about one third of the garrison imprisoned, which consisted of the said commander, a lieut. Feltham, a conductor of artillery, a gunner, two serjeants, and forty-four rank and file;

about one hundred pieces of cannon, one thirteen-inch mortar, and a number of swivels. This surprise was carried into execution in the gray of the morning of the tenth day of May, 1775. The sun seemed to rise that morning with a superior lustre; and Ticonderoga and its dependencies smiled on its conquerors, who tossed about the flowing bowl and wished success to Congress and the liberty and freedom of America.

FIFTY YEARS AFTER his first visit to Lake George as a college student on vacation, Francis Parkman noted his disgust at the transformed scene in a letter to a Canadian friend, the Abbé Casgrain:

> The *nouveau riche*, who is one of the pests of this country, has now got possession of the lake and its islands.
>
> For my part, I would gladly destroy all his works and restore Lake George to its native savagery.

Today, save for some 20,000 acres of forest preserve at the central part of Lake George, the Champlain-Lake George valley is the most highly developed area of the Adirondack Park. Originally this eastern fringe was well outside the Blue Line. In 1931, however, the park was expanded to include all of Lake George and part of the western shore of Lake Champlain (still more of the latter was included in the 1970s). Some Adirondackers of long memory regard this extension as a dilution. When I submitted the plan of the first edition of the *Reader* to Kenneth Durant, he protested the inclusion of the whole section titled "The Storied Path." This maverick of his family regarded Lake George as the end product of all that had gone wrong in the Adirondacks since his ancestors—Dr. Thomas, William West, and his own father, Frederick Durant—had invaded the woods with their fever of promotion. In a reference to the low elevation of Lake George, favorable to oaks and rattlesnakes, he wrote:

> When I was half as old as I am now we could say unctuously, "There are no venomous snakes in the Adirondacks," reciting a

bit of nature lore: "Rattlesnakes do not advance beyond the oaks." Then, when I was not looking, someone moved the Blue Line around Lake George and took in oaks and rattlesnakes— and worse. You may as well face it—though you don't—Lake George village of a Sunday in midsummer is in the Adirondacks. Put that in your anthology! . . . I prefer Eden without snakes.

Well, Eden without snakes is questionable in myth, theology, and reality. A slightly flawed paradise is probably the best we deserve; certainly the best we have been able to keep. And to an anthologist the rattlers, the overdeveloped shores, and the Sunday crowds seem a small price to pay for the addition of two hundred years of history, limited vistas of still unspoiled island and mainland, and Parkman and Cooper too.

In leaving now the Champlain-Lake George valley, we surrender two centuries of stirring history but gain a wilderness, significant parts of which remain to this day. It is a paradox that the Adirondack interior, so close to population centers of the Northeast, was virtually unknown till after the American Revolution. By 1820 a few hardy pioneers, mostly from Vermont, had penetrated into the interior. Systematic exploration did not begin till the 1830s. The next fifty years, however, witnessed an explosion of interest and development that threatened to overwhelm the woods till effective measures were taken.

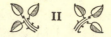

Possibilities Unbounded

All men are pioneers inside their hearts,
They are forever seeking wilderness....
They are dreaming of lands uncivilized that sprawl
Unfound, or unimagined, or forgot.

Lionel Wiggam

URING THE TWO-CENTURY conflict over the Champlain-Lake George corridor, the wilderness of northern New York was prized chiefly for its strategic value. Trappers meanwhile used it as a hunting ground. Otherwise the interior was a realm of mystery, unsurveyed and unexplored. Not until the fighting stopped was the way open for a variety of answers to the question: What is it good for?

Answers were not immediately forthcoming. A crude survey in 1772 ended abruptly on a hill where the going was rough and the rum gave out. Both before and after the Revolution, however, came a few large landowners with baronial ambitions. The first and most successful, Sir William Johnson, knighted by the Crown for his victory over the French in the Battle of Lake George and other services, flourished at his manorial hall in Johnstown prior to the Revolution. His land extended north from the Mohawk Valley into parts of the wilderness now within the Blue Line. There on the southernmost bend of the Sacandaga River he built two lodges for his leisure hours (the sites now flooded by the Sacandaga Reservoir), and thus became the first proprietor of something like a private park in the Adirondacks. While at Summer House and

[50]

Fish House, Sir William spent the day in sport and the night in exercising seignorial rights to a tenant's pretty daughters. Lucky in everything, this Old World aristocrat died on the eve of the Revolution; his heir, Sir John Johnson, fled to exile in Canada with his Tory supporters. Other would-be barons with lands in the Adirondacks were less fortunate. William Gilliland of Lake Champlain, returning to the ruins of his property after the Revolution, died of exposure in the forest; Charles Frederick Herreshoff of Brown's Tract killed himself when his enterprises failed. The ambitions of the barons have left little impress on the Adirondacks: a few clearings, a ruined forge, names on the map.

The westward surge of pioneers after the Revolution bypassed the Adirondacks. Repelled by harsh climate, rugged terrain, the more than usual impenetrability of Adirondack forests, pioneer families settled in the outlying valleys or pushed farther west. The few who did penetrate into the interior found the wilderness a threat to survival. Security and progress lay in enlarging the clearing around the homestead and improving communications. The wilderness became an enemy to be subdued. True, some of the children and grandchildren of the first-generation pioneer discovered the attractions of wild country. But most of the answers to What is it good for? came from the outside, from the city-bred.

The obvious resources of the region were the abundance of timber and game and the likelihood of mineral deposits. Exploiters of these resources appeared early in the last century. Logging began on the fringes of the uplift and, following the rivers, reached the center of the region by midcentury. Mines were opened.

Besides exploiters bent on taking wealth out of the woods, there were developers who sought to bring it in. Several of these men were wilderness lovers. The Reverend John Todd counted on his vacations in northern New York in the early 1840s to restore his health and spirits. Yet he had a vision of progress for the little pioneer settlement at Long Lake and others like it. The trees were to be cut down to make way for a prosperous Christian society.

Equally ambivalent was the Durant family a few decades later. They too were wilderness lovers, as much at home in the woods as in society. But they saw no incompatibility in bringing the

conveniences and luxuries of civilization into the woods. They
wanted the best of two worlds in their luxury camps, their railroads, telegraph lines, steamboats, and great resort hotel on Blue
Mountain Lake. Referring to this duality of his ancestors, Kenneth
Durant remarked that they all had the developer's urge: "all the
Durants except me—sitting on the piazza at Saratoga Springs,
dreaming of wealth in wild lands. . . . It is not so much that the
wilderness and Christian living are incompatible, but that the
parable of the talents teaches us that undeveloped land is a sin."

The woods have proved big and durable enough to contain,
isolate, or defeat the works of these developers of the Gilded Age
and early twentieth century. William West Durant's luxury camps
are now conference centers or historical monuments. Frederick
Durant's great hotel had only a short life. W. Seward Webb's
railroad, revived in the late 1970s for a few runs, is quiescent again,
and his private park is now largely state owned. Forest fires
destroyed A. Augustus Low's mercantile empire of timber products, bottled Adirondack spring water, products of his sophisticated
sugarbush, and preserves from berry crops on cut-over lands. Two
Boy Scout councils now sport in the regrown woods of his Bog
River domain.

The preservation of several large areas of wilderness and semi-
wilderness in the Adirondacks is largely due to the historical
accident that the interior was virtually unknown and unsettled
before the 1830s. One of the many paradoxes of the region is
that, though it is situated in the populous Northeast, its most salient
geographical feature, the height of its mountains, remained a
mystery till 1836, when Ebenezer Emmons and associated scientists
began the first systematic survey of the Adirondacks. Till then
Whiteface was assumed to be the highest peak, and its elevation
was stated as 2,600 feet above sea level, lower than the measured
elevation of some Catskill peaks. In 1836 Emmons climbed Whiteface and made a barometric measurement of 4,855 feet, close to
the recent reading of 4,867. At the same time he noted that there
were at least three higher summits to the south. In August of the
following year Emmons and other scientists made the first known
ascent of Mount Marcy, highest peak in the state. (Mount

Washington in New Hampshire had been climbed two centuries earlier in 1642.) The announcement of this discovery brought the first tourists into the high peak region and soon after into the central lake region.

By the 1830s and increasingly over the next generation a popular culture of love of nature was spreading among educated classes in the cities, on the wings of English romantic poets and American transcendentalists. Sentiments such as Byron's

> There is a pleasure in the pathless woods,
> There is a rapture in the lonely shore,
> There is a society, where none intrudes;

Emerson's "In the woods is perpetual youth"; and Thoreau's "In Wildness is the preservation of the world" were echoed in the popular press and seeped into the consciousness of literate persons. Wilderness came to be recognized as our unique national heritage, setting us apart from other nations. To keep in touch with our roots, we needed periodic escape from the city into the woods. The woods were a great reservoir of health, inspiration, and renewal.

When in the middle decades of the last century farmers, loggers, miners, and developers invaded the interior, there was a simultaneous countermovement of explorers, sportsmen, and tourists. Among the latter were conservationists who had by mid-century learned that the resources of the continent were not inexhaustible, as the first wave of pioneers had believed. Emmons himself cautioned in 1838 against the loggers' practice of clear-cutting in a mountainous region such as the Adirondacks. Some sportsmen were game hogs, but many others recognized the necessity of game regulations to insure sustained yield. The conservationists won a notable victory in 1885 with the creation of the Forest Preserve to protect the major watershed of the state.

But for many conservation of resources was not enough. They wanted outright preservation. Whereas the conservationist stressed the long-range material advantages of controlled use, the preservationist stressed the immaterial rewards of a pristine wilderness where man is only a temporary visitor. "Mountain parks and reservations are useful not only as fountains of timber and irrigating rivers," as John Muir said, "but as fountains of life." The preservationist view was recognized in the creation of the Adirondack Park in 1892 "for the free use of all the people for their health and pleasure" and again in 1894 with the adoption of the "forever-wild" constitutional amendment governing the Forest Preserve, a covenant to the defense of which, says preservationist Paul Schaefer, a man can devote the best hours of his life.

To the preservationist wilderness is a cornucopia of gifts to body and spirit. "The ultimate values of wilderness are spiritual values," says Paul Oehser, a frequent visitor to the Adirondacks. "No one man can define or predict what the wilderness may yield. Its secrets are inexhaustible, even as creation itself. It is a well of wonder and inspiration." In this section and others several articulate writers try to define the values Oehser has in mind. A composite definition emerges from these attempts. Preservationists are well represented in Adirondack literature.

It is the nature of wilderness to suggest unlimited possibilities. But limits there certainly are. Perhaps the most restrictive lie in the opposition of interests. With settlers, exploiters, developers, sportsmen, summer residents, tourists, conservationists, preservationists, and lately, since Rachel Carson's *Silent Spring*, environmentalists abroad in the woods, conflict is inevitable. Clear-cut, shining victories for any one side are few and far between. The record is full of compromises. The 1970 report of the Temporary Study Commission on the Future of the Adirondack Park is itself a masterpiece of compromise. It is slanted, maintains the Local Government Review Board, toward the preservationist side. But preservationists can legitimately respond that they get only a one-sixth slice of the pie in the million acres classified as wilderness. So the conflict goes on. And now, as Mason Smith points out in the last essay of this section, it has been institutionalized.

THE BARONET AND SUSANNAH
Jeptha R. Simms

Sir William Johnson, after establishing himself at his hall in Johnstown, no doubt lived in greater affluence, or more in the style of a European nobleman of that day, than ever did any other citizen of New York. His household was quite numerous at all times and not unfrequently was much increased by distinguished guests. . . .

Sir William was a large, well-looking and full-favored man. "Laugh and grow fat" is an old maxim of which his neighbors were reminded when they beheld this fun-loving man. He was well read for the times and uncommonly well versed in the study of human nature. . . .

Traversing the forest in the French war, from Ticonderoga to Fort Johnson, his then residence, no doubt first made Sir William Johnson familiar with the make of the country adjoining the Sacandaga River; and soon after the close of that war he erected a lodge for his convenience, while hunting and fishing, on the south side of the river, nearly eighteen miles distant from his own dwelling. The lodge was ever after called *The Fish House*. . . .

From the residence of Col. John I. Shew, situated on an eminence one and a half miles from Fonda's Bush and on the plank road to Fish House, is afforded the lover of natural science, in a clear day, one of the richest landscapes in this part of the state. Here the eye, looking north, seems to scan rather more than one-half of an amphitheatre an hundred miles in circuit, with rich and varied scenery. Within the view is overlooked the Sacandaga vlaie[now the Sacandaga Reservoir], a body of from ten to thirteen thousand acres of drowned lands. . . . One of the most interesting features about the vlaie is the fact that a little knoll or table of hard land elevated some ten or twelve feet extends into it toward the upper or western end. It is oblong in shape, level upon the top and gently sloping all round. It lies about northwest and southeast, the summit being some six hundred feet long by one hundred and fifty in breadth; and containing in the whole say ten to fifteen acres of very good land. This tongue of land is called *Summer-House Point*, from the fact that Sir William Johnson erected a beautiful cottage in the centre of it in 1772, and there spent much of his time in the summer for several seasons. From Johnstown to this point, which is just fourteen miles, the Baronet opened a carriage road. . . .

A large garden was cultivated on the point, two cows kept there, and when the Baronet was there two horses also; as he usually rode there in a carriage. He planted fruit trees there, and two antiquated apple trees of a dozen or more are still standing. The stone of which the cellar and well were made was brought from Fish House in a boat. . . .

Near the mouth of Han's Creek and about halfway from Summer-House Point to Fish House dwelt before the Revolution the family of Henry Wormwood. He had three daughters and two sons. The oldest daughter, whose name is now forgotten, married and went to Schoharie; the other two, Susannah and Elizabeth, lived at home. Susannah, the eldest of the two, was a beautiful girl of middling stature, charmingly formed, with a complexion fair as a water lily—contrasting with which she had a melting dark eye and raven hair. Elizabeth much resembled her sister, but was not quite as fair. An Irishman named Robert or Alexander Dunbar, a good-looking fellow, paid his addresses to Susannah, and soon after married her. The match was in some manner brought about by the Baronet; was an unhappy one, and they soon after parted. She however retained as her stock in trade a young Dunbar. What became of Dunbar is unknown.

Sir William was on very intimate terms with both the Wormwood girls, but the most so with Susannah, after she became a grass-widow—at which time she was about twenty years old. Those girls were often at the cottage on the point and not unfrequently at Fish House. As the latter place was not furnished, when Sir William went down there intending to stay overnight, he took down a bed from the point, which, "as the evening shades prevailed," was made up on the floor. In passing Wormwood's dwelling, some half a mile distant from his boat at the nearest point, if he desired an agreeable companion for the night, he discharged his double-barreled gun, and the two shots in quick succession was a signal that never failed to bring him a temporary housekeeper. Susannah was his favorite, and so pleased was she with his attentions that she often arrived on foot at the Fish House before he did, especially if he lingered to fish by the way.

Wormwood and his wife sometimes accompanied one of their daughters to the Fish House, where they occasionally remained overnight. The old man had the misfortune to break an arm, and by imprudence he kept it lame for a long time. Early one morning he called in at Shew's dwelling, situated over a knoll and perhaps one-fourth of a mile from the Fish House. Rubbing his arm he began to give a sorry picture of its lameness, in which he was suddenly interrupted by Mrs. Shew. "Poh!" said she, "you have made it lame by sleeping on the floor again at the Fish House."

"No I haven't," said he; "I slept on a good bed; for Sir William brought down from the point a very nice wide one, which was plenty large enough for four"—

"*Four?*" quickly interrogated Mrs. Shew, greatly surprised at the reply of Wormwood. "Pray how did you manage to sleep *four* in a bed?"

"Oh, easy enough. Susannah made it up very nicely on the floor, and then Sir William told us how to lay. He first directed the women to get in the middle, and now, said he to me, you get on that side and take care of your old woman next to you, and I'll get in on this side and try to take care of Susannah. No, I didn't make my arm lame by sleeping on the floor *last* night." It is unnecessary to add, Mrs. S. did not question her neighbor any farther.

To dispose of this family in a few words, which catered for

years to pamper the baser passions of an influential man, liberally endowed with Solomondic lust; the two sons went to Canada with Sir John Johnson; Elizabeth married *somebody* and moved to— *somewhere;* and Susannah, with an heir to the Sacandaga vlaie— sex unknown—remained about Johnstown with her parents until the Revolution was over and then went to Canada. Old Worm- wood was seen at Amsterdam after the war by a former neighbor, who enquired where he lived. "Anywhere," he replied, "where I can find a house." Poor weak man, he has beyond a doubt parted with his mortal coil long since; but his old bones, we hazard a conjecture, more than once felt the need of Sir William's "wide bed," or some other, before that solemn event.

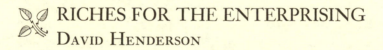

RICHES FOR THE ENTERPRISING
DAVID HENDERSON

The discovery of the iron ore deposits south of Indian Pass, between lakes Sanford and Henderson, is narrated in the following letter by David Henderson, one of the party of prospectors, to his partner and future father-in-law, Archibald McIntyre, of New York and Albany. Though the vein was rich, McIntyre Iron Works strug- gled against difficulties of production and transportation till its abandonment in 1857. Since 1941 the mines at Tahawus have been major producers of titanium, once considered an "impurity" in the ore.

Elba, Essex County, 14th October, 1826. We have now left the woods and intend returning home, for excellent reasons. We find it impossible to make a complete search for the silver ore this season. Duncan McMartin's time will not allow him to remain longer at present—to search all the likely ground, it would take seven men one month longer at least—but the principal cause of our quitting it just so soon is the discovery of the most extraordinary bed of iron ore, for singularity of situation and extent of vein, which perhaps this North American Continent affords. . . .

[We] got all in preparation for the woods pretty early—just before starting, a strapping young Indian of a Canadian tribe made his appearance at Darrow's gate, the first which had been seen in the settlement for three years. Enoch [a Negro servant], who by the bye we had been plaguing about Indians, and whose fears on that score were considerably excited, happened to be standing at the door at the time and made a precipitate retreat to the back settlements of the house. "Well now Missa Henderson this too bad —don't you collect I tells you not to bring me in among Indians— they be a people I wants nothing to do with."

The Indian opened his blanket and took out a small piece of iron ore about the size of a nut—"You want see 'em ore—me know 'em bed, all same"—Whereabouts did you find it? "Me know—over mountain" (pointing to the southwest). Does any other Indian know of it—"No—me hunt 'em beaver, all 'lone last spring—when me find 'em"—Have you shewn it to any white man?—"Yes me shewn him ore—no, bed—but no white man go see it"—How far to it?—"Me guess, twelve miles over that way"—The people about laughed at the idea and said altho' the ore was good—he had chip'd it from a rock, and thought the Indian would lead us a wild goose chase, etc. . . .

This Indian being a very modest, honest looking fellow, we concluded to take him along with us at any rate and enquired at him how much he would take to remain in the woods with us till Saturday night—"Dollar, half, and 'bacco." To this moderate demand we assented. So off we went with our packs on our backs —Our company consisted of Duncan and Malcolm McMartin, Dyer Thompson, our valiant nigger, the Indian, John [McIntyre] and myself. By the way the Indian's name is Lewis, his father's name Elija—and he calls himself therefore Lewis Elija—something like the *Highland* way of names, being another strong resemblance to the *Highlanders*—We (the descendants of Shem, Ham and Japheth) trudged along the road in a peaceable manner; although it was plain to be seen, that the descendant of Ham eyed the descendant of Shem with suspicion and kept at a most respectful distance. . . .

On Friday morning we all started with the Indian for the ore bed—our course to a notch in the south mountains, where the River Ausable has its source. After a fatiguing journey we arrived at the notch, as wild a place as I ever saw. On one side an immense rock rising perpendicularly from the narrow pass we had to travel through, filled in many places with large masses which had tumbled down from each side of the mountain. On the whole, it was a terrific place to think of travelling through. Our descendant of Ham gaz'd in a fit of astonishment— When he found that we were scrambling on and must go through what he saw so dreadful before him— Well now dis beat all! For God Almighty's sake! how can a body ever get over dis? What put it in your compurnihenshun ever to come in sich parts? I never thinks there be such horrificable place in all dis world.

We climb on—came to a place where we were all obliged to glide down on the breech with some caution. Enoch was brought to his trumps at this necessity—he liked not the idea of so long a voyage upon his beam ends—and declared to me with a good deal of pettishness—that "*dis was a compleat take in.*" A few minutes afterwards he made good his footing to a tree, but some green moss at its root having covered a deceitful hole, poor Enoch's leg was destined to fill it up, and down he came, camp-kettle and all— the one leg pointing to the heavens, and the other to the opposite direction, for it was a dreadful chasm below—the hole however fitted the leg pretty well— Well, says I, Enoch, that is a complete *take in* indeed!

We at length gained the summit of the notch, the very fountain head of the Ausable River, where we found another stream running south, which appears to be the principal source of the Hudson River. We proceeded down the notch on the other side, and at about halfway down [were] obliged to camp for the night. Our situation here was grand in the extreme—encamped at the head of the North River in a narrow pass—the moon glimmering by fits through the forest; the huge perpendicular rocks on each side, aspiring to the heavens, were our curtains—the clouds our canopy, the ground our bed—the infant murmurs of the giant River Hudson, the music which lull'd asleep— Astir by times next morning— had every appearance of a wet day, and therefore concluded to leave Enoch for the purpose of making the camp as rain proof as possible for the night. Took a little biscuit in our pocket by way of lunch and left Enoch all alone.

The Indian carried us over a hill, and after travelling about four miles came to the same stream on which we encamp'd the previous night, but of course much enlarged. On crossing this, found a great many pieces of pure iron ore laying in the channel—some as large as a pumpkin. We travelled *down* the stream about half a mile, when to our astonishment we found the bed of ore (which we had hitherto conceived to be on the side of a mountain) laying on the river— This river runs there nearly north and south, and the vein strikes over it in a northeast and southwest direction. He took us to a ledge five feet high running into the river, which was nothing but *pure ore*. The Indian however had no idea of the extent of the vein.

We went one hundred yards below the vein, where is a waterfall of ten feet. Mr. Duncan McMartin, his brother and the Indian proceeded down to a lake below (which is about four miles long) to make observations. Mr. Thompson, John and myself returned to the ore bed to make a particular examination and wait there till their return. We found the *breadth* of the vein to be about *fifty feet!*—traced it into the woods on both sides of the river. On the one side went eighty feet into the wood, and digging down about a foot of earth, found the pure ore bed there—and let me here remark this immense mass of ore is unmix'd with anything—in the middle of the river where the water runs over—the channel appears like the bottom of a smoothing iron—on the top of the vein are large junks which at first we thought stone, but lifting one up (as much as Thompson could do) and letting it fall it crumbled into a thousand pieces of pure ore. In short, the thing was past all our conceptions— We traced the vein most distinctly—the sides parallel to one another, and running into the earth on both sides of the stream. We had an opportunity to see the vein nearly five feet from the surface of it on the side of the ledge which falls perpendicular into the water, and at this depth we made a cavity of a foot or two, where we found the ore crumbled to pieces, which Thompson called *shot ore*—it was there of an indigo colour —the grain of the ore is large—on the top of the ledge it appears to be a little harder than below, but not so hard but a junk would break easily in throwing it down— Thompson considers it a rich ore, and as we have now ascertained, entirely free from sulphur.

Do not conceive it wonderful that this immense vein has never been discovered—it is in an extraordinary place—you might pass the whole and think it rock—it has been a received opinion that there was no ore *south* of the great ridge of mountains—a white man or even an Indian may not travel in that way for years—but certain it is, that here is the *great* mother vein of iron, which throws her little veins and sprinklings all over these mountains. Duncan and Malcolm and the Indian returned to us—they paced from the lake, and found it to be nearly a mile and a half from the ore bed. The nearest house, where one Newcomb lives, is from six to eight miles distant. The next is the Pendleton settlement— the stream is excellent for works—and a good chance for a road to Newcomb's where is a regular road.

When they returned to us, the rain began to pour in torrents— the day was nearly spent— We removed as much as possible all traces of marks on the ore bed, should it happen that any hunter might pass the spot— We hastened on our journey drench'd to the skin—the Indian our guide. What a wonderful sagacity these unsophisticated children of the forest display in the wilderness— let them see sun—rivers or distant hills—or failing these the most indistinct tracts [Scots for path] they are never at a loss—"Here 'em bear today—Moose here day 'fore yesterday—Wolf here hour ago"—were the frequent ejaculations of our Indian; and I may here observe when we were on the other side of the pass—he turned up three tier of leaves and said "Brigham and me here tree year ago" —but to go on with my narrative darkness came upon us, and soon found that we had turned back, for we found ourselves going south with the stream— We made great efforts after this discovery to go for the camp where we had left Enoch with our small stock of provisions which we had brought from our stationary camp but it rain'd so hard that we were weigh'd down with the weight of our clothes, and so dark that we could scarcely see our hand before our face—in short we at last knew not in what direction we were going. The Indian now was of no more use as a guide than any of us—for without sun, headlands or tract what could the poor Hebrew do? We were indeed on the stream on which we had left Enoch, but to travel along the banks of it in the dark over windfalls and rocks we found impossible. . . .

It cleared off towards the morning, and you may well conceive we gave daylight a hearty welcome. We found ourselves only one mile from the place where we left Enoch—we hastened to him as fast as stiff legs would carry us, and we found him asleep after a wakeful night of terrification. The storm howled "dreadly" he said all night—and he could not shut his eyes for the fear of bears, panthers, wolves and Indians—and the "horricate" thought of being left all alone in such a night and place. The very first thing we did was to drink up all the rum we had *raw* about a glass each —and a breakfast we made, finish'd everything but a piece of pork about two inches square. . . .

[After further difficulties and delays on the return journey, they reached North Elba after having been "in the woods eight days without having our clothes off."]

This enormous iron bed kept possession of our minds—I dreamt about it— We judge it best to lose no time in securing if possible— We will take the Indian with us to Albany—dare not well leave him in this country—Mr. McMartin has made all the observations he can—so as to come at it at Albany. The Indian has drawn us a complete map of all the country about. If it has been surveyed, there will be little difficulty—if not, there will be much—but it must be overcome. . . . Shew'd specimens of the ore to some bloomers—they said there was no doubt about it. I have written you very fully. Will write you on our arrival in Albany, after knowing what can be done. In the meantime, I am, Dear Sir, Yours truly,

D. Henderson.

AFTER THE TREES ARE CUT DOWN
REV. JOHN TODD

The First Visit—1841

Early in the month of September, 1841, in company with a learned friend, whose accurate skill has measured these mountains and these waters [probably Professor Farrand N. Benedict of Burlington College, Vermont], I first visited and became acquainted with this wilderness. Nearly in its centre we came to a beautiful sheet of water—the Long Lake—which is about twenty miles long and from half a mile to three miles wide. It is studded with islands and surrounded by a heavy forest and in the warm sky of summer seems like a fairy land. Scattered along towards the head of the lake, we found a little community of eight or nine families. They were here alone, shut out from the world. The hunter's axe alone had marked the trees when they came. They lived in their little log houses, and their little boats were their horses and the lake their only path. If they wanted to call a physician, or to go to a store, or even to get a bushel of rye ground, they must follow a wild footpath between forty and fifty miles to get out. A pocket compass was used as frequently as by the sailor. They were skilful in taking the moose, the deer, and the salmon-trout, and these were their world. But even here Death had followed and found them, and they had buried their flower, a girl of sixteen or seventeen years of age, just before we got there. The mother pointed me to the spot where they had cut down the lofty trees, that the sunlight might come in and rest upon the grave of the solitary sleeper. There was no knell, and no minister, and no prayer at her funeral—for there was no one to speak for God. Men had gone there to survey lands, to buy and sell, to hunt and fish, but no one to care for the soul. It was Saturday when we arrived, and as soon as it was known that a minister had come, two of the young ladies sprang into a little boat and rowed round to let the families know of the event. The ladies there can row and manage a boat as well as they can a horse in other places. In thus calling on their neighbors, they must have rowed twelve or fourteen miles. The Sabbath morning came, and no hounds were sent to chase the deer. No fish were caught. The loons screamed unmolested. It was the first Sabbath that ever broke upon the lake, and I was to preach the first sermon.

We met—the little boats coming up, some rowed by a father with all his family in it, some by the sisters, and some by the little brothers; and one huge bark canoe, with an old hunter who lived alone many miles further in the wilderness. We met in a little log house covered with hemlock bark. Men, women, children, and dogs were all there. We could not sing, for none had learned the songs of Zion in a strange land. I preached the first sermon which that wilderness ever heard. In the afternoon we met some four or five miles up the lake to accommodate one who was feeble. They were all there again. Our woodsman now recalled a half hunting tune or two, and so we had singing. Oh! what a meeting was that! They hung on the lips. They wept and remembered the days and privileges they once enjoyed. They came around like children and promised that if I would "come in" and stay with them, they would leave off hunting and fishing on the Sabbath and become good! And when we passed through the mighty forest, never yet degraded by the axe, down to the little bay, and when we all shot out of that sweet little bay together in our little boats, parted there, they broke out and sang. . . .

The Second Visit—1842

I organized them into a church of God, by the name of "The First Congregational Church on Long Lake." I baptized eight of their children, including six little boys belonging to Mr. S., who, with his wife, was among those who wept for joy and trembled in weakness on this occasion. It was a most solemn occasion. It was the most solemn season I ever witnessed. And when in the name of my own church and in the name of the beloved churches of New England, I gave them the right hand, I felt safe in assuring them that we should remember and sympathize with this young and feeble sister, who was thus "now planted in the wilderness." I ventured to assure this little flock that we would not forget her; that we would pray for her and would minister to her spiritual wants. They promised to have a weekly prayer meeting every Friday afternoon, to hold up the Sabbath by means of the Sabbath school, and to have sermons read on the Sabbath as soon as they could get some that are suitable, and to pray that God would in his own time and way send them a pastor. When I reached home and told the story, the children of my Sabbath school immediately set about making a collection to send them a Sabbath school library. . . .

As soon as the road is open, population will roll in, and I may yet live to see the day when a church shall be erected on one of their beautiful islands and a hundred little boats lie moored around while they keep holy time. What a day will that be! and how sweet will be the notes of the church-going bell as they float up and down and across these beautiful waters and are echoed from the mountains which stand around and glass themselves in the lake! This little church is to be at the head of a great population! May the handful of corn scattered upon the mountains shake like Lebanon.

I left the little band feeling feeble, though they were not forsaken, and believing that a brighter day is to come to them. Two little boys, whom I had baptized, rowed me down the lake very late Sabbath night, after the labors of the day, to my camp, and after they had landed me, for a long time I could see their little forms in the boat as they turned to go back to their home. They rowed away in silence and in the darkness, but I knew they were under the eye of Him to whom they had been given that day, and that they were safe. Though we were sick and out for twenty days and nights without shelter, and in storms, I felt on my return that it was all nothing in comparison with the joy of that Sabbath, in which the little church was "planted in the wilderness."

The Third Visit—1843

The fact is new and seems strange to many that there should be in the northeastern part of New York a wilderness almost unbroken and unexplored, embracing a territory considerably larger than the whole state of Massachusetts; a territory exhibiting every variety of soil, from the bold mountain that lifts its head up far beyond the limit of vegetable life to the most beautiful meadow land on which the eye ever rested. This territory, when as thickly inhabited as is Massachusetts, will contain over a million of inhabitants. It is for the most part primitive soil, composed of ranges and groups of lofty mountains and deep valleys, with beautiful intervals along side of the rivers, which have been washed down from the sides of the mountains. When the day shall arrive in which these forests shall be cut down, and along the lakes and valleys and around the base of these glorious mountains there shall be a virtuous, industrious and Christian population, I have no doubt it will easily support a million of people. Here are forests almost interminable, timber of great beauty and abundance; iron ore in quality very rich, and in quantity inexhaustible; waterfalls of great height, yielding any amount of power in all directions. Say what we will about the fertility and the glories of the everlasting flats of the West, the *primitive soil* is associated with what man loves and what makes men. It is connected with the blue mountains and the pure air which flows over them. It is associated with the leaping brook, the gushing waterfall, and the pure waters which come rushing down from their mountain home, with manufactories and industry, thrift, health, a bracing climate, and a virtuous community. Who would feel that if New England could, at a word, exchange her hard hills, her granite mountains, and her severe climate for the rich, exuberant plains and sunny climes of the south and west, that the exchange would not be most disastrous to the happiness of the present and of future generations? . . .

The scenery on these lakes is grand and beautiful beyond anything of which I ever conceived. The lakes of Scotland have been celebrated of old in story and in song; but the time will come, I doubt not, when these lakes will become the most interesting resort to be found in this country, for the great, the rich, the curious and the fashionable. Most of them are surrounded by forests which grow down to the water's edge and glass themselves in mirrors which reflect every leaf; most are studded with romantic islands covered with the mighty forests where the eagle finds a home unmolested. . . .

The Fourth Visit—1844

It has been intimated that there is but little good land in this immense forest. I wonder at the traveller who can say this. Did he ever follow the Racket River from Long Lake down to the Big

Bogs and see the valley it creates? Did he ever look at the two hundred acres where the Indians once had corn on the shore opposite the mouth of Stony Brook? Did he ever pass through townships No. 24 or 25, where the river winds and is twenty-two miles in advancing ten? Did he ever view the land near Fish Creek on the Upper Saranac Lake and between that and the St. Regis? Did he ever see the land at Cold River or the township which lies south of Great Tupper's Lake or the land on the Racket Lake or that which lies between Mud Lake and Handsome Pond? I think I might ask this question of at least twenty townships, each ten miles square, which we visited and pronounced among the most beautiful land we ever beheld.

Let no man think he can explore this wilderness in a few days or even weeks. The Rev. Mr. Allen and myself have spent two vacations in it, and very few men ever labored more severely. At our last visit we penetrated between eighty and ninety miles after leaving the last habitation of man. I believe out of the two hundred lakes which are already known, we visited only twenty-four in the two visits; and to do that, we worked early and late, camped where the night found us, and ate what we could obtain and when we could obtain it. We probably, including our return, travelled over three hundred miles in the forest at each visit. I think I speak advisedly, then, when I say that though it is an Alpine region, a country of mountains and rocks, of lakes and ponds, a region of storms and long winters, yet after all, there are immense tracts of as beautiful land as need be and such as will not suffer by comparison with the best anywhere found. Much of it—nay, most of it—was never visited except by the hunter. . . .

It is difficult to say what the climate will be after the forests are removed. Most suppose it will be colder than at present, inasmuch as the forests break and shut off the winds. If my own opinion is of any value, I think it will be milder after the removal of the trees. . . . The ground, covered with a thick forest, does not become warm and continue warm all night as it will when the trees are removed and as it does in an open country. Hence, though the waters are warm, the ground is always cold, and during the warmest night in the summer, a large fire at your feet and a buffalo robe around you are most comfortable. But when the sun shall be let in to warm the earth and the warmth shall be returned to the atmosphere, is it not reasonable to suppose the climate will be softened and milder? . . .

A most wonderful change had the Gospel wrought among that people since he [Mr. Parker, the missionary] went among them. The Sabbath has become holy time; the population almost universally are constant in attending public worship. . . . What an advancement in intellect! I think I never saw such a growth in intellect in a single year. By the light of their fires during the long winter evenings, they had read. The Bible class has a library of eighty-four volumes—the gift of Mr. Delavan of Albany—and some of the girls had understandingly read every book through. They could understand preaching, and very seldom have I heard a Bible class recite better. . . . The missionary teaches them how to read, to write, to think; how to catch their fish and how to make their rackets or snowshoes. He is now teaching all the elder part of the youth in a week-day school as well as on the Sabbath. And I am happy to feel that there are some things very encouraging in future prospect. . . . We wish to fulfil our pledge to the landholders and put up a neat little church and complete it. Then will the Sabbath be ever abiding there, and that settlement, now so remote and so lonely, will become a blessed community—sanctifying all who will hereafter fill the region. When I was with them on the Sabbath—when I looked upon my young friend, *Sabatas*, a noble Indian young man, whose violin leads the music in public worship—when I saw how much they had improved in intellect, morality, and character, I felt that all that has been done for them will yet return in blessings upon the friends who have done it. Nor do I believe it possible for any benevolent heart to visit these dwellers in the wilderness without feeling an interest in them which is amazing even to himself.

DON'T CUT DOWN THE TREES
JOEL T. HEADLEY

On visits to Long Lake in 1844 and 1846 Joel T. Headley drew different conclusions on the future of the pioneer settlement there from those formed three years earlier by John Todd ("After the Trees Are Cut Down"). The following reply to Todd appeared first in the New York *Observer*, which Todd had also used as a mouthpiece.

You have heretofore had a good many letters from Long Lake descriptive of its scenery, capabilities of its land, the interesting colony on its borders, etc. . . . I said once, through your paper, that this never could be a good farming country, in the common acceptation of that term; and I was asked if I had seen this and that and the other lake. I now repeat my former assertion and say, as then, that this might become a good wool-growing region, or dairy country, but nothing more.

It is, in the first place, the most mountainous portion of this state; indeed, I do not believe there is in the Union a territory three hundred miles in circumference so terribly rough and wild as this. It is not only mountainous but has the disadvantage of being the source of nearly all the waters of northern and eastern New York, and hence has less alluvial soil than equally rough districts lying along large rivers. All mountainous regions have more or less interval land, with a rich, deep soil; but here the intervals are lakes. Water occupies the place ordinarily appropriated to towns and meadows. There is good land here, no doubt, and large tracts which are arable and would be fruitful; but the question is, what proportion does this bear to that which cannot be cultivated? I have seen fields of waving grain in the vale of Chamouni and thousands of cattle grazing in rich pastures in Grindelwald and long stretches of meadow in the valley of Meyringen; but it would be ridiculous to call the Alpine district a good farming country, for all that. I venture to say that there are three hundred acres in this region a plough will never touch to one that it will. Besides, it is a cold climate here, and the summers are short. Neither corn nor wheat can be relied on as a crop. Grass, rye, oats, and potatoes may be grown, and these are all.

Now here is a colony, called the Long Lake Colony, about which much has been said, much sympathy excited, and on which more or less money has been expended. And what is its condition? It has been established for many years, and by this time it ought to furnish some inducements to the farmer who would locate here, nearly fifty miles from a post office or store and half that distance from a good mill. But what is the truth respecting it? *Not a man here supports himself from his farm;* and I can see no gain since I was here two years ago. Some of the best men have left, and those that remain depend on the money (some seven hundred dollars) furnished by the state for the making of roads, to buy their provisions with. The church which was organized some time since was never worthy of the name of one, the few men who composed it, with some few exceptions, being anything but religious men. I was told by one of the chief men here that one man now constituted the entire "Congregational Church of Long Lake." There are no meetings held on the Sabbath, not even a Sabbath school. As I went from house to house, I saw books scattered round belonging to the Long Lake Library, marked, some of them, with the names of the donors; but they seemed to me thrown away. The truth is, the people here, as a general thing, would not give a farthing for any religious privileges, indeed would rather be without them; and instead of this colony being a center from which shall radiate an immense population, covering the whole of this wild region, it will drag on a miserable existence, composed, two-thirds of it, by those who had rather hunt than work. I do not mean to disparage this central region of New York; but I would divest it of the romance of dreamers and the falsehoods of land speculators. . . .

I would like to see this desolate country settled; but it never will be till the West is all occupied. An overplus population will subdue it, nothing else. Crowding may drive farmers here, but no gentler means. Say what men will, it is an awfully rough, cold, and forbidding country to the farmer. The Swiss from the Alps or the Scotch from the Highlands might pitch their abodes here and stay —necessity alone will keep the rest; and when this forest-covered territory shall "support a million of people," the state of New York will show a census equal to that of the whole Union at present. . . .

He who comes into this region must expect to work hard with little recompense, see a rough stony farm reject his labor, and make up by economy what he lacks by acquirement.

Still, this is a glorious region to the hunter after the picturesque and grand in nature. I know nothing equal to it this side of the Alps. These lofty mountains folding their summits so calmly and solemnly away against the sky—these beautiful lakes in their green inclosures sparkling in the sun—these countless islands and winding rivers make it a land of beauty and sublimity that once seen is ever after remembered. Still, much of its interest is owing to its very wildness. The shores of these lakes look beautiful because a mantle of foliage sweeps down to the very margin of the waters; but where they are cultivated, rocks and stones present a sterile aspect to the beholder. Cut down the trees, and two-thirds of all the beauty of this region would depart. There would be no sloping shores, carrying the rich meadow or waving grain to the water's edge, as on the Cayuga and Skaneateles lakes, but in their place abrupt banks, covered with rocks that no cultivation could cover.

But it is with singular feelings one fresh from the city stands here and looks around on the interminable forests and remembers that it is a hard day's work to get out to civilized life, and yet that his feet are on the soil of New York, and a few roods of ground divide him from the waters of the Hudson. It is no small job to get here, and to one not accustomed to the woods it is absolutely frightful. Several companies from New York, after penetrating halfway into the forest, have become alarmed and disheartened and turned back, and I am not surprised at it. A young man with me, brought up in the country but along the Cayuga Lake, could not refrain from expressions almost of alarm. "How savage!" he would say; "it is really horrible, day after day, and nothing but woods." And how solemn it is to move all day through a majestic colonnade of trees and feel that you are in a boundless cathedral whose organ notes swell and die away with the passing wind like some grand requiem. Still more exciting is it to lie at midnight by your camp fire and watch the moon sailing up amid the trees or listen to the cry of the loon, wild and lonely, on the wild and lonely lake, or the hoot of the owl in the deep recesses of the forest.

THE VAGABOND SPIRIT
S. H. HAMMOND

Had I my way, I would mark out a circle of a hundred miles in diameter and throw around it the protecting aegis of the constitution. I would make it a forest forever. It should be a misdemeanor to chop down a tree and a felony to clear an acre within its boundaries. The old woods should stand here always as God made them, growing on until the earthworm ate away their roots, and the strong winds hurled them to the ground, and new woods should be permitted to supply the place of the old so long as the earth remained. There is room enough for civilization in regions better fitted for it. It has no business among these mountains, these rivers and lakes, these gigantic boulders, these tangled valleys and dark mountain gorges. Let it go where labor will garner a richer harvest and industry reap a better reward for its toil. It will be of stinted growth at best here.

"I like these old woods," said a gentleman whom I met on Racket last year; "I like them because one can do here just what he pleases. He can wear a shirt a week, have holes in his pantaloons, and be out at elbows, go with his boots unblacked, drink whisky in the raw, chew plug tobacco, and smoke a black pipe, and not lose his position in society. Now," continued he, "though I don't choose to do any of these things, yet I love the freedom, now and then, of doing just all of them if I choose, without human accountability. The truth is that it is natural as well as necessary for every man to be a vagabond occasionally, to throw off the restraints imposed upon him by the necessities and conventionalities of civilization, and turn savage for a season, and what place is left for such transformation save these northern forests?"

The idea was somewhat quaint, but to me it smacked of philosophy, and I yielded it a hearty assent. I would consecrate these old forests, these rivers and lakes, these mountains and valleys to the Vagabond Spirit, and make them a place wherein a man could turn savage and rest, for a fortnight or a month, from the toils and cares of life.

LORDS OF THIS REALM
(from "The Adirondacs")
RALPH WALDO EMERSON

> . . . The length of Follansbee we rowed,
> Under low mountains, whose unbroken ridge
> Ponderous with beechen forest sloped the shore.
> A pause and council: then, where near the head
> Due east a bay makes inward to the land
> Between two rocky arms, we climb the bank,
> And in the twilight of the forest noon
> Wield the first axe these echoes ever heard.
> We cut young trees to make our poles and thwarts,
> Barked the white spruce to weatherfend the roof,
> Then struck a light and kindled the camp-fire. . . .
>
> Ten scholars, wonted to lie warm and soft
> In well-hung chambers daintily bestowed,
> Lie here on hemlock-boughs, like Sacs and Sioux,
> And greet unanimous the joyful change.
> So fast will Nature acclimate her sons,
> Though late returning to her pristine ways.
> Off soundings, seamen do not suffer cold;
> And, in the forest, delicate clerks, unbrowned,
> Sleep on the fragrant brush as on down-beds.
> Up with the dawn, they fancied the light air
> That circled freshly in their forest dress
> Made them to boys again. Happier that they
> Slipped off their pack of duties, leagues behind,
> At the first mounting of the giant stairs.
> No placard on these rocks warned to the polls,
> No door-bell heralded a visitor,
> No courier waits, no letter came or went,
> Nothing was ploughed, or reaped, or bought, or sold;
> The frost might glitter, it would blight no crop,
> The falling rain will spoil no holiday.

We were made freemen of the forest laws,
All dressed, like Nature, fit for her own ends,
Essaying nothing she cannot perform. . . .

All day we swept the lake, searched every cove,
North from Camp Maple, south to Osprey Bay,
Watching when the loud dogs should drive in deer,
Or whipping its rough surface for a trout;
Or, bathers, diving from the rock at noon;
Challenging Echo by our guns and cries;
Or listening to the laughter of the loon;
Or, in the evening twilight's latest red,
Beholding the procession of the pines;
Or, later yet, beneath a lighted jack,
In the boat's bows, a silent night-hunter
Stealing with paddle to the feeding-grounds
Of the red deer, to aim at a square mist.
Hark to that muffled roar! a tree in the woods
Is fallen: but hush! it has not scared the buck
Who stands astonished at the meteor light,
Then turns to bound away—is it too late? . . .

Above, the eagle flew, the osprey screamed,
The raven croaked, owls hooted, the woodpecker
Loud hammered, and the heron rose in the swamp.
As water poured through hollows of the hills
To feed this wealth of lakes and rivulets,
So Nature shed all beauty lavishly
From her redundant horn.

               Lords of this realm,
Bounded by dawn and sunset, and the day
Rounded by hours where each outdid the last
In miracles of pomp, we must be proud,
As if associates of the sylvan gods.
We seemed the dwellers of the zodiac,
So pure the Alpine element we breathed,

So light, so lofty pictures came and went.
We trode on air, contemned the distant town,
Its timorous ways, big trifles, and we planned
That we should build, hard-by, a spacious lodge
And how we should come hither with our sons,
Hereafter—willing they, and more adroit.

PHILOSOPHERS' CAMP
WILLIAM JAMES STILLMAN

My Adirondack experiences and studies having excited the
desire on the part of several Cambridge friends to visit the Wilderness, I made up a party [1857] which comprised [James Russell]
Lowell and his two nephews, Charles and James Lowell (two
splendid young New Englanders afterwards killed during the Civil
War), Dr. Estes Howe, Lowell's brother-in-law, and John Holmes,
the brother of Oliver Wendell, considered by many of the Cambridge set the wittier and wiser of the two, but who, being extremely averse to publicity, was never known in literature. We
made a flying journey of inspection through the Saranac Lakes
and down the Raquette River to Tupper's Lake, and then across
a wild and at that day a little explored section to the head of Raquette Lake, and down the Raquette River back to the Saranacs;
the party returning home and I back to the headwaters of the
Raquette to spend the summer painting. . . .
   The next summer the party was formed which led to the foundation of the Adirondack Club, and the excursion it made [in
August, 1858] is commemorated by Emerson in his poem "The
Adirondacs." The company included Emerson, Agassiz, Dr. Howe,
Professor Jeffries Wyman, John Holmes—who became as fond as

I was of this wild life—Judge Hoar (later Attorney-General in the cabinet of President Grant), Horatio Woodman, Dr. Binney, [James Russell Lowell], and myself. Of this company, as I write, I am the only survivor. I did my best to enroll Longfellow in the party, but, though he was for a moment hesitating, I think the fact that Emerson was going with a gun settled him in the determination to decline. "Is it true that Emerson is going to take a gun?" he asked me; and when I said that he had finally decided to do so, he ejaculated, "Then somebody will be shot!" and would talk no more of going. . . .

The care of arranging the details of the excursion was left to me, and I had, therefore, to precede the company to the Wilderness and so missed what must have been to the others a very amusing experience. The rumor of the advent of the party spread through the country around Saranac, and at the frontier town [Keeseville] where they would begin the journey into the woods the whole community was on the *qui vive* to see, not Emerson or Lowell, of whom they knew nothing, but Agassiz, who had become famous in the commonplace world through having refused, not long before, an offer from the Emperor of the French of the keepership of the Jardin des Plantes and a senatorship if he would come to Paris and live. Such an incredible and disinterested love for America and science in our hemisphere had lifted Agassiz into an elevation of popularity which was beyond all scientific or political dignity, and the selectmen of the town appointed a deputation to welcome Agassiz and his friends to the region. A reception was accorded, and they came, having taken care to provide themselves with an engraved portrait of the scientist to guard against a personation and waste of their respects. The head of the deputation, after having carefully compared Agassiz to the engraving, turned gravely to his followers and said, "Yes, it's him"; and they proceeded with the same gravity to shake hands in their order, ignoring all the other luminaries.

I had in the mean time been into the Wilderness and selected a site for the camp on one of the most secluded lakes, out of the line of travel of the hunters and fisherfolk—a deep *cul de sac* of lake on a stream that led nowhere, known as Follansbee Pond. There, with my guide, I built a bark camp, prepared a landing-place, and then returned to Saranac in time to meet the arriving guests. I was unfortunately prevented from accompanying them up the lakes the next morning because a boat I had been building for the occasion was not ready for the water, and so I missed what was to me of the greatest interest—the first impressions of Emerson of the Wilderness, absolute nature. I joined them at night of the first day's journey, in a rainstorm such as our summer rarely gives in the mountains, and we made the unique and fascinating journey down the Raquette River together; Agassiz taking his place in my boat, each other member of the party having his own guide and boat.

The scene, like the company, exists no longer. There is a river which still flows where the other flowed; but, like the water that has passed its rapids and the guests that have gone the way of all those who have lived, it is something different. Then it was a deep, mysterious stream meandering through unbroken forests, walled up on either side in green shade, the trees of centuries leaning over to welcome and shelter the voyager, flowing silently in great sweeps of dark water, with, at long intervals, a lagoon setting back into the wider forest around, enameled with pond lilies and sagittaria, and the refuge of undisturbed waterfowl and browsing deer. Our lake lay at the head of such a lagoon, a devious outlet of the basin of which the lake occupied the principal expanse, reached through three miles of no-man's route, framed in green hills forest-clad up to their summits. The camp was a shelter of spruce bark, open wide in front and closed at the ends, drawn on three faces of an octohedron facing the fireplace. The beds were made of layers of spruce and other fir branches spread on the ground and covered with the fragrant twigs of the arbor vitae. Two huge maples overhung the camp, and at a distance of twenty feet from our lodge we entered the trackless, primeval forest. The hills around furnished us with venison, and the lake with trout, and there we passed the weeks of the summer heats. We were ten, with eight guides, and while we were camping there we received the news that the first Atlantic cable was laid and the first message sent under the sea from one hemisphere to the other—an event which Emerson did not forget to record in noble lines.

In the main, our occupations were those of a vacation, to kill time and escape from the daily groove. Some took their guides and made exploration, by land or water; after breakfast there was firing at a mark, a few rounds each, for those who were riflemen; then, if venison was needed, we put the dog out on the hills; one boat went to overhaul the set lines baited the evening before for the lake trout. When the hunt was over we generally went out to paddle on the lake, Agassiz and Wyman to dredge or botanize or dissect the animals caught or killed; those of us who had interest in natural history watching the naturalists, the others searching the nooks and corners of the pretty sheet of water with its inlet brooks and its bays and recesses, or bathing from the rocks. Lunch was at midday, and then long talks. . . .

To me the study of the great student [Emerson] was the dominant interest of the occasion. I was Agassiz's boatman on demand, for while all the others had their personal guides and attendants, I was his; but often when Emerson wanted a boat I managed to provide for Agassiz with one of the unoccupied guides and take the place of Emerson's own guide. Thus Emerson and I had many hours alone on the lake and in the wood. He seemed to be a living question, perpetually interrogating his impressions of all that there was to be seen. The rest of us were always at the surface of things —even the naturalists were only engaged with their anatomy; but Emerson in the forest or looking at the sunset from the lake seemed to be looking through the phenomena, studying them by their reflections on an inner speculum.

In such a great solitude, stripped of the social conventions and seeing men as they are, mind seems open to mind as it is quite impossible for it to be in society, even the most informal. Agassiz remarked one day, when a little personal question had shown the limitations of character of one of the company, that he had always found in his Alpine experiences, when the company were living on terms of compulsory intimacy, that men found each other out quickly. And so we found it in the Adirondacks: disguises were soon dropped, and one saw the real characters of his comrades as it was impossible to see them in society. Conventions faded out, masks became transparent, and for good or for ill the man stood naked before the questioning eye—pure personality. I think I gathered more insight into the character of my companions in our greener Arden, in the two or three weeks' meetings of the club, than all our lives in the city could have given me.

And Emerson was such a study as can but rarely be given any one. The crystalline limpidity of his character, free from all conventions, prejudices, or personal color, gave a facility for study of the man limited only by the range of vision of the student. . . .

Of all the mental experiences of my past life nothing else survives with the vividness of my summers in the Adirondacks with Emerson. The last sight I had of him was when, on his voyage to Egypt, he came to see me at my home in London, aged and showing the decay of age, but as alert and interrogative as ever with his insatiate intellectual activity. And as I look back from the distance of years to the days when we questioned together, he rises above all his contemporaries as Mont Blanc does above the intervening peaks when seen from afar, not the largest in mass, but loftiest in climb, soaring higher if not occupying the space of some of his companions, even in our little assemblies. . . .

His insatiability in the study of human nature was shown curiously in our first summer's camp. He had the utmost tenderness of animal life and had no sympathy with sport in any form—he "named the birds without a gun"—and when we were making up the outfit for the outing he at first refused to take a rifle; but as the discussion of make, calibre, and quality went on, and everybody else was provided, he at length decided, though no shot, to conform, and purchased a rifle. And when the routine of camp life brought the day of the hunt, the eagerness of the hunters and the passion of the chase, the strong return to our heredity of human primeval occupation gradually involved him and made him desire to enter into this experience as well as the rest of the forest emotions. He must understand this passion to kill. One Sunday morning, when all the others went out for the drive of the deer—necessary for the larder, as the drive the day before had failed—Emerson asked me to take him out on the lake to some quiet place for meditation. We landed in a deep bay where the seclusion was most complete, and he went into the woods to meditate. Presently we heard the baying of the hound as he circled round the lake, on the hillsides, for the deer at that season were reluctant to take to the water, and gave a long chase; and as he listened, he began to take in the excitement of the hunters and finally broke out abruptly, "Let us go after the deer"; and down the lake we went, flying at our best, but we arrived too late—Lowell had killed the deer.

He said to me later, and emphatically, "I must kill a deer"; and one night we went out "jack-hunting" to enable him to realize that ambition. This kind of hunting, as most people know, is a species of pot-hunting, much employed by the hunters for the market and so destructive to the deer that it is now forbidden by the law in all the Adirondack country. The deer are stalked by night along the shores, where they come in to feed, the hunter carrying in his boat a light so shaded that it illuminates only the space directly in front of the boat, the glare blinding the animal so that he does not see the boat or the boatman. In this way the deer may be approached within a few yards if the paddler is skillful; but as he stands perfectly still and is difficult to see in the dim light, the tyro generally misses him. We paddled up to within twenty yards of a buck, and the guide gave the signal to shoot; but Emerson could see nothing resembling a deer, and finally the creature took fright and ran, and all we got of him was the sound of galloping hoofs as he sped away, stopping a moment, when at a safe distance, to snort at the intruders, and then off again. We kept on and presently came upon another, toward which we drifted even nearer than to the first one, and still Emerson could see nothing to distinguish the deer from the boulders among which he stood; and we were scarcely the boat's length from him when, Emerson being unable to see him and not caring to run the risk of losing him, for we had no venison in camp and the luck of the morning drive was always uncertain, I shot him. We had no other opportunity for the jack-hunt, and so Emerson went home unsatisfied in this ambition—glad, no doubt, when he recalled the incident, that he had failed.

The guides—rude men of the woods, rough and illiterate, but with all their physical faculties at a maximum acuteness, senses on the alert and keen as no townsman could comprehend them—were Emerson's avid study. This he had never seen—the man at his simplest terms, unsophisticated and, to him, the nearest approach to the primitive savage he would ever be able to examine; and he studied every action. When the dinner was over and the twilight coming on, he sometimes asked me to row him out on the lake to see the nightfall and watch the "procession of the pines," that weird and ghostly phenomenon I have before alluded to [the east-ward inclination of the tops of a row of tall pines as a result of the prevailing westerly winds; the subject of a painting by Stillman].

More than a generation has passed since then. Twenty-five years afterward I went back to the scene of the meeting. Except myself, the whole company are dead, and the very scene of our acting and thinking has disappeared down to its geological basis, pillaged, burnt, and become a horror to see; but among the memories which are the only realities left to it, this image of Emerson claiming kin-ship with the forest stands out alone, and I feel as if I had stood for a moment on a mount of transfiguration and seen, as if in a vision, the typical American, the noblest in the idealization of the Amer-ican, of all the race. Lowell was of a more cosmopolitan type, of a wider range of sympathies and affections, accepted and bestowed, and to me a friend, loved as Jonathan loved David; but as a unique, idealized individuality, Emerson looms up in that Arcadian dream more and more the dominant personality. It is as character, and not as accomplishment or education, that he holds his own in all com-parisons with his contemporaries, the fine, crystallized mind, the keen, clear-faceted thinker and seer. I loved more Agassiz and Lowell, but we shall have many a Lowell and Agassiz before we see Emerson's like again. Attainments will be greater, and discovery and accomplishments will surpass themselves as we go on, but to *be*, as Emerson was, is absolute and complete existence.

Agassiz was, of all our company, the acknowledged master; loved by all, even to the unlettered woodsmen, who ran to meet his service as to no other of the company; by all the members of it reverenced as not even Emerson was; the largest in personality and in universality of knowledge of all the men I have ever known. No one who did not know him personally can conceive the hold he had on everybody who came into relations with him. His vast command of scientific facts and his ready command of them for all educational purposes, his enthusiasm for science and the diffusion of it, even his fascinating way of imparting it to others, had even less to do with his popularity than the magnetism of his presence and the sympathetic faculty which enabled him to find at once the plane on which he should meet whomever he had to deal with. . . .

The third magnate of our Club was Lowell, with whose personality the world at large is already well acquainted. . . . We were nearest each other in our Adirondack life, in which he had all the zest of a boy. He was the soul of the merriment of the company, fullest of witticisms, keenest in appreciation of the liberty of the occasion and the *genius loci.* One sees through all his nature-poetry the traces of the heredity of the early settler, the keen enjoyment of the fresh and unhackneyed in nature, even of the angularity of the New England farmhouse and the brightness and newness of the villages, so crude to the tastes founded in the picturesqueness of the Old World. Not even Emerson, with all his indifference to the mere form of things, took to unimproved and uncivilized nature as Lowell did, and his free delight in the Wilderness was a thing to remember, and perhaps by none so keenly appreciated as by me, to whom the joy of forest life was a satisfactory motive for living. . . .

The excursion had been so satisfactory that when the whole company had come together again in the autumn at Cambridge, the formal organization of the Club was called for, and to the number of those who had been at Camp Maple there was a large accession of the most prominent members of the intellectual society of Boston and Cambridge. It was decided to purchase a tract in the Adirondack Wilderness, the less accessible the better, and there to build a permanent club-house, and I was appointed to select the site and lay it out. The meeting was late in the autumn, and the winter had set in with heavy snow before I had my orders. . . . I pushed on into the Wilderness and drove from the settlements in to the Saranac in a storm, facing a northwesterly wind which, filling the air with a cold fog as penetrating as the wind, crystallized on every tree and twig and made the entire forest, as far as the eye could reach, like a forest of frosted silver. It was a spectacle for a lifetime and has never been offered to me again; but I reached Martin's [on Lower Saranac Lake], where we had to put up, dangerously chilled.

Next day, however, I had all the guides of the neighborhood in for consultation as to a certain tract which I had fixed on from report and general knowledge of the region, and we planned a survey in the snow. It was fourteen miles from any house to the lake I had fixed on—that known as Ampersand Pond; but fortunately, there were amongst the guides called in some who had been assistants in the official survey, and with their practical knowledge and memory of the lines, I was enabled, without leaving the inn, to draw a map of the section of a township which included the lake and determine its exact position, with the fact that it had been forfeited to the State at the last tax sale and was for sale at the land office in Albany. We bought the entire section, less 500 acres, taxes on which had been paid, for the sum of $600—thus securing for the Club a tract of 22,500 acres. . . .

I returned to my painting with the early summer and, when the season came, to the organization of the Club and the inauguration of its club-house and grounds. It was certainly the most beautiful site I have ever seen in the Adirondack country—virgin forest save where the trappers or hunters had cut wood for their campfires, the tall pines standing in their long ranks along the shores of a little lake that lay in the middle of the estate, encircled by mountains except on one side, where the lake found its outlet; and the mountains were cloaked to their summits in primeval woods. In a little valley where a crystal spring sent its water down to the lake and a grove of deciduous trees gave high and airy shelter, I pitched the camp—a repetition slightly enlarged of that on Follansbee Pond. As usual I preceded the Club party, accompanied by S. G. Ward and his son and also the son of Emerson, to prepare the ground. The solitude of the locality may be judged from the first hunt. We had arrived late in the day and had no food except the bread we took with us, and the next morning we had to kill our breakfast before we could eat it. I took Mr. Ward and the boys in my boat and paddled down to the foot of the lake, where was a wide beach, on which we found a two-year-old buck grazing. I paddled to within fifty yards of him, and though I found that my rifle would not go off and had to change it for another, with considerable movement, the deer took no notice of us, and I dropped him in his tracks with a feeling of compunction only overcome by the fact that we had no breakfast if he went away. So peaceful was our realm! I have often paddled within easy shot of a deer on other waters, but only by remaining motionless when he was looking round, for the movement of a hand would send him flying in panic; but this poor deer might have been reared in Eden.

The meeting of the Club that year was a most successful one; and when it was over . . . I was left alone to my painting. . . . I never enjoyed so entirely the forest life as that autumn. I had laid a line of sable traps for miles through the woods and caught several "prime" sable, which I intended as a present to my fiancée, and the long walks over the line in the absolute silence of the great forest, the snowfall, and the gorgeous autumn were more fascinating than ever before.

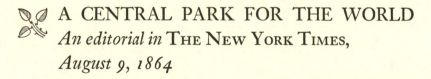

A CENTRAL PARK FOR THE WORLD
An editorial in THE NEW YORK TIMES,
August 9, 1864

Within an easy day's ride of our great city, as steam teaches us to measure distance, is a tract of country fitted to make a Central Park for the world. The jaded merchant or financier or litterateur or politician, feeling excited within him again the old passion for nature (which is never permitted entirely to die out) and longing for the inspiration of physical exercise and pure air and grand scenery, has only to take an early morning train in order, if he chooses, to sleep the same night in the shadow of kingly hills and waken with his memory filled with pleasant dreams, woven from the ceaseless music of mountain streams.

To people in general, Adirondack is still a realm of mystery. Although the waters of the Hudson, which today mingle with those of the ocean in our harbor, yesterday rippled over its rocks, and though on all sides of it have grown up villages and have been created busy thoroughfares, yet so little has this wonderful wilderness been penetrated by enterprise or art that our community is practically ignorant of its enormous capacities, both for the imparting of pleasure and the increase of wealth.

It is true that the desultory notes of a few summer tourists have given us a vague idea of its character. We know it as a region of hills and valleys and lakes; we believe it to abound in rocks and rivulets and have an ill-defined notion that it contains mines of iron. But as yet we have never been able to understand that it embraces a variety of mountain scenery unsurpassed, if even equalled, by any region of similar size in the world; that its lakes count by hundreds, fed by cool springs and connected mainly by watery threads which make them a network such as Switzerland might strive in vain to match; and that it affords facilities for hunting and fishing which our democratic sovereign-citizen could not afford to exchange for the preserves of the mightiest crowned monarch of Christendom. And still less do we understand that it abounds in mines which the famous iron mountains of Missouri cannot themselves equal for quality and ease of working; and that its resources of timber and lumber are so great that, once made easily accessible, their supply would regulate the prices of those articles in our market.

And this access is what we are now going to secure. The gay denizens of Saratoga this season are excited by an occasional glimpse of a railroad grade running north from that town toward the Upper Hudson and aiming directly at the heart of the wilderness. A thousand men are now cutting down and filling up and blasting and bridging "on this line." . . . With its completion, the Adirondack region will become a suburb of New York. The furnaces of our capitalists will line its valleys and create new fortunes to swell the aggregate of our wealth, while the hunting-lodges of our citizens will adorn its more remote mountainsides and the wooded islands of its delightful lakes. It will become to our whole community, on an ample scale, what Central Park is on a limited one. We shall sleep tonight on one of the magnificent steamers of the People's Line, ride a few cool hours in the morning by rail, and, if we choose, spend the afternoon in a solitude almost as complete as when the Deerslayer stalked his game in its fastnesses and unconsciously founded a school of romance equally true to sentiment with that of feudal ages.

And here we venture a suggestion to those of our citizens who desire to advance civilization by combining taste with luxury in their expenditures. Imitating the good example of one of their number who upon the eastern slopes of Orange Mountain has created a paradise, of which it is difficult to say whether its homes or its pleasure-grounds are more admirable, let them form combinations and, seizing upon the choicest of the Adirondack Mountains, before they are despoiled of their forests, make of them grand parks, owned in common and thinly dotted with hunting seats where, at little cost, they can enjoy equal amplitude and privacy of sporting, riding and driving whenever they are able, for a few days or weeks, to seek the country in pursuit of health or pleasure. In spite of all the din and dust of furnaces and foundries, the Adirondacks, thus husbanded, will furnish abundant seclusion for all time to come; and will admirably realize the true union which should always exist between utility and enjoyment.

THE VOICE THAT LAUNCHED A THOUSAND GUIDE-BOATS
William H. H. Murray

Not until you reach the Racquette do you get a glimpse of the magnificent scenery which makes this wilderness to rival Switzerland. There, on the very ridge-board of the vast watershed which slopes northward to the St. Lawrence, eastward to the Hudson, and southward to the Mohawk, you can enter upon a voyage the like of which, it is safe to say, the world does not anywhere else furnish. For hundreds of miles I have boated up and down that wilderness, going ashore only to "carry" around a fall or across some narrow ridge dividing the otherwise connected lakes. For weeks I have paddled my cedar shell in all directions, swinging northerly into the St. Regis chain, westward nearly to Potsdam, southerly to the Black River country, and from thence penetrated to that almost unvisited region, the South Branch, without seeing a face but my guide's, and the entire circuit, it must be remembered, was through a wilderness yet to echo to the lumberman's axe. It is estimated that a thousand lakes, many yet unvisited, lie embedded in this vast forest of pine and hemlock. From the summit of a mountain, two years ago, I counted, as seen by my naked eye, forty-four lakes gleaming amid the depths of the wilderness like gems of purest ray amid folds of emerald-colored velvet. Last summer I met a gentleman on the Racquette who had just received a letter from a brother in Switzerland, an artist by profession, in which he said that, "having travelled over all Switzerland and the Rhine and Rhone region, he had not met with scenery which, judged from a purely artistic point of view, combined so many beauties in connection with such grandeur as the lakes, mountains, and forest of the Adirondack region presented to the gazer's eye." And yet thousands are in Europe today as tourists who never gave a passing thought to this marvellous country lying as it were at their very doors.

Another reason why I visit the Adirondacks and urge others to do so is because I deem the excursion eminently adapted to restore impaired health. Indeed, it is marvellous what benefit physically is often derived from a trip of a few weeks to these woods. To such as are afflicted with that dire parent of ills, dyspepsia, or have lurking in their system consumptive tendencies, I most earnestly recommend a month's experience among the pines. The air which you there inhale is such as can be found only in high mountainous regions, pure, rarefied, and bracing. The amount of venison steak a consumptive will consume after a week's residence in that appetizing atmosphere is a subject of daily and increasing wonder. I have known delicate ladies and fragile schoolgirls, to whom all food at home was distasteful and eating a pure matter of duty, average a gain of a pound per day for the round trip. This is no exaggeration, as some who will read these lines know. The spruce, hemlock, balsam, and pine which largely compose this wilderness yield upon the air, and especially at night, all their curative qualities. Many a night have I laid down upon my bed of balsam-boughs and been lulled to sleep by the murmur of waters and the low sighing melody of the pines, while the air was laden with the mingled perfume of cedar, of balsam and the water lily.

Not a few, far advanced in that dread disease, consumption, have found in this wilderness renewal of life and health. I recall a young man, the son of wealthy parents in New York, who lay dying in that great city, attended as he was by the best skill that money could secure. A friend calling upon him one day chanced to speak of the Adirondacks, and that many had found help from a trip to their region. From that moment he pined for the woods. He insisted on what his family called "his insane idea," that the mountain air and the aroma of the forest would cure him. It was his daily request and entreaty that he might go. At last his parents consented, the more readily because the physicians assured them that their son's recovery was impossible, and his death a mere matter of time. They started with him for the north in search of life. When he arrived at the point where he was to meet his guide he was too reduced to walk. The guide seeing his condition refused to take him into the woods, fearing, as he plainly expressed it, that he would "die on his hands." At last another guide was prevailed upon to serve him, not so much for the money, as he afterwards told me, but because he pitied the young man and felt that "one so near death as he was should be gratified even in his whims."

The boat was half filled with cedar, pine, and balsam boughs, and the young man, carried in the arms of his guide from the house, was laid at full length upon them. The camp utensils were put at one end, the guide seated himself at the other, and the little boat passed with the living and the dying down the lake and was lost to the group watching them amid the islands to the south. This was in early June. The first week the guide carried the young man on his back over all the portages, lifting him in and out of the boat as he might a child. But the healing properties of the balsam and pine, which were his bed by day and night, began to exert their power. Awake or asleep, he inhaled their fragrance. Their pungent and healing odors penetrated his diseased and irritated lungs. The second day out his cough was less sharp and painful. At the end of the first week he could walk by leaning on the paddle. The second week he needed no support. The third week the cough ceased entirely. From that time he improved with wonderful rapidity.

He "went in" the first of June, carried in the arms of his guide. The second week of November he "came out" bronzed as an Indian and as hearty. In five months he had gained sixty-five pounds of flesh and flesh too "well packed on," as they say in the woods. Coming out he carried the boat over all portages; the very same over which a few months before the guide had carried him, and pulled as strong an oar as any amateur in the wilderness. His meeting with his family I leave the reader to imagine. The wilderness received him almost a corpse. It returned him to his home and the world as happy and healthy a man as ever bivouacked under its pines.

This, I am aware, is an extreme case and as such may seem exaggerated, but it is not. I might instance many other cases which, if less startling, are equally corroborative of the general statement. There is one sitting near me as I write, the color of whose cheek and the clear brightness of whose eye cause my heart to go out in ceaseless gratitude to the woods, amid which she found that health and strength of which they are the proof and sign. For five summers have we visited the wilderness. From four to seven weeks each year have we breathed the breath of the mountains, bathed in the waters which sleep at their base, and made our couch at night of moss and balsam-boughs, beneath the whispering trees. I feel, therefore, that I am able to speak from experience touching this matter; and I believe that, all things being considered, no portion of our country surpasses, if indeed equals, in health-giving qualities, the Adirondack Wilderness. . . .

Gentlemen often ask me to compare the North Woods with the Maine Wilderness. The fact is, it is difficult to make any comparison between the two sections, they are so unlike. But I am willing to give my reasons of preference for the Adirondacks. The fact is, nothing could induce me to visit Maine. If I was going east at all, I should keep on, nor stop until I reached the Provinces. I could never bring my mind to pass a month in Maine, with the North Woods within forty-eight hours of me. I will tell you why. Go where you will in Maine, the *lumbermen* have been before you; and lumbermen are the curse and scourge of the wilderness. Wherever the axe sounds, the pride and beauty of the forest disappear. A lumbered district is the most dreary and dismal region the eye of man ever beheld. . . . No number of deer, no quantities of trout can entice me to such a locality. He who fancies it can go; not I. In the Adirondack Wilderness you escape this. There the lumberman has never been [an inaccurate statement when Murray wrote in 1869]. No axe has sounded along its mountain sides or echoed across its peaceful waters. The forest stands as it has stood, from the beginning of time, in all its majesty of growth, in all the beauty of its unshorn foliage. No fires have blackened the hills; no logs obstruct the rivers; no sawdust taints and colors its crystal waters. The promontories which stretch themselves half across its lakes, the islands which hang as if suspended in their waveless and translucent depths have never been marred by the presence of men careless of all but gain. You choose the locality which best suits your eye, and build your lodge under unscarred trees and upon a carpet of moss untrampled by man or beast. There you live in silence, unbroken by any sounds save such as you yourself may make, away from all the business and cares of civilized life.

Another reason of my preference for the Adirondack region is based upon the *mode* and *manner* in which your sporting is done. Now I do not plead guilty to the vice of laziness. If necessary, I can work and work sharply; but I have no special love for labor in itself considered; and certain kinds of work, I am free to confess, I abhor; and if there is one kind of work which I detest more than another, it is *tramping;* and above all, tramping through a lumbered district. How the thorns lacerate you! How the brambles tear your clothes and pierce your flesh! How the meshwork of fallen treetops entangles you! I would not walk two miles through such a country for all the trout that swim; and as forever casting a fly from the slippery surface of an old milldam, no one ever saw me do it, nor ever will. I do not say that some may not find amusement in it. I only know that I could not. Now, in the North Woods, owing to their marvellous water-communication, you do all your sporting from your boat. If you wish to go one or ten miles for a fish, your guide paddles you to the spot and serves you while you handle the rod. This takes from recreation every trace of toil. You have all the excitement of sporting without any attending physical weariness. And what luxury it is to course along the shores of these secluded lakes or glide down the winding reaches of these rivers overhung by the outlying pines and fringed with water lilies, mingling their fragrance with the odors of cedar and balsam! To me this is better than *tramping*.

I have sported a month at a time without walking as many miles as there were weeks in the month. To my mind, this peculiarity elevates the Adirondack region above all its rivals, east or west, and more than all else justifies its otherwise pretentious claim as a "Sportsman's Paradise." In beauty of scenery, in health-giving qualities, in the easy and romantic manner of its sporting, it *is* a paradise, and so will it continue to be while a deer leaves his track upon the shores of its lakes or a trout shows himself above the surface of its waters. It is this peculiarity also which makes an excursion to this section so easy and delightful to ladies. There is nothing in the trip which the most delicate and fragile need fear. And it is safe to say that, of all who go into the woods, none enjoy the experiences more than ladies, and certain it is that none are more benefited by it.

But what about *game*, I hear the reader inquire. Are deer plenty? Is the fishing good? Well, I reply, every person has his own standard by which to measure a locality, and therefore it is difficult to answer with precision. Moreover, it is not alone the presence of game which makes good sporting. Many other considerations, such as the skill of the sportsman and the character and ability of the guide, enter into this problem and make the solution difficult. A poor shot and a green hand at the rod will have poor success anywhere, no matter how good the sporting is; and I have known parties to be "starved out" where other men, with better guides, were meeting with royal success. With a guide who understands his business I would undertake to feed a party of twenty persons the season through, and seldom should they sit down to a meal lacking either trout or venison. I passed six weeks on the Racquette last summer and never, save at one meal, failed to see both of the two delicious articles of diet on my table. Generally speaking, no inconvenience is experienced in this direction. Always observing the rule not to kill more than the camp can eat, which a true sportsman never transgresses, I have paddled past more deer within easy range than I ever lifted my rifle at. The same is true in reference to trout. I have unjointed my rod when the water was alive with leaping fish and experienced more pleasure as I sat and saw them rise for food or play than any thoughtless violator of God's laws could feel in wasting the stores which Nature so bountifully opens for our need. . . .

To sum up what I have thus far written, I say to all brother sportsmen that, all things considered, the sporting, both with rifle and rod, in the North Woods is good—good enough to satisfy any reasonable desire. In this please remember that I refer to the wilderness proper and not to the lumbered and inhabited and therefore over-hunted borders of it. . . .

It is in the ministry that you find the very men who would be the most benefited by this trip. Whether they should go as sportsmen or tourists or in both capacities, a visit to the North Woods could not fail of giving them precisely such a change as is most desirable and needed by them. In the wilderness they would find that perfect relaxation which all jaded minds require. In its vast solitude is a total absence of sights and sounds and duties which keep the clergyman's brain and heart strung up, the long year through, to an intense, unnatural, and often fatal tension. There, from a thousand sources of invigoration, flow into the exhausted mind and enfeebled body currents of strength and life. There sleep woos you as the shadows deepen along the lake, and retains you in its gentle embrace until frightened away by the guide's merry call to breakfast. You would be astonished to learn, if I felt disposed to tell you, how many consecutive hours a certain minister sleeps during the first week of his annual visit to the woods!

Ah me, the nights I have passed in the woods! How they haunt me with their sweet, suggestive memories of silence and repose! How harshly the steel-shod hoofs smite against the flinty pavement beneath my window and clash with rude interruptions upon my ear as I sit recalling the tranquil hours I have spent beneath the trees! What restful slumber was mine; and not less gently than the close of day itself did it fall upon me as I stretched myself upon my bed of balsam-boughs, with Rover at my side, not twenty feet from the shore where the ripples were playing coyly with the sand; and lulled by the low monotone of the pines, whose branches were my only shelter from the dew which gathered like gems upon their spear-like stems, sank, as a falling star fades from sight, into forgetfulness. And then the waking! The air fresh with the aroma of the wilderness. The morning blowing its perfumed breezes into your face. . . .

If every church would make up a purse and pack its worn and weary pastor off to the North Woods for a four weeks' jaunt in the hot months of July and August, it would do a very sensible as well as pleasant act. For when the good dominie came back swarth and tough as an Indian, elasticity in his step, fire in his eye, depth and clearness in his reinvigorated voice, wouldn't there be some preaching! And what texts he would have from which to talk to the little folks in the Sabbath school! How their bright eyes would open and enlarge as he narrated his adventures and told them how the good Father feeds the fish that swim and clothes the mink and beaver with their warm and sheeny fur. The preacher sees God in the original there and often translates him better from his unwritten works than from his written word. He will get more instructive spiritual material from such a trip than from all the "Sabbath-school festivals" and "pastoral tea-parties" with which the poor smiling creature was ever tormented. It is astonishing how much a loving, spiritually-minded people can bore their minister. . . .

If you go in by way of the Saranacs, do not camp down in that section as some do, but pass over Indian Carry, through the Spectacle Lakes and Ramshorn Creek (called by some Stony Creek), into the Racquette River. Then turn up or down as you please. If you desire to see some of the finest scenery imaginable, pass up the Racquette to Long Lake and, when some two miles up the lake, turn your face toward the north, and you will behold what is worth the entire journey to see. Then go on and do not camp until you do so on the southern or western shore of Racquette Lake. Here you will find good sporting and scenery unsurpassed. Build here your central camp and, as soon as you are established, take your boat and go over to the "Wood's Place," and from the knoll on which the house stands you will gaze upon one of the finest water views in the world. Then visit Terrace Lodge on an island to the front and left of you, and, climbing up the ledge, you will either find the writer there to welcome you or see where he and one better than he have passed many delightful hours. Only beware how you appropriate it, for we have a sort of life-lease on that campground and may appear to claim possession when you least expect us.

Then paddle to Beaver Bay and find that point in it from which you can arouse a whole family of sleeping echoes along the western ridge and the heavy woods opposite. Then go to Constable Point and quench your thirst at the coolest, sweetest spring of pure water from which you ever drank. Go next to the southern part of the lake, so hidden behind the islands that you would never suspect such a lovely sheet of water lay beyond, with its two beautiful reaches of softly shining sand, one white as silver, the other yellow as gold; and in the waters which lave the golden, find the best bathing in the whole wilderness. Do not leave this region until you have made an excursion to that Lake George in miniature, Blue Mountain Lake, and fill your mind with an impression which will remain in memory as one of the sweet and never-to-be-forgotten recollections of life.

When you have retraced your progress up and reached the mouth of Ramshorn Creek [Stony Creek], keep on down the Racquette until you have swung round to Big Tupper Lake and lunched on the sloping ledge over which the outlet of Round Lake and Little Tupper pours its full tide in thunder and foam; and, if it be not too late in the season and you know how to use the rod, you will raise, amid the froth and eddies of the falls, some of the largest, gamiest, brightest-tinted trout that ever gladdened a sportsman's eye. Then, if you are robust and full of pluck, force your way over the four-mile carry between the Falls and Round Lake and, hurrying on through its sluggish waters, do not pause until you enter the narrow, secluded stretch of Little Tupper. But the moment you enter stop, joint your rod, and noose on your strongest leader and largest flies, for you will find right there, at the entrance of Bog Creek, trout that will put your skill and tackle to the severest test. . . .

As you pass out, visit the St. Regis waters by the way of Big Wolf and Rollin's Pond and Long Pine [Long Pond], and so circle down to mine host at Martin's [Lower Saranac Lake]. What a trip you will have had, what wonders seen, what rare experiences enjoyed! How many evenings will pass on golden wings at home, as friends draw close their circle around the glowing grate and listen as you rehearse the story of your adventures—shoot over again your "first buck" and land for the hundredth time your "biggest" trout!

MURRAY VINDICATED
KATE FIELD

First, let me deal with the patron saint of the Adirondack Lakes, the Rev. Mr. Murray. Far away from newspapers, sublimely indifferent to and ignorant of the state of the country, and whether it is at peace or in pieces, there yet come to me significant echoes that make this, indeed, a "howling wilderness." And the echoes from the hills are scolding after this fashion. "Murray is a humbug." "Murray is a liar." "I am one of Murray's fools." "Murray ought to be assassinated." "Murray is responsible for more than one death." To all of which and to much more of like nature I reply, that the authors of those echoes are far more guilty of exaggeration than he whom they vilify.

Early in the spring there appeared a breezy, hearty book entitled *Adventures in the Wilderness*, written by a young and enthusiastic clergyman. It had a great success for three excellent reasons: because the public hungered for a taste of nature pure and undefiled; they thought they saw their way to Paradise through the portals of the Adirondacks, and shouted "Eureka" before they had even got into the woods. Because the book was graphically if not elegantly written and therefore impressed the most careless reader. Because it was published by a responsible firm and had the benefit of extensive advertising. There is no accounting for the vagaries of human nature; hence it is useless to be astonished at the consequences that followed the reading of this book. Certainly Mr. Murray never dreamed of such results, or he would have walked through a fiery furnace before giving to the public his impressions of wood-life. Everybody determined to visit the Adirondacks and, wonderful to relate, everybody insisted upon taking every incident of Mr. Murray's adventures *au pied de la lettre*. When people put their common sense in their darkest and deepest pockets, and then abuse some one else for the blunders entailed thereby, an impartial jury is likely to render a verdict of "unreasonable." Intelligent readers are in the habit of taking adventures with several grains of allowance. . . .

Mr. Murray relates the marvelous recovery of a consumptive

who went into the Adirondacks as a last hope, but he does not urge all last hopes to follow what was undoubtedly an exceptional example. If consumptives with both legs in the grave visit the Adirondacks, and after a few days or weeks leave the woods somewhat less alive than when they entered, surely their friends display the most extraordinary absence of reason in attributing their decease to Mr. Murray's book. Yet this is being done. Several persons have come here, in a dying condition, and have died, whereupon relatives and lookers on have denounced Mr. Murray in most offensive language. Newspaper writers multiply two or three dead men by a fertile imagination, and produce "numbers of dead and dying." Such criticism is outrageous, and such reports are willfully malignant. . . .

I do not doubt that incipient consumption may be stayed, if not cured, by breathing this dry air, redolent of balsam, but lost lungs are rarely, if ever, found, although there are those here living on one lung who believe in this climate for their particular cases. I say thus much with no desire to attract more invalids to the Adirondacks. After the thanks Mr. Murray has received from the traveling public, I should be daring indeed did I offer inducements to my best friends. I am merely doing justice to this delightful climate. I do not know its superior, and the time is not far distant when the Adirondacks will be the greatest summer resort in America, if not in the world. There are those in our camp who average a gain of four pounds a week, and whose appetites, in spite of mosquitoes, beggar description.

THE BLOOMER GIRLS
KATE FIELD

I had sought the Adirondacks in many a summer dream, and on a sunny day in July, 1869, I found my horizon bounded by the waving summits of its mountains and my boat gliding over the yielding bosom of its lakes.

It all came to pass in consequence of reading one small book. That book was "Murray." . . .

After a weary day's journey, creeping up and sliding down hills, pulling through sand and wading through mire, we arrive at Martin's. The *terra incognita* is found at last! Trunks lie about in hopeless confusion, guns peer from every corner, fishing rods bow from every window, flannel shirts and ambiguous boots proclaim the downfall of that tyrant Fashion, and everybody looks as if the business of life were to lounge and despise "store" clothes. At least this is the impression produced by everybody of the masculine gender. Men know the meaning of personal comfort and take it whenever they can get it without violating the social decalogue. Women glory in discomfort. Crinoline, panier, corsets, and trailing dresses are dearer to their souls than health, nature, muscle, and children. Regardless of eternal fitness, they flaunt their muslins in the face of the backwoodsman and hover on the outskirts of the Wilderness, as if to say to their sex, "So far shalt thou go and no farther," while fathers, brothers, husbands, and sons grow away from them as they grow into sympathy with outdoor life. "God made the country and man made the town," says the old saw. It is a mistake. Woman made the town, and with all the ills to which she is heir and from which she will not emancipate herself. Even the beaver has its town house and country house, but wherever woman goes she carries brick walls and ballrooms with her. And she it is who is to mould the world anew! Can sound minds be made out of weak bodies?

Helter skelter, off with silks, kid gloves, and linen collars, on with bloomer, stout boots, and felt hat, and we helpless women are transformed into helpful human beings. The guides, having packed our baggage into the middle of each boat, are waiting for us to step aboard. "You are maniacs," cry women in muslin, who stand upon the pier to wonder at our madness, as we glide away from our "kind" and are at last on Adirondack waters. . . .

Variety? The *blasé* man of the world, in search of novelty, the *ennuyée*, who despairs of killing time, know not the latent capacities of the Adirondacks. First comes the broad surface of a lake, dotted with islands that are each an invitation and an interrogation to the mind. Its shores are rich with the fringe of countless trees, and in the distant landscape an Adirondack spur towers up as some grand sentinel to watch over and guard the wilderness. Then suddenly lake yields to creek or river. Casting oars aside, the guide stands up in the bow and paddles the boat over beds of lilies, yellow and white, that look up into our faces and ask if nature is not beautiful, after all, and better than paving stones. Wild roses peep out of the thicket of some "slew," and pines and hemlocks bend over the banks to tell us how soft and pure the air is. Just as we are beginning to long for a brisk walk through the woods, a sound of noisy water greets the ear. "Them's rapids," says the guide. "You'll have to get out and walk a mile, for this here's the carry." Out we jump; then follows the "loading up." Our guides disappear beneath the boats, which they carry on their shoulders as a turtle carries its shell and striding ahead, with nothing visible but legs, leave us to follow.

Perhaps the way may lie through a narrow trail, perhaps it may be over a muddy road, perhaps it may rain, perhaps the sun may be showering the foliage with gold. True-hearted Adirondackers declare that "whatever is, is right," and though midges burn, black flies bite, and mosquitoes perform their favorite airs before our eyes and in our ears, we are as bright as the sun—and as warm. Arrived at the end of the carry, we sit down to await the return of our guides, who start off for a second load. Now comes the initiation in smudges. If one does not grow merry over smudge-building and does not enjoy disappointing the insect kingdom by sitting in a glory of smoke, such a one was never made to camp out and had better retrace his steps.

All aboard again, and we are off through an inlet tortuous as a corkscrew, fallen trees blocking the channel and sharp-visaged rocks darting up to dispute the right of way. One moment we are aground, the next we are shooting over a very good apology for rapids. First it is broadside, then stern foremost, and finally back again to first principles. Hungry? We never were so hungry in all our lives. Wild ducks are hardly safe in the presence of our capacious maws, and if larks were only to fall from heaven ready cooked, we would devour them whole. In the nick of time our boats are drawn up on the shore, and we wend our way to a cabin that has sat down in the woods on purpose to take in the passer by. . . .

And here we are in camp. . . . We cannot sleep the first night. The novelty of the situation, the light of the fire, the strange sounds, the unusual out-of-door feeling, excite the brain and create wilder dreams than those invoked by slumber. Getting up in the morning too is no less peculiar than going to bed. The dressing which is not dressing, the washing which is not washing, the total disregard of appearances, the unmitigated contempt which we entertain for our looking-glass denote so marvelous a change of heart that it is doubtful whether we are ourselves or somebody else. . . . Whether any man ever fell in love with any woman arrayed in tar and sweet oil, or *vice versa*, are questions worthy of consideration. If love-making were the only occupation in the world, perhaps those who entered the wilderness would leave all hope behind. Certainly tar-oil combined with mosquitoes would kill even the passion of Romeo and Juliet. But fortunately the Romeos and the Juliets do not hunt in couples, and thus the charm remains unbroken. . . .

I would go into the woods taking the heart of home with me. What is the heart? Why the kitchen to be sure. With a fine commissary department, camp life is Arcadia. . . .

Days come, days go, and life grows richer, fuller, until the thought of old harness and bit become the *bête noire* of existence. Nevertheless, it is right to work in harness; so last words are spoken, last glances taken, last flapjacks and tears are swallowed together, we break up camp sounder in body and mind, and go out of the wilderness weighing many more pounds than when we came in. What are the annoyances of mosquitoes, midges, and black flies when cast in this balance? . . .

Who ought to go? Women, because they are in greatest need

of just such a life. Yet they are the last that I would advise to go, because of their horror of the bare ground, a little dirt, and freedom from restraint. They sleep on featherbeds without a murmur but shudder at the suggestion of a blanket in the open air. They go mad over the biting of mosquitoes but accept an attack of diphtheria at Saratoga without complaint. They deride a bloomer dress, in which every muscle has full play, and drag unwholesome fashions through streets and parlors with infinite satisfaction. The open air means tan and freckles. Shall health be considered when complexion is in danger? Expansion of the lungs means expansion of the ribs. Can this be tolerated at the expense of an enlarged waist? But there are women who are willing to be tanned, freckled, and even made to resemble antique statuary, for the sake of renewed youth. Let such try the wilderness. "Life consists in wildness." "The most alive is the wildest. Dulness is but another name for tameness." Do you not believe me? Ask Thoreau.

THE PLEASURE OF LIFE
JAMES BRYCE

The first point in which the difference from England strikes a stranger [in the United States] is the liberty allowed to girls and young men of going about together. They walk out in the country or in the streets of a town not merely in groups but a couple all alone, unaccompanied by aunts or brothers, without asking any permission and without attracting any notice. . . .

Of all American devices for enjoying the delicious autumn, the very pleasantest, and to a European at least the most romantic, is a party in the woods. A group of friends arrange to go together into some mountain and forest region, usually into the great Adirondack wilderness to the west of Lake Champlain, carrying with them guns and fishing-rods, tents, blankets, and an ample store of groceries and engaging three or four guides. They embark with all their equipments and pass in their boats up the rivers and across the lakes of this great wild country through sixty or eighty miles of trackless forest, glowing with a brilliance of scarlet and yellow that no words can render, to their chosen camping ground at the foot of some tall rock that rises from the still crystal of the lake. Here they build their bark hut and spread their beds of elastic and fragrant hemlock boughs; the men roam about during the day tracking the deer or now and then, if such luck befall, the wary painter [panther], the ladies read and work and bake the corn cakes; at night there is a merry gathering and a row in the soft moonlight. On these expeditions brothers will take sisters and cousins, their sisters and cousins bringing, perhaps, lady friends with them; the brothers' friends will come too, and all will live together in a fraternal way for weeks or months, though no elderly relative or married lady be of the party. . . .

Society in America is altogether easier than ours, simpler, more elastic, more variable, more gay and sparkling, more tolerant (spite of De Tocqueville's reflections on democratic uniformity) of individual divergences from the common type. . . .

Youths and maidens in America certainly have, in their own emphatic language, "a good time." They can see as much of one another as they please; they can do so without the sense of being watched and criticized; and, what is more than all, they can be friendly and mutually interested without fearing to be misunderstood. . . .

Looking at the matter simply as a question of human enjoyment, the success of the American system may be pronounced complete. It makes a staid middle-aged man long to have his youth to live over again, to see the bright, cheery, hearty, simple ways of the young people whom he meets straying on the sands at Newport or picnicking beside the waterfalls of the White Mountains, safe in their own innocence, meeting one another on the natural footing of human creatures, without affections of innuendo on the one side or prudery on the other. Little overtures and coquetries there may sometimes be, but it is all, as the attorneys say, "without prejudice." . . .

There is an idea afloat in the world, an idea which the Americans themselves are fond of, and which an Englishman living among them finds it hard to resist, that the United States is the land of the future, that its institutions, social and political, represent a type towards which the other English-speaking peoples are unconsciously, and it may be unwillingly, moving. As respects politics, at any rate, one hopes and believes that this is false; but as respects social arrangements, there is some truth in it. . . . The times have been when it would have been thought dreadful for girls to go bowling along Piccadilly all alone in hansoms; and England may see the day when, instead of being driven to suggest half furtive meetings at the Academy or the Horticultural, a young gentleman will ask a lady to come for a walk in Kensington Gardens tomorrow from half-past five till seven. Meanwhile, until that happy day arrives, it is pleasant to remember that beyond the Atlantic there is a land where youths and maidens have "a lovely time," where flirtation is harmless because it is understood and permitted, where friendship is honoured along with love, where friendship leads up to love, and love is all the truer and more lasting because friendship has gone before.

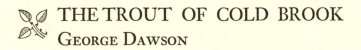

THE TROUT OF COLD BROOK
George Dawson

Having . . . passed over the five miles which intervene between Martin's and the river [Saranac] entrance to Cold and Ray brooks, where I went the last two Augusts, I wish only to say that, in the proper season, they will afford, with moderate skill and patience, such sport as is rarely vouchsafed to any angler anywhere. At least, such was my experience two years ago [c. 1874] when during a short afternoon I landed from a deep pool in Cold Brook fifty splendid trout *and fished three hours for one*. It was on this wise: For an hour or more before sunset, a trout which I estimated to weigh more than three pounds kept the water in constant agitation and myself in a fever of excitement. I cast for him a hundred times at least. With almost every cast he would rise but would not strike. He would come up with a rush, leap his full length out of the water, shake his broad tail at me as if in derision, and retire to repeat his aggravating exploits as often as the fly struck the water. Other trout rose, almost his equal in dimensions, and were taken, but their capture soon ceased to afford me the slightest pleasure. The sun was rapidly declining. We had eight miles to row, and prudence dictated a speedy departure. But I was bound to land that trout if it took all summer.

I tried almost every fly in my book in vain; I simply witnessed the same provoking gyrations at every cast. If, however, I threw him a grasshopper disconnected from my line, he would take it with a gulp; but the moment I affixed one to the hook and cast it ever so gently, up he came and down he went unhooked, with the grasshopper intact. I was puzzled, and as a last resort I sat quietly down hopeless of achieving success so long as light enough remained for the wary fellow to detect the shadow of rod or line. The sun soon set. Twilight gently began its work of obscuration, and in due time just the shadow I desired fell upon the surface of the pool. I then disrobed my leader of its quartette of flies, put on a large miller, and with as much caution as if commissioned to surprise a rebel camp and with like trepidation, I chose my position. Then, with a twist of the wrist which experts will comprehend, I dropped my fly as gently as a zephyr just where the monster had made his last tantalizing leap, when, with the ferocity of a mad bull and with a quick dash which fairly startled me in the dim twilight, he rose to my miller, and with another twist of the wrist as quick and sudden as his rise, I struck him!

I have been present in crowds when grand victories have been suddenly announced, and when my blood has run like electric currents through my veins as I joined in the spontaneous shout of the multitude, but I have passed through no moment of more intense exhilaration than when I knew, by the graceful curve of my rod and by the steady tension of my trusty line, that I was master of the situation. He pulled like a Canastoga stallion and gave me all I knew to hold him within the restricted circle of the deep pool, whose edges were lined with roots and stumps and things equivalent. It was a half hour's stirring contest, and the hooting of the owl in the midst of the darkness which enveloped us was the trout's requiem. When I had landed him and had him fairly in quad, will it be deemed silly for me to say that I made the old woods ring with such a shout as one can only give when conscious of having achieved a great victory?

═══════════

❧ INVALID AT PAUL SMITH'S
EDWARD LIVINGSTON TRUDEAU, M.D.

I was influenced in my choice of the Adirondacks only by my love for the great forest and the wild life and not at all because I thought the climate would be beneficial in any way, for the Adirondacks were then [1873] visited only by hunters and fishermen and it was looked upon as a rough, inaccessible region and considered a most inclement and trying climate. I had been to Paul Smith's in the summer on two occasions before on short visits with my friend Lou Livingston and his mother, and had been greatly attracted by the beautiful lakes, the great forest, the hunting and fishing, and the novelty of the free and wild life there. If I had but a short time to live, I yearned for surroundings that appealed to me, and it seemed to me a longing I had for rest and the peace of the great wilderness.

It was a sad home-leaving, as my wife and my friends considered me most seriously if not hopelessly ill, and she was still in bed with the baby at her side and little Chatte in the nurse's arms. Dr. Walton saw me off and comforted me by his promises to look after "the wife and kids" and help my little family to move down to the rectory at Little Neck for the summer. I finally tore myself away and was helped into the cab by my friend Lou, who at once began to dilate on what sport we should have at Paul's; but my heart was heavier than it had been since my brother's death.

The first day we went to Saratoga by train and rested there overnight, and the next day by train to Whitehall and by boat through Lake Champlain, reaching Plattsburg at supper time. I had a raging fever all day, went to bed at once on reaching the Fouquet House, and was too ill and weak the next morning to attempt the long trip into the wilderness to Paul Smith's, so we had to wait at Plattsburg two days. Lou Livingston told me afterwards that the hotel people had tried to dissuade him from taking me on such a long journey and to such a rough and remote place as Paul Smith's and had urged him to induce me to return home. Whenever he hinted at a return home, however, I was evidently so upset at the idea that he decided to go on with me.

On the third day we started on a little branch iron-ore road for Ausable Forks, where the mines were, and from there we had to drive forty-two miles to Paul Smith's, most of which was over a rough corduroy road. While I was resting Lou hired an old-fashioned two-horse stage-wagon, put a board between the seats, and with a mattress and a couple of pillows arranged me so that I could lie down all the way quite comfortably. All day long we crept up the hills at a snail's pace and trotted down the hills and on the level road until I thought we must have gone fifty miles at least. I stood the jolting pretty well until afternoon, when the fever and the fatigue made the rough shaking of the wagon almost unbearable. Lou Livingston smoked innumerable pipes, conversed with the driver, with whom he made friends over occasional little nips from his flask, and they seemed very happy and comfortable; but for me it certainly was an afternoon of misery.

The sun was just setting as I caught sight of the great pines around Paul Smith's, and in a minute we were driving up to the door of the hostelry, a swarm of guides and fishermen were clambering off the steps and the horse-block, and many hands extended in welcome. Fred Martin, Mrs. Paul Smith's brother and one of the most splendid, sturdy specimens of manhood I have ever seen, was about to give my hand a squeeze that would, no doubt, have finished me when I whispered to him I was sick and wanted to be carried up to my room. He picked me up as if I had been an infant and went up two flights of stairs two steps at a time, opened the door of a room I had occupied before, and put me down on the bed with a pained expression and the comforting remark—

"Why, Doctor, you don't weigh no more than a dried lamb-skin!"

We both laughed, and indeed I was so happy at reaching my destination and seeing the beautiful lake again, the mountains and the forest all around me, that I could hardly have been depressed by anything Fred Martin could have said.

During the entire journey I had felt gloomy forebodings as to the hopelessness of my case, but under the magic influence of the surroundings I had longed for, these all disappeared and I felt convinced I was going to recover. How little I knew, as I shook hands with the great, strong men who came up to my room that evening to say a word of cheer to me, that forty-two years later most of them would be dead and that I should still be in the Adirondacks and trying to describe my first arrival at Paul Smith's as an invalid!

Soon Katie Martin, Mrs. Paul Smith's pretty sister, came in with a word of welcome and cheer and a tray on which were eggs, brook trout, pancakes and coffee, and I ate heartily and with a real relish for the first time in many a long week. . . .

I slept well and woke full of hope and anticipation and interest in my new surroundings. The first thing I did was to secure a guide, and Warren Flanders was engaged by me and George Martin by Lou Livingston. . . .

Warren Flanders came to my room after breakfast and told me he had fixed the boat "comfortable" with balsam boughs and blankets so that I could lie down in it, had put my rifle in, and if I felt up to it we would row down the river to Keese's Mill "kind of slow" and see what we could see. My hunting blood responded at once and I was soon in the boat. It was a beautiful sunny June day, the sky and water were blue, and the trees resplendent in their spring foliage; and as I lay comfortably on the soft boughs in the stern of the boat, with my rifle in reach across the gunwale, my spirits were high and I forgot all the misery and sickness I had gone through in the past two months.

The guide kept looking ahead from time to time. All at once he stopped, suddenly turning the boat sidewise. On a point about two hundred yards away I saw two deer: a buck and a doe were feeding. I never sat up, but rested my rifle on the side of the boat and fired at the buck, who, after a few jumps, fell dead at the edge of the woods. Warren went ashore, loaded the deer in the boat, and we returned to the hotel. If any game laws existed in those days they didn't apply to the Adirondack wilderness, for it was the custom to shoot game and catch fish at any season, provided they were used as food and not sent out of the woods for sale.

I got back quite triumphant to the hotel, and Lou Livingston, Paul Smith and the guides, who were very sympathetic about my illness, seemed delighted that I had had such good sport on the first day of my arrival.

This was my first personal experience as a patient in the Adirondacks and rather different from the first day spent by most patients who come now to Saranac Lake as ill as I was then! The change, the stimulus of renewed hope, and the constant open-air life had a wonderful effect on my health. I soon began to eat and sleep and lost my fever. At that time we had no idea of the essential value of rest, but as I often spent the entire day in the boat, fishing or being rowed about from place to place or watching the lake for deer, I unconsciously was kept at rest. My anxiety about my family was entirely relieved by frequent letters from my wife and good friend Walton, who sent me regular reports of "the brats" every two weeks, in which he fulminated, after his usual manner, on the nuisance of having to go out into the country to see them; but the reports were all good, and my improvement day by day became more manifest.

SCHOLAR'S UNWINDING
WILLIAM JAMES

To Charles Renouvier. Keene Valley, August 5, 1883. I have been here myself just a week. The virgin forest comes close to our house, and the diversity of walks through it, the brooks and the ascensions of hilltops are infinite. I doubt if there be anything like it in Europe. Your mountains are grander, but you have nowhere this carpet of absolutely primitive forest, with its indescribably sweet exhalations, spreading in every direction unbroken. I shall stay here doing hardly any work till late in September. I need to lead a purely animal life for at least two months to carry me through the teaching year.

To Mrs. Henry Whitman. Springfield Centre, N.Y., June 16, 1895. I will come if you command it; but reflect on my situation ere you do so. Just reviving from the addled and corrupted condition in which the Cambridge year has left me; just at the portals of that Adirondack wilderness for the breath of which I have sighed for years, unable to escape the cares of domesticity and get there; just about to get a little health into me, a little simplification and solidification and purification and sanification—things which will never come again if this one chance be lost; just filled to satiety with all the simpering conventions and vacuous excitements of so-called civilization; hungering for their opposite, the smell of the spruce, the feel of the moss, the sound of the cataract, the bath in its waters, the divine outlook from the cliff or hilltop over the unbroken forest—oh, Madam, Madam! do you know what medicinal things you ask me to give up? Alas!

I aspire downwards, and really *am* nothing, *not becoming* a savage as I would be, and failing to be the civilizee that I really ought to be content with being! But I wish that *you* also aspired to the wilderness. There are some nooks and summits in that Adirondack region where one can really "recline on one's divine composure" and, as long as one stays up there, seem for a while to enjoy one's birthright of freedom and relief from every fever and falsity. Stretched out on such a shelf—with thee beside me singing in the wilderness—what babblings might go on, what judgment-day discourse!

════════════

APPROACH TO THE MOUNTAINS
George Marshall

Fortunately our family did not have an automobile. Therefore we took it as a matter of course that when we wished to climb the high peaks of the Adirondacks, we should approach them on foot. This had the double advantage of being a pleasure in itself and of helping prepare us physically and psychologically for the wilder country beyond the ends of roads.

When Bob Marshall, Herb Clark and I first climbed Tahawus in 1918, we hiked the eight miles of dirt road between Lake Placid Station and South Meadows. In fact, on each trip to or from the high mountains during the following seven years or more, we walked and usually carried packs. . . .

The joys of road walking in those days before pavements and heavy traffic were to us only second to those of tramping and climbing in the back woods. The road lacked the freshness, superlative beauty, wildness, and sense of great adventure and complete freedom of the wilderness; but it nonetheless possessed many of these elements and also awarded us with that satisfying sense of physical and mental exhilaration and well-being which can only be obtained through physical accomplishment. As we swung along, the dust rising from our feet, our energy seemed to be kinetic—the more we walked, the easier it seemed to be to walk. This process, especially when the sun was shining, also stimulated good conversation and the gaiety of open country. If at times fatigue stole upon us, it was banished readily by a short rest, a bite of food, a drink of water or a good night's sleep. After all, two of us in 1918 had the good fortune of being fourteen and seventeen.

The road from Lake Placid Station to South Meadows wound over old glacial beaches and lake bottoms covered with second growth trees and pastures. It afforded numerous inspiring views of the surrounding wooded mountains, which were constantly changing from hour to hour and season to season with shifts in vegetation, light and color. We never tired of this route. The bright field flowers and humming insects welcomed us in June. The sticky hot, lazy days of July at some times tested our endurance and at others were strangely relaxing. The crystal clear blue skies of August gave promise of perfect views from the high peaks. The intervening dark days of rain settled the dust and made the world fresher and greener. The chill, windblown, snow-blocked lanes of February brought the power of the wilderness nearer to civilization. . . .

The road climbs steeply from the river to North Elba. On the first trip on which we carried packbaskets, the straps began to pull a bit as the road mounted. Suddenly Herb burst into song:

> "I saw three wayworn travelers,
>   In tattered garments clad.
>   They were struggling up the mountain
>   And it seemed that they were sad.
>   Their backs were heavy laden,
>   Their strength was almost gone,
>   And they shouted as they journeyed,
>   'Deliverance will come.'
>   Then, crowns of victory, palms of glory,
>   Crowns of victory they will wear."

As our laughter subsided, we gained our "palms of glory" by taking a shortcut across pastures and through the woods. This enabled us to escape the heat of the road and the remainder of the climb to North Elba Corners. Just before leaving the road, we looked with happy anticipation across the flower-studded Plains of Abraham to the high mountains, dominated by Tahawus and Mac-

Intyre and cut dramatically by Avalanche and Indian passes. These, with their encircling wild country, were our objectives. . . .

Before continuing, we also looked back across the Ausable River towards John Brown's Farm and grave marked by the American flag flying above the trees. We thought of his courage, and that of his family and neighbors, in farming here in those difficult pioneer days, and of his far greater bravery and foresight in his historic blows against slavery. We stood for a moment between these two great symbols of freedom—the wild mountains and the man of righteous passion.

We rested under a spreading maple at the far end of the pasture. Our serious mood vanished as Herb regaled us with a yarn about seventeen milk cows which had been chased down the grassy hill above us by a grizzly and had died of heart failure. . . .

We continued on our way to South Meadows. A mile or so beyond Woods' the road passes a shoulder of Van Hoevenberg Mountain. Herb claimed it was called "Calamity Mountain" after Joe McGinnis, who had the misfortune to contract the "fantod" right there. This dread disease made Joe shrink into a knot the size of a baseball. . . .

South Meadows was a jumping-off place for several of our trips into the roadless area which is the wilderness of the high peaks. From here, we made our first climb of Tahawus; circled the MacIntyre Range in a day; explored the wild Wallface-Scott Pond-Lost Pond plateau; packed to Panther Gorge to climb the Gothics Range; walked to the Saranacs by way of Indian Pass, Preston Ponds, Big Ampersand, and Kettle Mt. Pass; and took numerous other trips into the backwoods.

When we entered these wilder regions, our eight-mile hike to the last frontier at the road's end had prepared us in ways that cannot be equalled today by driving an auto to the beginning of a trail. The road walk was a gradual transition, physically and psychologically, between the twentieth-century world and the primeval. . . .

Road walking having become a thing of the past, the transition to the mood of forest and mountain now must take place entirely within the wilderness itself. It really cannot occur by fiat at the car door or the trail-head with the speed and ease of switching off the ignition. Hours of walking and plenty of space are required for the transition alone. Much more of time and of big roadless country are needed to give the opportunity for that complete and satisfying wilderness experience which thousands of people seek each year on their vacations into the backwoods. This re-emphasizes the continuing importance both to guard the boundaries of our Forest Preserve and to protect the wild forest atmosphere within in order to preserve the wilderness and its unique, superlative values for generations to come.

 OLYMPIC VILLAGE
George Christian Ortloff
The following article appeared in Adirondack Life
on the eve of the 1980 Winter Olympics

February 4, 1932, dawned cold and clear, and for the first time all winter, there was just enough snow on the ground to cover the dead, dry grass completely. It was the warmest winter in U.S. Weather Service history, and in Lake Placid three years of planning for the Olympic Winter Games were jeopardized by the one thing planning can't control: the weather.

The crowd gathered around the gleaming speed skating oval for the opening ceremony as the brilliant sun rose higher over the Adirondack peaks. In seats designed for nearly 7,000, there were fewer than 3,000 people. It was two and a half years since the stock market crash had sent the whole world into a deep economic depression, and there weren't that many people who could afford the $5 ticket price for the opening ceremony. Besides, the fence around the stadium was only about six feet tall, and thousands of non-paying spectators were getting as good a view as the ticket holders.

As the teams wheeled around the track in the traditional parade of nations, only seventeen flags represented their countries. There had been more teams at St. Moritz in 1928, but the Depression had affected the finances of participants, too. The hockey schedule featured only four teams—so few that, in addition to the actual tournament for the medals, each team would play exhibition games against American club teams to flesh out the competition.

Weather and money might have ruined the III Olympic Winter Games, but they did not. The Games were held, and Lake Placid was praised by the International Olympic Committee for having staged the Games under the most severe financial obstacles the modern world had yet seen.

It had been a great adventure for a little backwoods town in the Adirondacks. The III Olympic Winter Games, from the first time Lake Placid had heard of them, had propelled the community— sometimes kicking and screaming—into the limelight as a glamorous international resort.

The sports themselves had not awed Lake Placid. Since the turn of the century, winter had become more and more of a playground every year. In the 'teens, speed-skating had become so popular in Lake Placid and neighboring Saranac Lake that more world records were set and broken in the two towns than in all the other speed-skating centers in North America combined. . . .

The 1932 Olympic Winter Games at Lake Placid are remembered for several important things:

1) They popularized winter sports in America.
2) In the long run, they were responsible for creating a whole new industry around winter sports.
3) They put Lake Placid on the map.
4) And they secured the position of the community in the tourist market for many years thereafter.

Moreover, for the U.S. Olympic Team, Lake Placid provided the setting for its best performance in all of the first twelve Winter Olympics.

The gold medal-winning spree of the 1932 U.S. speed-skating team alone has never been equalled [until 1980]. In fact, just two men, Jack Shea and Irving Jaffee (who took four golds between them) did better than any *entire* U.S. Winter Olympic team in all sports combined, before or since. In addition to sweeping all four speed-skating events, the American 1932 team took both bobsledding events, picked up silver medals in 5,000-meter speed-skating, pairs, figure skating, hockey, and four-man bobsledding; and took bronze medals in two-man bobsledding and women's figure skating. It was enough to dethrone Norway as the two-time unofficial Olympic team champion, the only time the U.S. has held that title in the Winter Games. . . .

The differences between 1932 and 1980 are . . . dramatic. Alpine skiing was not even on the Olympic calendar in 1932. Now, at Whiteface Mountain, millions of dollars later, the largest of the Olympic facilities is also a recreational complex attracting thousands of visitors a year.

Alongside the bobrun snakes a similar serpentine chute of concrete, the luge run. Like the bobrun, it is the only one in North America, and it is also refrigerated. Both runs are lighted for night practice.

In 1932, the athletes from every nation stayed in hotels and rented homes. Now, athletes stay together in one large "Olympic Village."

The ceremonies in 1932 were rudimentary, and unpolished. Since 1936, the pageantry of an Olympic Games has become the paradigm of modern pomp and circumstance, and the 1980 Winter Olympics will usher the participants in and out with a 1,000-mile relay of the Olympic flame, original music performed by as many as six hundred musicians at a time, fireworks each night over Mirror Lake, and the latest in artistic technology—laser projections on the mountainsides.

The skies will be full of helicopters in 1980, shuttling television cameras back and forth to different locations, providing aerial platforms for security and traffic control officers, and speeding injured participants to the nearest major hospital in Burlington, Vermont.

The images of Lake Placid's Olympics will be seen, as they happen, by as many as 600 million people around the world. Television will ensure that the impact of 1980 will be many times that of 1932.

The 1932 Olympics made Lake Placid a household word for

at least a decade and kept the village alive as a resort. The 1980 Olympics were sought by Lake Placid for much the same reasons, and they will undoubtedly accomplish those objectives. But without realizing it when they began, Lake Placid's Olympic organizers have already accomplished something far more important to the Olympic movement.

In 1972, the last year of Avery Brundage's long term as president of the IOC, it seemed that the Winter Olympics were headed for the scrap heap. Brundage himself was against them because they were too commercialized for his taste. Then Denver, which had been planning for the 1976 Games, backed out. A minority of the IOC Executive Committee actually introduced a resolution calling for the end of the Winter Olympics.

Enter Lake Placid. Two months after the Denver debacle, Lake Placid was presenting its case to the IOC in an effort to pick up the 1976 pieces. So was Innsbruck, Austria, another previous Olympic host. The IOC picked Innsbruck to replace Denver, but Lake Placid's presentation gave them confidence in the future, and they pointedly asked that the Adirondacks come back with a bid for 1980. As it turned out, it was a good thing they did. By the time IOC met in Vienna to pick the 1980 site, every other city but Lake Placid had dropped out of the running.

Lake Placid did not so much win by default, as because it was in the right place with the right idea at the right time. The "Olympics in perspective" which Lake Placid proposed, not only fit the IOC's needs at the time, but, because it also became a reality, it led the way for other small cities which, by 1972, had become intimidated by the formidable job of trying to stage the Olympic Games. The bidding for the 1984 Winter Olympics was healthy, with four cities eagerly competing, and several cities are already putting together their bid packages for 1988.

Most of the folks around Olympic headquarters in the North Elba Town Hall won't say so, but there's no question that Lake Placid, by persisting with its own dream, has saved the Winter Olympics from oblivion.

CONFLICT OF INTERESTS
MASON SMITH

In the summer of 1971, Peter S. Paine, Jr., who had been a member of the Temporary Study Commission on the Future of the Adirondack Park—the Nelson Rockefeller-appointed body that had recommended the creation of the fledgling Adirondack Park Agency—issued a warning to the environmentalists. "The conservation organizations that are interested in the Adirondacks are really going to have to get to work," Paine said, "and, in my judgment, it is going to take one full-time paid employee of the Adirondack Mountain Club, the Association for the Protection of the Adirondacks, the Sierra Club, and the whole cast of characters throughout the conservation spectrum, to sit there and dog that Agency. Citizen support and citizen criticism and appearance at public hearings are absolutely indispensable . . . if you are going to keep this Agency honest."

At the time, environmentalists were busy fighting the huge Horizon and Ton-Da-Lay second home developments. Then, as the State Land Master Plan and afterwards the Park Agency's Land Use and Development Plan came out, and as it fumbled to develop an efficient permit system, what the APA seemed to need was defending, not dogging. When the Adirondack Council was formed at last, in 1975, it was in response to efforts to abolish the APA, and its primary activity was to intervene in court cases and administrative hearings to defend the constitutionality of the Adirondack Park Agency Act.

This the Council did, successfully enough, under its founding chairman R. Courtney Jones, but it still had no regular staff and no continuous presence in the Park. The full import of Paine's remarks was not appreciated until 1977. That year, state and local political power massed behind the siting of the new Olympic ski jumps at Intervale, where they would be extremely conspicuous from every vantage for many miles around, including several of the High Peaks. The Council vigorously advocated an impact study and a search for other sites. But the beleaguered Agency, fearful of the charge of obstructing the Olympics, allowed the Intervale site to be steam-rollered through hearings and gave its conceptual approval to the construction of the jumps there without even the most cursory consideration of alternatives. Earlier threats that the Adirondacks would "swallow" the APA suddenly seemed quite real.

At this point, the Adirondack Council had a choice: lick its wounds, pay off the $39,000 legal debt it had run up on the ski jump issue, and dissolve; or reorganize, expand its activities, not only to fight the Agency's battles for it in court but to do just what Paine had foreseen would be needed: "to sit there and dog that Agency."

It chose the second path. Courtney Jones turned over the chairmanship to a self-described "environmental hard-liner," Harold A. Jerry, Jr., the former Executive Director of the Temporary Study Commission and to a great extent the author of its recommendations, which had led to the creation of the APA itself. Jerry hired away a valued staff member of the APA, Gary Randorf. The Adirondack Council established an office in the Park. In the few years since, the Adirondack Council has established itself firmly as the preeminent exponent of environmentalism in the Adirondack Park; and the APA no longer finds itself out on the radical fringe of land use planning to protect the wilderness. . . .

The agenda of the Adirondack Council reads a lot like the *Report of the Temporary Study Commission*. In a talk given before the Park Agency in 1977 and still remembered, Jerry reminded the commissioners that the Study Commission "has a dream . . . to create a vibrant, viable, visible Adirondack Park." He ticked off the components of that dream: a program of acquisitions of choice parcels of open space by fee purchase or easement; unit management of state lands; wildlife management; control of overuse, including a permit system; protection of trail-less peaks; visitor information centers; state aid for local government to compensate for tax losses when development easements reduced the market value of private lands; land-use controls that more effectively guaranteed open space remaining open; protection of lakes and ponds as well as rivers. . . .

The Agency itself had survived its battles so far but in the process had evolved a too-defensive posture. It tried to discharge its statutory duties inconspicuously and certainly didn't look hard to see what it could do to improve and protect the region's wilderness character. It was beginning, Jerry charged, to sound like an economic development agency, surrendering authority to local governments, appeasing the very regional legislators whose "main goal in life" was its destruction. "What do you hope to gain by these maneuvers?" he asked. "It has been said that the support of environmentalists is not enough to guarantee your continued existence. I ask you, how long do you expect to exist if the environmentalists abandon you completely?"

The Adirondack Park was supposed to connote something more than a line on the ground, a sign law, and a place where you had to get a permit to build a house. If the APA had forgotten what the Temporary Study Commission had envisioned, Jerry hadn't. The Adirondack Council under Jerry would fight the Agency's fights for it, and help to educate a larger constituency for it, so that Agency people could "sit down before dinner, drink that highball slowly, and think about planning." The Council had its eye on the goal, the whole campaign firmly in mind, and promised not to let the Agency forget it. . . .

Jerry has proposed a $100 million bond issue for the purpose of buying from landowners the right to develop their land. By buying "scenic easements," the state would simultaneously secure more open space in perpetuity and improve the viability of the timber industry, because without development rights attached, the land's market value falls to the value for timber production or wilderness value alone. What landowners would save in taxes, the towns of course would lose—if the proposal ended there. It doesn't. Jerry stresses that under his proposal the people of the entire state would make up the difference to the towns. They would pay taxes on the easements, just as they now pay taxes on the public lands. . . .

The Adirondack Council . . . has become an integral part of a *de facto* system of communication and influence on Park-related issues. The struggle that has always characterized Adirondack history, between those who would exploit and those who would set aside and save can now be said to be, for all practical purposes, institutionalized: on the one hand, the Local Government Review Board, the local governments themselves, and the alliance of hunting and fishing associations known as the Conservation Council; in the middle, the APA and DEC; and on the other hand, the Adirondack Council, committed above all to the ideal of wilderness.

Everything in its program—even things that might seem contradictory—flows from that ideal. The promotion of a stronger national image of the Adirondacks, which might seem to be asking for overuse, flows from the reasoning that the more people who are aware of a great Adirondack Park of six million acres containing wonderful wilderness areas, the more assured its protection. Again, country-wide recognition of the Park will help an intelligent, non-destructive tourist industry to thrive, and that industry, knowing its self-interest, will protect the wilderness. A canoe route across Whitney Park, a highway overlook with a view of the High Peaks, a sign identifying Giant Mountain to Northway travelers, a system of visitor information centers—everything that enhances public awareness will protect it, as will a more profitable lumber industry. And finally, a resident population awakened to its extraordinary privilege of living in a park-like environment, breathing clean air, drinking clean, safe water, with wilderness in its back yard, will gladly surrender some of the options people elsewhere use and abuse, and they will also protect it.

As Harold Jerry studied the national parks, and as he became involved with nationwide environmental groups, his perspective became national, and he found himself comparing "what we were doing here" with practices long established in the national parks. He sees the Adirondack Park as being far behind in its public image, its natural resource management, its interpretive services, its systems of controlling high use pressures. He, perhaps more extremely than the Council as a whole, wishes it to be a place apart. But the Park is unique and really incomparable to anything anywhere else, with its in-held towns and industries and 3.6 million acres of private land—not to mention 125,000 people living inside it. Many Adirondackers would rather feel a different difference. We cling to the feeling (too inarticulate to be a belief) that the Big Woods are still a real, natural wilderness, undeveloped because inhospitable, as it was for the Bark-Eaters who gave it a name, beyond a frontier whose progress stalled at its edges, through poverty and neglect—thank God.

It isn't, of course. The Adirondack Park is a deliberately and still tenuously preserved place, whose forests were once all but clear-cut and burned off, whose beaver were once all but extirpated, whose wolves and lynx and cougars were, whose eagles well may be. And its history instructs that it has only been preserved as well as it has by the vigilance of such citizen groups as the Adirondack Council. Environmental extremism isn't a danger. It's a flat necessity. As Clarence Petty, who was raised the son of a guide at Indian Carry, observes, "This controversy will always go on. It's always been that way."

III

Guide and Party

I believe that Adam in paradise was not so favorably situated on the whole as is the backwoodsman in America.
Henry David Thoreau

THE BOND BETWEEN the guide and his patron was love of the woods and of hunting, fishing, or exploring. When this was genuine, barriers between the city-bred party (one patron or more) and the backwoodsman vanished. A friendship was formed which sometimes lasted a lifetime.

A relationship as emotional as this attracts traditions and legends. In the last century especially, when guide service was more essential than today, the Adirondack guide was a celebrated figure in the nation, proverbial for woodcraft, honesty, resourcefulness, patience and good humor, and backwoods philosophy. These merits, often real enough, were enhanced in the mind of the patron, particularly if he was a writer acquainted with the myths of the age. Myth and reality combined to make the guide the most attractive figure in Adirondack life and literature.

The reality was a man who had lived all or nearly all his life in the woods, killed his first deer at twelve, and operated a trap line between bouts of schooling; now in maturity, with an intimate knowledge of the woods and waters of his own area and muscles hardened by a winter's logging, he could row a boat all day, pack it and the duffel over the carries, build a shelter wherever needed, find the best spring holes, organize a hunt with dogs or float noiselessly into shore behind a jack light. He could cook passably well, had a few picturesque oaths and other expressions not in the lexicon and a collection of hunting stories for the campfire. Besides all this, he had an assortment of odd, ornery, or amiable traits that made him a character among characters.

From the beginning of guiding as a profession, a myth was ready-made for attachment to this reality. It was the myth of the American as a new man, innocent, unburdened by the sins of the past, and optimistic about his chances of making a new life in a new world. If this American was a backwoodsman, Thoreau held, his chances were all the better. R. W. B. Lewis traces the growth of this myth in *The American Adam*. The first great exemplar of it in fiction is Cooper's hero Leatherstocking, the woodsman-guide as he ought to be.

Natty Bumppo, or Leatherstocking, appears under various nick-names in five of Cooper's novels published between 1823 and 1841. In only one of the five, *The Last of the Mohicans*, is he shown in an Adirondack setting, as the scout Hawkeye in the Lake George region. Nevertheless, he was promptly adopted as the spiritual father of Adirondack guides. Coincidence helped. In the midst of the Leatherstocking series, during the world's first enchantment over Natty Bumppo, the Adirondacks were opened to tourists with news of the first ascent of Mount Marcy in 1837. John Cheney was one of the local guides on that expedition. A month later Charles Fenno Hoffman, magazine editor and Cooper enthusiast, came to see for himself and make a report. He engaged Cheney as guide, and in the first popular travel book about the Adirondacks two years later announced to the world that he had found the living counterpart of Natty Bumppo. If it were not for the anachronism, he declared, he would swear that his friend John Cheney was the model for Cooper's hero. In the next decade two other tourists and writers, Charles Lanman and Joel T. Headley, rounded out the portrait begun by Hoffman, and Cheney was established as a Leatherstocking of the Adirondacks. For the next half century tourists and sportsmen expected to find Leatherstockings in their guides, and what was missing in the reality was often supplied by the imagination. So general did the association become that in 1883 Lester A. Beardslee, writing in *Forest and Stream*, attached the name to a whole class of guides he believed passing:

"The very best guides . . . were men of the Leather Stocking type."
To have such a guide was not only an open sesame to the pleasures
of the woods but also, among a rising middle class, a matter of
prestige. The best guides were in high demand and booked a year
in advance.

Some patrons were unlucky. At all times there have been lazy,
inept, bad-mannered guides who could spoil a camping trip, just as
the starch and dignity Sam Dunning associated with Boston parties
could spoil things for the guide. The party who delayed booking
a guide or made a random choice was sometimes disappointed. Kate
Field, a journalist not easily taken in by myths, gave a balanced
appraisal: "Guides are exceedingly human. There are saints among
them, and there are sinners." Verplanck Colvin, who in his official
survey of the Adirondacks came in contact with more guides than
anyone else, said of the fifty-one who served him in the crowded
survey year of 1873, "Almost all of them were faithful, intelligent
and skillful men, ready to labor night and day for the success of
the survey."

The surly and uncommunicative guide that F. Trench Towns-
hend, a captain in the British Life Guards, complained of was
probably the exception. Many guides had a collection of hunting
stories with which to entertain the patron. James Haughton, writing in the *Harvard Magazine* in 1860, described Cort Moody as
follows: "Tall and gaunt, dressed in a blue shirt, his brown face
expressing much shrewdness and determination, he is a perfect
Leatherstocking, only less laconic; for Cort is a real sailor for telling yarns." Although Sam Dunning and Mart Moody had a certain
reputation for drollery, humor was usually absent from guide
stories. It is a product of urban sophistication. The funniest of all
Adirondack bear stories, quoted in Section V, was told by a city
man, Charles Dudley Warner, friend and one-time collaborator of
Mark Twain. Warner himself did not give the guides much credit
for humor or art: "[They] cheer the night with bear fights, and
catamount encounters, and frozen-to-death experiences, and simple
tales of great prolixity and no point, and jokes of primitive lucid-
ity." After a long day's hunt, the party could readily tolerate
soporific yarns.

Natty Bumppo himself is a kind of backwoods angel who totes

a gun. He is the one man whom power does not spoil. Though a lord in the forest, he is incorruptible in his innocence. He is Adam before the Fall living in a wild, shaggy American Eden and holding the key to it.

This lovely fiction was the party's ideal for his guide. The guides themselves did not read Cooper. If they had, they might have criticized Natty Bumppo's woodcraft. But the smarter ones had an inkling of what the party expected, and some were willing to oblige, within limits. John Cheney kept his legend bright. John Plumley, celebrated as "Honest John" by Adirondack Murray, never belied the reputation. Mitchell Sabattis faithfully kept his promise to a patron never again to touch drink, or so it was said. Only by imitating the angels, says a twentieth century romanticist, can we hope to become by painful small degrees somewhat better than the chimpanzee. A slight danger existed that a guide might try too hard. After Warner had drawn his fetching profile of Orson Phelps as the primitive man, Phelps himself, admiring the portrait, took to posturing a little and lost some of his naturalness. But few guides ever tried that hard.

The Leatherstocking legend embodies one substantial truth: the good guide was lord of the forest and held the key to it for the townsman, especially in the days before roads, trails, and topographic maps. Without him the city man was a fumbler in the woods; his life there might be as vexatious and complicated as in the city—not what he came for at all. He came to kill deer and catch trout. But he wanted more—no less than a change within himself. Like many Americans, he was a pioneer at heart. The writers of midcentury had a ready explanation for his case. In the town innocence is corrupted, needs multiplied, vitality sapped. Things are in the saddle and ride mankind. Men live sterile lives of quiet desperation. On the frontier, in the wilderness, however, it is possible to regain innocence, freedom, and vitality; to begin a new life free from the past. As Emerson puts the theory:

> Whoso walks in solitude
> And inhabiteth the wood,
> Choosing light, wave, rock and bird,
> Before the money-loving herd,

Into that forester shall pass,
From these companions, power and grace.
Clean shall he be, without, within.

Not many could become that forester. But if they were bound to the city for eleven months, they could satisfy their need of wilderness in the remaining one. It is surprising how many midcentury tourists came into the Adirondacks suffering from what they called "brain-fever" and came out with a cheer for the forest life that some "honest John" had taught them. "Everything," wrote Henry van Dyke, "depends in the Adirondacks upon your guide." The guides could not only find game for the city man to kill but also induct him into that forest Eden where purification takes place, for, says Murray, they "are uncontaminated with the vicious habits of civilized life" and "the wilderness has unfolded to them its mysteries." But now we are back with the myth and must tread softly not to disturb the illusion that Old Mountain Phelps could "hallow a 'random scoot' through the forests into something akin to questing for the Holy Grail."

Anyway, the gratitude of patrons is a matter of record. The wealthy paid tips sometimes exceeding pay for a successful outing. Grover Cleveland created a post office named Moody and appointed as its first postmaster Mart Moody, the guide who had served him before he became President. Irving Bacheller wrote a novel (*Silas Strong*), a poem "Him an' Me," and a memoir in *From Stores of Memory* in tribute to "the most remarkable character I have known," Philo Scott, guide of the Cranberry Lake region.

The hotel guides, according to Murray, were as a class inferior to the independent ones. Not responsible to the party, they lacked incentive to please. Of the independents Murray writes: "A more honest, cheerful, and patient class of men cannot be found the world over. Born and bred, as many were, in this wilderness, skilled in all the lore of woodcraft, handy with the rod, superb at the paddle, modest in demeanor and speech, honest to a proverb, they deserve and receive the admiration of all who make their acquaintance."

But the conditions that once made guiding a flourishing profession have passed. The best period was the forty years after the first ascent of Mount Marcy. Then a guide was essential to tourist and sportsman. Large areas were yet unsurveyed, maps sketchy and inaccurate, roads few and miserable, trails almost nonexistent except on the carries. The waterways were the traffic lanes, and here the guide and his guide-boat (made in the region and skillfully adapted to travel there) were indispensable. By the 1880s, however, transportation had become easier. Roads were improved, railroads were penetrating the Blue Line. Steamboats were introduced on the lakes. Colvin's survey made possible reliable maps. In the high peak region blazed trails could be followed without a guide. And in three cruises in the early eighties George Washington Sears (Nessmuk) proved that a visitor in a lightweight canoe, even if he had three-score years and uncertain health, could be his own skipper—especially when indulgent guides sometimes helped him over the carries and let him share a few trade secrets. Nessmuk granted that the guide was still the controlling element in the North Woods but warned that the day of his sovereignty was nearing an end. The independent guide was being undermined by first-class hotels, stage coaches, and steamers. He was assisting in his own decline by padding his bill with such items as travel time from and to his home (often mythical) and "doubling the carries" when, as often happened, the city man broke down under his share of the load. The guide who for two weeks or more had been the considerate nurse, teacher, cook, entertainer, philosopher, and friend turned sly and impersonal on presenting his bill. Leatherstocking was losing his innocence.

Other observers of the eighties agreed with Nessmuk. Captain Beardslee complained about the growing number of young, unqualified guides that lacked familiarity even with their own area but were artists in running up a bill and evading hard work. Dr. Arpad Gerster, who in better days had had Alvah Dunning as guide, came to prefer traveling alone to the "impatience of guides who were always in a 'stew' to reach the next hotel on the route, where 'grub' was awaiting them." He adds that even in the eighties the guide began to change his character from woodsman to a mere machine for transportation, "losing his woodcraft, his leisurely and knowing ways, and his aplomb."

In the nineties the guides themselves tried to mend matters by organizing an association pledged to standard rates and adherence to the game laws. Guides of the old school lingered on, and their example helped to keep the tradition alive in times grown uncongenial. For in the present century it is the Conservation Department (lately known as the Department of Environmental Conservation), not the guide, that rules the woods. Guides are required to register with the department. The list still bears the names of several hundred distributed throughout the Adirondacks. Among them a rare son or grandson of an oldtime guide tries to uphold the tradition. A few others who register with the DEC never plan to work for pay but want to associate themselves with an honored tradition. They are familiar with their part of the woods and are pleased to show you its wonders—an esker as yet unmapped by geologists, a giant white pine, a colony of showy lady's slippers, an active osprey nest, or a peat bog of exceptional depth. In these few Natty Bumppo lives on after a fashion.

Gurth Whipple wrote in 1935 a somewhat belated requiem to the great age of guiding: "The latter-day guides are like the latter-day saints; they can't compare in genuineness with the old orthodox patriarchs; they are a different race. Their hunting ground is no longer a free domain; they can no longer take game at will and build camps wherever their fancy dictates. They are all regimented, registered, licensed, and badged, which proclaims to the public that they are qualified persons. The old-timers would rest uneasy in their graves if they knew this. No member of the gnarled and woolly coterie could ever be mistaken for anyone else. He needed no badge and no government mandate to designate his business or support his qualifications."

Most guides today make their living by other work and go out with parties only during the hunting season. On a summer weekend they may, if they can bear it, lead a party of picnicking schoolteachers to a pond where water lilies grow. The more fortunate have year-round jobs with game clubs, guiding in season and taking care of club property the rest of the year. The individual hiker, mountain climber, camper, or canoeist almost never hires a guide.

How does the party fare without Leatherstocking? His guides

are the impersonal bulletins of the Department of Environmental Conservation, the marked trails, the guidebooks of the Adirondack Mountain Club, topographic maps, and a compass. These don't chew tobacco and tell yarns. They can't give the gradual initiation to woods life, adjusted to mental and physical capacities, that Leatherstocking knew by instinct and experience how to do. It is harder to find Eden today. But it is still there; maybe an improved version where the woods have grown back. It is better protected now than then against despoilers, including guide and party. And there is much satisfaction in finding it on your own.

LEATHERSTOCKING THE SECOND
C. F. HOFFMAN

Attracted by press reports of the first ascent of Marcy, Charles
Fenno Hoffman was on the scene a month later, in September, 1837.
His happy suggestion of "Tahawus," Indian word meaning "cloud-
splitter," as a name for Marcy came too late; Emmons had named
the peak in August. Hoffman tried to climb Marcy and wept on
finding it impossible with his one leg, even with John Cheney as
guide. Cheney guided him through Indian Pass, however.

If it did not involve an anachronism, I could swear that
Cooper took the character of Natty Bumpo [Bumppo] from my
mountaineer friend, John Cheney. The same silent, simple, deep
love of the woods—the same gentleness and benevolence of feeling toward all who love his craft—the same unobtrusive kindness
toward all others; and lastly, the same shrewdness as a woodsman
and gamesomeness of spirit as a hunter are common to both. . . .

The walk to the Indian Pass is difficult enough at any time, but
soon after leaving our boat at the inlet of Lake Henderson, the
morning, which had hitherto been cloudy, broke into a cold rain
which, wetting our clothes through, increased the weight that
we had to drag through a primitive swamp, where each step was
upon some slippery log affording a precarious foothold; some
decayed tree, into whose spongy body you would sink kneedeep
or upon quaking mosses that threatened to swallow one up

entirely. Here, though, while wading through the frequent pools or stumbling over the fallen boughs which centuries had accumulated, I would often pause to admire some gigantic pine which, drawing vigour from the dankness and decay around it, would throw its enormous column into the air, towering a hundred feet above hemlocks and cedars near, which would themselves seem forest giants when planted beside the modern growth of our Atlantic border. . . .

Though winding up and down continually, we were in the main ascending gradually to a lofty elevation. The number of the swamps were diminished, the frequent rills flashed more rapidly amid the loose boulders of rock, which soon began to cover the soil entirely; while the boulders themselves became lofty hillocks of solid stone, covered with moss and sustaining a vigorous growth of the birch, the mountain-ash, or clumps of the hardy white cedar upon their summits.

Wet, bruised, and weary, we sat down beneath one of those enormous masses of displaced rock, after scaling a difficult ascent, and purposed to encamp there for the night; but looking up through an opening in the trees, we saw the cliffs of the Indian Pass almost immediately above us, as they were swathed in mist, and the heavy scud, impelled by the wind which drew strongly through the gap, drifted past the gray precipice and made the wall look as if in motion to crush us when just entering the jaws of the ravine.

But there were still two hours of daylight left, and though the mile that was yet to be traversed before we gained the centre of the pass was the most arduous task of the whole route, we again commenced the ascent. It took the whole two hours to accomplish this mile, but as the glen narrowed, our further advance was animated by a new object of interest, in the shape of a fresh moose-track; and we followed the trail until it broke abruptly in a rocky gorge, wilder than any I had yet beheld. . . .

We are now in the bosom of the pass, and the shadows of night are veiling the awful precipice which forms the background of the picture. We have climbed the last ascent, steeper than all the rest, and here, in a clump of birches and balsam-firs,

surrounded by steeps and precipices on every side, is our place
to bivouac for the night.

"It ain't so bad a place for camping out," said John Cheney, as
he rose from slaking his thirst at a feeble rill which trickled from
beneath the roots of a rifted cedar over which he leaned—"it
ain't so bad a place to camp if it didn't rain so like all natur. I
wouldn't mind the rain much, nother, if we had a good shantee;
but you see the birch bark won't run at this season, and it's pretty
hard to make a water-proof thatch unless you have hemlock
boughs—hows'ever, gentlemen, I'll do the best by ye."

And so he did! Honest John Cheney, thou art at once as stanch
a hunter and as true and gentle a practiser of woodcraft as ever
roamed the broad forest; and beshrew me when I forget thy
services that night in Indian Pass.

The frame of a wigwam used by some former party was still
standing, and Cheney went to work industriously tying poles
across it with withes of yellow birch and thatching the roof and
sides with boughs of balsam-fir. Having but one axe with us, my
friend and myself were, in the mean time, unemployed, and
nothing could be more disconsolate than our situation as we stood
dripping in the cold rain and thrashing our arms, like hackney-
coachmen, to keep the blood in circulation. My hardy friend,
indeed, was in a much worse condition than myself. He had been
indisposed when he started upon the expedition and was now so
hoarse that I could scarcely hear him speak amid the gusts of
wind which swept through the ravine. We both shivered as if in
an ague, but he suffered under a fever which was soon super-
added. We made repeated attempts to strike a fire, but our "loco
foco" matches would not ignite, and when we had recourse to
flint and steel, everything was so damp around us that our fire
would not kindle. John began to look exceedingly anxious:

"Now, if we only had a little daylight left, I would make
some shackleberry-tea for you; but it will never do to get sick
here, for if this storm prove a northeaster, God only knows
whether all of us may ever get away from this notch again. I guess
I had better leave the camp as it is and first make a fire for you."

Saying this, Cheney shouldered his axe, and striking off a few yards, he felled a dead tree, split it open, and took some dry chips from the heart. I then spread my cloak over the spot where he laid them to keep off the rain, and stooping under it, he soon kindled a blaze, which we employed ourselves in feeding until the "camp" was completed. And now came the task of laying in a supply of fuel for the night. This the woodsman effected by himself with an expedition that was marvellous. Measuring three or four trees with his eye, to see that they would fall near the fire without touching our wigwam, he attacked them with his axe, felled, and chopped them into logs, and made his woodpile in less time than could a city sawyer, who had all his timber carted to hand. Blankets were then produced from a pack which he had carried on his back; and these, when stretched over a carpeting of leaves and branches, would have made a comfortable bed if the latter had not been saturated with rain. Matters, however, seemed to assume a comfortable aspect as we now sat under the shade of boughs, drying our clothes by the fire, while John busied himself in broiling some bacon, which we had brought with us. But our troubles had only yet begun; and I must indulge in some details of a night in the woods for the benefit of "gentlemen who sit at home at ease."

Our camp, which was nothing more than a shed of boughs open on the side toward the fire, promised a sufficient protection against the rain so long as the wind should blow from the right quarter; and an outlying deer-stalker might have been content with our means and appliances for comfort during the night. Cheney, indeed, seemed perfectly satisfied as he watched the savoury slices which were to form our supper steaming up from the coals.

"Well," said the woodsman, "you see there's no place but what if a man bestirs himself to do his best, he may find some comfort in it. Now, many's the time that I have been in the woods on a worse night than this, and having no axe nor nothing to make a fire with, have crept into a hollow log and lay shivering till morning; but here, now, with such a fire as that—"

As he spoke a sudden puff of wind drove the smoke from the green and wet timber full into our faces and filled the shantee to a degree so stifling that we all rushed out into the rain, that blew in blinding torrents against us.

"Tormented lightning!" cried John, aghast at this new annoyance. "This is too pesky bad; but I can manage that smoke if the wind doesn't blow from more than three quarters at a time." Seizing his axe upon the instant, he plunged into the darkness beyond the fire, and in a moment or two a large tree came crashing with all its leafy honours, bearing down with it two or three saplings to our feet. With the green boughs of these he made a wall around the fire to shut out the wind, leaving it open only on the side toward the shantee. The supper was now cooked without further interruption. My friend was too ill to eat; but though under some anxiety on his account, I myself did full justice to the culinary skill of our guide and began to find some enjoyment amid all the discomfort of our situation. The recollection of similar scenes in other days gave a relish to the wildness of the present and inspired that complacent feeling which a man of less active pursuits sometimes realizes when he finds that the sedentary habits of two or three years have not yet warped and destroyed the stirring tastes of his youth.

We told stories and recounted adventures. I could speak of these northern hills from having passed some time among them upon a western branch of the Hudson when a lad of fourteen; while the mountain-hunter would listen with interest to the sporting scenes that I could describe to him upon the open plains of the far west; though I found it impossible to make him understand how men could find their way in a new country where there were so few trees! With regard to the incidents and legends that I gathered in turn from him, I may hereafter enlighten the reader. But our discourse was suddenly cut short by a catastrophe which had nearly proved a very serious one. This was nothing more nor less than the piles of brush which encircled our fire, to keep the wind away, suddenly kindling into a blaze and for a moment or two threatening to consume our wigwam. The wind, at the same time, poured down the gorge in shifting, angry blasts which whirled the flames in reeling eddies high into the air, bringing the gray cliffs into momentary light—touching the dark evergreens with a ruddy glow—and lighting up the stems of the pale birches, that looked like sheeted ghosts amid the surrounding gloom.

A finishing touch of the elements was yet wanting to complete the agreeableness of our situation, and finally, just as the curtain of brush on the windward side of the fire was consumed, the cold rain changed into a flurry of snow; and the quickly-melted flakes were driven with the smoke into the innermost parts of our wigwam. Conversation was now out of the question. John did, indeed, struggle on with a panther story for a moment or two, and one or two attempts were made to joke upon our miserable situation, but sleet and smoke alternately damped and stifled every effort, and then all was still except the roar of the elements. My sick friend must have passed a horrible night, as he woke me once or twice with his coughing; but I wrapped myself in my cloak, and placing my mouth upon the ground to avoid choking from the smoke, I was soon dreaming as quietly as if in a curtained chamber at home. The last words I heard John utter, as he coiled himself in a blanket, were—

"Well, it's one comfort, since it's taken on to blow so, I've cut down most of the trees around us that would be likely to fall and crush us during the night."

The ringing of Cheney's axe was the first sound that met my ear in the morning, which broke excessively cold. The fire had burnt low, though frequently replenished by him during the night, and he was now engaged in renewing it to cook our breakfast, which was soon ready, and for which the frosty mountain-air gave me a keen appetite. The kind fellow, too, prepared some toast and a hot draught for my enterprising companion, whom nothing could prevent from further exploring the pass.

DOWN THE RAQUETTE WITH MITCHELL J. M. M. (John MacMullen)

Thirty-seven years ago (1843) the Adirondacks were not fashionable. The Raquette River appeared upon the map running through the midst of them, but even diligent research on my part brought almost no information about either the region or the river. My desire to penetrate these unknown wilds was very great, for I was then young and enthusiastic and indemnified myself for the confinement of my winter's teaching by such excursions as would bring me nearest to the delightful wildness of savage life.

The early summer of this year found me teaching mathematics to my young friend Jim R. The room in which we sat looked out on Union Square, and as the leaves of the city trees waved in the gentle breeze, my longing for the wildwood rose higher and higher until it flowed out into my talk, and soon, without at all intending it, I found I had inoculated my pupil with this same strong desire. Forthwith close siege was laid by him to father and to mother; the barriers of parental caution were gradually sapped and a reluctant assent won. Just then, however, I was asked to "coach" an aspirant for college, and as I could not afford to lose the compensation, a stout attack was made on the parental purse that brought me full indemnity, and so we started. . . .

[A heavy yawl, the only boat they were able to purchase on Long Lake, proved unmanageable in the rapids of the Raquette. They abandoned it and tried to go on in an improvised raft.]

Poling steadily along on our reluctant raft, we finally reached a place where the stream was completely choked with driftwood. Mooring our clumsy craft to the east bank, we set to work with axe and pole to cut and push away the logs, to win a passage for our blunt-headed bark. While thus engaged in what seemed a vast solitude, we were both startled at hearing voices, and while standing, lost in wonder, we saw a birchbark canoe shooting around the upper bend of the river and bearing down upon us. Before the canoe-men came within earshot I told Jim that our only choice was between starving down the river or engaging one of these men as a guide and running the risk of what they might choose to do. Jim said he had had enough of starving and would prefer to run the risk with them. They appeared as much surprised as we were at our encounter. When I said, "Good day," they preserved an ominous silence; but when asked whether they would take charge of us and guide us down the river, they talked together for a moment in their lingo and then agreed to do it. The terms were a dollar a day for each of us. We therefore placed ourselves and our baggage in a compartment of their canoe, squatting down, Indian fashion, because it was impossible to do anything else. When we first saw them the side of the canoe was about six inches above the water. When we got into it we brought it down about three inches.

The party we embarked with consisted of three half-breed men, one half-breed young woman, and one full-blooded squaw, with the high, clear-cut features of the Mohawks and a clear, translucent, light copper-colored skin that told at once her high health and her race. Her dress consisted of a neat calico short gown over a dark woolen skirt, under which appeared leggings and moccasins. Her whole attention seemed given to her baby or papoose, which was strapped on a piece of board in the usual Indian fashion. She never by any chance looked at us, at least we never saw her do so, and when we looked at her she was usually looking far ahead or else down at her little treasure, and a true little treasure it was. I have since had several babies of my own and thus have learned to appreciate that little forestling. To think of spending a week on tolerably intimate terms with a baby and never hear it cry! . . .

The mother's name we never heard, nor that of her husband. We called them the chief and the chief's wife. He was a half-breed with a skin that looked like a dull white cheese, and plenty of hair, cut in a style at once Yankee and classical, making a regular circle so that each hair was a crooked radius. He never spoke to us, and I doubted whether he understood English until one day his smiling at a joke betrayed him. His only answer to the few questions he did answer was a nod or a gesture. The young woman was half-breed also with the same cheesy complexion and rather lumpy features but a very keen eye. She was usually the first to see a wild duck far away on the water, and her paddle was handled as skilfully and with as enduring vigor as that of any man in our party. . . . A quick low grunt from her and a finger pointing for one brief moment were enough for Mitchell. His long, heavy, rifled pistol was raised like a gun with both hands, a quick but careful aim was taken, and one more duck was added to our larder.

This Mitchell was the most intelligent of all the men. His features were finer, his skin clearer, his eye brighter, and he was the man with whom we transacted all our business. Occasionally he consulted the others in their lingo, but generally decided for himself. The remaining half-breed was a young man of cheesy complexion and heavy features whose name was Pete. The only thing I envied him was his handling of the paddle.

As soon as we were embarked with our baggage, off we started in that light and frail canoe that thus held and carried safely five men, two women, and a baby. As we sped rapidly on, the Indians kept their usual bright lookout for game. After paddling some distance the canoe was turned into a little cove, or rather a rounded indentation in the river bank, which seemed a well-hole full of trout, for as fast as hook and line could be put down so fast up came the trout, each weighing a pound or two. When our navigators had enough we turned again into the stream and sped on our way to Tupper's Lake. There we found a log cabin built by a man who came in from the East, made a clearing, and planted potatoes. He was tired of his experiment and concluded to go back. We were very glad to see him, but much more glad to see his potatoes. . . .

Next morning the half-breeds began to build us a canoe of spruce bark. This kind of craft is made of a single piece of bark, while a birch canoe is made of many pieces fastened together. Birch bark is hard and therefore slips over any pointed knot that would pierce the thicker but softer bark of the spruce, but it is on the other hand ground away if allowed to rub against stones, while over these same stones the soft and slippery spruce bark passes with impunity.

The process of making our canoe was very interesting. A fine large spruce tree about a foot and a half in diameter was chosen that grew in an open space near the river and had fifteen feet of good thick bark without break or knot-hole. The tree was cut down, the three half-breeds relieving one another in the work, a ring was cut around the tree at the upper end of the clear bark, then a line was cut through the bark along the trunk, "spuds" were made, and the whole clear sheet of bark, fifteen feet long and four feet wide, was laid upon the ground with the inner side down. "The chief" then cut away a slender triangular piece of the thick outer bark, about six inches at the base and about twelve inches long, in four places, about three feet from each end, leaving the flexible inner bark to fold over, so that when the corners were brought together and the ends closed up, the bow and stern might both be somewhat higher out of the water, and the sides need not sag out so much in the middle. . . .

The ends of our boat were sewed up with the roots of the spruce tree. These slender roots or rootlets can be had of six feet in length and running from a quarter of an inch down to a point. The smaller part is taken to use as thread. A hole is made in the bark with a sharp stick and the rootlet thus inserted. The sewing is what the ladies call overhand. The spruce gum is used to make the inside of the seam water-tight. Thus this tree supplied for our boat bark, thread, and gum. Sewing with the roots of a tree seemed to me so strange that I concluded, as we often do, that it must be peculiar to this locality. My astonishment may be imagined when, as I was arranging my books after I got home and was casually glancing over a copy of the Latin work of Olaus Magnus, in which he gives an account of the inhabitants of northern Europe, to find, on reading the first few lines of a chapter headed, "*De navibus nervis et radicibus colligatis*," that this very thing had been done by them hundreds of years ago. . . .

The half-breeds appeared to be well-trained woodsmen, understanding perfectly the peculiar qualities of the different trees and profiting by them all. Mitchell put the axe into the birch canoe and crossing the river returned with some long, narrow pieces of cedar, he having of course with his keen eyes seen these treetops from our side. I had read in Homer and in Spenser of the "easily split cedar," but when I saw pieces of it fifteen feet long by two inches wide, and only three quarters of an inch thick, split almost as smoothly as if they had been sawed, I had increased respect for the "fissile cedar." These pieces were used as gunwales and tied on with strips of tough and flexible bark passed through punched holes. Strips of wood thin enough to bend were cut just of the proper length and then forced in so that they followed the curve of the boat, their ends coming in snugly under the gunwales to stiffen the craft. This boat thus constructed of a single piece of bark carried safely, through many a rapid, Mitchell, Pete, Jim, and myself—three full grown men and one nearly so—with about a hundred pounds of baggage. "The chief," with his wife and Martha, were in the birch canoe. This naval construction took the better part of two days. . . .

At length we embarked, and as the swift but silent paddles urged our slippery-bottomed boats along we passed point after point and bend after bend, enjoying to the fullest every sylvan scene in that wild solitude, shooting a duck occasionally or stopping to get some fish where our guide knew so well where to find them, until we stopped in some pleasant places at noon to cook and eat, enjoying every mouthful; then again into the boats to paddle on through the bright, breezy afternoon, enjoying everything as if life were but one long holiday, until the time came for supper and for sleep, nor had we long to wait before slumber closed our eyelids, and when they opened in the morning how refreshed and vigorous we felt. What a pity that civilized man does not attend to his rations of fresh air and exercise so as to keep abreast of the savage in the intense healthfulness of his existence.

One morning as I lay awake, just before rising, I saw Mitchell go up to our canoe, which lay as usual bottom up, and kiss it in several places. Now a half-breed in the woods is about the last man to be suspected of sentimentality, and I felt that I owed it to the world to inquire into this instance of more than Eastern devotion. Jumping up nimbly, therefore, I approached the phenomenon and ejaculated:

"What are you doing, Mitchell?"

Down came my fine-spun theory with a thump, as his gruff answer struck my ear:

"Suckin' for holes."

While I was looking, the air did come through at one place where he sucked, and now I noticed that he had in one hand a small brand from the fire, and in the other a small piece of old rag. He was also chewing something, which on inquiry I ascertained to be spruce gum. Tearing off a small corner of the rag and putting it on the hole, he placed a small piece of the gum upon it, and blowing up his firebrand so as to get the greatest heat, he melted the gum so that it went through the rag into the hole, and so closed it securely. Mitchell's rag getting used up after a while, he was looking about one morning for some other material when Jim asked him what he wanted, and was told that he was looking for a little piece of rag. Now the button had, in the wear and tear of woodland life, come off from the wrist of Jim's shirt sleeve and the cuff had been torn away a little, so that the sleeve presented a convenient corner which Jim immediately took hold of, and gave Mitchell what he wanted. Having once found such a storehouse, Mitchell returned to it again and again, and the last I saw of Jim's sleeve was an irregular fringe just on his shoulder. . . .

We had also another illustration of the truth that to good woodsmen like these trees are as closets from which they take whatever they may need. Jim had got hold of a small piece of board of irregular shape about twelve inches long by six broad, which may have floated all the way down from Long Lake. After washing it carefully in the river, he put it on his knees to serve him as a plate. While I was expressing in extravagant terms my astonishment at such luxury and my envy of such happiness, Mitchell quietly took the axe and, walking up to the nearest tree, made one cut that penetrated a little further than the bark, then another about a foot above it, and then a nearly vertical cut in the same place as this latter one, thus slicing off a thin piece of wood with the bark attached, and pleasantly presented to me this fresh, sweet and fragrant plate thus artistically improvised. Of course I profited by the lesson, and when at any meal thereafter I needed a fresh plate I simply went up to one of the sylvan closets with the proper key and took one out.

At length we neared the settlements, and our delightful woodland life drew quietly to its close. The first small village, or rather hamlet, we encountered rejoiced in the sentimental name of Matildaville [now Colton]. A good sturdy specimen of the American farmer in his shirt-sleeves was standing on the bank and appeared to look at us in astonishment.

"Why, where did you come from?" said he to me, who happened to be first.

"From Long Lake."

"What! all the way from up south?"

Having been all my life accustomed to rivers that ran from north to south, this seemed to me a very strange expression, but when I came to reflect I saw that Long Lake was upstream to him, so that his phrase was after all correct. He told me afterward that we were the first white men that ever came down Raquette River. How this may be I do not know. . . .

After parting pleasantly, with thanks on both sides, from our guides, whom we never saw again and of whom we never heard anything, except that Mitchell at length became a leader in the Methodist Episcopal Church, Jim and myself sat down to a good square meal whose crowning joy was pancakes with maple syrup.

MITCHELL SABATTIS' REFORM
L. E. CHITTENDEN

My guides were Mitchell Sabattis and Alonzo Wetherby.
Sabattis was a St. Francis Indian, a skilful hunter, and became
afterward one of the finest characters I ever knew. At that time he
got howling drunk at every opportunity. It is a pleasure to remember that he always attributed his reformation to his connection
with me, and that for the last thirty years of his life he was a kind
husband, an excellent father to worthy children, and a most repu-
table citizen. He died only a few years ago, a class-leader in the
Methodist Church, universally respected. "Lon" Wetherby was an
equally good hunter, a giant in strength, and a Yankee by birth.
To hear the rich, liquid sound with which he rolled out his only
oath, "By Ga-u-ull!" was worth a journey to the outlet of Long
Lake. . . . .

We were much in need of venison. We were expecting company
and there was no fresh meat in the camp. One rainy, foggy night
Sabattis and myself went to . . . Moose Creek to try for a deer. The
water had suddenly risen and the adjacent marshes were over-
flowed. We had ascended the creek as far as it would carry our
boat and had found nothing. On our return about half-way to the
river, we heard a deer. He was standing in the shallow water on
the marsh and outside the curtain of willows which grew upon the
bank. Mitchell stopped the boat opposite where he stood, so near
that we could hear him chewing the leaves. It was impossible to
get a sight of any part of him. If we made any disturbance he was
certain to disappear instantly in the darkness.

Five minutes we stood endeavoring to pierce that curtain with
our eyes. Then I estimated as well as I could his height above the
water, aimed where I thought his chest ought to be, and gave him
one barrel. Away he went across the broad marsh, dashing through
the water until he reached the solid ground, where his measured
gallop grew fainter, until to my ear it was no longer to be heard
on account of distance.

"Well! We have lost him," I said in a tone of disappointment. "I
am sorry, for he was a noble buck. I got one glance at his antlers."

"How can we lose what we never had?" was Mitchell's pertinent inquiry. "But we will have him yet before daylight. He is hard hit and will not run very far."

"Why do you say that?" I asked. "He bounded away in a very lively manner as if he was uninjured."

"For two reasons," he answered. "He did not snort or whistle as an unwounded deer always does when suddenly startled. Then one of his forelegs appeared, by the sound, to be crippled."

He pushed the boat rapidly across the marsh to the hard ground, and with the light in his hand soon found where the deer had passed through the thick weeds and grasses. "It is all right," he said. "Here is where he went out, and it's as bloody as a butcher's shop."

I came near where he stood. "Show me the blood," I said.

"Why there! and there! and there! all over! Don't you see it?" he exclaimed.

"I see nothing but wet leaves and bushes," I replied. "Now stop and show me what you call blood."

He plucked a leaf with incurved edges, on the wet surface of which there was a discoloration which he said was blood. "It is as plain as can be," he said; "you would not expect a wounded buck in a hurry to stop and paint a United States flag for our benefit. I am going for him," he continued. "You stay in the boat until you hear a shot, which may mean that I have found him or that I have given him up. Then you fire a pistol, which will give me my bearings and save time."

With the lantern in one hand and my gun in the other, he disappeared in the foggy night. How long I lay stiffening in the boat or stamped along the shore in an effort to keep my blood in circulation, I do not know. But after what seemed hours of weary waiting, away up on the side of the mountain I heard the faint report of a gun. I fired the revolver in answer and waited again until I heard something threshing down the hill.

"Is that you, Mitchell?" I shouted.

"Yes," he answered. "I have got him. He is a splendid buck; not too old and in prime condition. He will provision the camp for a week."

He now appeared, dragging the deer after him.

"How did you find him?" I asked.

"I followed his track over the wet leaves," he answered. "Where he stopped the spot was marked by a pool of blood. These were nearer together as we went up the hill. Finally I overtook him. He was standing with his head down and I saw he had been hard hit. I held the jack in one hand and shot him with the gun held in the other."

Mark, now, what this Indian had done. His ear had detected an injury to one of the animal's forelegs. In the dark and rainy night, by the light of the jack, he had found his path out of the marsh, had followed it over fallen trees, through the thick brushwood, a mile or more up the steep hillside, until he had overtaken the wounded deer, and holding the light in one hand and the gun in the other had given him the fatal shot. Such a story seems incredible. Had I not seen the results I think I would not myself believe it. . . .

In those delightful five weeks I formed an attachment for these guides which lasted as long as they lived. From Wetherby, and later from others, I learned that Sabattis was a generous fellow whom every one liked, but he would get drunk upon every opportunity, and then he was a madman. His wife was a worthy white woman. They had five children. The sons were as skilled in woodcraft as their father and inherited the excellent qualities of their mother. One of them grew up with the figure of Apollo, and when I last saw him I thought that physically he was the most perfect man I had ever seen. . . .

I spent my last night at Mitchell's home. . . . Mitchell and his wife appeared depressed by some impending calamity. I made them tell me their trouble. There was a mortgage upon their home and little farm. It was due, the property was to be sold about four weeks later, and they saw no way of avoiding this, to them, ruinous result. If his home was sold, Mitchell's habits would be worse than ever.

Mitchell's wife assured me that he was proud of the fact that he had never broken his word; she said he was a kind husband, and if she could induce him to promise not to drink, she would even be reconciled to the loss of her home.

The next morning when the horses were at the door and I was about to leave, I called Mitchell and his wife into their little "square room," seated myself between them, and asked:

"Mitchell, what would you give to one who would buy your mortgage and give you time in which to pay it?"

"I would give my life," he exclaimed, "the day after I had paid the debt. I would give it now if I could leave this little place to my Bessie and her children."

"It will not cost you so much as that," I said. "I am going to Elizabethtown. I shall buy or pay your mortgage. Your home will not be sold. On the morning of the second day of August next year [1860], I want you and 'Lon' with your boats to meet me at Bartlett's, between the Upper and Lower Saranac Lakes. If you there tell me that you have not drunk a glass of strong liquor since I saw you last, your mortgage shall not trouble you so long as you will keep your promise not to drink. If you break your promise, I do not know what I shall do, but I shall lose all my confidence in Mitchell Sabattis. Your wife and children will not be driven from their home until you get drunk again."

He promised instantly, solemnly. He rose from his chair. I thought he looked every inch the chief which by birth he claimed to be as he said: "You may think you cannot trust me, but you can! Sabattis when he was sober never told a lie. He will never lie to his friend." . . .

I bought, took an assignment of the mortgage and carried it to my home. Other duties occupied me, and Sabattis had long been out of my mind. One evening late in the following February, just at nightfall, I was watching the falling snow from my library window in Burlington when a singular conveyance stopped almost in front of my door. It was a long, unpainted sled, the runners hewn from natural crooks, with stakes some five feet high inclosing an oblong box of rough boards, to which were harnessed two unmatched horses. The driver travelled by the side of the horses, carrying a long gad of unpainted wood having no lash. He wore a cap and coat of bearskin, which concealed his features.

Taking him to be some stranger who had lost his way, I went to his assistance. As I made some observation, a voice deep down inside the bearskin said: "Why! it's Mr. Chittenden. I was looking for you and your house."

"Mitchell Sabattis!" I exclaimed. "In the name of all that is astonishing, what are you doing here?" . . .

Good fortune had attended him from the time when he was relieved from anxiety about the mortgage. He had employment as a guide until the season for trapping and shooting for market began. He had never killed so many deer nor got so good prices in money for venison. He had paid all his little debts and saved one hundred dollars, which his wife said he ought to bring to me. They thought I would like a little game. So he had built a sled, borrowed two horses, made up a little load, and he had travelled that long and hard road from the head of Long Lake to Crown Point and thence to Burlington, not less than one hundred and fifty miles.

A refusal of his gift was not to be thought of. The next morning I took my butcher to his little load of game. There were the saddles or hind quarters of twenty-five fat deer in their skins, two carcasses of black bear dressed and returned to their skins, the skin of a magnificent catamount, with the skull and claws attached, which he had heard me say I would like to have, a half-dozen skins of the beautiful fur of the pine marten or the American sable, more than one hundred pounds of brook trout, ten dozen of ruffed grouse all dressed and braided into bunches of a half-dozen, and some smaller game, with some specimen skins of the mink and fox. There was more game than my family could have consumed in a year.

I selected a liberal supply of the game and took the skins intended for myself and family. For the balance my butcher paid him liberally, and this money with his savings would have more than paid his mortgage. But I would not so soon lose my hold upon him. He had told me that if he could build an addition to his house his wife could keep four boarders while he was guiding in the summer. I induced him to save money enough for this addition and to purchase the furniture then and there. He paid the interest and costs and a part of the principal of his mortgage and went home loaded with presents for Bessie and the children—a very happy man. . . .

In 1885 the old feeling came over me, and with such of my family as had not gone out from me into homes of their own, I went to a new and fashionable hotel some thirty miles from Long Lake. From an old resident who knew it thoroughly I had the subsequent history of Mitchell Sabattis. He had never broken his promise to me. He united with the Methodist Church and became one of its leaders, and in a few years was the leading citizen in the Long Lake settlement. In worldly matters he prospered. His wife kept a favorite resort for summer visitors. Their children were educated, the daughters married well—two of the sons served their country with courage and gallantry through the war, returned home unwounded with honorable discharges, and now guided in summer and built the celebrated Adirondack boats in the winter. Mitchell, now a hale and healthy veteran of eighty-four years, still lived at Long Lake in the very house of which I was once the mortgagee.

The next morning I heard a light step on the uncarpeted hall and a knock at my door. I opened it and Sabattis entered. He was as glad to see me as I was to grasp his true and honest hand. But I was profoundly surprised. Had the world with him stood still? He did not look a day older than when I last saw him, more than twenty-five years ago. The same keen, clear eye, transparent skin with the play of the muscles under it, the same elastic step, ringing voice and kindly heart. His eye was not dim nor his natural force abated. We spent a memorable day together—at nightfall we parted forever. Not long afterward he died full of years, full of honors, that noblest work of God, an honest man.

RED FLANNEL
Ralph Waldo Emerson

                    In Adirondac lakes,
At morn or noon, the guide rows bareheaded:
Shoes, flannel shirt, and kersey trousers make
His brief toilette: at night, or in the rain,
He dons a surcoat which he doffs at morn:
A paddle in the right hand, or an oar,
And in the left, a gun, his needful arms.
By turns we praised the stature of our guides,
Their rival strength and suppleness, their skill
To row, to swim, to shoot, to build a camp,
To climb a lofty stem, clean without boughs
Full fifty feet, and bring the eaglet down:
Temper to face wolf, bear, or catamount,
And wit to trap or take him in his lair.
Sound, ruddy men, frolic and innocent,
In winter, lumberers; in summer, guides;
Their sinewy arms pull at the oar untired
Three times ten thousand strokes, from morn to eve.

   Look to yourselves, ye polished gentlemen!
No city airs or arts pass current here.
Your rank is all reversed; let men of cloth
Bow to the stalwart churls in overalls:
They are the doctors of the wilderness,
And we the low-prized laymen.
In sooth, red flannel is a saucy test
Which few can put on with impunity.
What make you, master, fumbling at the oar?
Will you catch crabs? Truth tries pretension here.
The sallow knows the basket-maker's thumb;
The oar, the guide's. Dare you accept the tasks
He shall impose, to find a spring, trap foxes,
Tell the sun's time, determine the true north,
Or stumbling on through vast self-similar woods
To thread by night the nearest way to camp?

❧ NO NONSENSE, PROFESSOR
F. S. STALLKNECHT

Sam Dunning, a noted wag among guides at Martin's in Saranac, contributed to the fun of a sporting tour in August, 1858, taken by the author and his artist friend, Charles E. Whitehead.

Unaccustomed to being the whole day exposed to sun and weather, I fall back on the seat of the boat and doze off in a sweet slumber, dreaming that I float off from the river's bosom into the air, above the tops of the trees, looking down upon the birds cooing so sweetly over the young in their undisturbed nests. The boat goes off in the clouds and I try to catch at the stars, which, without burning, hang all around, till Sam's gruff voice awakens me. He is swearing away at a hidden rock which threatened to rub a hole in the bottom of his boat, and the moment he sees my eyes open begins with one of his similes, which, if not the most apt for the occasion, always end in making Sam, his boat and passenger, all three, shake with laughter. . . .

Says Sam, "That rub of the boat reminds me of rubbing agin a good-looking widder down in Essex County last winter. I suppose she was a widder, anyhow she was in black, and she might have been a *grass*, for with all her black drygoods her eyes a kind o' glistened when I helped her out of the stage. Well, it begun to rain, and as she had a couple of miles to go the boys about the hotel were in a pucker how to get up her trunk, which was one of them big square black shanties on wheels with yellow skylights all over; the horses were out ahead and it was three miles to the nearest cart, and as for leaving her bandbox and finery for a minute, no woman in the world could be expected to do that, so says I to myself, 'Darn it all, I'll break the rule,' for let me tell ye, the moment I am out of the woods for my winter tour down to old Essex, to hug the big hotel stove for five or six weeks, and hear what is a going on out in the world, I am the gentleman. . . . But, says I on taking a look at the widder in trouble, 'Marm,' says I, 'I'll see you over the carry,' so off goes my coat, and in less than ten minutes I had her hundred and fifty pounder safely landed over to the house. Well, there warnt nobody home except the old black cat, so of course I sot down and had a little familiar. Says I, 'Sam's in clover for this 'ere lay'; but dang it all, I had her to myself for only three days, when up comes a chap in the stage and walks off my widder to the nearest minister, and off they went without saying as much as a good-bye. So says I, 'I'll stick to Brave and the woods; never will I find a woman so true to me as this here old dog.' When we two are off on a lay, I'd like to see the man what'll rob us of our game."

When Sam's story was done we were at the mouth of Follensbee Creek, a very narrow brook which for a mile or more winds a sinuous course into the pond. . . . It was a relief to get out of the brook, which swarmed with mosquitoes and midges. Follensbee Pond is about three miles long to a half mile wide. As we rowed into it the sun was just setting, and the shadow of the unbroken woods surrounding it on all sides lay on the bosom of the water, almost across. . . .

Whitehead's boat was ahead, so to find out where he was I blew my hunting horn; the blast was answered by echoes innumerable till I heard his manly "Halloo!" under the bank where he was awaiting us in the shade. . . .

We paddled down to the lower end of the pond and soon espied a boat shooting off from a sequestered nook. It came down to meet us and was found to contain three gentlemen, one of them Mr. John Holmes, whom I hunted with on Tupper's Lake last year. Another boat appears, containing Professor Agassiz at the stern, Ralph Waldo Emerson at the prow, and James Russell Lowell rowing. They address Whitehead, point out their camp and courteously invite us to lay in and pay them a visit. We accept their kind offer, although it seems hardly fair to disturb such men, who have come so far to seek the solitude of nature. On landing we are met by Professor Jeffries Wyman, whom I often met in Paris seventeen years ago this summer and am indebted to for many kindnesses. He was attending to drying the stomach of a buck for a specimen. We follow him to their camp.

Their ten guides have built a spacious bark shanty, quite open in front. Mr. Binney is busy hoisting the American flag, the same that has accompanied him in the East and waved over his bateau on the Nile. They have shot two deer and caught abundance of trout. Most of the party are away for a row. We pitch our tent at a convenient distance and cook a nice venison steak off one of their deer, which, with a cup of warm tea, sets us all in a good contented frame. It has got to be ten o'clock, we light our pipes and again visit the "Philosophers' Camp" (as Sam Dunning calls it); they are all at home now, and a pleasant hour is passed in familiar chitchat. They are a party of ten in all, with ten guides; Judge Hoar, Dr. Estes Howe and Mr. Stillman, the artist, are among them. We tell them of the news telegraphed from New York to Burlington the day we passed there that the *Niagara* has safely landed the American end of the cable at Newfoundland and is in communication with the *Agamemnon*, then near the Irish coast. At hearing this three hearty cheers rend the air, and a hope is expressed it may prove true. The sportsmen talk over their former hunts.

Ralph Waldo Emerson shakes me by the hand and invites me, looking upwards, to admire the dome. We look up and find ourselves standing under a clump of hoary pines with large naked trunks and spreading green tops, forming a lofty green cathedral, and the stars are all twinkling in the blue arch above, so Mr. Emerson's brief words of ecstasy strike as ever and need no other illustration than to follow his eyes.

Agassiz is rolled up in his blanket, discussing with Wyman the subject of snakes swallowing and re-ejecting their young, when he eyes a bug, gets up for his fly-net, and with an adroit swing and back fling bags the game and very neatly takes his prey out by the tips of his fingers. He catches a few more, and Whitehead plucks one of the same genus off his coat, which he hands him, and it is accepted with the pleasant politeness none but a Frenchman can express.

Sam Dunning, hearing from the guides that they have a French chap among them great on bugs and snakes [professor of natural history at Harvard] and opening every fish and animal that comes in his way, edges his way up, bent, as he tells them, on tackling him on his (Sam's) theory on the copulation of trout. Sam declares, with a little pepper in the expression, that the old theory of the trout depositing their eggs and the males then impregnating them with their milt is a humbug; he has experimented and found it is not so. Agassiz listens to all he says, but fails to be convinced by Sam's logic and trials; even Sam's last argument, that if he wasn't right the things would have nothing worth living for, fails, so when we come down to bunk in at the tent Sam expresses his supreme disgust with Mr. Agassiz.

"He may be a nice man and pleasant enough, and I might be willin' to go guide with him, but," says he, "it must be great consolation for a man to come away off here in the woods to catch boogs and mice; I should think he might find enough on 'em where he came from; but if you tell me he knows anything about breeding trout, I tell you he don't know northing about it. Pshaw!"

_____

MORE DIGNITY THAN DOLLARS
JOEL T. HEADLEY

Everything is democratic in the woods, and several guides, engaged to go out with different parties the coming week, dropped in [at Martin's, Lower Saranac Lake] to have a chat with the gentlemen. One of these, whom they called "Sam" [probably Sam Dunning], was an original. He was a capital guide, willing, cheerful, a good cook, and strong as an ox. Standing full six feet in his stockings, he thought no more of putting his boat on his head, paddles, oars, and all, and carrying it for three miles over streams and logs and hills and through swamps than I would an empty basket. Sam has only one fault—his tongue never stops. He says a great many queer, laughable things and a great deal that is stale, flat, and unprofitable. Still he is an honest, kind, capable, and accommodating guide. Last year [1857] he went out with a party from Boston and Cambridge, and his democratic notions received a shock from which he will never recover. His harmless rattle was considered disrespectful, and Sam, who had never before seen anybody too good for him, was taken wholly aback by the distance at which he was kept. He was treated simply as a paid servant at home. This was a new revelation to him. In his long life in the woods he had seen nothing like it before. A rollicking, free-and-easy set he had always been with hitherto, and so much stateliness and dignity in camp life quite bewildered him. He said, however, that he had his revenge on one of them. On a long and uneven carrying-place, over which he was floundering with his boat on his head, the gentleman began to grumble at the difficulties of the way and repeatedly asked Sam if there was no way for him to get across except by walking. "Yes," replied the latter, at last, "ketch a sucker and put him between your legs and scull over." Sam said that ever after the man regarded him as some strange animal whose company should be carefully avoided.

His dislike of Bostonians and Cambridge men, as he calls them, has become chronic, and he will run on for hours about them. He has a large tent, which my companions wish to take along with them. But I dislike tents; they are heavy to carry, in a rain they are damp, while you are afraid to build up those roaring fires near them which make a bark shanty so comfortable by serving the double purpose of driving off the mosquitoes and of keeping you warm. They were, however, determined to strike a bargain with Sam, and I, who had hitherto been a mere listener, asked him how many his tent would hold. "Just two Boston men—I have tried it—they will fill it full, but it will hold *six New Yorkers easy.*" "Why, Sam," I replied, "I did not know the Bostonians were so much larger than New Yorkers." "Well, they are," said he; "I have measured them with my tent. One takes up just as much room as three New Yorkers." "It seems to me," I added, "that you bear the Bostonians some malice. What is the matter—why don't you like them?" He drew himself up, *à la* Webster, and in a severe, grave tone, replied: "Sir, *they have got more dignity than dollars.*"

OLD MOUNTAIN PHELPS
CHARLES DUDLEY WARNER

The primitive man is one who owes more to nature than to the forces of civilization. What we seek in him are the primal and original traits, unmixed with the sophistications of society and unimpaired by the refinements of an artificial culture. He would retain the primitive instincts which are cultivated out of the ordinary, commonplace man. . . . It is our good fortune to know such a man. . . . He emigrated from somewhat limited conditions in Vermont at an early age, nearly half a century ago, and sought freedom for his natural development backward in the wilds of the Adirondacks.

Sometimes it is a love of adventure and freedom that sends men out of the more civilized conditions into the less; sometimes it is a constitutional physical lassitude which leads them to prefer the rod to the hoe, the trap to the sickle, and the society of bears to town-meetings and taxes. I think that Old Mountain Phelps had merely the instincts of the primitive man, and never any hostile civilizing intent as to the wilderness into which he plunged. Why should he want to slash away the forest and plough up the ancient mould, when it is infinitely pleasanter to roam about in the leafy solitudes or sit upon a mossy log and listen to the chatter of birds and the stir of beasts? Are there not trout in the streams, gum exuding from the spruce, sugar in the maples, honey in the hollow trees, fur on the sables, warmth in hickory logs? Will not a few days' planting and scratching in the "open" yield potatoes and rye? And if there is steadier diet needed than venison and bear, is the pig an expensive animal? . . .

He was a true citizen of the wilderness. Thoreau would have liked him, as he liked Indians and woodchucks and the smell of pine forests; and if Old Phelps had seen Thoreau, he would probably have said to him, "Why on airth, Mr. Thoreau, don't you live accordin' to your preachin'?" You might be misled by the shaggy suggestion of Old Phelps's given name—Orson—into the notion that he was a mighty hunter, with the fierce spirit of the Berserkers in his veins. Nothing could be farther from the truth. The hirsute and grisly sound of Orson expresses only his entire affinity with the

untamed and the natural, an uncouth but gentle passion for the
freedom and wildness of the forest. Orson Phelps has only those
unconventional and humorous qualities of the bear which make the
animal so beloved in literature; and one does not think of Old
Phelps so much as a lover of nature—to use the sentimental slang
of the period—as a part of nature itself.

His appearance at the time when as a "guide" he began to come
into public notice fostered this impression—a sturdy figure, with
long body and short legs, clad in a woolen shirt and butternut-
colored trousers repaired to the point of picturesqueness, his head
surmounted by a limp, light-brown felt hat, frayed away at the
top, so that his yellowish hair grew out of it like some nameless
fern out of a pot. His tawny hair was long and tangled, matted
now many years past the possibility of being entered by a comb.
His features were small and delicate and set in the frame of a reddish beard, the razor having mowed away a clearing about the
sensitive mouth, which was not seldom wreathed with a child-like
and charming smile. Out of this hirsute environment looked the
small gray eyes, set near together; eyes keen to observe and quick
to express change of thought; eyes that made you believe instinct
can grow into philosophic judgment. His feet and hands were of
aristocratic smallness, although the latter were not worn away by
ablutions; in fact, they assisted his toilet to give you the impression
that here was a man who had just come out of the ground—a real
son of the soil, whose appearance was partially explained by his
humorous relation to soap. "Soap is a thing," he said, "that I hain't
no kinder use for." His clothes seemed to have been put on him
once for all, like the bark of a tree, a long time ago. The observant
stranger was sure to be puzzled by the contrast of this realistic and
uncouth exterior with the internal fineness, amounting to refinement and culture, that shone through it all. What communion had
supplied the place of our artificial breeding to this man?

Perhaps his most characteristic attitude was sitting on a log with
a short pipe in his mouth. If ever man was formed to sit on a log,
it was Old Phelps. He was essentially a contemplative person.
Walking on a country road or anywhere in the "open" was irk-
some to him. He had a shambling, loose-jointed gait, not unlike

that of the bear; his short legs bowed out, as if they had been more in the habit of climbing trees than of walking. On land, if we may use that expression, he was something like a sailor; but once in the rugged trail or the unmarked route of his native forest, he was a different person, and few pedestrians could compete with him. The vulgar estimate of his contemporaries that reckoned Old Phelps "lazy" was simply a failure to comprehend the conditions of his being. It is the unjustness of civilization that it sets up uniform and artificial standards for all persons. The primitive man suffers by them much as the contemplative philosopher does, when one happens to arrive in this busy, fussy world.

If the appearance of Old Phelps attracts attention, his voice, when first heard, invariably startles the listener. A small, high-pitched, half-querulous voice, it easily rises into the shrillest falsetto; and it has a quality in it that makes it audible in all the tempests of the forest or the roar of rapids, like the piping of a boatswain's whistle at sea in a gale. He has a way of letting it rise as his sentence goes on, or when he is opposed in argument, or wishes to mount above other voices in the conversation, until it dominates everything. Heard in the depths of the woods, quavering aloft, it is felt to be as much a part of nature, an original force, as the northwest wind or the scream of the hen-hawk. When he is pottering about the camp fire, trying to light his pipe with a twig held in the flame, he is apt to begin some philosophical observation in a small, slow, stumbling voice which seems about to end in defeat; when he puts on some unsuspected force, and the sentence ends in an insistent shriek. Horace Greeley had such a voice and could regulate it in the same manner. But Phelps's voice is not seldom plaintive, as if touched by the dreamy sadness of the woods themselves.

When Old Mountain Phelps was discovered, he was, as the reader has already guessed, not understood by his contemporaries. His neighbors, farmers in the secluded valley, had many of them grown thrifty and prosperous, cultivating the fertile meadows and vigorously attacking the timbered mountains; while Phelps, with not much more faculty of acquiring property than the roaming deer, had pursued the even tenor of the life in the forest on which he set out. They would have been surprised to be told that Old Phelps owned more of what makes the value of the Adirondacks than all of them put together, but it was true. This woodsman, this trapper, this hunter, this fisherman, this sitter on a log and philosopher was the real proprietor of the region over which he was ready to guide the stranger. It is true that he had not a monopoly of its geography or its topography (though his knowledge was superior in these respects); there were other trappers and more deadly hunters and as intrepid guides; but Old Phelps was the discoverer of the beauties and sublimities of the mountains; and when city strangers broke into the region, he monopolized the appreciation of these delights and wonders of nature. I suppose that, in all that country, he alone had noticed the sunsets and observed the delightful processes of the seasons, taken pleasure in the woods for themselves, and climbed mountains solely for the sake of the prospect. He alone understood what was meant by "scenery." In the eyes of his neighbors, who did not know that he was a poet and a philosopher, I dare say he appeared to be a slack provider, a rather shiftless trapper and fisherman; and his passionate love of the forest and the mountains, if it was noticed, was accounted to him for idleness. When the appreciative tourist arrived, Phelps was ready, as guide, to open to him all the wonders of his possessions; he, for the first time, found an outlet for his enthusiasm and a response to his own passion. It then became known what manner of man this was who had grown up here in the companionship of forests, mountains, and wild animals; that these scenes had highly developed in him the love of beauty, the aesthetic sense, delicacy of appreciation, refinement of feeling; and that, in his solitary wanderings and musings, the primitive man, self-taught, had evolved for himself a philosophy and a system of things. And it was a sufficient system, so long as it was not disturbed by external scepticism. When the outer world came to him, perhaps he had about as much to give to it as to receive from it; probably more, in his own estimation; for there is no conceit like that of isolation.

Phelps loved his mountains. He was the discoverer of Marcy and caused the first trail to be cut to its summit, so that others could enjoy the noble views from its round and rocky top. To him it was, in noble symmetry and beauty, the chief mountain of the globe. To stand on it gave him, as he said, "a feeling of heaven up-h'istedness." He heard with impatience that Mount Washington was a thousand feet higher, and he had a child-like incredulity about the surpassing sublimity of the Alps. Praise of any other elevation he seemed to consider a slight to Mount Marcy and did not willingly hear it, any more than a lover hears the laudation of the beauty of another woman than the one he loves. When he showed us scenery he loved, it made him melancholy to have us speak of scenery else-where that was finer. And yet there was this delicacy about him that he never over-praised what he brought us to see, any more than one would over-praise a friend of whom he was fond. I remember that when for the first time, after a toilsome journey through the forest, the splendors of the Lower Ausable Pond broke upon our vision—that low-lying silver lake, imprisoned by the precipices which it reflected in its bosom—he made no outward response to our burst of admiration; only a quiet gleam of the eye showed the pleasure our appreciation gave him. As some one said, it was as if his friend had been admired—a friend about whom he was unwill-ing to say much himself, but well pleased to have others praise.

Thus far we have considered Old Phelps as simply the product of the Adirondacks; not so much a self-made man (as the doubtful phrase has it) as a natural growth amid primal forces. But our study is interrupted by another influence, which complicates the problem but increases its interest. No scientific observer, so far as we know, has ever been able to watch the development of the primitive man played upon and fashioned by the hebdomadal iteration of "Gree-ley's Weekly Tri-bune." Old Phelps educated by the woods is a fascinating study; educated by the woods *and* the Tri-bune, he is a phenomenon. No one at this day can reasonably conceive exactly what this newspaper was to such a mountain valley as Keene. If it was not a Providence, it was a Bible. It was no doubt owing to it that Democrats became as scarce as moose in the Adirondacks. . . .

The first driblets of professional tourists and summer boarders who arrived among the Adirondack Mountains a few years ago found Old Phelps the chief and best guide of the region. Those who were eager to throw off the usages of civilization and tramp and camp in the wilderness could not but be well satisfied with the aboriginal appearance of this guide; and when he led off into the woods, axe in hand and a huge canvas sack upon his shoulders, they seemed to be following the Wandering Jew. The contents of this sack would have furnished a modern industrial exhibition—provisions cooked and raw, blankets, maple sugar, tinware, clothing, pork, Indian meal, flour, coffee, tea, etc. Phelps was the ideal guide. He knew every foot of the pathless forest; he knew all woodcraft, all the signs of the weather or, what is the same thing, how to make a Delphic prediction about it. He was fisherman and hunter and had been the comrade of sportsmen and explorers; and his enthusiasm for the beauty and sublimity of the region and for its untamable wildness amounted to a passion. He loved his profession, and yet it very soon appeared that he exercised it with reluctance for those who had neither ideality nor love for the woods. Their presence was a profanation amid the scenery he loved. To guide into his private and secret haunts a party that had no appreciation of their loveliness disgusted him. It was a waste of his time to conduct flippant young men and giddy girls who made a noisy and irreverent lark of the expedition. And, for their part, they did not appreciate the benefit of being accompanied by a poet and a philosopher. They neither understood nor valued his special knowledge and his shrewd observations. They didn't even like his shrill voice; his quaint talk bored them. It was true that, at this period, Phelps had lost something of the activity of his youth, and the habit of contemplative sitting on a log and talking increased with the infirmities induced by the hard life of the woodsman. Perhaps he would rather talk, either about the woods life or the various problems of existence, than cut wood or busy himself in the drudgery of the camp. His critics went so far as to say, "Old Phelps is a fraud." They would have said the same of Socrates. Xantippe, who never appreciated the world in which Socrates lived, thought he was lazy. Probably Socrates could cook no better than Old Phelps and no doubt went "gumming" about Athens with very little care of what was in the pot for dinner.

If the summer visitors measured Old Phelps, he also measured them by his own standards. He used to write out what he called "short-faced descriptions" of his comrades in the woods, which were never so flattering as true. It was curious to see how the various qualities which are esteemed in society appeared in his eyes, looked at merely in their relation to the limited world he knew and judged by their adaptation to the primitive life. It was a much subtler comparison than that of the ordinary guide, who rates his traveller by his ability to endure on a march, to carry a pack, use an oar, hit a mark, or sing a song. Phelps brought his people to a test of their naturalness and sincerity, tried by contact with the verities of the woods. If a person failed to appreciate the woods, Phelps had no opinion of him or his culture; and yet, although he was perfectly satisfied with his own philosophy of life, worked out by close observation of nature and study of the Tri-bune, he was always eager for converse with superior minds—with those who had the advantage of travel and much reading and, above all, with those who had any original "speckerlation." Of all the society he was ever permitted to enjoy, I think he prized most that of Dr. Bushnell. The doctor [Rev. Horace Bushnell, D.D.] enjoyed the quaint and firsthand observations of the old woodsman, and Phelps found new worlds open to him in the wide ranges of the doctor's mind. They talked by the hour upon all sorts of themes—the growth of the tree, the habits of wild animals, the migration of seeds, the succession of oak and pine, not to mention theology and the mysteries of the supernatural. . . .

The view from Marcy is peculiar. It is without softness or relief. The narrow valleys are only dark shadows; the lakes are bits of broken mirror. From horizon to horizon there is a tumultuous sea of billows turned to stone. You stand upon the highest billow; you command the situation; you have surprised Nature in a high creative act; the mighty primal energy has only just become repose. This was a supreme hour to Old Phelps. Tea! I believe the boys succeeded in kindling a fire; but the enthusiastic stoic had no reason to complain of want of appreciation in the rest of the party. When we were descending, he told us, with mingled humor and scorn, of a party of ladies he once led to the top of the mountain on a still day who began immediately to talk about the fashions! As he related the scene, stopping and facing us in the trail, his mild, far-in eyes came to the front, and his voice rose with his language to a kind of scream.

"Why, there they were, right before the greatest view they ever *saw*, talkin' about the *fashions*!"

Impossible to convey the accent of contempt in which he pronounced the word "fashions," and then added, with a sort of regretful bitterness—

"I was a great mind to come down and leave 'em there." . . .

The first time we went into camp on the Upper Ausable Pond, which has been justly celebrated as the most prettily set sheet of water in the region, we were disposed to build our shanty on the south side, so that we could have in full view the Gothics and that loveliest of mountain contours. To our surprise Old Phelps, whose sentimental weakness for these mountains we knew, opposed this. His favorite camping-ground was on the north side—a pretty site in itself but with no special view. In order to enjoy the lovely mountains, we should be obliged to row out into the lake; we wanted them always before our eyes—at sunrise and sunset and in the blaze of noon. With deliberate speech, as if weighing our arguments and disposing of them, he replied, "Waal, now, them Gothics ain't the kinder scenery you want ter *hog down*!"

It was on quiet Sundays in the woods or in talks by the camp fire that Phelps came out as the philosopher and commonly contributed the light of his observations. Unfortunate marriages and marriages in general were, on one occasion, the subject of discussion; and a good deal of darkness had been cast on it by various speakers when Phelps suddenly piped up, from a log where he had sat silent, almost invisible, in the shadow and smoke—

"Waal, now, when you've said all there is to be said, marriage is mostly for discipline."

Discipline, certainly, the old man had, in one way or another; and years of solitary communing in the forest had given him, perhaps, a childlike insight into spiritual concerns. Whether he had formulated any creed or what faith he had, I never knew. Keene Valley had a reputation of not ripening Christians any more successfully than maize, the season there being short; and on our first visit it was said to contain but one Bible Christian, though I think an accurate census disclosed three. Old Phelps, who sometimes made abrupt remarks in trying situations, was not included in this census; but he was the disciple of supernaturalism in a most charming form. . . .

The sentiment of the man about nature, or his poetic sensibility was frequently not to be distinguished from a natural religion and was always tinged with the devoutness of Wordsworth's verse. Climbing slowly one day up the Balcony—he was more than usually calm and slow—he espied an exquisite fragile flower in the crevice of a rock in a very lonely spot.

"It seems as if," he said, or rather dreamed out—"it seems as if the Creator had kept something just to look at himself."

To a lady whom he had taken to Chapel Pond (a retired but rather uninteresting spot) and who expressed a little disappointment at its tameness, saying,

"Why, Mr. Phelps, the principal charm of this place seems to be its loneliness,"—

"Yes," he replied in gentle and lingering tones, "and its *nativeness*. It lies here just where it was born."

Rest and quiet had infinite attractions for him. A secluded opening in the woods was a "calm spot." He told of seeing once, or rather being *in*, a circular rainbow. He stood on Indian Head, overlooking the Lower Lake, so that he saw the whole bow in the sky and the lake and seemed to be in the midst of it; "only at one place there was an indentation in it, where it rested on the lake, just enough to keep it from rolling off." This "resting" of the sphere seemed to give him great comfort. . . .

Is this philosopher contented with what life has brought him? Speaking of money one day, when we had asked him if he should do differently if he had his life to live over again, he said, "Yes, but not about money. To have had hours such as I have had in these mountains and with such men as Dr. Bushnell and Dr. Shaw and Mr. Twichell, and others I could name, is worth all the money the world could give."

HITCH UP, MATILDA
S. R. STODDARD

"Come, Bill—how about that adventure of yours at Avalanche Lake?" said one of the party gathered around the blazing fire. We all had heard of it, but wanted the facts from the principal actor.

"What adventure?" said Nye [William B. Nye, guide of North Elba].

"Oh, come, you know what one we mean; go ahead." So, after considerable innocent beating about the bush to ascertain the one meant, although it was perfectly evident that he knew all the time, Nye told his story:

"Well, boys, some of you may remember a party of three— Mr. and Mrs. Fielding and their niece, from somewhere or other on the Hudson—that I went guiding for in 1868. Mr. Fielding was rather a little man, one of those quick-motioned, impulsive sort who make up their minds quick and is liable to change it in five minutes afterward, but a very generous gentleman withal; his wife was taller and heavier than he, would look things carefully over before she expressed an opinion, and when she made up her mind to do a thing she did it. The niece—Dolly they called her—was about seventeen years old, a splendid girl, handsome as a picture, and she knew it too, all very sociable and willing to talk with anyone; and I tell you boys, when I look at such a girl I sometimes feel as though may be I have made a mistake in living alone so long, but I'm too old a dog now to think of learning new tricks, so we will go on.

"Well, our trip was to be from Nash's through Indian Pass to the iron works, then on to Mount Marcy and back by way of Avalanche Pass. We got rather a late start from Nash's, and all the boarders told Mrs. Fielding she could not go through that day. She says, 'You'll see I shall if the guide will show me the way.' She *did* go through, though she traveled the last three or four miles by torch-light. I tried to have her let me build a little camp and stay till daylight; she said, 'No, you know what they said when we started. If you can find the way I am going through.' I told her I could find the way if it was darker than a stack of black cats. She says, 'Lead on, I will follow.' The last mile she carried her shoes in her hand, but she *beat*, and that was enough. The next day we went to Lake Colden and camped; the next to Mount Marcy and back to Colden camp again.

"The following day we started to go through Avalanche Pass to North Elba—you will remember the walls, hundreds of feet high on either side, that you can neither get over nor around without going around the mountain; well, along one side is a shelf from two to four feet wide and as many under water, and when we got there they wondered how we were to get past. I said I could carry them or I could build a raft, but to build a raft would take too much time, while I could carry them past in a few minutes. Provisions were getting short and time set to be at North Elba, so Mr. Fielding says, 'Well, Matilda, what say you? Will you be carried over, or shall we make a raft?' Mrs. Fielding says, 'If Mr. Nye can do it and thinks it safe, I will be carried over, to save time.' 'Well, Dolly, what do *you* say?' 'Oh, if Mr. Nye can carry Aunt over he can *me*, of course; I think it would be a novelty.' Mr. Fielding says, 'Well, we have concluded to be carried over if you can do it safely.' . . . I waded across and back to see if there had been any change in the bottom since I was there before. When in the deepest place the water is nearly up to my arms for a step or two; I had nothing with me then. When I got back Mrs. Fielding said she did not see how I was going to carry them across and keep them out of the water. I said, 'I will show you. Who is going to ride first?'

"Mr. F. said, 'It is politeness to see the ladies safe first; so Matilda must make the first trip.' *She* would 'let the politeness go and would like to see Mr. F. go over first.' But he said she had agreed to ride if I said it was safe; now he wanted to see her do it. 'And *so I will!*' said she. 'How am I to do it?' I set down with my back against a rock that came nearly to the top of my shoulders, told her to step on the rock, put one foot over one side of my neck, the other over the other side, and sit down. That was what she did not feel inclined to do, and was going to climb on with both feet on one side, but her husband told her to throw away her delicacy and do as I told her, reminding her of her word, which was enough. She finally sat down very carefully, so far down on my back that I could not carry her. I told her it wouldn't do, and at last she got on and I waded in.

"'Hurrah! there they go!' 'Cling tight, Matilda!' shouted the young lady and the husband in the same breath. 'Hold your horse, Aunt!' laughed Dolly. 'Your reputation as a rider is at stake; three cheers for Aunt Mazeppa!—I mean Aunt Matty. Novel, isn't it? Unique and pleasing; you beat Rarey, Auntie, that's what you do!'

"I had just barely got into the deep water, steadying myself with one hand against the rocks and holding on to her feet with the other, when, in spite of all I could do, she managed to work half way down my back.

"'Hitch up, Matilda! hitch up, Matilda! why *don't* you hitch up?' screamed Mr. Fielding, and I could hear him dancing around among the rocks and stones, while I thought Dolly would have died laughing, and the more he yelled 'hitch *up*,' the more *she* hitched *down*, and I began to think I would have to change ends, or she would get wet; but by leaning way over forward, I managed to get her across safe and dry. Then how was she to get off? I said, 'I will show you.' So I bent down until her feet touched the ground, and she just walked off over my head, the two on the other side laughing and shouting all the time.

"Then came Dolly's turn. I told her that she must sit straight as a major general; she said she would—she'd let them see that all the money spent at riding schools hadn't been thrown away in *her* case. Wondered if any poet would immortalize her as they had Phil Sheridan; then with some kind of a conundrum about Balaam (I never thought much of conundrums anyway) she got on and I took her over and unloaded her the same as I did her aunt. The rest was easy enough, rather more in my line too, and we got back all right. Of course I did no more than my duty at the time, but you can bet I kept pretty still about it for some time until at last it leaked out. But there is one thing I would say, the ladies never told of the adventure or made the slightest allusion to it in public as some would, in my presence at least, and for thus showing so much regard for the feelings of a bashful man and a bachelor I shall be grateful to them to my dying day."

ALVAH DUNNING
FRED MATHER

Only men who possess strongly marked personalities are capable of making strong friends and as equally strong enemies. The truth of this has been well shown in the replies to letters asking for information about the old woodsman who is probably the oldest of Adirondack guides [in 1897]. Carefully sifting these replies, it seems that Alvah is well liked by sportsmen whom he has served, and by a few dwellers in and around the great region of mountains and lakes which comprises about one-third of the great State of New York. Others dislike him, and among Adirondack guides he is, for some reason, the most unpopular man in the woods. To me any old man in the woods is interesting, and as individuality crops out more strongly in men who have never assumed the mask of civilization, we will try to see him with unprejudiced eyes.

Alvah will be eighty-one years old next June. He is tall, spare and wiry. A look at his picture, taken a few years ago by Stoddard, will show that his strongly marked face is full of character, grit and determination, and it looks like a face that could not be developed outside the woods. . . .

It was in 1865 that I first met Alvah and fished for trout with him in the Brown Tract Inlet and Racquette Lake. I was then regaining health after a long struggle all summer, and a couple of weeks with Alvah put on the finishing touches.

The old man—he was "old" to me then—took good care of me, and I returned much improved. His talk of woods life was very entertaining, and it was only a few weeks afterward that I became acquainted with his mortal enemy, Ned Buntline [Edward Zane Carroll Judson, dime novelist], also a fishing companion, so that I got Alvah's story while it was fresh. . . .

My trouting on this trip is skipped and the man is taken up. Said he: "These woods is a-gittin' too full o' people fer comfort—that is, in summer time; fer they don't bother the trappin' in the winter; but they're a-runnin' all over here in summer a-shootin' an' a-fishin', but they don't kill much, nor catch many fish; but they git in the way, an' they ain't got no business here disturbin' the woods."

"They pay you well for working for them, don't they, Alvah?"

"Yes, they do, durn 'em; or I wouldn't bother with 'em; but I druther they'd stay out o' my woods. They'll come anyhow, an' I might as well guide 'em, fer ef I don't some un else will, but I druther they'd keep their money and stay out of the woods. I can make a livin' without 'em, an' they'd starve to death here without me. They're the durndest lot of cur'osities you ever seen; know more about guns an' killin' deer than any man in the woods, but when it comes to fishin' tackle you'd oughter see it."

This talk occurred after we had fished several days and had looked over the otter "uses" and other interesting things to be found in the wilderness, and the old man's remarks seemed to be so severely personal that they provoked me to say: "I am very sorry to have disturbed you and will go back home in the morning."

The old man looked up and said: "I didn't mean you; 'cause you seem to know how to sit inter a boat an' to know the voices of the birds an' how to fish. Now don't you go an' take a meanin' outer my words that I didn't mean."

"All right, Alvah! But if these people don't kill much game or fish they can't disturb you much, and I'm a little curious to know why you object so much to their coming here. The woods belong largely to the State, and they certainly have the right to come in here." This had the desired effect; it made the old man angry and drew his fire.

"Yes," he said, after turning the thing over in his mind in the deliberate manner common to men of the woods, "that's the worst of it; they've got a right to come here and disturb men who've made their homes in these woods all their lives, and many of 'em 's fools. I hate fools, don't you?"

Here was a chance to classify fools and to quote Touchstone: "I met a fool in the forest"; but that course might not have drawn the old man out, so I simply said: "I dunno, why?"

"Oh, they pester one so. A few years ago one came up here and tried to make me believe the world is round and turns over upside down in the night, and they all believe it, all of 'em, every durned one that I've spoke to about it. What d'ye think o' that?"

"I think they're wrong, of course, for we can see that these lakes don't spill out in the night. Yet this world can't be as flat as a pancake, for here are the mountains which disprove that, and as for turning over—"

"You don't believe it?"

"Not a word of it!" And we were friends.

When we met again in 1882 he recalled the trip, and at his camp on Racquette Lake he said: "Times is different now, an' wus. In them days nobody said a word if a poor man wanted a little meat an' killed it, but now they're a-savin' it until the dudes get time to come up here an' kill it, an' some of 'em leave a deer to rot in the woods, an' on'y take the horns ef it's a buck or the tail ef it's a doe, just so's they can brag about it when they go home, an' they'd put me in jail ef I killed a deer when I needed meat. I dunno what we're a-comin' to in this free country."

There was nothing to be said on this subject, and I said it. When dinner time came he called me from the lake, and as we two sat at table said: "There's some cold boiled ham and here's a stew o' mountain mutton. Mebbe it's agin your principles to eat our mutton in June, so I sot out the ham. I'm goin' to eat the mutton; you can do as you like."

Ham can be had at any lunch counter. The deer had been killed, and a refusal to eat a portion of it would not restore it to life. . . .

Mr. [Charles H.] Bennett, of The Antlers, tells me that Alvah will not write any more, but in a recent interview with him he got the following from Alvah: "In 1858 Ned Buntline came into the woods to get away from civilization and write novels. Ned built a cabin on Eagle Lake which he called Eagle's Nest and hired Alvah to work for him. They quarreled and Ned killed Alvah's hounds and they threatened to kill each other. In 1865 Alvah built a camp on Racquette Lake, where he lived alone, trapping, drawing his fur on a hand sled fifty-five miles to Boonville and bringing back provisions. It took a week to make the trip. One winter his skins of otter, fisher, marten, mink and bear brought him $743. In 1874 his camp on Sunny Island was burned and he lost everything he owned. That fall he built a camp on Eighth Lake, Fulton Chain, to get out of the way of travel, but in a few years returned to Racquette and built at Brown's Tract Inlet, where he now lives, a much disgruntled man, who says the people are wandering all over and spoiling the woods. Fifty years ago the Adirondacks was indeed a wilderness known to but a few sportsmen. There were but few boats in it and no mode of travel except by water. Here Alvah Dunning lived, hunted, and reigned supreme in his woods." . . .

When I met Alvah the last time—some half dozen years ago—he was living in the past. The future had nothing in store but the destruction of the forests, or, what was as bad, their being run over by tourists or the building of expensive "camps" by wealthy men. The good times were in the distant past, when he never saw a strange face unless he went into the settlements. "They're puttin' steamboats on the lakes to scare the trout to death, an' have built a railroad into Old Forge. They've put a lot o' black bass into Racquette Lake to eat up the few trout that's left, an' what good anyone sees in a black bass is more'n I know." . . .

Young men, some little concession—charity, if you will—should be extended to this man who was born in the woods and considers it his by right of prior discovery and settlement years before you were born. . . . The strict letter need not be enforced on the man whose whole life has been spent in a struggle for existence in the forest, and who could not live out of it. Put yourself in his place! [Five years after this sketch was written Alvah Dunning died, at eighty-five, in a hotel room in Utica on his way home from a Sportsmen's Show in New York. He was asphyxiated in his bed; the gas-jet in his room had been leaking all night.]

THE SPORTSMAN AND HIS GUIDE
Harry V. Radford

From an address delivered at the annual banquet of the Brown's
Tract Guide Association at Old Forge, January 8, 1903.

The sportsman's relation to his guide is scarcely less close,
scarcely less sacred than that of child to mother; for no matter
how much experience we of the city and town may have had in the
ways of the wilderness, when we leave the beaten paths and the
settlements and head for the backwoods with our faithful guide as
sole companion, we cannot but feel, as we follow the unblazed trail
at his side, that compared with the trained, inborn woodcraft of
this lifelong woodsman, we are but children in our partial knowledge of the woods and of how to live in them. . . .

In the fourteen seasons which I spent here in the Adirondacks
. . . it has been my good fortune to bivouac in the same camp,
under the same blanket, with scores of trusty woodsmen—some of
whom are here tonight—on many a lonely lake, in many a gloomy
mountain pass, and under stars that shone upon as wild, remote
and beautiful regions as sun ever set over in the Empire State; and
I can say—and it gives me pleasure to say it—that on every occasion I have found the hardy, keen-witted woodsmen whom we en-
gage in the triple capacity of "guide, philosopher, and friend" to
be fully worthy of this wide-embracing designation. . . .

What varied experiences we have had together, my guide and
I! Now we are working our way, side by side, up the rugged, forbidding slopes of Mt. Marcy—I a stripling of fourteen, he a stalwart weather-beaten woodsman of fifty. Again, we are pushing our
light boat up a narrowing creek in the St. Regis or Fish Creek
waters, or carrying it over to an isolated, little-known chain of
ponds to the southwest of Mud Lake. Now threading the water-
mazes of those wilderness ponds between Forked Lake and Little
Tupper, or exploring the wild, trackless country round about Cold
River and Mounts Seward and Santanoni. Again, we are penetrating the mysterious fastnesses of Indian Pass, or descending the precipitous wall of Panther Gorge, or wetting our feet in the immacu-

late waters of Lake Tear-of-the-Clouds. Up the broad Raquette we sweep in our graceful guide boat—my guide and I. . . . Always my guide is the same patient, faithful, assistful companion; bearing the burdens with me (and bearing more than his share); making camp at nightfall wherever we might find ourselves; cooking meals that kings might envy—kindly, considerate, attentive. Is it any wonder that the guide and the sportsman are inseparable friends through life; that no matter how exalted may be the social or official rank of a sportsman, his guide is always made to feel one with him—on equal footing? Scores of guides there are who have been the camp-mates and have slept under one blanket with Presidents of the United States, with statesmen, generals, poets, philosophers, scientists—the greatest men of the land—nor can the greatest of the land think it other than an honor to share companionship with these sturdy, resolute men of honor, courage, and tact who of all men deserve the designation, "Nature's noblemen."

I cannot adequately express to you in my own words the strength of this familiar fellowship which exists between the sportsman and his guide; this rooted friendship which years of separation cannot shake; this admiration in which the man of the city holds his brother man who has lived his life amid the ennobling environments of the forest; this strange, magnetic bond which unites the city-bred woodlover and his guide. And, so, I shall quote for you a few lines which were written at my request, a year or two ago, about an old guide whom most of you have known well, by one whose name is familiar to every sportsman in America and whom many of you guides have known personally . . . the man who is called the "Father of the Out-of-Doors Idea"—W. H. H. Murray —to whom you guides and thousands of others have lovingly given the sobriquet he earned so well, "Adirondack Murray."

Well, as you all know, Mr. Murray's favorite guide used to be John Plumley of Long Lake. . . . About two years ago, Plumley, then an old man of seventy-four, reached the end of the last carry. . . . When I learned that Plumley had passed away, I sent word to Mr. Murray, who I knew was planning to rejoin his old guide here in the Adirondacks the following summer, after an absence from this region of just twenty years; for, when guide and sportsman had last parted (both then in the prime of life), a compact had been entered into between them that if both lived to see twenty years more, they would meet here again in the woods the twentieth summer and live over again their former experiences. In the course of a few weeks Mr. Murray sent me the following "In Memoriam" sketch for publication in *Woods and Waters*. . . . I shall close these remarks with the beautiful, pathetic eulogy which W. H. H. Murray wrote of his oldtime guide and camp-companion, Honest John Plumley:

"He taught me a faultless knowledge of the woods, the name and nature of plant and herb and tree, the languages of the night, and the occultism of silent places and soundless shores. I blunderingly expounded to him the knowledge of the skies, the names of stars, of planets and constellations and of the splendor beyond that was invisible as yet and would forever be until our eyes became clearer and purer. He had a most gentle and mannerly reticence and that sweetest of all habits in man or woman—the habit of silence. He could look and see, listen and hear, and say nothing. He was natured for reception of all fine impressions that come to the best and the finest of the earth out of the still depths of woods and the quietude of far-stretching, moonlighted waters. His knowledge of woodcraft was intuitive. . . . He was the only guide I ever knew of either race, red or white, that could not in any circumstance lose himself or his way.

"They tell me that he is dead. It is a foolish fashion of speech and not true. Not until the woods are destroyed to the last tree, the mountains crumbled to their bases, the lakes and streams dried up to their parched beds and the woods and wood life are forgotten, will the saying become fact. For John Plumley was so much of the woods, the mountains, and the streams that he personified them. He was a type that is deathless. Memory, affection, imagination, literature—until these die, the great guide of the woods will live with ever enlarging life as the years are added to years and the lovers of nature and of sport multiply. . . .

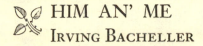

HIM AN' ME
IRVING BACHELLER

Being a story of the Adirondacks told by me in the words of him.

We'd greased our tongues with bacon 'til they'd shy at food an'
    fork
An' the trails o' thought were slippery an' slopin' towards New
    York;
An' our gizzards shook an' trembled an' were most uncommon hot
An' the oaths were slippin' easy from the tongue o' Philo Scott.

Then skyward rose a flapjack an' a hefty oath he swore
An' he spoke of all his sufferin' which he couldn't stan' no more;
An' the flapjack got to jumpin' like a rabbit on the run
As he give his compliments to them who couldn't p'int a gun.

He told how deer would let 'em come an' stan' an' rest an' shoot
An' how bold an' how insultin' they would eye the tenderfoot;
How he—Fide Scott—was hankerin' fer suthin' fit to eat
"———!" says he. "Let's you an' me go out an' find some meat."

We paddled off a-whisperin' beneath the long birch limbs
An' we snooked along as silent as a sucker when he swims;
I could hear him slow his paddle as eroun' the turns he bore;
I could hear his neck a-creakin' while his eye run up the shore.

An' soon we come acrost a buck as big an' bold as sin
An' Philo took t' swallerin' to keep his feelin's in;
An' every time he swallered, as he slowly swung eroun',
I could hear his Adam's apple go a-squeakin' up an' down.

He sot an' worked his paddle jest as skilful as he could
An' we went on slow an' careless, like a chunk o' floatin' wood:
An' I kind o' shook an' shivered an' the pesky ol' canoe
It seemed to feel as I did, for it shook an' shivered too.

I sot there, full o' deviltry, a-p'intin' with the gun,
An' we come up clost and closter, but the deer he didn't run;
An' Philo shet his teeth so hard he split his briarroot
As he held his breath a-waitin' an' expectin' me to shoot.

I could kind o' feel him hanker, I could kind o' hear him think,
An' we'd come so nigh the animal we didn't dast to wink,
But I kep' on a-p'intin' of the rifle at the deer
Jest as if I was expectin' fer to stick it in his ear.

An' Philo tetched the gunnel soft an' shook it with his knee;
I kind o' felt him nudgin' an' a-wishin' he was me,
But I kep' on a-p'intin' with a foolish kind o' grin,
Enjoyin' all the wickedness that he was holdin' in.

An' of a sudden I could feel a tremble in his feet;
I knew that he was gettin' mad an' fillin' up with heat.
An' his blood it kind o' simmered, but he couldn't say a damn—
He'd the feelin's of a panther an' the quiet of a lamb.

But I only sot a-p'intin' at the shoulder of the deer
An' we snooked along as ca-areful an' we kep' a-drawin' near;
An' Philo—so deceivin'—as if frozen into rock,
Was all het up with sinfulness from headgear unto sock.

An' his foot come creepin' for'ards an' he tetched me with his boot
An' he whispered low an' anxious, an' says he: "Why don't ye
    shoot?"
An' the buck he see the time had come fer him an' us to part
An' he flung the spray as Philo pulled the trigger of his heart.

He had panthers in his bosom, he had horns upon his mind;
An' the panthers spit an' rassled an' their fur riz up behind;
An' he gored me with his languidge an' he clawed me with his eye
'Til I wisht that, when I done him dirt, I hadn't been so nigh.

He scairt the fish beneath us an' the birds upon the shore
An' he spoke of all his sufferin' which he couldn't stan' no more;

Then he sot an' thought an' muttered as he pushed a mile or so
Like a man that's lost an' weary on the mountain of his woe.

An' he eyed me over cur'ous an' with pity on his face
An' he seemed to be a sortin' words to make 'em fit the case.
"Of all the harmless critters that I ever met," says he,
"There ain't not none more harmlesser—my God!—than what you
  be."

An' he added, kind o' sorrowful, an' hove a mighty sigh:
"I'd be 'shamed t' meet another deer an' look him in the eye.
God knows a man that p'ints so never orter hev no grub,
What game are you expectin' fer t' slaughter with a club?"

An' I answered with a riddle: "It has head an' eyes an' feet
An' is black an' white an' harmless, but a fearful thing to meet;
It's a long an' pesky animal as any in the county:
Can't ye guess?—I've ketched a pome an' I'll give ye half the
  bounty."

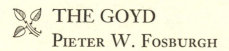

THE GOYD
PIETER W. FOSBURGH

    Among the mammals of New York fast moving toward ex-
tinction and already more legendary than real is the old-fashioned
Adirondack guide (pronounced goyd). The few remaining members of the two species, those with the double-bitted coffee-dunked
strainer-type mustachio and those without, have now attained the
status of local characters (they are aware of this) and spend most
of their time beguiling themselves and their prey with stories of
how things used to be. Things were better then. Some still do a
little guiding (pronounced goydin), but most are now holed up
behind a woodpile cut by their grandchildren, in the mountain
towns where they were born.

We speak here of the second generation of guide, the generation that reached maturity along about 1900. But before enlarging on this North Woods phenomenon, it might be fitting to say something about those that came before and have come after him. The first was a more rugged generation, a product of the post Civil War days when the Adirondacks were a real rather than a preserved wilderness, when the first sizeable run of tourists was "staging in" from Port Kent to Keeseville to Lower Saranac, or from Lake George to Minerva to Long Lake, or from Albany to Boonville and thence on horseback to the Fulton Chain.

Guides in those days were the native sons of the wilderness. Most famous of them all was Mitchell Sabattis of Long Lake, but there were others—Alvah Dunning, John Cheney, the Plumleys, Cash McGraw, George Ring, Alonzo Dudley, the Sweeneys—who knew the woods and who for two-fifty a day fee and one dollar a week for food would undertake to make camp, cook, comfort, and guide for the gentlemen who hired them. There were scamps in the crowd even then, but with the help of Adirondack Murray and other writer-sports the guides of the period established themselves as rough diamonds and frontier philosophers with whom any gentleman might indulge himself in a fireside chat before turning in for the night. . . .

Before returning to our fast disappearing guide of the second generation, we might inquire into those of the third or present. In order to guide for hire, all 532 [licensed guides] are required to have a license and wear a badge issued by [the Conservation] Department. . . . The application for the license must be endorsed by a game protector and by a licensed guide and must be approved by the district game protector of the district in which the applicant lives. On the application the prospective guide is required to state the type of party he feels himself qualified to take out and also the territory that he knows well enough to operate in. He is required to answer questions about his experience and about his ability to swim, handle boats and canoes, read a U.S. Geological Survey map, and cook. At the conclusion of his application he signs a sworn statement that he has never been convicted of a violation of the fish and game laws. . . .

Having brought the guide-and-guiding situation roughly up to date [mid-nineteenth century], we return now to our starting point. The guide of the first generation, the Noble Frontiersman like Sabattis, has had many historians; the guide of the third generation is still with us and awaits development and subsequent recording; but the guide of the middle period is passing on and needs preservation, if not by taxidermy, then otherwise. A physical description would appear to be indicated; the term *goyd* will be used throughout to indicate the product of the middle period.

The size and shape of the goyd is determined primarily by the amount of pork fat (pronounced sausage gravy) consumed, and only secondarily by genes and inheritance. In early years the goyd is able to adjust the pork fat by dint of hard work; in later years, with less work but the same appetite, the pork fat adjusts the goyd. In general it may be said that at any age and regardless of height the goyd cuts an impressive figure; the older, the more impressive.

We proceed now to the dressing of this figure. At the top of the goyd is his hat. Next to his 32 Special this is his most prized possession, but whereas he has only one gun he is likely to have two or three hats because he feels that in order to dress properly for a variety of occasions it is necessary to change only hats, not clothes. The *visiting* or *store* hat sits awkwardly and is always conspicuously new, no matter how many years it has been kept in the box it was bought in; the *character* hat, not owned by all goyds and worn only for an audience, is a broad-brimmed affair requiring special carriage; the *wearin'* hat, on the other hand, has been molded to the head by many years of steady use and yet is capable of minor adjustments of brim and crown to express the mood of the moment.

Contrary to general opinion, none of these hats is ever adorned with trout flies or other paraphernalia; the hat must stand on its own or else it's time to secretly break in another one.

The inner vestment of the goyd is the union suit, regardless of season, but this appears outwardly at neck, wrist and ankle on warmer days and even on colder ones if the effect seems to justify the exposure. In order to adjust himself to drops in temperature, the goyd customarily relies upon the addition of both shirts and pants, the maximum number of pants observed by this writer being four, although our correspondent in Owls Head claims that five was the average during the winter of '47. The problem of supporting these pants is solved by a suspenders-and-belt combination which this writer does not even pretend to understand.

At the bottom of the goyd appear his feet. These are prominently displayed not just because of their size but because the various pants above are narrow-cuffed and cut off four inches above the ankle, permitting a view of union suit as it disappears into socks (wool, knitted by wife or aunt) and shoes. The shoes are high leather, similar to the type that the Army considers appropriate, and are replaced only when absolutely necessary with a rubber type.

Several other peculiarities with regard to clothing distinguish the goyd. (1) He never wears a raincoat, possibly because he hates rain like a chicken and is seldom to be found out in it. (2) He has a profound distrust of buttons. The reason for this is not known, but it results in the use of king-size safety pins to secure important openings, even though such openings are already secured with healthy buttons. Neither is it known what of value the goyd fears to lose in the event that either type of fastening gives way; apparently a sense of personal security is involved. (3) Watch chains, the heavier the better, are standard equipment, and are removed with the store teeth only upon retiring. In addition, a number of worn but carefully knotted cords, suspended at various points about the person of the goyd, disappear into his pockets and presumably provide direct connection with articles of importance.

Such is the goyd. We encountered one of these characters last fall. It was during the hunting season and he was sitting on a rock in the sun, just beside the dirt road where he'd left his car.

"Afternoon, Sam," we said. "What you doing?"

"Goydin. Been here goydin all day."

"That so? Don't see your hunters."

"Well," Sam said, "I got a party about forty rod over down in under thataway. He's settin' on a blowdown. Been settin' six hours. Then I got another party down back in over thataway. He's settin' on a rock. Them fellers is deer huntin' and I'm drawin' ten dollars a day."

O Tempora, O Goydin!

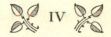

IV

The Angle of Vision

I am for the woods against the world,
But are the woods for me?
Edmund Blunden

Enter these enchanted woods,
You who dare.
George Meredith

IN THE TWO preceding sections the Adirondacks are viewed as friendly and hospitable: a realm of opportunity for the enterprising, a sanctuary for the jaded city man, and a second Garden of Eden for the backwoodsman to realize the American dream of a new life free from the past. But there is a minority report. Wilderness, as Roderick Nash says, tends to be a state of mind, and minds are notoriously diverse. The spectrum between love and hate is a broad one. Some visitors experience a mixture of attraction and repulsion.

Father Jogues, the first white man of record to cross the Adirondacks from north to south, looked on the wilderness as anti-Christian, a breeding ground of savagery and heathenism. But the greatest hate-monger of all time was a clergyman, the Reverend John Lundy, who went to Saranac Lake in the late 1870s as a health seeker. His *Saranac Exiles* (1880) is conceived, says Alfred Donaldson, in malice and written in spite. If Lundy had been a better and more convincing writer, he might have checked the headlong influx of invalids and tourists in the 1880s. But his testy diatribes validate the disclaimer on his title page—"not by W. Shakespeare."

Peter Kalm, a Swedish naturalist and student of Linnaeus, was excited over the flora of the Champlain-Lake George valley on his 1749 tour. Having heard stories of Indian atrocities from the French soldiers in his escort, however, he was apprehensive over crackling sounds in the woods at night. "The long autumn nights are rather terrifying in these vast wildernesses," he noted in his journal during a bivouac on Lake George. "May God be with us!" Primitive dread of the dark forest did not disappear along with hostile Indians. Its imaginary object was simply transferred to wild beasts.

A more tangible cause of discontent was the inconvenience and discomfort of life in the woods. During the Murray rush there was much grumbling when too many tourists chased too few guides. Others complained that Murray had deceived them by belittling the plague of insects, the muddy carries, the leaking shelters, and so forth.

Tourists and sportsmen were free to visit the Adirondacks during a benign season of the year. But year-round tubercular patients in Saranac Lake, beset by intimations of mortality, had to endure besides the harshness of Adirondack winters. While Dr. Trudeau found fulfillment in permanent residence, his patient Robert Louis Stevenson discovered that even a Scot was unprepared for the austerity of a long winter climaxed by the blizzard of 1888. Complaining of the "bleak, blackguard, beggarly climate" and taking advantage of improved health, he fled rejoicing to the South Seas.

An Adirondack winter could change the perspective even of the nature lover in good health. Watching a deer starving to death during a blizzard forces recognition of another side of nature than that known to the summer visitor, its indifference or cruelty.

The Europeanized American, George William Curtis, dissents on aesthetic grounds. A wilderness lake for him falls short of ideal beauty. He prefers Lake Como with its villas and terraced gardens to the monotony of trees around Lake George.

There is dissent too on moral grounds. The optimist, believing in the natural goodness of man, praises the freedom of the wilderness; but the sceptic or pessimist may see that freedom as an encouragement to immoral or criminal acts. Who would see? asks Dreiser's Clyde Griffiths as he conceives of a way to resolve economic and social tensions originating outside the woods. Likewise a native in Jean Rikhoff's chronicle of the Buttes family observes that the greed and rapacity of outsiders are destroying the woods and, with them, the dream of a virtuous society rooted in the soil. The artist William Stillman, on prolonged visits, finds that isolation may drive the backwoodsman himself to brutish behavior.

"In the forest, possibility was unbounded; but just because of that," says R. W. B. Lewis, "evil inclination was unchecked, and witches could flourish there." Historically, the witch population of the Adirondacks has fallen far short of that of the old woods of Massachusetts. But the potential has always existed. Verplanck Colvin, who crisscrossed the region for thirty years in a state survey, insisted that the forest, spread out over a vast extent of uneven ground, remained a mystery to him. There is witchery in Alfred Street's boisterous owls, though they may be harmless poltergeists. And in the night forest Stillman hears voices and sees visions.

But it was reserved for a very recent writer, Joyce Carol Oates, to realize the full potential of our woods for witchery. Her *Bellefleur* (1980) is the chronicle of several generations of a demon-ridden family in a setting more like the Adirondacks than any other geographical entity. The woods of Cotton Mather and Nathaniel Hawthorne must now yield their preeminence in the black arts. *Bellefleur*, a magnificent gothic romance, sees to that. As you come to any gnarled, hoary tree in the forest, take care to say the name of your patron saint.

LAKE GEORGE AND LAKE COMO
George William Curtis

Lake George is a simple mountain lake upon the verge of the wilderness. You ascend from its banks westward and plunge into a wild region. The hills that frame the water are low and when not bare—for fires frequently consume many miles of woodland on the hillsides—covered with the stiffly outlined, dark and cold foliage of evergreens. Among these are no signs of life. You might well fancy the populace of the primeval forest yet holding those retreats. You might still dream in the twilight that it were not impossible to catch the ring of a French or English rifle or the wild whoop of the Indian; sure that the landscape you see [in 1852] was the same they saw, and their remotest ancestors.

From the water rise the rocks, sometimes solitary and bearing a single tree, sometimes massed into a bowery island.

The boat-boys count the isles of the lake by the days of the year and tell you of three hundred and sixty-five. It is a story agreeable enough to hear, but wearisome when the same thing is told at every pretty stretch of islanded water. In the late afternoon or by moon-light, it is pleasant to skim the quiet lake to the little Tea Island, which has a tree-sheltered cove for harbor and on which stands a ruined temple to T. But whether bohea, or gunpowder, or some more mysterious divinity, the boat-boys reluct to say, and you must rely on fancy to suggest. . . .

All this does not make a lake as beautiful as Como. Here, at Lake George, is no variety of foliage. The solemn evergreens emphasize the fact of a wild primeval landscape. Were there brilliant, full-foliaged chestnuts or lustrous vines to vary the monotony of hue, or spiring cypresses and domed stone pines to multiply different forms, or long reaches of terraced shore, the melancholy monotony of impression which is now so prominent would be alleviated. The scene is too sad and lonely. The eye is tortured by the doomed ranks of firs and hemlocks that descend like resigned martyrs to the shore. It is not sublime, it is not the perfection of loneliness, it is not the best of its kind. Yet in the August moonlight the empress asked me if it was not more beautiful than Como.

Consider Como. That strip of water blends the most characteristic Swiss and Italian beauty. From the dark and awful shadow of the Snow-Alps which brood over its northern extremity, the lake stretches under waving vines and shimmering olives (that look as if they grew only by moonlight, said Mrs. Jameson's niece), under orange terraces and lemons and oleanders, under sumptuous chestnuts and funereal cypresses and ponderous pines and all that they imply of luxurious palaces, marble balusters, steps, statues, vases and fountains, under these and through all the imagery of ideal Italy, deep and far into the very heart of southern Italian loveliness. And on the shores near the town of Como, among the garden paths or hills that overhang the villas, you may look from the embrace of Italy straight at the eternal snow-peaks of Switzerland—as if on the divinest midsummer day your thought could cleave the year and behold December as distinctly as June.

Lake Como is the finest combination of natural sublimity and beauty with the artistic results which that sublimity and beauty have inspired. This is the combination essential to a perfect and permanently satisfactory enjoyment of landscape. We modern men cannot be satisfied with the satisfaction of the savage, nor with that of any partial nature and education. . . .

So when the empress said to me, "Is it not more beautiful than Como?" I said, no. Yet it is impossible not to perceive the great capabilities of Lake George.

The gleam of marble palaces or of summer retreats of any

genuine beauty, even a margin of grain-goldened shore or ranges of whispering rushes beneath stately terraces—indeed, any amelioration of nature by art would perfect the loveliness of Lake George and legitimate the empress's praises. At present it is invested with none of that enchanted atmosphere of romance in which every landscape is more alluring. Its interest and charm is the difference between an Indian and a Greek, between pigments and a picture.

Do not suppose that I am maligning so fair an object as the lake, even while I regard it as a good type of the quality of our landscape compared with the European. Space and wildness are the proper praises of American scenery. . . . In the general vague vastness of the impression produced, this is a genuine triumph. But it is a superiority which appeals more to the mind than to the eye. The moment you travel in America the victory of Europe is sure. . . . We have none of the charms that follow long history. We have only vast and unimproved extent and the interest with which the possible grandeur of a mysterious future may invest it. One would be loth to exhort a European to visit America for other reasons than social and political observation or buffalo hunting. We have nothing so grand and accessible as Switzerland, nothing so beautiful as Italy, nothing so civilized as Paris, nothing so comfortable as England. The *idea* of the great western rivers and of lakes as shoreless to the eye as the sea, or of a magnificent monotony of grass or forest, is as impressive and much less wearisome than the actual sight of them. . . .

The "No" of my reply meant all that. And when, the next morning, we steamed in a stiff gale from Caldwell to Crown Point, the unhumanized solitude of the shores accorded well with the dusky legends of Indian wars that haunt the lake.

Lake George should be the motto of a song rather than the text of a sermon, I know. But it is beautiful enough to make moralizing poetry. It is the beauty of a country cousin, the diamond in the rough, when compared with the absolute elegance and fascination of Como. Nor will I quarrel with those whom the peasant pleases most—especially if they have never been to court.

✿ ILLUSION AND REALITY
WILLIAM JAMES STILLMAN

Under the stimulus, in part, of the desire for something out of the ordinary line of subject for pictures and in part from the hope that going into the "desert" might quicken the spiritual faculties . . . I decided to pass the next summer [1854] in the great primeval forest in the northern part of New York State, known as the Adirondack wilderness. It was then little known or visited; a few sportsmen and anglers had penetrated it, but for the most part it was known only to the lumberers. Here and there, at intervals of ten to twenty miles, there were log houses, some of which gave hospitality in the summer to the sportsmen and in the winter to the loggers who worked for the great lumber companies. It was a tract of a hundred miles, more or less, across, mainly unbroken wildwood, cut up by rapid rivers, impossible of navigation otherwise than by canoes and light skiffs which could be carried from one sheet of water to another on the backs of the woodsmen, around the cascades and over tracts of intervening land through virgin forests without roads and, to a large extent, without paths. I hoped here to find new subjects for art, spiritual freedom, and a closer contact with the spiritual world—something beyond the material existence. I was ignorant of the fact that art does not depend on a subject, nor spiritual life on isolation from the rest of humanity, and I found, what a correct philosophy would have before told me, nature with no suggestion of art and the dullest form of intellectual or spiritual existence. . . .

I found on Upper Saranac Lake a log cabin inhabited by a farmer whose family consisted of a wife, a son, and a daughter. There I enjoyed a backwoods hospitality at the cost of two dollars a week for board and lodging and passed the whole summer, finding a subject near the cabin at which I painted assiduously for nearly three months. I passed the whole day in the open air, wore no hat, and only cloth shoes, hoping that thus the spiritual life would have easier access to me. I carried no gun and held the lives of beast and bird sacred, but I drew the line at fishing, and my rod and fly-book provided in a large degree the food of the household, for trout swarmed. I caught in an hour during that summer, in a stream where there has not been a trout for years, as large a string as I could carry a mile. All the time that I was not painting I was in the boat on the lake or wandering in the forest.

My quest was an illusion. The humanity of the backwoods was on a lower level than that of a New England village—more material if less worldly; the men got intoxicated, and some of the women —nothing less like an apostle could I have found in the streets of New York. I saw one day a hunter who had come into the woods with a motive in some degree like mine—impatience of the restraints and burdens of civilization and pure love of solitude. He had become, not bestialized like most of the men I saw, but animalized—he had drifted back into the condition of his dog, with his higher intellect inert. He had built himself a cabin in the depth of the woods, and there he lived in the most complete isolation from human society he could attain. He interested me greatly, and as he stopped for the night at the cabin where I was living, we had considerable conversation. He cared nothing for books, but enjoyed nature and only hunted in order to live, respecting the lives of his fellow-creatures within that limit. He only went to the settlements when he needed supplies, abstained from alcoholic drinks, the great enemy of the backwoodsman, and was happy in his solitude. . . .

In his solitary life, in the unbroken silence which reigned around him, he heard mysterious voices, and only the year before he had heard one say that he was wanted at home. He paid no attention to it, thinking it only an illusion, but after an interval it was repeated so distinctly that he packed his knapsack, took his dog, and went out with the intention of going home. On the way he met a messenger sent after him who told him that his brother had met with an accident which disabled him from all work, and begged him to come to his assistance. The voice had come to him at the time of the accident. As a rule, however, the voices seemed vagarious, and he attached no importance to them, except as phenomena which interested him slightly. . . .

The backwoods life, as a rule, I found led to hard drinking, and even the old settler with whom I had taken quarters, though an excellent and affectionate head of his family and in his ordinary life temperate and hard-working, used at long intervals to break bounds and, taking his savings down to the settlement, drink till he could neither pay for more nor "get it on trust," and then come home penitent and humiliated. . . .

In the solitude of the great wilderness, where I have passed months at a time, generally alone, or with only my dog to keep me company, airy nothings became sensible; and in the silence of those nights in the forest, the whisperings of the night wind through the trees forced meanings on the expecting ear. I came to hear voices in the air, words so clearly spoken that even an incredulous mind could not ignore them. I sat in my boat one evening, out on the lake, watching the effects of the sky between the gaunt pines which, under the prevalence of the west winds, grew up with an easterly inclination of their tops, like that of a man walking, and thus seemed to be marching eastward into the gathering darkness. They gave a sudden impression of a procession, and I heard as distinctly as I ever heard human speech a voice in the air which said "the procession of the Anakim." Over and over again as I sat alone by my camp fire at night, dreaming awake, I have heard a voice from across the lake calling me to come over and fetch it, and one night I rowed my boat in the darkness more than a mile to find no one. Watching for deer from a treetop one day, in broad sunlight, and looking over a mountain range along the crest of which were pointed firs and long level ridges of rock in irregular alternation, the eerie feeling suddenly came over me, and the mountain-top seemed a city with spires and walls, and I heard bands of music and then hunting-horns coming down with the wind, and there was a perfect illusion of the sound of a hunting party hurrying down into the valley, which gave me a positive panic, as if I were being pursued and must run. I remember also on another occasion a transformation—transfiguration rather—of the entire landscape in colors such as neither Titian nor Turner ever has shown me. It was a glorification of nature such as I had never conceived and cannot now comprehend.

The fascination of indulgence in this illusory life became such that I lingered every summer longer and finally until November, when, in that high and northerly locality, the snow had fallen and the lake began to freeze, living only under a bark roof, open to the air and to the snow, which fell on my bed during the night. I can easily imagine the life leading to insanity. Probably my interest in nature and my painting kept me measurably free from this danger, but not from illusions as unaccountable as spiritism and sometimes more real than the physical facts. I had one evening, when I was lying awake in a troubled state of mind, a vision of a woman's face, utterly unlike anybody I had ever seen and so beautiful that with the sheer delight of its beauty I remained for several days in a state of ecstasy, as if it were constantly before me, and I remember it still, after more than forty years, as more beautiful than any face I ever saw in the flesh. It was as real while it lasted as any material object could have been, though it was a head without a body, like one of the vignetted portraits which used to be so fashionable in my early days.

NIGHT SOUNDS ON THE RAQUETTE
ALFRED B. STREET

Again came the distant hoot of the owl floating over the dark silence.

"Shut up there!" exclaimed Corey. "What d'ye think we care for you!"

"Them owls is a sassy thing; them and loons," said Harvey, lighting his pipe with a match. "They seem to hev a notion nobody haint no business in the woods but them."

"I tell ye, shut up and mind yer business!" said Corey, as another hooting was heard, but this time appearing to come from a considerable distance. "If I hear another word, I'll give ye a bullet to feed on."

"How can you shoot him, Corey?" said I. "He must be, from the sound, certainly a quarter if not half a mile away."

"He isn't twenty rods!" replied Corey; "that's a way the critters hev of hootin' in their throat so as to seem a long way off when they're close by."

"That's a true bill," chimed in Harvey. "And they're just the revarse o' wolves. Let them howl and you'd think yourself nigh enough to look down their throats a'most when they're mebby so fur off they couldn't smell ye if their noses was as long as pine trees. They'll go y-o-w-l, y-o-w-l, one beginnin' fust and the rest strikin' in, jest as they sing in meetin' when the parson lines the hymn." . . .

A sudden crack sounded and then a dull, reverberating report.

"A tree fallin'," said Corey, as I gave a slight start. "They'll fall sometimes in the woods without any warnin', jest as human bein's will in apoplex."

"That's so," said Harvey. "I've bin out afore now, and a tree that looked jest as sound as a trout 'ud give a quick shrick like, as a deer'll bleat when tackled by the hounds, and then fall with a most onmassyful noise. It takes a two-hoss pettyfogger to git out o' the way."

At this moment came the most singular sound I ever heard. It was a sharp whine, half smothered in a thick wheeze, or a loud hiss with a fine whistle cutting through it, like an exhausted blacksmith's bellows or a person breathing in asthma.

"What on earth is that, Corey?" asked I.

"It's a young owl tryin' to whistle," answered he, "and a rael doleful sound 'tis. It sounds as if his throat was dry, and he couldn't pucker his mouth."

"It sounds as if he had the phthisic," said Harvey, "and was tryin' to breathe through a holler knittin' needle."

A hollow, choking ubble-bubble now sounded close at hand.

"There's somebody drowning there in the river, boys! do make haste—quick!"

But the "boys" only laughed.

"That's another of the owls agin; the big horned critters, or cat owls, as they're called," said Corey.

"An owl again!" exclaimed I. "Why, how many noises do the creatures make?"

"As many a'most as ridin' skimington," answered Harvey. "Sometimes they'll screech like a catamount; then they'll whine like an old woman at camp-meetin'. Another sounds like a bell—a leetle owl, not much bigger'n a couple o' white lily-blows. Another sounds for all the world like the whet-whet of a saw—and that isn't a great sight bigger'n a pine knot. I've heerd some bark like a dog, some mew like a cat, and spit 'pit 'pit they will and snarl and growl as ugly as Satan. Others agin'll c-r-y out so doleful, you'd think they had the belly-ache. Others agin'll whu-i-stle clear as a nigger. They're great hands to steal, too, 'specially the big horned ones. I've seen 'em spyin' round my traps for what they could git, time and agin. And I've ketched 'em tearin' rats they've found in traps all to pieces and lookin' farse as wildcats."

"What do they live on?"

"Well, ducks and patridges and dead fish; the last is old hunderd to 'em. I've seen 'em skim cluss to the ground and then fall quick as a wink on a squirrel, or muskrat, or rabbit, mebby. I've shot, afore now, and wounded 'em, and they'd throw themselves on their back and lift up their long, black claws and snap their beaks and wink their round eyes, they would, and sw-e-l-l like a big puffball. They're all sorts o' colors, too, grey and brown and white and brindle; and one kind's red at fust, as ef 'twas singed by the camp fire, and then grows mottled like. This 'ere makes sounds like a body's teeth a-chatterin' and clickin' t'gether with the cold. The fust time I heerd one I couldn't think what on airth 'twas. I looked round and round, and finally at last I see the leetle red sarpent a p-e-e-kin' out of a holler low down in a maple, lookin' like a konkus on a pine tree."

We now glided along in silence past the grim, ghostly trees. I almost fancied we were spectres flitting through a phantom scene, bound in a spell, and I feared to draw breath lest I should break it and incur some dreadful punishment. Now and then I imagined the darkness gathering into a vast demon and threatening to whelm us in the gloom of his frown; sometimes I thought the somber walls on each side were closing to annihilate us.

Suddenly another hissing was heard, but this time accompanied with a sound between a snarl and a snore. It filled the woods in the stillness until I thought it might be the demon napping on his lonely vigil.

Corey clattered one of the oars, and immediately, with a keen shriek, a large black object burst from the shore and, sailing over our heads, became lost in the darkness.

"An eagle," said Corey, unconcernedly. "He was sleepin'; and though he snores like a nor'wester, the least leetle sound'll wake him, and off he goes."

A sudden light now gleamed from the gloom in front, and Harvey exclaimed—

"Here we are cluss to camp. I'm glad on't; my j'nts feel rayther creaky in the damp air so long." . . .

Just as we had slouched our felt hats over our ears and were wrapping ourselves in our blankets, a most horrible uproar burst from the opposite bank. It sounded like imps in convulsions of laughter. The tones and the echoes were so blended it was impossible to tell the number of the voices.

"Harvey!" shouted Bingham to that worthy at the camp fire. "Are the ghosts of the Saranac tribe pealing out their war-whoops preparatory to an onslaught, or have all the panthers in the woods become suddenly mad and are coming to attack the camp?"

"Them's owls," said Harvey laconically.

"Owls once more!" cried I. "Are the woods made of owls, and every owl with a different voice?"

"The sort of owl that makes this noise," said Harvey, "is a part of my almynack of the weather. We shell hev a rainy day tomorrer depend on't."

SOME WERE NOT CHARMED
WACHUSETT

The instant popularity of the Reverend William Murray's *Adventures in the Wilderness* in the spring of 1869 led that very summer to the phenomenon known as the Murray Rush, satirized in a somewhat labored effort at Pickwickian humor in Charles Hallock's "Raquette Club" (*Harper's*, August, 1870). Less well known but crisper are the observations of a special correspondent, "Wachusett," in a series of articles in the Boston *Daily Advertiser* for July, 1869.

Mr. Murray's pen has brought a host of visitors into the wilderness such as it has never seen before—consumptives craving pure air, dyspeptics wandering after appetites, sportsmen hitherto content with small game and few fish, veteran tourists in search of novelty, weary workers hungering for perfect rest, ladies who have thought climbing the White Mountains the utmost possible achievement of feminine strength, journalists and lecturers of both sexes looking for fresh material for the dainty palate of the public, come in parties of twos and dozens and make up in the aggregate a multitude which crowds the hotels and clamors for guides and threatens to turn the wilderness into a Saratoga of fashionable costliness. . . .

When you quit your wagon at the door of Martin's, lame and soiled and hungry as you are, the chances are ten to one that you postpone the sofa, the supper-table and the wash basin that you may catch the extended hand of the hospitable proprietor of the inn and selfishly strive to get ahead of the occupants of the next team by whispering eagerly in his ear, "How about a guide?" Perhaps you have written to Mr. Martin a month in advance to secure you in this respect; perhaps you have come in trusting to luck. In either case the answer is the same. You will have to wait. There are some people in the house who have waited several days already, and who must be supplied ahead of you. But guides are coming in every day, and the delay will probably not be long. Meanwhile there is excellent fishing in the neighborhood, and everything will be done to make the time pass pleasantly. . . .

As you mingle with the guests of the inn, you discover that one thought is dominant with all. People collect into knots to talk over their chances of guides; they form combinations to secure the desired end; they watch each other jealously to see that no individual gets an unfair advantage; they stand guard on the pier to catch the first glimpse of an incoming boat; they make furtive expeditions up the lake on the dim chance of catching a disengaged guide coming down. Arrivals at first indifferent catch the fever, as sober people at Baden get infected with the passion of the place for gambling. One would think that Mr. Martin's pleasant hostelry was a prison-house by the eagerness of its inmates to secure the means of getting away.

If it were a simple question of four times as many tourists wanting guides as there are guides open to engagement, and the lists long since closed, there would be room only for despair and none for excitement in the pursuit. But there are other elements to the problem. Mr. Martin himself has about forty guides in his employment, and there is no more certainty when any of them will come in than into what number the ball on the roulette board will come to a stop. Parties who go off for four weeks will come back after three days, moaning about the black flies or some other annoyance, and throw their guides upon the market. Parties who have engaged six guides for a certain day will arrive in diminished numbers and only want four, releasing the surplus men to be snapped up by those in waiting. And on the other hand, parties once off for the woods will overstay their time, throwing the most elaborately arranged slate into confusion. Once away from Mr. Martin's wharf there is no communication. No telegram nor letter can send a summons or an inquiry; nor can a messenger find a particular party in the vast expanse of lake and woods much more easily than a hunter can find a particular deer. Thus there are all the elements of an exciting chase in the search for guides, and the people at the hotels enter into it with a zest which they will not feel for the pursuit of deer or trout. . . .

I have spoken of the prevalence of the mosquitoes. With these must be included the black flies. Either these insects have not read Mr. Murray's book; or they have mislaid their almanac; or, what is more probable, the lateness and wetness of the season has prolonged their term of life; for certainly the first week of July finds them here in undiminished numbers. Mr. Murray makes light of these insect pests; and from my own experience I shall not venture to contradict him; but I can simply tell what I have seen and heard. I have seen parties hurrying back to the haunts of men from camps which they had sought but a few days before with high hopes of pleasure, driven away solely and simply by the stings of these little torments. I have heard of a gentleman, a sportsman, a journalist, the representative of a sporting paper, who came into the woods for a long stay, bringing four hundred pounds of baggage, and who discharged his guide after five days and sped back to the city to tell how a reverend author had gulled him and the public. I have seen a gentleman so disfigured by mosquitoes that he sought a resting place where his bites might heal before he would present himself to his friends. I have known those temporarily deprived of sight and hearing by mosquito bites. I have been told by these sufferers that they used every ointment prescribed by guide or apothecary and had resort to every variety of net for the head, window, and lodge front without the least relief. I have seen people going through lovely scenery with heads muffled up like those of the assassination conspirators in the Washington prison; and yet the faces thus enveloped were all covered with mosquito bites.

And yet it seems to me that Mr. Murray is in the right of the matter in so far as he asserts the possibility by proper management of avoiding and defying the stingers and biters. There are some people so physically constituted that the bite of a mosquito is as serious a matter to them as the sting of a scorpion. These people should never come into the woods; or, having unwisely come, they should hasten away as soon as their tenderness of skin and blood is discovered. But the majority of people can get along without serious inconvenience. . . .

There are some of the hotels in which the mosquitoes reign and are not to be dethroned. Screens are put in the windows, but the insects mind them no more than they would a painted sign warning them to "Stick No Bills." The landlord advises you to go to bed without a light, but it makes no difference. You cover yourself with tar; but the buzzing keeps you from sleeping until it has evaporated, and then the bites wake you. But on the other hand there are hotels in which never a mosquito ventures, some mysterious charm or peculiar advantage of situation operating to keep them away. If one will flee the first class and stick to the latter, he may make the tour of the wilderness with comfort. I presume the same distinction holds good in regard to camps, since some live out of doors and come back unscathed, while others find the torment unendurable. . . .

To a large majority even of the heterogeneous host who have come here this summer, the sport to be found in the Adirondack wilderness is the first consideration. Those who have no interest in such matters at home breathe it in here with the other novel qualities of the air; languid invalids borrow a gun to take into the woods; and fashionable ladies whose fingers are accustomed to the fan and the crochet needle burden their belts with useless pistols and savage knives and soon learn to learnedly discuss the merits of flies and fishing-rods. The hotels offer no other amusement; the billiard table and bowling alley are unknown; and the incongruous gentleman who has brought his croquet set from home and forced his guide to carry the heavy, awkward box over a long series of portages finds no spot of level, unencumbered earth big enough to play so much as a game of marbles on. We must find excitement and occupation in shooting and fishing or die of ennui when the novelty of the strange method of travel is past.

In the chronic habit of grumbling which the famine of guides and the surfeit of mosquitoes has created at Martin's, growls are aimed at the sporting; and indeed it is not to be wondered at that some discontent is generated by the condition of things in this respect at the outer edge of the wilderness. The deer, with all their foolishness, have learned not to venture into the neighborhood of the Lower Saranac Lake; and venison is about as rare there as it is in Boston. One hears of good fishing; but one sees only gentlemen going out laboriously for all day and returning half ashamed of a scanty string of little four-inch trout such as they would have thrown contemptuously back into the water had any larger fish risen to their flies.

Thus there will naturally be two reports as to the character of the sport in the wilderness this year, those whom the lack of guides has kept in the north telling one story, full of the bitterness of disappointment, while the lucky ones who get the means of getting where the sport is, will come back with a record of enjoyment and victory only less glowing in its colors than Mr. Murray's own. For though the multitude invading the wilderness this summer is very unfavorable for sport of some kinds, there is still a great deal of pleasure to be had by those who get beyond the limbo of the Saranac lakes. We have seen no single fish so large as those we have read of; but we have paused in a shady stretch of the Raquette River where the trout jumping eagerly out of the water were almost as numerous as the flies which lazily flitted above the surface to tempt their appetites. . . .

With the sportsmen . . . there mingles this year a larger proportion than ever before of invalids attracted here by the reports of marvellous healing properties in the air, of especial benefit in cases of lung diseases. The great majority of these people derive invaluable benefit from their visit because the great majority are those who come in time, in the first stages of a malady at first capable of cure. The singular sweetness of the air is apparent to all. . . . But there is another class who come here this summer equally filled with hope of thorough recovery who find nothing but the bitterest disappointment, bringing perhaps an accelerated death in its train. These are the consumptives in the later stages of disease who have tried everything else in vain. . . . It is the saddest of sights to see one of these sufferers arrested in the forest by the coming of death, the comforts with which home would surround him absolutely unattainable by any expenditure of money, no means at hand of summoning friends, no physician to be found, even departure by the route of entrance impossible now that the stimulus of hope has been withdrawn. . . .

The table at one of the hotels the other day was greatly entertained by the torrent of indignation poured forth by a lady who considered that she had been induced to come into the Adirandacks on false pretences, and promised to "show up Mr. Murray in the N'York Her'ld." But I cannot join this crusade. I think there is no lady who could not heartily enjoy the tranquil row from

Martin's to Bartlett's [on the Saranac River between Middle and
Upper Saranac lakes], comfortably established in a light boat,
conscious of the becoming novelty of a Highland costume with
natty boots and red stockings, graceful sash and jaunty cap, and
the unaccustomed but fascinating ornaments of pearl-handled
pistols, a glittering hunting knife, and a chased silver drinking cup
hung about the waist, with a coquettish ivory whistle suspended
from the neck. But I think I have known ladies who would not
enjoy, even in the same array, crossing a carry in a rain storm, face
and hands dripping with tar and oil, mosquito bites smarting on
wrists and temples, the boots soaked through and through, the reserve stockings in the carpet bag equally wet, guide and escort so
loaded with boat and baggage as to be incapable of rendering assistance, and a slippery log tempting to a tumble into a shallow pool
with a muddy bottom. Ladies who can pass such an ordeal without
a loss of temper which would make all its evils tenfold worse can
safely make their plans for the Adirondacks.

SOURING OF THE DREAM
JEAN RIKHOFF

The New World was like a blank piece of paper on which
men might write the outlines of a better world, a world in which
the mistakes of the past were not to be repeated and perpetuated,
where the minority did not break the majority to their wishes,
where one man did not hold power over countless others. The red
men did not fit into these plans. They were unfortunate intruders
on the dream, and so they were pushed back, shunted outside the
dream, and when occasionally they rebelled at being shoved out of
the way, the brutal wars broke out. Red and white flew at one another; it was difficult to distinguish the hunter and the hunted.

But the white man had guns. He had machines of war. He had pieces of paper which proved in his own courts of law that he now owned the land. The Indian gave way—he had no choice, and up through Albany poured hundreds of eager settlers, pressing into the last of the wilderness along the Northeast, opening up vast tracts of hostile lands where the winters were so bitter that the strongest shelters could not keep out the bitter winter cold and where the summers were so brief that the first fruits came only to be caught by the early frosts. But the land was free and it belonged to those who took and subdued it. Men were no longer serfs or peasants or bonded men; they owned land, thousands of acres of land. It was theirs to do with what they wished. And often what they wished— most often—was to make money, so they put the land up as it had been put up in the past, as a pawn for power, and the bright white paper began to be written on in the same words and phrases as before—*greed*, *graft*, *conniving*, *betrayal*, showed up oftener and oftener in bold print, a tale of conspiracies and sell-outs that linked the land from one person to another until it was time for new plunderers to come and rob the earth of the greatest of its treasures, the great forests which greened the hills and valleys as if, indeed, this were the New Beginning.

Lumbermen were making drives as early as 1813 down the Hudson to Wings—then changed to Glens—Falls, but no one was paying much attention, no one except old Mowatt Raymond down in Albany, who had an eye for the future if ever one had been put in the head of a man. In the 1840s he began buying the land adjoining the Butteses along with thousands of forest acres, big, wild unroaded areas, around Racquette, Tupper and Long Lakes. People tapped their heads and said, *loco*, and turned with one of those superior little smiles that meant, Of course I got a lot more sense, too bad I ain't got his money, I'd really put it to use. . . .

It was timber men talked of now, lumber and board feet and how many logs could be hauled out in a season. The woods resounded with the sound of axes, the crash of felled trees, the footsteps of hard drinking, foolhardy, irresponsible, maniacal sons-of-bitches who were, Cobus's grandfather said, cutting all the wood in sight and killing themselves in river tie-ups or those deadly brawls in town along the spring river run when they got drunk and out of hand and stomped one another with cleated shoes, and he was glad of it. Odder Buttes predicted that when they were finished, those sons-of-bitches, only small pockets of forest here and there would be left, and that only because they had been overlooked in the excitement and rush to push on, and that first growth, virgin wood that had been here since the beginning, would have vanished under the woodsman's axe.

"Terrible men," he said because he was unable to understand them. They had no interest in land. Owning land, farming it, were meaningless concepts to them. The traits that made them heroes in the woods were the very ones that branded them trash in town. Cobus found the idea that the same man could be entirely opposite things simply depending upon the place he was in bewildering. It was impossible for him to balance opposite notions at the same time and come out with any kind of proper picture. Were these men giants? That was what the woodsmen said. They claimed there were men back in the woods who could perform feats no other man in town or on a farm could even attempt. But the townspeople scoffed; fools, they said, reckless fools who ain't got no sense of responsibility, ain't got no sense of proportion—who cares if they can do some of them blame things they say they can. Do them things make any difference? Who will even remember them fool things in three, four years?

We will, the woodsmen said, angry, banging huge fists on the bar slab.

You'll move on, but we'll still be here, the townspeople thought smugly.

Everything was changed. Cobus's grandfather kept saying so, and it was true enough. "Fools runnin' around in Washington *and* fools in the forest," he said, "both of them ruinin' what God made to be set up right, the Landing fillin' up with thieves and Irish, the country gone to hell, and no place better to see it than right here with these land robbers, like the Raymonds, loggin' everythin' in sight."

THE STEVENSONS IN SARANAC
ROBERT LOUIS STEVENSON, MARGARET BALFOUR STEVENSON, AND LLOYD OSBOURNE

In quest of health Robert Louis Stevenson made his home at Baker's in Saranac Lake from October, 1887, to April, 1888. The party included his wife, Fanny; his mother, Margaret Balfour Stevenson; his stepson, Lloyd Osbourne; and Valentine Roch, a Swiss maid. Selections are from the letters of RLS and his mother and from the memoir of his stepson.

Mother, October. The house is built of wooden boards, painted white, with green shutters, and a verandah around it. It belongs to a guide, who takes parties into the woods for shooting and fishing excursions; he usually has boarders, but he and his wife have agreed to give over to us part of the house, their own portion being entirely shut off by double doors. Into our part you enter by the kitchen! . . .

Everything is of the plainest and simplest, but sufficiently comfortable. We are about ten minutes' walk distant from the village and beautifully situated above the river, upon which we look down; the view from our windows is best described as "very highland," but the chief glory just now lies in the autumn colourings, which Louis declares are exactly like the Skelt's theatre scenes, the "two-pence coloured" ones that we used to think so impossible! He is consequently delighted and declares it reminds him of Leith Street and home. . . . Fortunately he has been none the worse of the journey and the long drive in the rain and says that he already feels the air of Saranac doing him good, so I trust we have hit on a place that will really suit him.

Yesterday was a charming day, with Mentone skies and the brightest of sunshines; certainly, if we have a good deal of weather like this we shall think ourselves very well off. And the air is delicious, with a sweetness that again and again reminds me of the Highlands. We now go out for frequent drives.

RLS, October (to Henry James). I know not the day; but the month it is the drear October by the ghoul-haunted woodland of Weir. . . . Our house—emphatically "Baker's"—is on a hill and has a sight of a stream turning a corner in the valley—bless the face of running water!—and sees some hills too, and the paganly prosaic roofs of Saranac itself; the lake it does not see, nor do I regret that; I like water (fresh water I mean) either running swiftly among stones, or else largely qualified with whisky.

Mother, October 27. The weather we find very variable: one day it is fine and almost warm, and the next is very cold with a little snow. I feel very well and strong and can take long walks without being tired; and Louis is wonderfully well for him, though the keen wind prevents him from getting out every day. But every one is enthusiastic about the climate here: I went one day to visit a lady who has been here for four years, and she says she delights in the winter, and is just longing for the frost to set in; the air is delicious then, and you don't feel the cold nearly as much as just now. She told me, also, that a man was once asked to take over the livery stables here, to which he replied, "What, go to Saranac, where the sick folk ride out in all weathers! I should think not, it's enough to kill any horse!"

You call your house the "Barracks"; well, ours is the "Hunters' Home," and Louis will not allow anything to be done that interferes with that illusion. We have in the living room a plain deal table covered with stains; I wanted to put a nice cloth on it, but he would not hear of it. "For what," he cries, "have hunters to do with table-covers?" There is not a footstool in the house, and the draughts along the floor make my feet very cold; so as a special favour to me, a log of wood is to be sawn into suitable pieces to serve as stools and still be in keeping with the "Hunters' Home." There was neither a teapot nor a coffeepot amongst the furnishings, as we believe that here both of these beverages are usually boiled in a saucepan; but we did not mind this, as we had utensils of our own bought for use on the voyage.

What we did suffer from was the absence of a single egg-cup. I went yesterday to the village to see if I could buy any at the store; no such thing was to be had, and the man seemed surprised at our wanting them. He at last suggested that he might give us a small jug that would do, and presently produced one that would certainly have held a full pint! Lloyd gravely asked if he could also supply eggs that would fit it. . . . This morning I bethought myself of my pointed medicine-glass, but alas! the egg was lost in its depths; however, I stuffed the bottom of it with paper and finally ate my egg in triumph. Nothing gives me more pleasure or a better appetite than an obstacle overcome, and these incidents of backwoods life are quite entertaining.

I must give you some account of how we pass our days here. My stove is lit about 6:30 in the morning and warms the room very quickly, so that I can soon sit up to read or write. Louis and Lloyd breakfast rather early and work until lunchtime; when Lou writes in the sitting room, I keep up the fire in my stove and stay in my own room, which is very bright and cheery. If I want to go out without disturbing the two authors, I get out by the window; I wish you could see the performance. . . . At 12:30 we all meet at lunch, and work is pretty well over for the day; at two the buggy arrives, and two of us go for a drive. Louis always takes his walks quite alone and hates even to meet any one when he is out; so it is fortunate that we are some way from the village, and that there is a private pine-wood close behind the house. When he comes in he generally goes to bed till dinner-time, at six o'clock. After dinner we talk and read aloud and play at cards till ten, when we are all ready for bed. You see it is a long day for Louis, who is often up very early; and that he is able for it proves that he is keeping wonderfully well.

RLS, November 21 (to John Addington Symonds). Here we are in a kind of wilderness of hills and fir-woods and boulders and snow and wooden houses. So far as we have gone the climate is grey and harsh, but hungry and somnolent; and although not charming like that of Davos, essentially bracing and briskening. The country is a kind of insane mixture of Scotland and a touch of Switzerland and a dash of America and a thought of the British Channel in the skies.

Mother, November. We have had more snow and very severe frost, with the thermometer down to twenty-five degrees below zero, so you see we were fairly off on one of "Kane's Arctic Voyages." Water froze in our rooms with the stoves kept burning all night; the ink froze on the table beside my bed. Louis woke one night dreaming that a rat was biting his ears, and the cause was a slight frost-bite; and Valentine found her handkerchief, *under her pillow*, frozen into a ball in the morning. How would you like, too, to have your kitchen floor turned into a nice shining sheet of ice the moment you had washed it—with hot water, mind—and a good fire in the room? . . .

Our life here is made up of small interests, and just now, while Louis and I are left to ourselves, it seems oddly like the old days at Heriot Row. Then, when "Papa dined out," Lou and I used to indulge in dishes we were not allowed at other times—particularly rabbit-pie, I remember—and so we do still. I sometimes almost forget that my baby has grown up!

RLS, December (to Miss Adelaide Boodle). I am very well; better than for years: that is for good. But then my wife is no great shakes; the place does not suit her—it is my private opinion that no place does—and she is now away down to New York for a change, which (as Lloyd is in Boston) leaves my mother and me and Valentine alone in our wind-beleaguered hilltop hatbox of a house. You should hear the cows butt against the walls in the early morning while they feed; you should also see our back log when the thermometer goes (as it does go) away—away below zero, till it can be seen no more by the eye of man—not the thermometer, which is still perfectly visible, but the mercury, which curls up into the bulb like a hibernating bear; you should also see the lad who "does chores" for us, with his red stockings and his thirteen-year-old face, and his highly manly tramp into the room; and his two alternative answers to all questions about the weather: either "Cold," or with a really lyrical movement of the voice, "*Lovely—raining!*"

RLS, December (to Sidney Colvin). I walk in my verandy in the

snaw, sir, looking down over one of those dabbled wintry landscapes that are (to be frank) so chilly to the human bosom, and up
at a grey, English—nay, *mehercle*, Scottish—heaven; and I think
it pretty bleak; and the wind swoops at me round the corner, like
a lion, and fluffs the snow in my face; and I could aspire to be elsewhere; but yet I do not catch cold, and yet, when I come in, I eat.
So that hitherto Saranac, if not deliriously delectable, has not been
a failure; nay, from the mere point of view of the wicked body, it
has proved a success. But I wish I could still get to the woods; alas,
nous n'irons plus au bois is my poor song; the paths are buried, the
dingles drifted full, a little walk is grown a long one; till spring
comes, I fear the burthen will hold good.

Mother, January 14. I have a wonderful piece of news for you.
Louis has got a pair of skates and has actually been out skating twice
on the pond at the back of our house, and last Sunday he went for
a sleigh-ride on Saranac Lake. He came back delighted and none
the worse of it; and really he is not only keeping well, but is distinctly a little fatter. We all thought it, but did not like to trust our
eyes till some friends noticed it also.

Yesterday the thermometer never rose above zero even in the
sun, and yet Lloyd and I drove ten miles and enjoyed it. I must,
however, tell you the garments I wore. I had my sealskin jacket
under my fur-lined cloak, my tweed cap, with knitted ear-covers
added under the tweed ones, and thick knitted veil, and my long
wool wrap twisted round and round over all. Then I had muffatees,
silk, and double woollen mittens on top, *and* a muff! We had each
a hot soap-stone for our feet, and if we had only had the small ones
which I have ordered (but which have not yet arrived) for our
hands, I think we would have been very complete. We felt exactly
as if we were travelling in Siberia, all the people we met looked so
like pictures one has seen of life there. We begin to think, now,
that if the climate is like this, the exiles may have a better time than
we used to suppose. For, as I said before, we really do not feel the
cold so much as we often do at home, and we all keep well, Louis
quite wonderfully so. Indeed he seems to feel the cold less than any

of us, and he skates a little every day and enjoys it, which is a capital sign of his health.

This morning I found both milk and water frozen quite hard in my bedroom, and the thermometer has been down to forty degrees below zero during the night. Hence some further experiences from "Kane's Voyages": Louis's buffalo coat was frozen fast to the kitchen door, behind which it hangs, though the fire was kept alight in the stove all through the night.

RLS, March (to Sidney Colvin). I am, as you may gather from this, wonderfully better: this harsh, grey, glum, doleful climate has done me good. You cannot fancy how sad a climate it is. When the thermometer stays all day below 10°, it is really cold; and when the wind blows, O commend me to the result. Pleasure in life is all delete; there is no red spot left, fires do not radiate, you burn your hands all the time on what seem to be cold stones. It is odd, zero is like summer heat to us now; and we like, when the thermometer outside is really low, a room at about 48°: 60° we find oppressive. Yet the natives keep their holes at 90° or even 100°.

Mother, March. I got back here on Friday, very much worn out, and much as I had enjoyed my visit, very happy to return home and find Louis really getting *quite fat* on his koumiss, and remarkably well. But when a few hours had elapsed, I had good cause to feel even more thankful to find myself safe at home; for we have just had the worst snowstorm of the season [the blizzard of '88, March 11-14], and our house was nearly buried in lovely snowdrifts. They looked so pure and so exquisite when seen through the window that I longed to dive into their downy softness, but refrained; I suspect it was a case in which distance lent enchantment to the view. All the railroad lines were blocked up, telegraphic and telephonic communication stopped, and we were for three days completely shut off from the outer world; but this is the first time that Saranac has been so entirely isolated, and even this time we really suffered on the whole less than in most parts, and save when the snow was falling there has been a good deal of sunshine and not much severe cold. Imagine how thankful I am, however, to have been snowed *in,* and not *out of,* the "Hunter's Home"!

RLS, April (to Miss Ferrier). A bleak, blackguard, beggarly climate, of which I can say no good except that it suits me and some others of the same or similar persuasions whom (by all rights) it ought to kill. It is a form of Arctic St. Andrews, I should imagine; and the miseries of forty degrees below zero, with a high wind, have to be felt to be appreciated. The greyness of the heavens here is a circumstance eminently revolting to the soul; I have near forgot the aspect of the sun—I doubt if this be news; it is certainly no news to us. My mother suffers a little from the inclemency of the place, but less on the whole than would be imagined. Among other wild schemes, we have been projecting yacht voyages.

Mother, April 7. It is odd that now, the beginning of April, we feel the cold much more than we did in midwinter. We have had many showers of snow, interspersed with thaws, and there is a generally dirty look everywhere; last night it froze again, the thermometer was down to six degrees above zero, and today it has never been higher than twenty degrees; and that is really too much of a good thing on the seventh of April. Louis has been a good deal in bed this week, as much to keep himself warm as for any more serious reason; he cannot write in this weather, and yet he wants to finish some work before we start on our travels. The doctor is anxious he should return here in July and camp out in the woods.

Mother, April 15. Louis and I left Saranac suddenly on Friday. Louis had been wearying for a change, and we had proposed to start on our travels tomorrow; Lloyd was in quarantine with a cold, I was low and out of sorts, and the weather was simply detestable. . . . He is looking wonderfully well and fatter than he has done for long, so we have much reason to be thankful for what Saranac has done for us. —It certainly is a wonderful place.

Lloyd Osbourne. Saranac suited R L S extremely well. He gained in weight; his spectral aspect disappeared; in a buffalo coat and astrakhan cap he would pace the veranda for hours, inhaling that piercing air which was so noticeably benefiting him. He worked hard, hard and well, first on a series of essays for *Scribner's Magazine*—"Random Memories," "A Chapter on Dreams," "Beggars," "The Lantern-Bearers," "Letters to a Young Gentleman Who Proposes to Embrace the Career of Art," "Pulvis et Umbra," "A Christmas Sermon," and others; then on *The Master of Ballantrae*, which he half finished; and then, at the close of our stay and in a whirlwind three weeks of industry, on *The Wrong Box*—my own book, which had cost me a winter's toil.

This collaboration, if so it may be called, was conceived on the spur of the moment. R L S had finished the reading of my final draft, and I was sitting on the side of his bed in no little suspense for his verdict. It meant a great deal to me, for S. S. McClure had promised to publish the book if R L S thought it good enough.

"Lloyd, it is really not at all bad," he said musingly. . . . "It made my fingers itch as I read it. Why, I could take up that book and in one quick, easy rewriting could make it sing!"

Our eyes met; it was all decided in that one glance.

"By God, why shouldn't I!" he exclaimed. "That is, if you don't mind?"

Mind!

I was transported with joy. What would-be writer of nineteen would not have been? It was my vindication; the proof I had not been living in a fool's paradise, and had indeed talent, and a future.

McClure, to whom I have just alluded, was then in the beginning of his meteoric career. . . . He was ready at a moment's notice to take fire with excitement and to soar into the azure of dreams and millions from which Stevenson had constantly to pull him down by the legs, so to speak.

But to one of his many plans R L S responded with unqualified enthusiasm—to charter a large yacht and to sail away for half a year or more in the Indian or Pacific oceans, supporting the enterprise by monthly letters, which McClure was to syndicate at enormous mutual profit, guaranteed beforehand. It was undeniably practicable—no azure here, no pulling down of those slender legs— all R L S had to say was which ocean and when.

Ah, the happy times we had, with outspread maps and Findlay's Directories of the World! . . . Such was our reading, such the stuff our dreams were made of as the snow drove against our frozen windows; as the Arctic day closed in, gloomy and wild, and snow-shoes and buffalo coats were put by to steam in corners while we gathered round the lamp. Visions of palms while our ears were yet tingling from the snow we had rubbed on to save them from frostbite; cascading streams in tropic Arcadies, with water as clear as crystal, while our own bedroom jugs upstairs were as solid as so much rock; undraped womanhood, bedecked with flowers, frisking in vales of Eden, while we were wooled to the neck like polar explorers and dared not even thaw too quickly for fear of chilblains. . . .

When my mother left us in the spring to visit her sister in California . . . R L S had said at parting:

"If you *should* find a yacht out there, mind you take it."

Six weeks later came the telegram that was to have such a far-reaching effect on our lives.

"*Can secure splendid sea-going schooner yacht 'Casco' for seven hundred and fifty a month with most comfortable accommodation for six aft and six forward. Can be ready for sea in ten days. Reply immediately,*

Fanny."

Stevenson answered:

"*Blessed girl, take the yacht and expect us in ten days,*

Louis."

❧ THE WAY OF THE LAKE
Theodore Dreiser

The following scene from *An American Tragedy* is more imagina-
tive than the narration of the murder itself, in which Dreiser reproduced with painstaking fidelity the circumstances of the drowning
of Grace Brown (Roberta) by Chester E. Gillette (Clyde Griffiths)
in a Herkimer County lake on July 11, 1906.

The preceding day—a day of somewhat reduced activities
on the lakes from which he had just returned—he and Sondra and
Stuart and Bertine, together with Nina Temple and a youth named
Harley Baggott, then visiting the Thurstons, had motored first
from Twelfth Lake to Three Mile Bay, a small lakeside resort
some twenty-five miles north, and from thence, between towering
walls of pines, to Big Bittern and some other smaller lakes lost
in the recesses of the tall pines of the region to the north of Trine
Lake. And en route, Clyde, as he now recalled, had been most
strangely impressed at moments and in spots by the desolate and
for the most part lonely character of the region. The narrow and
rain-washed and even rutted nature of the dirt roads that wound
between tall, silent and darksome trees—forests in the largest sense
of the word—that extended for miles and miles apparently on
either hand. The decadent and weird nature of some of the bogs
and tarns on either side of the only comparatively passable dirt
roads which here and there were festooned with funereal or viper-
ous vines, and strewn like deserted battlefields with soggy and
decayed piles of fallen and criss-crossed logs—in places as many
as four deep—one above the other—in the green slime that an
undrained depression in the earth had accumulated. The eyes and
backs of occasional frogs that, upon lichen or vine or moss-covered
stumps and rotting logs in this warm June weather, there sunned
themselves apparently undisturbed; the spirals of gnats, the solitary
flick of a snake's tail as disturbed by the sudden approach of the
machine, one made off into the muck and the poisonous grasses
and water-plants which were thickly imbedded in it.

And in seeing one of these Clyde, for some reason, had thought of the accident at Pass Lake. He did not realize it, but at the moment his own subconscious need was contemplating the loneliness and the usefulness at times of such a lone spot as this. And at one point it was that a wier-wier, one of the solitary water-birds of this region, uttered its ouphe and barghest cry, flying from somewhere near into some darker recess within the woods. And at this sound it was that Clyde had stirred nervously and then sat up in the car. It was so very different to any bird-cry he had ever heard anywhere.

"What was that?" he asked of Harley Baggott, who sat next him.

"What?"

"Why, that bird or something that just flew away back there just now?"

"I didn't hear any bird."

"Gee! That was a queer sound. It makes me feel creepy."

As interesting and impressive as anything else to him in this almost tenantless region had been the fact that there were so many lonesome lakes, not one of which he had ever heard of before. The territory through which they were speeding as fast as the dirt roads would permit, was dotted with them in these deep forests of pine. And only occasionally in passing near one were there any signs indicating a camp or lodge, and those to be reached only by some half-blazed trail or rutty or sandy road disappearing through darker trees. In the main, the shores of the more remote lakes passed were all but untenanted, or so sparsely that a cabin or a distant lodge to be seen across the smooth waters of some pine-encircled gem was an object of interest to all.

Why must he think of that other lake in Massachusetts! That boat! The body of that girl found—but not that of the man who accompanied her! How terrible, really!

He recalled afterwards—here in his room, after this last conversation with Roberta—that the car, after a few more miles, had finally swung into an open space at the north end of a long narrow lake—the south prospect of which appeared to be divided by a point or an island suggesting a greater length and further windings or curves than were visible from where the car had stopped. And except for the small lodge and boathouse at this upper end it had appeared so very lonesome—not a launch or canoe on it at the time their party arrived. And as in the case of all the other lakes seen this day, the banks to the very shore line were sentineled with those same green pines—tall, spear-shaped—their arms widespread like one outside his window here in Lycurgus. And beyond them in the distance, to the south and west, rose the humped and still smooth and green backs of the nearer Adirondacks. And the water before them, now ruffled by a light wind and glowing in the after-noon sun, was of an intense Prussian blue, almost black, which suggested, as was afterwards confirmed by a guide who was loung-ing upon the low veranda of the small inn, that it was very deep —"all of seventy feet not more than a hundred feet out from that boathouse."

And at this point Harley Baggott, who was interested to learn more about the fishing possibilities of this lake in behalf of his father, who contemplated coming to this region in a few days, had inquired of the guide who appeared not to look at the others in the car: "How long is this lake, anyhow?"

"Oh, about seven miles." "Any fish in it?" "Throw a line in and see. The best place for black bass and the like of that almost anywhere around here. Off the island down yonder, or just to the south of it round on the other side there, there's a little bay that's said to be one of the best fishin' holes in any of the lakes up this way. I've seen a coupla men bring back as many as seventy-five fish in two hours. That oughta satisfy anybody that ain't tryin' to ruin the place for the rest of us."

The guide, a thinnish, tall and wizened type, with a long, narrow head and small, keen, bright blue eyes laughed a yokelish laugh as he studied the group. "Not thinkin' of tryin' your luck today?"

"No, just inquiring for my dad. He's coming up here next week, maybe. I want to see about accommodations."

"Well, they ain't what they are down to Racquette, of course, but then the fish down there ain't what they are up here, either." He visited all with a sly and wry and knowing smile.

Clyde had never seen the type before. He was interested by all the anomalies and contrarities of this lonesome world as contrasted with cities he had known almost exclusively, as well as the decidedly exotic and material life and equipment with which, at the Cranstons' and elsewhere, he was then surrounded. The strange and comparatively deserted nature of this region as contrasted with the brisk and vigorous life of Lycurgus, less than a hundred miles to the south.

"The country up here kills me," commented Stuart Finchley at this point. "It's so near the Chain and yet it's so different, scarcely any one living up here at all, it seems."

"Well, except for the camps in summer and the fellows that come up to hunt moose and deer in the fall, there ain't much of anybody or anything around here after September first," commented the guide. "I've been guidin' and trappin' for nigh onto seventeen years now around here and 'cept for more and more people around some of the lakes below here—the Chain principally in summer—I ain't see much change. You need to know this country purty well if yer goin' to strike out anywhere away from the main roads, though o' course about five miles to the west o' here is the railroad. Gun Lodge is the station. We bring 'em by bus from there in the summer. And from the south end down there is a sorta road leadin' down to Greys Lake and Three Mile Bay. You musta come along a part of it, since it's the only road up into this country as yet. They're talkin' of cuttin' one through to Long Lake sometime, but so far it's mostly talk. But from most of these other lakes around here, there's no road at all, not that an automobile could make. Just trails and there's not even a decent camp on some o' 'em. You have to bring your own outfit. But Ellis and me was over to Gun Lake last summer—that's thirty miles west o' here and we had to walk every inch of the way and carry our packs. But, oh, say, the fishin' and moose and deer come right down to the shore in places to drink. See 'em as plain as that stump across the lake."

And Clyde remembered that, along with the others, he had carried away the impression that for solitude and charm—or at least mystery—this region could scarcely be matched. And to think it was all so comparatively near Lycurgus—not more than a hundred miles by road; not more than seventy by rail, as he eventually came to know.

But now once more in Lycurgus and back in his room after just explaining to Roberta, as he had, he once more encountered on his writing desk the identical paper containing the item concerning the tragedy at Pass Lake. And in spite of himself, his eye once more followed nervously and yet unwaveringly to the last word all the suggestive and provocative details. The uncomplicated and apparently easy way in which the lost couple had first arrived at the boathouse; the commonplace and entirely unsuspicious way in which they had hired a boat and set forth for a row; the manner in which they had disappeared to the north end; and then the up-turned boat, the floating oars and hats near the shore. He stood reading in the still strong evening light. Outside the windows were the dark boughs of the fir tree of which he had thought the preceding day and which now suggested all those firs and pines about the shores of Big Bittern.

But, good God! What was he thinking of anyhow? He, Clyde Griffiths! The nephew of Samuel Griffiths! What was "getting into" him? Murder! That's what it was. This terrible item—this devil's accident or machination that was constantly putting it before him! A most horrible crime, and one for which they electrocuted people if they were caught. Besides, he could not murder anybody—not Roberta, anyhow. Oh, no! Surely not after all that had been between them. And yet—this other world!—Sondra—which he was certain to lose now unless he acted in some way—

His hands shook, his eyelids twitched—then his hair at the roots tingled and over his body ran chill nervous titillations in waves. Murder! Or upsetting a boat at any rate in deep water, which of course might happen anywhere, and by accident, as at Pass Lake. And Roberta could not swim. He knew that. But she might save herself at that—scream—cling to the boat—and then—if there were any to hear—and she told afterwards! An icy perspiration now sprang to his forehead; his lips trembled and suddenly his throat felt parched and dry. To prevent a thing like that he would have to—to—but no—he was not like that. He could not do a thing like that—hit any one—a girl—Roberta—and when drowning or struggling. Oh, no, no—no such thing as that! Impossible.

He took his straw hat and went out, almost before any one heard him *think*, as he would have phrased it to himself, such horrible, terrible thoughts. He could not and would not think them from now on. He was no such person. And yet—and yet—these thoughts. The solution—if he wanted one. The way to stay here —not leave—marry Sondra—be rid of Roberta and all—all—for the price of a little courage or daring. But no!

He walked and walked—away from Lycurgus—out on a road to the southeast which passed through a poor and decidedly unfrequented rural section, and so left him alone to think—or, as he felt, not to be heard in his thinking.

Day was fading into dark. Lamps were beginning to glow in the cottages here and there. Trees in groups in fields or along the road were beginning to blur or smokily blend. And although it was warm—the air lifeless and lethargic—he walked fast, thinking, and perspiring as he did so, as though he were seeking to outwalk and outthink or divert some inner self that preferred to be still and think.

That gloomy, lonely lake up there!

That island to the south!

Who would see?

Who could hear?

🌿 DEER IN THE STORM
HUGH FOSBURGH

This is one of those days when a man doesn't go out unless he has to—there is a fiendish blizzard in progress. The wind is blasting out of the northwest, driving a heavy granular snow that is swirling and drifting in the lees, the visibility is about fifty yards and the thermometer reads ten below zero. From where I sit in the warmth and snug security of the living room, it is a cruel, lovely thing to watch.

A while ago, I saw a small deer on the edge of the woods—for some reason it came into the open, stood in abject drooping despair for a minute or two, then turned and wallowed back into the balsams.

I wondered how long it was going to live and where it would lie down to die.

I don't remember by exactly what sequence of whimsies it came about, but I got to thinking about American landscape painters and the treatment they give to the wilderness and the world of nature. I concluded, arbitrarily, that the treatment was generally superficial indeed. Our painters, with few exceptions, notably Winslow Homer, rarely come to grips with nature—they carry on a sporadic good-time flirtation with it which in the end results merely in the evocation of nostalgia. Nostalgia is a fine genuine sentiment, with nothing sentimental about it, and it has a proper and rightful place in landscape painting, but it's not enough because it precludes the very essence of nature—its innate cruelty. You can't evoke any nostalgia from the storm that is presently raging or from the predicament of that deer down there in the woods.

I turned to thinking about how I would paint the wilderness world if I could (a ridiculous hypothesis) and started making a list.

I would paint that deer I just saw. I would paint it newly dead and enjoying the first tranquillity it has ever known and, staring at it, would be a lovely sleek bobcat.

I would paint another deer—a doe just delivered of her fawn, with the fawn standing on shaky legs and trying to suck, and the snow swirling about them. I would call it "Spring Blizzard."

I would paint that lovely sleek bobcat, dead and just removed from a trap, and the man who has caught it is testing the sharpness of his skinning knife against the hairs on his wrist.

I would paint that trapper—he has broken through the ice far from shore and he is fighting to live; and all the tools of his trade

—his snowshoes, his pack basket, his traps, his ax, and the rifle on his back—are weighing him down. I would call it "Rotten Ice."

I would paint the men who work in the wilderness and get their living from it and who, by working in it, necessarily destroy some part of it. I would paint the lumberjacks and hunters and loggers and trappers at their ruthless work, and I would try to show that what they were doing was inevitable and right and that they loved the thing they were destroying.

I would paint abandoned lumber camps, and tumbledown cabins, and rotting sawdust piles—the feeble monuments these men leave.

In my still-lifes I would paint the tools of destruction they use —the axes, carbines, saws, cant hooks, knives, and chains—all of them lethal and efficient and beautiful. In particular I would paint an old bear trap that I have—a monstrous hand-forged fascinating thing, perhaps an evil thing.

The wilderness world is like that trap, and I would try to paint it that way.

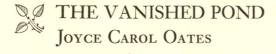

THE VANISHED POND
Joyce Carol Oates

Whenever he can, the child Raphael Bellefleur flees the robust and often violent life of the Bellefleur castle on Lake Noir, set in a half real, half mythical Adirondacks. He finds a private world of solace and delight at Mink Pond, his discovery. The pond whispers to him, "Come here, come here to me, I will take you in. I will give you new life." Then one day—

Where, everyone wondered, was poor Raphael . . .?
The undersized child with his pale, clammy skin, and that furtive expression tinged with a melancholy irony, the son of Ewan's

who could not possibly *be*, Ewan thought, his son, or the son of
any Bellefleur, was seen less and less frequently that summer until,
finally, one morning, it was discovered that he had simply vanished.

Raphael, they called, Raphael . . .?

Where are you hiding?

At family gatherings Raphael had always been distracted and
reluctant, and he was so frequently absent (he hadn't, for instance,
gone to Morna's wedding) that it was several days before anyone
actually *missed* him. And then only because one of the upstairs
maids reported to Lily that his bed hadn't been slept in for three
nights running.

They went in search of him to Mink Pond, of course. Albert led
the way, shouting his name. . . . But where was Mink Pond? It
seemed, oddly, that Mink Pond too had vanished.

By midsummer the pond had shrunk to a half-dozen shallow
puddles, grown over with grasses and willow shrubs; by late summer, when Raphael was discovered missing, nothing remained but
a marshy area. It was a meadow, really. Part of the large grassy
meadow below the cemetery.

Where was Mink Pond, the Bellefleurs asked in astonishment.

A low-lying marshy ground, where bright mustard grew, and
lush green grasses, and willow trees. It gave off a rich pleasant
odor of damp and decay, even in the bright sunshine.

We must be standing in it, they said. Standing on it. Where it
once was.

But looking down they saw nothing: only a meadow.

Raphael, they cried. Raphael. . . . Where have you gone? Why
are you hiding from us?

Their feet sank in the spongy earth, and their shoes were soon
wet and muddy. How cold, their surprised wriggling toes . . .!
Germaine ran and chattered and giggled and slipped and fell but
immediately scrambled to her feet again. Then they saw that she
wasn't giggling: she had begun to cry. Her face was contorted.

Raphael! Raphael! Raphael!

In Lily's arms she hid her face, and pointed toward the ground.
Raphael—*there*.

After a search of many hours, up along Mink Creek (which had narrowed to a trickle of peculiar rust-tinged water that smelled flat and metallic) and back through the cemetery into the woods, and a mile or two into the hills, they returned to Mink Pond again —to what had been Mink Pond—and saw that their footprints were covered over, in rich green grass.

Raphael? Raphael?

Was there a pond here, really, one of the visiting cousins asked.

It was here. Or maybe over there.

Here, below the cemetery.

By those willows.

No—by that stump. Where the redwings are roosting.

A pond? Here? But when? How long ago?

Only a week ago!

No, a month ago.

Last year.

They wandered about, calling Raphael's name, though they knew it was hopeless. He had been so slight-bodied, so furtive and pale, no one had known him well, none of the children had liked him, Lily wept to think she hadn't loved him enough—not *enough* —and now he had gone to live beneath the earth (for, after Germaine's hysterical outburst, Lily was never to be placated, or argued out of her absurd conviction) and would not heed her cries.

Raphael, she called, where have you gone? Why are you hiding from us?

Ewan, hearing about the pond, and his little niece's words, went out to investigate. But the pond of course was gone: there *was* no pond.

He stamped about, a thickset, muscular man, graying, ruddy-faced, somewhat short of breath. His stomach strained against the attractive blue-gray material of his officer's shirt; his booted heels came down hard in the moist soil. Long ago he had shaved off his beard (for it displeased his mistress Rosalind) but now an irregular patch of gray stubble covered his jaw and a good deal of his cheeks.

It was absurd, this business about the pond. There had never been a pond here. Ewan remembered quite clearly a pond over back of the apple orchard, in which he and his brothers had played as children—*that* pond still remained, probably—but he hadn't the energy to search for it.

Nor, curiously, had he the energy to search for Raphael. After losing Yolande, and then Garth . . .

He stared down at the moist marshy earth beneath his feet. It was just a meadow, good grazing land, rich with grass, probably fertile beneath. If it were fifty years ago they would plow it up and plant it, possibly in winter wheat; but now everything was changed; now. . . . He could not remember what he had been thinking.

For a long while Leah's and Gideon's strange little girl (about whom her grandmother Cornelia said with a mysterious smile, Ah, but Germaine isn't as odd as she *might* be!) refused to walk on the lawn, even in the walled garden where she had always played. She wept, she began to scream hysterically, if someone tried to lead her out; the graveled walks were all right but the lawns terrified her. If it was absolutely necessary that she cross a lawn, why then Nightshade (who did not at all mind the task, and reddened, like a proud papa, with pleasure) had to carry her.

But aren't you a silly, willful girl, Leah scolded. And all because of some nonsense about your cousin Raphael. . . .

The little girl frequently began to cry at the very mention of that name, and so the others, even Leah, soon stopped pronouncing it in her presence. And very soon they stopped pronouncing it at all: for, it seemed, young Raphael had simply vanished: there *was* no Raphael.

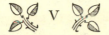

As It Happened

There was funny things that happened in the woods.
Bub Stowe, quoted in Robert Bethke's *Adirondack Voices*

ADIRONDACK PEOPLE were puzzled by W. H. H. Murray's book *Adventures in the Wilderness*. The reverend author said many nice things about the people and the places of the Adirondacks, and these things were true. But there were also those chapters about the trout of Nameless Creek and the ghost of Phantom Falls. Murray must be a liar, some concluded. So many strange things happen in the woods that Adirondack people don't see why anyone has to make up fiction.

True, tall tales about the exploits of Paul Bunyan and other heroes circulated in the lumber camps around the turn of the century. Most of these were migratory and were imported by roving lumberjacks. A superficial air of belonging was grafted on them by the introduction of local place names. But Paul Bunyan was never really at home in the Adirondacks. In the long run Adirondack people like the plain truth, or the truth only slightly elaborated. The hero who suits them best is not the outsized Paul but the little census-taker up in Keene, Anson Allen, who when forced to fight the bear, limited his expectation of Providence to the modest prayer:

"If you don't help me, don't help the bear."

Likewise a genuinely indigenous story-teller shied away from immoderate boasting when the yarn concerned himself. Mart Moody of Big Tupper, who entertained two Presidents, was not above acknowledging that there were some fixes he couldn't get out of. One of his most celebrated stories concerned two bears that were chasing him. Thinking fast, he led the bears into a ravine so narrow that they could attack him only one at a time. Then Mart saw a third bear up front. At this point his story came to an abrupt halt. He started to walk away. Only under pressure would he tell the outcome, with the admission that he was no Paul Bunyan. "The bears et me," he would say, and turning to his wife if she was around, "Ain't that so, Minervy?"

There are several collections of Adirondack folk songs and yarns. The latest and certainly one of the best, dealing with the northwest sector of the park, is *Adirondack Voices* (1981). In it Robert Bethke, a trained folklorist, captures the remnants of a tradition that would soon have passed into oblivion. These native yarns are mostly of oral provenance. They need a voice and a personality to breathe life into them and to bridge the occasional prolixity. When reduced to print, they are of great interest to the folklorist and the sociologist but have limited appeal to the general reader. That is my apology for including only two native ballads.

Most of the stories in this section were intended for the printed page. They are by city men for whom the woods were a periodic escape from their ordinary lives. This double life of escape and return gives their stories a perspective absent from native yarns: a heightened sense of wonder, a source of humor in the fumbles of the urbanite when left to his own devices in the woods. Both of these resources, the wonder and the comedy, are present in Charles Dudley Warner's *In the Wilderness*. The stories and essays of this book are a necessary corrective to the heroic posture of Murray's city man in the woods in *Adventures in the Wilderness*. Warner introduces us to the anti-hero or, as in "How I Killed a Bear" here excerpted, to the hero in spite of himself. His book is as fresh today as it was a century ago. It is a neglected classic of Adirondack literature and of American humor.

AT CALAMITY POND
ALFRED L. DONALDSON

The works [McIntyre Iron Works] had grown so that the supply of water was sometimes inadequate in dry weather. Various plans for increasing it were discussed, but no steps were taken till September, 1845. Then the company's engineer Daniel Taylor suggested combining the two branches of the Hudson River at a point where they were only a few miles apart. To investigate the feasibility of doing this a party was formed, consisting of Mr. [David] Henderson, his ten-year-old son Archie, Mr. Taylor, and "Tony" Snyder and John Cheney, the well-known guides. They took knapsacks and provisions with them and prepared to camp out over night. They had not gone very far when they came to a little pond known as "the duck hole." A number of ducks were swimming about it.

"Take my pistol and kill some of those ducks," said Mr. Henderson to Cheney. The guide took the pistol, but before he could get a shot at the ducks they flew away. He thereupon handed the pistol back to Mr. Henderson, who slipped it into his belt and moved away to join the rest of the party at the head of the little lake.

John Cheney stayed behind to catch some trout in place of the lost ducks. Just as he had fixed his line and dropped it into the water, he heard the report of a pistol. Looking in the direction whence it came, he saw Mr. Henderson in a stooping posture, and Mr. Taylor and Snyder, who had been gathering wood, hurrying to his side. Cheney then realized that something was wrong and ran to the spot. Mr. Henderson had meanwhile fallen to the ground, and when Cheney reached him he looked up and said:

"John, you must have left the pistol cocked."

The guide was too overwhelmed to make any answer. Then Mr. Henderson looked around him and said:

"This is a horrible place for a man to die." A moment later he motioned his son to his side and added, gently: "Archie, be a good boy, and give my love to your mother."

That was all. His lips kept moving a while as if in prayer, and then, fifteen minutes after being shot, he breathed his last. He had thrown his knapsack and belt, in which was the pistol, on a rock, and in falling the open hammer was struck and the weapon discharged. A bed of balsam boughs was made and the body laid upon it. This done, Snyder hurried to the village to get help. On reaching it he kept his errand as quiet as possible, but as he started back with a number of men carrying lanterns, axes, and other tools, so unusual a sight could not fail to attract attention in the little hamlet. Women ran out of the houses to inquire what had happened, and among them were Mrs. Henderson and her little daughter Maggie. On learning that an accident had occurred, the child had an intuitive foreboding of the truth and began crying out: "Papa is shot! Papa is shot!" And so the fact transpired.

On the way back Snyder detailed some of the men to cut out trees and bushes and widen the narrow trail for the passing of the corpse. This became the path used by tourists on their way to Mount Marcy. J. T. Headley, the historian, passed over it the following year with John Cheney as his guide. The latter pointed out the spot where the returning party, overtaken by darkness, had been forced to spend the night. The rough poles on which the corpse had rested and the signs of the big fire that had been built were still visible. "Here," said Cheney, indicating a log, "I sat all night and held Mr. Henderson's little son in my arms. It was a dreadful night."

The remains reached the village the next morning, and a rude coffin was constructed for them. A despatch was sent to Russell Root of Root's Center, on the Schroon River, requesting him to meet the funeral party at Wise's Shanty on the "cartage" road. This was only partly completed at the time, and the body had to be taken to Tahawus first. From there it had to be carried ten miles on men's shoulders over a rough trail till the road was reached. Here Root was waiting with a team and drove the party to Lake Champlain, where they took a steamboat en route to Jersey City. . . .

Mr. Henderson was a man of unusual business ability. He had great energy and enterprise, backed by sound principles, financial acumen, and considerable scientific knowledge. He was of a genial, cordial, cheery disposition and very popular with the men at the works, in whose lives and welfare he took a personal interest. He was a player on the violin and would often help to while away the long evenings by playing for the men and their families to sing and dance.

The "duck hole" where he was shot has ever since been called "Calamity Pond," and the brook that flows from it and a near-by mountain now bear the same name. The tiny pond lies about a three hours' tramp to the east of Lake Henderson and near Lake Colden, and in this remote, deserted spot, where only a straggling hunter or fisherman strays, stands one of the most unexpected sights in the wilderness—a beautifully carved stone memorial, bearing this inscription:

THIS MONUMENT
ERECTED BY FILIAL AFFECTION
TO THE MEMORY OF
OUR DEAR FATHER
DAVID HENDERSON
WHO ACCIDENTALLY LOST
HIS LIFE ON THIS SPOT
3RD SEPTEMBER 1845

Beneath the inscription, in high relief, are a chalice, a book, and an anchor. The monument is of Nova Scotia freestone, eight feet high, and weighs a ton. The difficulties and expense of placing it where it stands were, naturally, great. It was drawn in by oxen in winter over a specially improvised roadway, and there it stands, a touching tribute of affection and yet a strange anomaly, for seldom indeed does a human being pass that way to gaze upon it.

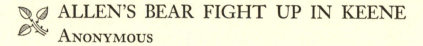

ALLEN'S BEAR FIGHT UP IN KEENE
ANONYMOUS

> Anson H. Allen, printer and newspaper editor, while taking the census of Essex County in 1840, encountered a bear on the wild and lonely "tight-nipping" Biddlecome road from Keene Flats to North Elba. He boasted of his exploit, and an unknown poet of the people commemorated it in the best and most widely known popular ballad of Adirondack origin.

Of all the wonders of the day,
There's one that I can safely say
Will stand upon the rolls of fame,
To let all know bold Allen's name.
The greatest fight that e'er was seen
Was Allen's bear fight up in Keene.

In 1840, as I've heard,
To take the census off he steered.
Through bush and wood for little gain,
He walked from Keene to Abram's plain;
But naught of this—it is not well
His secret motives thus to tell.

As through the wood he trudged his way,
His mind unruffled as the day,

He heard a deep convulsive sound
Which shook the earth and trees around,
And looking up with dread amaze,
An old she-bear there met his gaze.

The bear with threatening aspect stood
To prove her title to the wood.
This Allen saw with darkening frown;
He reached and pulled a young tree down;
Then on his guard, with cautious care,
He watched the movements of the bear.

Against the rock with giant strength
He held her out at his arm's length.
"Oh, God!" he cried in deep despair,
"If you don't help me, don't help the bear."
'Twas rough and tumble, tit for tat,
The nut cakes fell from Allen's hat.

Then from his pocket forth he drew
A large jack-knife for her to view.
He raised his arm high in the air,
And butcher-like, he killed the bear.

Let old men talk of courage bold,
Of battles fought in days of old,
Ten times as bad, but none I ween
Can match a bear fight up in Keene.

HOW I KILLED A BEAR
CHARLES DUDLEY WARNER

So many conflicting accounts have appeared about my casual encounter with an Adirondack bear last summer that in justice to the public, to myself, and to the bear it is necessary to make a plain statement of the facts. Besides, it is so seldom I have occasion to kill a bear that the celebration of the exploit may be excused.

The encounter was unpremeditated on both sides. I was not hunting for a bear, and I have no reason to suppose that a bear was looking for me. The fact is that we were both out blackberrying and met by chance—the usual way. There is among the Adirondack visitors always a great deal of conversation about bears—a general expression of the wish to see one in the woods and much speculation as to how a person would act if he or she chanced to meet one. But bears are scarce and timid, and appear only to a favored few.

It was a warm day in August, just the sort of day when an adventure of any kind seemed impossible. But it occurred to the housekeepers at our cottage—there were four of them—to send me to the clearing on the mountain back of the house to pick blackberries. It was rather a series of small clearings, running up into the forest, much overgrown with bushes and briers and not unromantic. Cows pastured there, penetrating through the leafy passages from one opening to another and browsing among the bushes. I was kindly furnished with a six-quart pail and told not to be gone long.

Not from any predatory instinct, but to save appearances, I took a gun. It adds to the manly aspect of a person with a tin pail if he also carries a gun. It was possible I might start up a partridge; though how I was to hit him, if he started up instead of standing still, puzzled me. Many people use a shot-gun for partridges. I prefer the rifle: it makes a clean job of death and does not prematurely stuff the bird with globules of lead. . . .

In this blackberry-patch bears had been seen. The summer before, our colored cook, accompanied by a little girl of the vicinage, was picking berries there one day when a bear came out of the woods and walked towards them. The girl took to her heels and escaped. Aunt Chloe was paralyzed with terror. Instead of attempting to run, she sat down on the ground where she was standing and began to weep and scream, giving herself up for lost. The bear was bewildered by this conduct. He approached and looked at her; he walked around and surveyed her. Probably he had never seen a colored person before and did not know whether she would agree with him; at any rate, after watching her a few moments, he turned about and went into the forest. This is an authentic instance of the delicate consideration of a bear and is much more remarkable than the forbearance towards the African slave of the well-known lion, because the bear had no thorn in his foot.

When I had climbed the hill, I set up my rifle against a tree and began picking berries, lured on from bush to bush by the black gleam of fruit (that always promises more in the distance than it realizes when you reach it); penetrating farther and farther, through leaf-shaded cow-paths flecked with sunlight, into clearing after clearing. I could hear on all sides the tinkle of bells, the cracking of sticks, and the stamping of cattle that were taking refuge in the thicket from the flies. Occasionally, as I broke through a covert, I encountered a meek cow, who stared at me stupidly for a second and then shambled off into the brush. I became accustomed to this dumb society and picked on in silence, attributing all the wood-noises to the cattle, thinking nothing of any real bear. . . .

I happened to look some rods away to the other edge of the clearing, and there was a bear! He was standing on his hind-legs and doing just what I was doing—picking blackberries. With one paw he bent down the bush while with the other he clawed the berries into his mouth—green ones and all. To say that I was astonished is inside the mark. I suddenly discovered that I didn't want to see a bear, after all. At about the same moment the bear saw me, stopped eating berries, and regarded me with a glad surprise. It is all very well to imagine what you would do under such circumstances. Probably you wouldn't do it; I didn't. The bear dropped down on his fore-feet and came slowly towards me. Climbing a

tree was of no use, with so good a climber in the rear. If I started
to run, I had no doubt the bear would give chase; and although a
bear cannot run down hill as fast as he can run up hill, yet I felt
that he could get over this rough, brush-tangled ground faster than
I could.

The bear was approaching. It suddenly occurred to me how I
could divert his mind until I could fall back upon my military base.
My pail was nearly full of excellent berries—much better than the
bear could pick himself. I put the pail on the ground and slowly
backed away from it, keeping my eye, as beast-tamers do, on the
bear. The ruse succeeded.

The bear came up to the berries and stopped. Not accustomed to
eat out of a pail, he tipped it over and nosed about in the fruit,
"gorming" (if there is such a word) it down, mixed with leaves
and dirt, like a pig. The bear is a worse feeder than the pig. Whenever he disturbs a maple-sugar camp in the spring, he always up-
sets the buckets of sirup and tramples round in the sticky sweets,
wasting more than he eats. The bear's manners are thoroughly disagreeable.

As soon as my enemy's head was down, I started and ran. Somewhat out of breath and shaky, I reached my faithful rifle. It was not
a moment too soon. I heard the bear crashing through the brush
after me. Enraged at my duplicity, he was now coming on with
blood in his eye. I felt that the time of one of us was probably
short. The rapidity of thought at such moments of peril is well
known. I thought an octavo volume, had it illustrated and published, sold fifty thousand copies, and went to Europe on the pro-
ceeds, while that bear was loping across the clearing. As I was cock-
ing the gun, I made a hasty and unsatisfactory review of my whole
life. I noted that, even in such a compulsory review, it is almost
impossible to think of any good thing you have done. The sins
come out uncommonly strong. I recollected a newspaper subscription I had delayed paying years and years ago, until both editor
and newspaper were dead, and which now never could be paid to
all eternity.

The bear was coming on.

I tried to remember what I had read about encounters with bears.

I couldn't recall an instance in which a man had run away from a bear in the woods and escaped, although I recalled plenty where the bear had run from the man and got off. I tried to think what is the best way to kill a bear with a gun when you are not near enough to club him with the stock. My first thought was to fire at his head, to plant the ball between his eyes; but this is a dangerous experiment. The bear's brain is very small; and unless you hit that, the bear does not mind a bullet in his head; that is, not at the time. I remembered that the instant death of the bear would follow a bullet planted just back of his fore-leg and sent into his heart. This spot is also difficult to reach, unless the bear stands off, side towards you, like a target. I finally determined to fire at him generally.

The bear was coming on. . . .

I tried to fix my last thoughts upon my family. As my family is small, this was not difficult. Dread of displeasing my wife or hurting her feelings was uppermost in my mind. What would be her anxiety as hour after hour passed on, and I did not return! What would the rest of the household think as the afternoon passed, and no blackberries came! What would be my wife's mortification when the news was brought that her husband had been eaten by a bear! I cannot imagine anything more ignominious than to have a husband eaten by a bear. And this was not my only anxiety. The mind at such times is not under control. With the gravest fears the most whimsical ideas will occur. I looked beyond the mourning friends and thought what kind of an epitaph they would be compelled to put upon the stone. Something like this:—

HERE LIE THE REMAINS
OF
_____ _____
EATEN BY A BEAR
Aug. 20, 1877

It is a very unheroic and even disagreeable epitaph. That "eaten by a bear" is intolerable. It is grotesque. And then I thought what an inadequate language the English is for compact expression. It would not answer to put upon the stone simply "eaten"; for that is indefinite and requires explanation: it might mean eaten by a cannibal. This difficulty could not occur in the German, where _essen_ signifies the act of feeding by a man and *fressen* by a beast. How simple the thing would be in German!——

HIER LIEGT
HOCHWOHLGEBOREN
HERR ——— ———,
GEFRESSEN
Aug. 20, 1877

That explains itself. The well-born one was eaten by a beast, and presumably eaten by a bear—an animal that has a bad reputation since the days of Elisha.

The bear was coming on; he had, in fact, come on. I judged that he could see the whites of my eyes. All my subsequent reflections were confused. I raised the gun, covered the bear's breast with the sight, and let drive. Then I turned and ran like a deer. I did not hear the bear pursuing. I looked back. The bear had stopped. He was lying down. I then remembered that the best thing to do after having fired your gun is to reload it. I slipped in a charge, keeping my eyes on the bear. He never stirred. I walked back suspiciously. There was a quiver in the hind-legs, but no other motion. Still he might be shamming: bears often sham. To make sure, I approached and put a ball into his head. He didn't mind it now: he minded nothing. Death had come to him with a merciful suddenness. He was calm in death. In order that he might remain so, I blew his brains out and then started for home. I had killed a bear!

Notwithstanding my excitement, I managed to saunter into the house with an unconcerned air. There was a chorus of voices:—

"Where are your blackberries?"

"Why were you gone so long?"

"Where's your pail?"

"I left the pail."

"Left the pail? What for?"

"A bear wanted it."

"Oh, nonsense!"

"Well, the last I saw of it, a bear had it."

"Oh, come! You didn't really see a bear?"

"Yes, but I did really see a real bear."

"Did he run?"

"Yes: he ran after me."

"I don't believe a word of it. What did you do?"

"Oh! nothing particular—except kill the bear."

Cries of "Gammon!" "Don't believe it!" "Where's the bear?"

"If you want to see the bear, you must go up into the woods. I couldn't bring him down alone."

Having satisfied the household that something extraordinary had occurred, and excited the posthumous fear of some of them for my own safety, I went down into the valley to get help. The great bear-hunter, who keeps one of the summer boarding-houses, received my story with a smile of incredulity; and the incredulity spread to the other inhabitants and to the boarders as soon as the story was known. However, as I insisted in all soberness and offered to lead them to the bear, a party of forty or fifty people at last started off with me to bring the bear in. Nobody believed there was any bear in the case; but everybody who could get a gun carried one; and we went into the woods armed with guns, pistols, pitchforks, and sticks, against all contingencies or surprises—a crowd made up mostly of scoffers and jeerers.

But when I led the way to the fatal spot and pointed out the bear, lying peacefully wrapped in his own skin, something like terror seized the boarders, and genuine excitement the natives. It was a no-mistake bear, by George! and the hero of the fight— well, I will not insist upon that. But what a procession that was, carrying the bear home! and what a congregation was speedily gathered in the valley to see the bear! Our best preacher up there never drew anything like it on Sunday.

And I must say that my particular friends, who were sportsmen, behaved very well, on the whole. They didn't deny that it was a bear, although they said it was small for a bear. Mr. Deane, who is equally good with a rifle and a rod, admitted that it was a very fair shot. He is probably the best salmon-fisher in the United States, and he is an equally good hunter. I suppose there is no person in America who is more desirous to kill a moose than he.

But he needlessly remarked, after he had examined the wound in the bear, that he had seen that kind of a shot made by a cow's horn.

This sort of talk affected me not. When I went to sleep that night, my last delicious thought was, "I've killed a bear!"

SERMON IN THE BUSH
WILLIAM H. BOARDMAN

"It's queer," said John, "how many ministers do come to these woods. I've seen a good many in my time, more'n a dozen, I reckon, and gen'lly good ones. It's probably the best of 'em that comes, but I don't know. I haven't seen one outside since I was a boy. One September I was a few miles above here on the river with my boat. It was about two o'clock and I had stepped back on the hardwood flat to where the Colonel had a cache under the big maple by the hemlock stub. There's a spring brook there and I was cookin' a meal of vittels when I heard two rifle shots in the line of my boat, and of course I stepped out to see what was goin' on. Two men were restin' on the bank opposite. They said they'd seen my boat and noticed it was fresh grounded on the bank and thought they'd find the owner of it by firin' a couple of shots, so's to ask on which side the trail led down the river.

"I brought 'em over and didn't ask questions, though it was puzzlin' to locate 'em. Course I noticed they stepped in a boat right and knew how to take care of themselves, though they were strange to this country. Their shoes was good, but the strings had been broke and knotted. Their pants was tore in a good many places, but mended good, except a few places fixed with safety pins, so it was pretty sure they'd come from Indian River way, through the big burnt ground. They were gritty and didn't ask for help, but I could see things wa'n't altogether pleasant, so I asked 'em to take a meal with me.

"Seemed as if I could hear their teeth click when they accepted, so I stepped across to the Colonel's maple for some more provisions. I dug out his bottle and put it with a tin cup by the spring where they was washin' up. Then I could see they was all right, for they took only about an ounce apiece. You can find out a good deal about a man by the way he treats whiskey. They were tender of it and showed they took it only when't was needed. . . .

"The old man asked if there was a camp where they could stay over Sunday, so I told 'em all about the Colonel and his camp, and how glad he'd be, when he come up in the spring, to hear from me that his camp had been of use to people who loved the woods. I told 'em they was all right, and would be well fixed after about two hours' tramp; and that's where I made a break, for, as it turned out, it was a good while before they saw Wilderness camp.

"The weather had changed while we was talkin', and I'd been careless, not noticin'. It was growin' black, and south of west I could see a cloud risin' that looked like a bag of bluin'. I struck off through the woods fast as I could make it, for we had five miles to go. The ministers kep' up well. We could hear roarin' and crashin' ahead of us, and we hadn't gone fur before the tops near us begun to whistle and moan, and I knew it wouldn't be long before they'd begin twistin' and breakin'. We was on a ridge, and I wanted to get down where some high rocks would shelter us, but it was black dark, except when it was lightnin', which was most of the time. When I saw a birch, about two foot through, that had fell acrost a little gully, I dodged down by it and called to the ministers to come in and make themselves small. They crawled in careful, without a word. The old one was the coolest man I ever see in these woods. When a hemlock come down across our birch and broke in two, it lightened and I could see his face. It was shiny, and he was smilin'.

"A flurry of rain come and stopped, and the wind stopped, and everything was dead for a minute before the whirlwind struck us.

I never heard such a noise since we bombarded Fort Fisher—roarin', hissin', and snappin', with thud, thud, thud, as the big trunks struck the ground. It was a long time passin', and we were just about the middle of the path, where there wasn't a big tree left standin'. We never got a scratch, but our birch was pretty well covered with tops. Then the rain come and it poured stiddy and was cold. I got dry curl off the birch and started a little fire and fed it with branches until it made light enough for me to work with the minister's little two-pound axe. It was slow, but I done it. The evenin' was gone and 't was late night when I got a fire the rain couldn't drown. It lit up the windfall and we could see what had happened.

"It's wonderful how comfortable you can be a-standin' straight up in a pourin' rain before a hot fire. The old man asked me about the war, and I told him about our defeat at Drury's Bluff, where I was taken prisoner. I must 'a' made it a long story, for when I stopped, the young man turned the face of his watch to the fire and said it was Sunday. I asked the old minister if he wouldn't preach me a sermon. I hadn't heard one since I was a boy. He seemed to forget about the rain, for he stepped to his pack and took out two leather-covered books, but he covered 'em up again and stood on the far side of the fire, a-facin' me acrost it. Then he said, 'Hymn number four hundred and fourteen,' and the young man sung with him. . . .

"I never heard such music, and didn't know folks could sing so. They sung all the verses, standin' there in the windfall, and the rain comin' all the while. When they begun the last verse—

"'When I tread the verge of Jordan,
Bid my anxious fears subside,'
I found I was cryin', not because I felt bad, but I seemed to be a little child again, and it was natural. Then he said:

"'The Lord is in His holy temple: Let all the earth keep silence before Him.'

"He repeated Scripture word for word and said prayers, sometimes kneelin' and sometimes standin'. I knelt when he did, and when he come to the Lord's prayer I remembered it and cried again, for I was a little child.

"Before he begun his sermon, he said:

" 'For we must needs die, and are as water spilt on the ground, which cannot be gathered up again; neither doth God respect any person; yet doth He devise means that His banished be not expelled from Him.'

"Then he stood, a-lookin' at me acrost the fire, and preached. It was all to me, me all alone, and I couldn't take my eyes off him. I can remember a good deal of what he said, and I'll never forget it. The fire lit up the downed tops, and he stood with his back to the felled hemlock, preachin' a sermon to me through the hot flame. He glowed and shone and seemed to rise up tall in the firelight. He must 'a' talked for hours, but I didn't know it until he said, 'Let us pray,' and we knelt down.

"When I stood up and turned away from the fire, the rain had stopped, and it was sun-up. He was a good man!"

NESSMUK IN TROUBLE
FRED MATHER

George Washington Sears ("Nessmuk"), contributor to *Forest and Stream* and author of *Woodcraft*, made three cruises in the Adirondacks in light-weight canoes in the summers of 1880, 1881, and 1883.

Jupiter Pluvius! How it did rain! We had seen it coming while at supper, and I said to my companion, Hon. James Geddes, of Syracuse, N. Y., "Jim, we must deepen the ditch around this tent or be drowned out. That's an angry sky, and the sun is only just down, yet it is dark as midnight. It's no ordinary shower that is promised us."

"That's so," replied the Hon. Jim, "and we've got to do it right quick, too. It's lucky that the land falls away so much from our tent; we will not have to dig far to have complete drainage."

We went at it with case knives and tin plates and finished widening and deepening the ditch on the back and sides of our wall tent —the front needed no ditch—when the first wind which precedes such a storm began to roar in the treetops, and in a few minutes the advance guard of St. Swithin began letting great drops resound through the forest. We felt secure; wind could not harm us unless it felled a tree across our tent, and as it was to be a camp for a week or more I had avoided all old and partially dead trees whose roots might also be partly dead, and before the rain beat the wind down we were inside, the door-flap buttoned and a candle lighted. I had prepared for the light by getting one of the flat fungi ("funguses," I want to call 'em, and only use the Latin plural to show my learning), and by dropping some melted candle on this and quickly standing the cold end in it, there was a candlestick. We had just got comfortably down on our blankets when the storm burst in all its fury. "Jim Geddes," said I, "you made an offensive remark to me before this storm got under way. We will have no quarrels over it because you intended no offense, and only a fool takes offense where none was intended, but when you reconsider your words you will see wherein you were wrong."

"Well, I'm surprised! Tell me all about it. We don't want to fight in this little ten by twelve tent when all nature is engaged in a combat outside. There! Did you notice how quick that clap of thunder followed the flash? That hit near us; but go on and tell me what it was that I said that has injured your feelings. I never thought you were so thin-skinned."

I looked at the surprise pictured on his honest, goodnatured face and said: "While I make no claim to being thin-skinned, I don't care to have my knowledge of woodcraft credited to accident. I selected this campsite and put up the tent while you were taking trout for supper, and when the storm was in sight you said: 'It's lucky that the land falls away so much from our tent.' Now, my dear Jim, luck was not in it at any stage of the game. That's the trouble. The word 'luck' sort o' soured on my stomach, and I couldn't digest it. Do you get my meaning?"

"I've got it," said Mr. Geddes, "and I still maintain that your skin is too thin to make a woman's glove. Just listen to that rain! Did you ever hear anything come down harder? Hark! What was that?"

"Oh, I don't know! Some echo of thunder in the mountains, for here in the Adirondacks the sounds of a storm will appall one not accustomed to mountain echoes."

"Hush! There it is again!"

We listened. Then came an unmistakable *"Da whoop!"*

"Somebody down at the landing," said Jim, "and he must be quite damp."

We left all our clothing, except our shoes, in the tent and went down to the lake to learn what sort of man might be abroad in a storm like this. The wind had subsided, but the rain still came in torrents. We called and a man said something which was drowned by the roar of the rain in the woods and on the lake. The next flash of lightning revealed a man waist deep in water holding to the side of a canoe. He was about twenty feet away and I rushed in and led him to the landing, which was a small opening in the bushes. After we had pulled his canoe well ashore we led him to the tent, which was easily seen by its light, for a candle shows up well through canvas on a dark night, and then we looked him over. He was a little man, about five feet nothing; about fifty years old, but one of those thin, wiry fellows without an ounce of fat who look as old at forty as they do a score of years later. He was chilled in his wet clothing while we were aglow, and we got him stripped and under the blankets as soon as possible and gave him such restoratives as we had. Divested of clothing he was nearly as big as a pound of soap after a hard day's washing, and until he became warm he had merely answered questions as to the things in his boat. He did not want them brought up. They could get no wetter. We questioned him no further and awaited the pleasure of our guest to begin the conversation.

Finally he said: "It's lucky for me that I saw the light in your tent. I had lost my paddle and the wind was making a plaything of my canoe. When I saw the light I jumped overboard to swim and drag the canoe, but I couldn't find a landing and was wading about when you came."

"Were you going up or down the lake?" asked Geddes.

"Neither. I'd been fishing on the other side and started to come across to where I left some duffle when the storm caught me."

I caught the word "duffle," which I had never heard until I had read Nessmuk's article in *Forest and Stream,* and I knew that he traveled in a canoe and camped alone, a very economical way of enjoying life, and a delightful one if we add a companion, to those who can care for themselves in the woods. So, without much chance of error, I said: "If I should hazard a guess, it would be that you are a Pennsylvania man who goes alone when he goes at all, writes up what he sees, thinks or imagines that he sees and thinks, and signs himself 'Nessmuk.' "

"That's a bull's-eye guess; how did you make it?"

"Well, partly because you called your camp stores 'duffle' and partly because you travel alone in a toy canoe, and again because you are built to sail in a chopping bowl. And let me introduce my friend, Mr. Geddes, of Syracuse, and myself. My name is Mather. At present I am the fishery editor of *Forest and Stream* and have written for it from its first number. Last year I was with the Adirondack survey as ichthyologist and wrote up our trip and discoveries. I also wrote a series of sketches headed: 'Trouting on the Bigosh.' "

"Yes," said our guest, "I've known of Mr. Geddes at the sportsmen's conventions. What did you say your name was—Murphy?"

"Correct; you have a good ear and a good memory. My family is descended from King Brian Boroimhe, who defeated the Norsemen in 1014 near Dublin, and whose name has been corrupted into Brian Boru and then into Murphy, just as your name, Sears, became shortened from Seersucker, the fabric of linen and silk, to its present form. There was no need to retain the last part of the name because it was known of all men."

The rescued man raised himself on his elbow and said: "You've got it straight, Fred; and now let up, as the rain has done, and I will make a fire and dry my clothes."

We opened the tent, for the rain had ceased and only for the drip from the trees there was no sign of the terrible storm. The earth was damp, but the drainage was good, and a fire soon threw its heat into the tent as our guest dried his clothing in the smoke. I was glad to have a chance to study him at close range. You may read what a man writes, but he only shows you the side he cares to have you see, the dress parade side, so to speak; or you may meet him daily for years and your vision will get no further; but camp with him a week when provisions are low and weather is bad, and if there is only one hog's bristle on his back that bristle will be erect and assert itself. . . .

In the morning we all had dry clothing, and started out after breakfast to fish in our two boats. Nessmuk had a little frail canoe, while ours was of the regular Adirondack pattern and weighed about eighty pounds. But the rod that our friend proceeded to join up was a wonder; it had originally been one of those four-piece abominations which are called "trunk rods," with joints shortened to allow the thing to be carried in a trunk. Originally it had been about ten feet eight inches long; now it was seven feet six inches, without a regular taper and too stiff to cast a fly. "What do you call that thing?" asked Geddes, as he picked up the rod and looked it over critically.

"That's a trout rod made after my own ideas, and it just suits me to a T. It's a good ash and lancewood rod cut down as I ordered."

I handled the rod and said: "It's elegant; the finest thing I ever saw. I didn't quite understand it at first, but just look it over carefully, Jim, and you will see that a canal driver can whale his mules to the queen's taste with that. You came up by the Black River Canal, didn't you?"

"I'll show you what it is for when we get where the fish are, and it will beat your long, limber-go-shiftless split-bamboos and give 'em ten in the game. They're too willowy, too limber, too aesthetic, too costly, and too high-toned to cruise in the *Nipper;* but just wait."

We waited, and towed the *Nipper* until we got to where its

skipper thought its paddle had drifted in the storm. He found it on shore, and then, with a light breeze, just enough to make a ripple, we drifted and began to fish. We watched the old man. He had a reel and a gut leader on his line, and soon said: "Lend me a couple of flies; I have lost mine." We stocked him up and began taking trout freely. I was busy replacing a fly when Geddes whispered: "Look at old Nessmuk; he never tried to cast a fly before."

I looked. He was standing in his canoe, balancing himself as it rocked, trying to get out his line, which would sometimes fall ten feet from the boat and sometimes in his boat. He saw our flies go out thirty and forty feet and saw the trout rise and strike, to be reeled in. He thought he could do it, but had to own up. He paddled alongside and said: "I never tried this rod with flies before, and it doesn't seem to work. There are no angleworms in the Adirondacks, and I think I'll have to ask you for some trout fins and livers for bait."

We tossed a couple of small trout into his canoe, and he removed his flies, put on some bare hooks, baited them, and began fishing. Geddes said: "The old fellow is a bait fisher and nothing else. He would have drifted off by himself if he had bait, but we drifted with him, and he had to own up. He said that his rod was not a fly rod. That's most certain, but it's dollars to doughnuts that he couldn't get a fly out with either of our rods. I'll ask him to try it."

"No, Jim," I said, "don't do it. It would only embarrass him and make him feel uncomfortable. He is a first-class woodsman and has made the mistake of trying to cast a fly with a rod which cannot cast one, and he has tried it before two experts and failed."

"You're right," said the great-hearted Geddes; "he's a good old fellow in his way, and we don't wish to make him uncomfortable. He's 'bit off more'n he can chaw,' as the saying goes, and we will turn our backs and not see it. He's not only using bait, but see the little twig he has tied on the line as a float. That's the last evidence of primitive methods."

Nessmuk took a few trout, and before noon we went back to our camp and had a grand woods dinner of hardtack, bean soup with salt pork, and fried trout. If I had never been within one thousand miles of New York I would say: "The dinner exceeded the wildest dreams of Delmonico," for the man of Nessmukian type thinks that there is only one place to eat in New York and somehow gets the idea that good cooking and service culminate under one roof. I can show him quiet, out-of-the-way places—but we have strayed from the camp on the Fulton chain of lakes.

When dinner was to be cooked Nessmuk shone as a bright particular star. He took charge, hustled around and did all the work while we looked on. He cleaned the fish, washed and boiled the beans while Geddes and I lay off, chatted and slept, Jim's last remark being: "He's a mighty good man in camp." . . .

Later I ran into his camp on the Fulton Chain, and I would have known it was Nessmuk's camp if I had not heard that he was ahead of me. A little tent of very light duck, which was just big enough for a small man to crawl into, was his shelter. A gum blanket and a woolen one were his bed, with no leaves nor balsam boughs under it, and a frying-pan, small tin pail to serve as a camp kettle, another containing salt pork for frying, a tin box of hardtack or pilot bread, and a coffee pot was all that was in sight, and all made of the lightest materials and just sufficient for one man. I gave his war cry—"Da-whoop!"—and soon he came paddling around a point and landed. After salutation I looked over his boat and outfit.

And such a boat! He had been experimenting in boat building with the sole idea of reducing weight, which he had to pack over the Adirondack carries, where the portages vary from a few yards to three miles or more. The *Nipper* was very light, too light for most men; it weighed about twenty-five pounds [sixteen]. The *Bucktail*, which I never saw, he told me weighed nineteen pounds, and now I beheld the *Sairy Gamp*, so named, he said, "because she never took water" [Sairey Gamp in *Martin Chuzzlewit*]. This latter creation of the Nessmukian brain and hand [actually built in Canton, New York, by the boat-builder J. Henry Rushton] was, as I remembered it, about eight and a half feet long and weighed between ten and eleven pounds [ten and a half]. These figures are from memory; my volumes of *Forest and Stream* are boxed and in storage and I am writing at a distance. This boat formed part of the exhibit of *Forest and Stream* at the World's Fair [1893, Chicago], being loaned for the occasion by the National Museum at Washington, where it has been deposited. . . .

I fished with him that afternoon, and he took me to a spring hole where trout were plenty and we had good sport; he fishing with venison for bait within ten feet of the boat and I using the fly where it did not interfere with him. He was the same old "snatch 'em in" potfisher and enjoyed it; but he loved the woods and their solitude and was perfectly able to take care of himself in them alone, with either rod or gun. He was bright, poetic, and witty. . . .

After the events recorded in this more or less veracious sketch, old Nessmuk came down the Hudson River, camping all the way, until he reached New York City, when he beached the *Sairy Gamp* and pitched his tent in Central Park, procured wood from some source, and proceeded to cook his supper. A gray-coated park policeman, who is generally known as a "sparrow cop," ran him in, and he spent the night in a cell at a police station.

What if his neighbors say that he was idle and preferred loafing in the woods to doing anything else? That is nothing to me; I enjoyed his society, which, if he had been thrifty, would never have come my way. I only know that I would like to meet him in the woods and on the streams again.

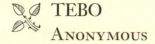

TEBO

Anonymous

This localized version of a migratory lumbermen's chantey is said to be based on an actual happening. A river driver named Joe Thibault (Tebo), working with the A. Sherman Lumber Company, lost his life in breaking a log jam on the Jordan River near its confluence with the Raquette. The site of the small waterfall is known today as Tebo Falls. I am indebted to the Potsdam Museum for this version.

It was on the sixth of May, my boys, as you will understand,
When Sherman ordered out his men all for to break the jam.
The logs were piled up mountains high, the water was so dreadful
   strong,
That it washed away poor Tebo and the logs that he was on.

He nobly faced the water and manly swam away,
He tried his best to save himself in every shape and way.
The jam soon overtook him towards sad grief and woe
And we found his drownded body in the Racket River, ho.

Young Akey came from Saranac and this I do explain
He tried his best to save him, but it was all in vain.
The waters they roared over him, he was forced to let him go:
And away then went poor Tebo for to meet his God we know.

Oh, Tebo was an able man, drove many a different stream,
It appeared that every morning that his last hours had come.
He had served his time on Earth that he was here for to stay,
He bid goodbye to all his boys all on the sixth of May.

Oh, Tebo leaves a widow and five young children small,
All at the mercy of his friends who drove the Racket fall.
A subscription was made up for them, each man their share did pay
To feed and clothe the orphans he left behind that day.

About four o'clock in the afternoon on the twenty-ninth of May
We found his drownded body and we laid it in the clay.

I hope his soul is in Paradise with God on High to rest,
While we carve upon his headstone, "He always done his best."

It is now I bid you all goodbye, my time has come to go
To answer at the Judgment bar for sins on earth below.
The past is bad, the future hidden, no earthly tongue can tell
The agony of that poor old man when into the waters he fell.

THEODORE ROOSEVELT'S MIDNIGHT RIDE Alfred L. Donaldson

On September 6th of that year [1901], President McKinley was shot by an anarchist in Buffalo. Mr. Roosevelt, then Vice-President, hastened to that city and remained there until assured that the wounded President was considered out of danger. He then went to the Adirondacks and joined his family, some of whom had preceded him to Tahawus Club.

On Friday, September 13th, he and some friends—Mr. James MacNaughton, Messrs. B. and H. Robinson, and Noah LaCasse as guide—made an ascent of Mount Marcy. On the afternoon of the day before these gentlemen and the ladies in their party left the main club-house at the Upper Works and went to a rough camp on Lake Colden. Here they spent the night. The following morning the ladies returned to the club-house, and the men proceeded to climb Marcy. They left Lake Colden at 9 a.m. and by noon had reached the summit of the mountain. They remained there about fifteen minutes only, and then descended a few hundred feet to the shelf of land that holds Lake Tear-of-the-Clouds, where they rested and ate lunch. While chatting and looking around, they saw a hurrying guide emerge from the woods below. A few moments later this man, Harrison Hall, handed Mr. Roosevelt a telegram which told him that President McKinley's condition had suddenly changed for the worse.

This was at half-past one. The party immediately hurried down the mountain and reached the club-house at half-past five. Finding no further news there, Mr. Roosevelt reluctantly consented to spend the night, but made arrangements to leave at the earliest possible moment in the morning. At eleven o'clock that night, however, Mr. MacNaughton brought him another message saying that the President was dying. Without a moment's hesitation Mr. Roosevelt declared his intention of starting immediately for Buffalo, and asked for a conveyance. At this his friends, seconded by the guides, urged him to wait till daylight. The roads were so rough and treacherous as to be considered impassable of a dark night, and this night was of the darkest. The men around the club were not the kind to balk at any ordinary risk, but none of them cared to be the driver in this one. Being informed of this, Mr. Roosevelt said he would take a lantern and go afoot. This threat, backed by preparatory action, induced one of the guides, Dave Hunter, to volunteer as a driver. A little later the start was made in a now historic night ride from one of the most isolated spots in the wilderness to the nearest railway station at North Creek, forty miles away.

The trip was planned in relays, for Mr. Roosevelt not only insisted on going, he insisted on going fast. The result was an utterly reckless dash through the darkness—a race with death in more senses than one. That the nation did not lose two Presidents that night was little short of miraculous, but, as we now know, fate was reserving this devotee of danger for the most peaceful of endings.

The first relay of the journey was driven by Dave Hunter; the second by Orrin Kellogg; the third and last by Mike Cronin, who was waiting at Aden Lair with a team of gaunt black horses, restless for the final dash. At 3 a.m. Mr. Roosevelt arrived, jumped from one buckboard to the other, and plunged wildly into the night again. At 4:39 a.m. he alighted at the North Creek station, where a special train was waiting and he was met by Secretary Loeb, who gave him the news that he was President of the United States.

As driver of the last lap in this famous ride, Mike Cronin became a sort of national hero. He was written to and interviewed about it until he gradually evolved a recital of the adventure that connected some thrilling detail with every bump and turn in the road. He also gave away more souvenir horseshoes than his team of blacks could have worn in a lifetime. [According to William Chapman White, about four hundred homes in the Adirondacks used to cherish an authentic shoe from Cronin's team of black horses.]

 THE PURLOINED TROUT
HENRY ABBOTT

That evening after supper, while Bige was cutting some firewood, I took the boat and my rod and went out on the pond to get some trout for breakfast.

It was just as the sun was dropping below the western hills, and there was a gorgeous golden glow in the sky. The breeze had dropped to a gentle zephyr that hardly caused a ripple on the surface of the water, so I allowed the boat to slowly drift while I was casting. A tree had fallen into the pond, and sitting in its branches near the treetop, close to the water and about fifty feet from the shore, I discovered a coon. He, also, was fishing, and I was curious to learn just how he operated.

I soon found that the coon was not without curiosity since he, just as eagerly, was watching my operations. As the boat slowly approached the treetop his sharp, beady eyes followed the movement of my flies as the rod whipped back and forth. It occurred to me that he might be seriously considering the advisability of adopting a fly rod for use in his fishing business.

Just as the boat passed the treetop and but a few feet from it, a good sized trout appeared at the surface and with a swirl and slap of his tail grabbed one of my flies and made off with it toward the bottom. Instantly the coon became very excited. His body appeared tense; his ring-banded tail swished from side to side; his feet nervously stepped up and down on the tree branch, like a crouching cat who sees a mouse approaching, and his snapping eyes followed the movement of my line as it sawed through the water while the fish rushed about, up and down, under the boat and back again. And when the trout made a jump above the surface and shook himself, the coon seemed to fairly dance with joy. Presently, the fish, now completely exhausted, appeared at the surface lying on his side, while I was reeling in the line; when the coon slipped into the water, grabbed the fish in his mouth and swam ashore. Climbing up the bank he turned, grinned at me and went into the bushes with my trout, now his trout, in his mouth and about three feet of leader trailing behind.

 A VISUAL HAPPENING
Harold Weston

In the early 1920s the Conservation Department had a very limited budget and welcomed outside help in the construction and maintenance of lean-tos. A group at the Lake Placid Club, which called itself the Adirondack Camp and Trail Club but was known during its short existence as The Sno Birds, offered to cover the costs of building a lean-to between Haystack and Basin on property owned by the Adirondack Mountain Reserve, if the latter gave permission for state maintenance of a camp there. The lean-to was constructed in late September 1923. Faith and I were the first persons to spend a night in Sno Bird Camp as it was and is named.

We had been told that the lean-to was "finished" and assumed that meant it was in condition for hikers to spend the night there. We planned to go from camp at the Upper [Ausable Lake] over Haystack, spend the night at Sno Bird and do the rest of the Range the next day. The date was October 1, 1923. We reached the camp towards dusk because I stopped to paint on Haystack. I always have a hard time tearing myself away from a mountaintop, especially from this focal point among the High Peaks—the massive thrust of Marcy looming up from the crevasses of Panther Gorge to tower above us, the impressive sequence of pyramids formed by the receding ridges of Basin, Saddleback, and Gothics, the rhythmic repetition of lateral mountain ranges of Sawteeth, Colvin, and Dix, one over the other, with the distant flatlands of the lower Champlain Valley as a backdrop, the pearl-like string of opal colors from the waters of the Upper Ausable, the Inlet, Stillwater, and Boreas Ponds with lucid blues of successive low ranges fading away to the south. Any attempt to pin down these visual happenings realistically was all the more futile because the colors were fast losing their resiliency in the fading light of a sky becoming overcast. One had to absorb the essence of the moment and then transmute it into form and color later on.

Upon reaching Sno Bird we were dismayed to find the walls and roof of the lean-to were finished, but on the floor of the camp, where some day a springy depth of balsam boughs might presumably be found, the tops of the trees cut for the logs that made the walls were nailed about five inches apart above some rocks and muddy ground. Unfortunately the person who lopped off the branches was in a hurry and left sharp stubs sticking out in all directions composing a spurred corduroy bed for its first guests to repose upon. I may not mind hardships of a kind, but I'm no guru with a yen to sleep on a bed of spikes. Hurriedly, because it was getting dark and about to rain, I gathered as many evergreen branches as I could to form a two-foot wide base for a "mattress" of boughs at one end of the camp, adding boughs which I cut in short lengths and stuck into the "mattress" sharply to take advantage of the natural springiness of the curve of the branch. In the meantime, as rain began, Faith was cooking supper over a very smoky fire made from the countless chips of all sizes from the camp logs, which of course had just been cut. The bedding proved as dismal as the fire, which constantly threatened to go out. Soon after we lay down, the firm spikes of the corduroy began to assert their manhood. Then, after we got a real fire going because it was getting colder, the wind shifted, smoke filled our end of the lean-to and we wished it would rain harder and put that damned fire out. Never on a mountain have I shivered and wept through a more miserable night.

In the predawn light we could see that every twig, every balsam needle, every fern and blade of grass was covered with a thick hoar frost. In some places between trees fantastic frost wreaths had formed, actually frost clinging to sturdy spider webs. Here and there on the ground lacelike accumulations of snow formed weird patterns by edging irregular patches of ice over black rocks. It would be madness to try to go on over the Range. Spots on Saddleback and Gothics would be impassable without special equipment. The clouds, scurrying past just overhead, seemed to be lifting. I predicted it would clear soon. After a leisurely breakfast, leaving our packs but taking my sketch box, we cautiously climbed the short distance to the top of Basin.

By now there were breaks in the clouds sweeping over us. As we reached the top and looked toward Johns Brook suddenly there was a glimpse of autumn trees blazing in sunlight in the valley below us. A bit later in almost the opposite direction the cold shoulder of Haystack emerged from the clouds and a moment later to the left of it Boreas Ponds silvery and shimmering. It was tantalizing because the vision was wiped away before you could grasp it all. The tempo of the moving clouds calmed down after a while and it cleared as we watched the movement of sun patches and shadows sweep up and over the bare glistening slides of the western ridge of Gothics, with Giant in the distance now benignly warming up in steady sunlight. I did four paintings in a frenzy. The wild exuberance of the day and its successive orgasms of wilderness beauty called for a shorthand method in paint to capture rapidly changing emotional reactions, methods that predated abstract expressionism. It was indeed a morning of glory.

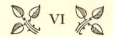

VI

Lost and Found

Something hidden. Go and find it. Go and look behind the Ranges—
Something lost behind the Ranges. Lost and waiting for you. Go!
                                                    Rudyard Kipling

THE ADIRONDACK WILDERNESS, said Verplanck Colvin, is a mystery even to those who know it best. To the motor tourist today, confined to the circuit of resort towns, motels, and highways, the fringes of woodland he speeds by may seem monotonous. But the forest has not lost its mystery and promise for those who enter it on foot or by canoe. Large wilderness areas are still untamed by roads. In them the mystery of the woods can still be experienced, and with it two interesting possibilities—getting lost and making a discovery.

No season passes without its quota of news stories about hunters or hikers lost in the woods. In rare instances the lost person never emerges, either through his own devices or through the intensive efforts of search parties. The risk is greatest in winter mountaineering. Even experienced, well-equipped winter climbers may go astray during a whiteout above timberline when blowing and drifting snow wipes out all trace of trail and footprints. One recent event of this kind is included here.

While risk of getting lost lessens with experience in woodcraft, the awareness making for discovery continues to grow. The happiest woodsmen are those for whom discovery becomes an end in itself. This was the lure that kept a New York City inventor,

[255]

Henry Abbott, on backpacking trips for over thirty years with his guide, Bige Smith. "Repeated excursions into the shade of the wilderness serve only to increase the pulling power and multiply the enticements of this attractive forest," he wrote. "The chief charm of exploration lies in the uncertainty of always finding what one starts out to find, and in the equal certainty that one may find something else."

Every woodsman has his own set of discoveries. I know a former Adirondack guide who is filled with nostalgia whenever he thinks of the remote spots in the bush where he once had camps or planned them. The locations are marked on his topographic maps as carefully as if they were hidden treasure. He never shows these maps. Maybe it is just as well that he can't bring himself to do so. Sharing another's discoveries is only a warmed-over pleasure. Everyone must make his own. It is not necessary that they impress others. A boulder with a garden of moss and ferns on its top, a grove of virgin white pines on a ridge, a deer caught unaware nuzzling in fallen leaves for beechnuts, a golden eagle nest on a crag, an esker overlooked by glacial geologists, a colony of yellow or showy lady's slippers will do as well to bring the sensation of discovery to a bushranger today as the lost ponds and unclimbed mountains of a century ago. Discovery is a never-ending experience in the woods.

HOW WE MET JOHN BROWN
RICHARD HENRY DANA, JR.

In the summer of 1849 Mr. Metcalf and I went into the Adirondacks, then but little known to tourists. Our journey up the valley of the Connecticut, across Vermont, and up Lake Champlain, full of beauties as it was, presented nothing that would be new to most readers. At Westport, near the head of Lake Champlain, on the New York side, we found a delightful colony of New England friends. . . . Here we took up a companion for our wild tour, Mr. Aikens, in theory a lawyer, but in practice a traveller, sportsman, and woodsman; and Mr. Jackson lent us a wagon with a pair of mules, and a boy Tommy to commissary and persuade the mules, and we drove out of Westport in the afternoon of a very hot day and made for the mountains.

Our route lay through Pleasant Valley, along the pretty Bouquet River, which flows from the mountains, winding among graceful hills, into the lake. We baited at Elizabethtown and spent the night at Ford's tavern in the township of Keene, sleeping on the floor and finding that we were expected to wash in the river, and were on our way again before sunrise. From Keene westward we began to meet signs of frontier life—log cabins, little clearings, bad roads overshadowed by forests, mountain torrents, and the refreshing odor of balsam firs and hemlocks. The next morning we stopped at a log house to breakfast, and found a guide to take us through the

Indian Pass, and sent Tommy and his mules forward to Osgood's tavern; and with no luggage but such as we could easily carry on our backs, began our walk to Lake Sandford [Sanford], Tahawus, and the Adirondack Iron Works. . . .

In the afternoon we came into the Indian Pass. This is a ravine, or gorge, formed by two close and parallel walls of nearly perpendicular cliffs, of about thirteen hundred feet in height, and almost black in their hue. Before I had seen the Yosemite Valley, these cliffs satisfied my ideal of steep mountain walls. From the highest level of the pass flow two mountain torrents in opposite directions—one the source of the Hudson, and so reaching the Atlantic; and the other the source of the Au Sable, which runs into Lake Champlain and at last into the Gulf of St. Lawrence—but no larger when they begin, trickling from the rocks, than streams from the nose of a teapot. . . .

Coming out of the pass, a few miles of rough walking on a downward grade brought us again to small clearings, cuttings of wood piled up to be carried off when the snow should make sledding over the stumps of trees practicable; and about sundown we straggled into the little extemporized iron-workers' village of Adirondack.

This was as wild a spot for a manufacturing village as can well be imagined—in the heart of the mountains, with a difficult communication to the southward and none at all in any other direction —a mere clearing in a forest that stretches into Canada. . . .

The three or four days we were here we gave to excursions up and down Lake Sandford, to Newcomb's farm, and Dan Gates's camp, and to the top of Tahawus. A small company of woodsmen, professional hunters and trappers, took us under their charge—as good a set of honest, decent, kind-hearted, sensible men as one could expect to meet with, having, I thought, more propriety of talk and manners, more enlargement of mind and general knowledge, than the same number of common sailors taken equally at random would have shown. There was Dan Gates and Tone Snyder—I suppose an abbreviation of Anthony or Antoine—and John Cheney and Jack Wright, names redolent in memory of rifles and sable-traps, and hemlock camps and deer, and trout and hard walks and good talks. We rode up Lake Sandford at dawn and back by moon-light, visiting the Newcomb farm and drinking of the spring on the hill by the side of Lake Delia, to which opinion had attached marvellous restorative powers. . . .

The Opalescent, which comes down from Tahawus, is a cap-tivating mountain stream, with very irregular courses, often broken by cascades and rapids, tumbling into deep basins, running through steep gorges, and from under overlying banks, always clear and sparkling and cool. The last mile of the ascent was then—doubt-less the axe has been at work upon it since—a toilsome struggle through a dense growth of scrub cedars and spruces, and it is only the summit that is bare. With this and the summit of Mount Washington, now probably but three or four days apart, the traveller can get the two extreme opposites of North American mountain scenery; the view from Mount Washington being a wild sea of bald bare tops and sides with but little wood or water, while that from Tahawus is a limitless expanse of forest with mountains green to their tops and all the landscape dotted and lined with the wide mirrors of large lakes, glittering bits of small lakes, silver threads of streams, and ribbons of waterfalls.

As we lay on the boughs with the fire sparkling before us, a good many stories were told, marvellous, funny, or pathetic, which have long since floated off from their moorings in memory.

But it is time to take leave of our excellent friends, whose companionship I shall never forget, and move on towards the promised point of my journey.

We had sent back the guide who had brought us through the Indian Pass; for Mr. Aikens was a good woodsman and had no doubt he could take us back. About the middle of the day we bade good-by to Dan and Tone and John, and took our last look at the straggling, struggling village—in a few years, I believe, abandoned altogether—and went through the pass and crossed the first branch of the Au Sable, and ought to have crossed the second before five o'clock; but the sun was far declined, it was getting to be six o'clock and after, and yet no river! Aikens became silent; but it was soon too evident that he had lost the trail. We had been led off by a blazed line that went to sable-traps; and here we were at nightfall

lost in a forest that stretched to Canada, and, for aught I know
to the contrary, to the Polar Circle, with no food, no gun, blanket
nor overcoat. Expecting to get through in six hours, we had taken
nothing with us. We consulted, and determined to strike through
the woods, steering by the sun—for we had no compass—in the
direction we thought the river lay. Our course should be north;
and we went on, keeping the setting sun a little forward of our
left shoulders—or as a sailor would say, a little on the port bow—
and struggled over fallen timber and through underbrush, and
climbed hills and tried to get a view of Whiteface, but to no
purpose, and the darkness overtook us in low ground by the side
of a small stream. We were very hungry, very much fatigued, and
not a little anxious; and the stories they had told us at the village of
parties lost in the forest—one especially, of three men who failed to
come in and were searched for and found, after several days, little
better than skeletons and almost crazed—these recurred pretty
vividly to our fancies. We drank at the stream, and Aikens, never
at a loss, cut a bit of red flannel from his shirt and bent a pin and
managed to catch one little trout in the twilight. He insisted on our
taking it all. He said he had got us into the trouble by his over-
confidence; but we resisted. It was, to be sure, a question of a square
inch of trout more or less, for the fish was not more than four
inches long by one inch thick; yet it was a point of honor with Mr.
Aikens, so we yielded and got one fair mouthful apiece.

The place was low and damp, and there was a light frost, and we
passed a miserable night, having no clothing but our shirts and
trousers. The black flies were very active, and our faces and arms
and necks were blotched and pitted in the saddest fashion. It was
with anxious eyes that we watched the dawn; for if the day was
clear, we could travel by the sun until it got high, but if it was thick
or foggy, we must stay still; for everyone used to the woods knows
that one may go round and round and make no progress if he has no
compass or point of sight. The day did break clear; and as soon as
there was light enough, Aikens groped about the skirts of the
little opening and made out signs that a path had once come into it.
He thought the brush grew differently at one place from what it did
elsewhere. Very well! We gave ourselves up to him and began

another day's struggle with fallen timber, hillsides, swamps, and undergrowth, on very faint stomachs, but with every show to each other of confidence and strength. In an hour or so plainer signs of a path rewarded Aikens's sagacity. I was glad for him especially; for he was a good deal annoyed at the trouble we were put to; and a better woodsman, for an amateur, or a more intelligent and generous fellow-traveller, we could not have desired. At last came some welcome traces of domesticated animals, and then a trodden path, and about noon we came out upon the road.

We were out, and the danger was over. But where were we? We held a council and agreed that we must have got far to the left, or westward, of our place of destination and must turn off to the right. It was of some consequence, for houses on this road were four to seven miles apart. But the right was up hill, and a long steep hill it seemed. Mr. Metcalf plunged down hill in contempt of his and our united grave conclusions, saying we did not *know*, and had better do what was easier. And well it was we did, for a near turn in the road brought us in sight of a log house and half-cleared farm, while had we gone to the right, we should have found it seven miles to the nearest dwelling.

Three more worn, wearied, hungry, black-fly-bitten travellers seldom came to this humble, hospitable door. The people received us with cheerful sympathy, and while we lay down on the grass under the shadow of the house, where a *smutch* kept off the black flies, prepared something for our comfort. The master of the house had gone down to the settlements and was expected back before dark. His wife was rather an invalid, and we did not see much of her at first. There were a great many sons and daughters— I never knew how many; one a bonny, buxom young woman of some twenty summers, with fair skin and red hair, whose name was Ruth, and whose good-humor, hearty kindness, good sense and helpfulness quite won our hearts. She would not let us eat much at a time and cut us resolutely off from the quantities of milk and cool water we were disposed to drink, and persuaded us to wait until something could be cooked for us, more safe and wholesome for faint stomachs; and we were just weak enough to be submissive subjects to this backwoods queen. A man came along in a wagon and stopped to water his horses, and they asked him if he had seen anything of Mr. Brown below—which it seemed was the name of the family. Yes, he had seen him. He would be along in an hour or so. "He has two Negroes along with him," said the man, in a confidential, significant tone, "a man and a woman." Ruth smiled as if she understood him. Mr. Aikens told us that the country about here belonged to Gerrit Smith; that Negro families, mostly fugitive slaves, were largely settled upon it, trying to learn farming; and that this Mr. Brown was a strong abolitionist and a kind of king among them. This neighborhood was thought to be one of the termini of the Underground Railroad.

The farm was a mere recent clearing. The stumps of trees stood out, blackened by burning, and crops were growing among them, and there was a plenty of felled timber. The dwelling was a small log house of one story in height and the outbuildings were slight. The whole had the air of a recent enterprise, on a moderate scale, although there were a good many neat cattle and horses. The position was a grand one for a lover of mountain effects; but how good for farming I could not tell. Old Whiteface, the only exception to the uniform green and brown and black hues of the Adirondack hills, stood plain in view, rising at the head of Lake Placid, its white or pale gray side caused, we were told, by a landslide. All about were the distant highest summits of the Adirondacks.

Late in the afternoon a long buckboard wagon came in sight, and on it were seated a Negro man and woman, with bundles; while a tall, gaunt, dark-complexioned man walked before, having his theodolite and other surveyor's instruments with him, while a youth followed by the side of the wagon. The team turned into the sheds, and the man entered the house. This was "father." The sons came out and put up the cattle, and soon we were asked in to the meal. Mr. Brown came forward and received us with kindness; a grave, serious man he seemed, with a marked countenance and a natural dignity of manner—that dignity which is unconscious and comes from a superior habit of mind.

We were all ranged at a long table, some dozen of us more or less; and these two Negros and one other had their places with us. Mr.

Brown said a solemn grace. I observed that he called the Negroes by their surnames, with the prefixes of Mr. and Mrs. The man was "Mr. Jefferson," and the woman "Mrs. Wait." He introduced us to them in due form, "Mr. Dana, Mr. Jefferson," "Mr. Metcalf, Mrs. Wait." It was plain they had not been so treated or spoken to often before, perhaps never until that day, for they had all the awkward-ness of field hands on a plantation; and what to do on the introduc-tion was quite beyond their experience. There was an unrestricted supply of Ruth's best bread, butter, and corn-cakes, and we had some meat and tea and a plenty of the best of milk.

We had some talk with Mr. Brown, who interested us very much. He told us he came here from the western part of Mas-sachusetts. As some persons may distrust recollections, after very striking intervening events, I ask pardon for taking an extract from a journal I was in the habit of keeping at those times:—

"The place belonged to a man named Brown, originally from Berkshire in Massachusetts, a thin, sinewy, hard-favored, clear-headed, honest-minded man, who had spent all his days as a frontier farmer. On conversing with him, we found him well-informed on most subjects, especially in the natural sciences. He had books and had evidently made a diligent use of them. Having acquired some property, he was able to keep a good farm and had confessedly the best cattle and best farming utensils for miles round. His wife looked superior to the poor place they lived in, which was a cabin with only four rooms. She appeared to be out of health. He seemed to have an unlimited family of children, from a cheerful, nice, healthy woman of twenty or so, and a full-sized red-haired son, who seemed to be foreman of the farm, through every grade of boy and girl to a couple that could hardly speak plain." . . .

In these regions it is the custom for farmers to receive travellers; and while they do not take out licences as inn-holders or receive strictly pay for what they furnish, they always accept something in the way of remuneration from the traveller. When we attempted to leave something with Ruth, which was intended to express our gratitude and good-will, we found her inflexible. She would receive the bare cost of what we had taken, if we wished it, but nothing for attentions or house-room or as a gratuity. We had some five-dollar bills and some bills of one dollar each. She took one of the one-dollar bills and went up into the garret and returned with some change! It was too piteous. We could not help smiling, and told her we should feel guilty of highway robbery if we took her silver. She consented to keep the one dollar, for three of us—one meal apiece and some extra cooking in the morning—as we seemed to think that was right. It was plain this family acted on a principle in the smallest matters. They knew pretty well the cost price of the food they gave; and if the traveller preferred to pay, they would receive that, but nothing more. There was no shamefacedness about the money transaction either. It was business or nothing; and if we preferred to make it business, it was to be upon a rule.

After a day spent on Lake Placid and in ascending Whiteface, we returned to Osgood's, and the next day we took the road in our wagon on our return to Westport. We could not pass the Browns' house without stopping. . . .

How mysterious is the touch of Fate which gives a man immortality on earth! It would have been past belief had we been told that this quiet frontier farmer, already at or beyond middle life, with no noticeable past, would within ten years be the central figure of a great tragic scene, gazed upon with wonder, pity, admiration, or execration by half a continent! That this man should be thought to have imperiled the slave empire in America and added a new danger to the stability of the Union! That his almost undistinguishable name of John Brown should be whispered among four millions of slaves, and sung wherever the English tongue is spoken, and incorporated into an anthem to whose solemn cadences men should march to battle by the tens of thousands! That he should have done something toward changing the face of civilization itself!

In 1859-60 my inveterate habit of overworking gave me, as you know, a vacation and the advantage of a voyage round the world. Somewhere at the antipodes I picked up from time to time, in a disjointed way, out of all chronological order, reports of the expedition of one John Brown into Virginia, his execution, and the political excitement attending it; but I learned little of much value. That was the time when slavery ruled all. There was scarce an

American consul or political agent in any quarter of the globe or on any island of the seas who was not a supporter of the slave power. . . . I returned home at the height of the Lincoln campaign of 1860, on which followed secession and war; and it was not until after the war, when reading back into its history, that I met with those unsurpassed narratives by Mr. Wentworth Higginson and Mr. Wendell Phillips of their visits to the home of John Brown about the time of his execution, full of solemn touches and marked by that restraint which good taste and right feeling accept in the presence of a great subject, itself so expressive of awe. Reading on, it went through me with a thrill— This is the man under whose roof I received shelter and kindness! These were the mother and daughters and sons who have suffered or shed their blood! This was the family whose artless heroism, whose plain fidelity and fortitude, seemed to have cast chivalry and romance into the shade! . . .

It seems as if those few days of ours in the Adirondacks in 1849 had been passed under a spell which held my senses from knowing what we saw. All is now become a region of peculiar sacredness. That plain, bare farm amid the blackened stumps, the attempts at scientific agriculture under such disadvantages, the simple dwelling, the surveyor's tools, the setting of the little scene amid grand, awful mountain ranges, the Negro colony and inmates, the family bred to duty and principle, and held to them by a power recognized as being from above—all these now come back on my memory with a character nowise changed, indeed, in substance, but, as it were, illuminated. . . .

It is not owing to subsequent events that John Brown and his family are so impressed on my mind. The impression was made at the time. The short extract from a journal which set down but little, and nothing that was not of a marked character, will, I trust, satisfy the most incredulous that I am not beating up memory for impressions. I have tried to recollect something more of John Brown's conversation, but in vain, nor can either of my companions help me in that. . . .

My journal speaks of the house as a "log cabin." I observe that Mr. Higginson and some of the biographers describe it as a frame building. Mr. Brown had been but a few months on the place when we were there, and he may have put up a frame house afterwards; or it is quite as likely that I was not careful to note the difference, and got that impression from its small size and plain surroundings. [Dana's observation was correct. John Brown built a second house later at the site of his grave, a little over a mile west of the original log cabin.]

Nearly all that the writers in December, 1859, have described lies clear in my memory. There can have been little change there in ten years. Ruth had become the wife of Henry Thompson, whose brother was killed at Harper's Ferry; and the son I speak of as apparently the foreman of the farm was probably Owen, who was with his father at Ossawatomie and Harper's Ferry and escaped. Frederick, who was killed at Ossawatomie in 1856, was probably the lad whom we saw coming home with his father, bringing the Negroes on the wagon. Among the small boys playing and working about the house were Watson and Oliver, who were killed at Harper's Ferry. I do not recollect seeing—perhaps it was not there then—the gravestone of his grandfather of the Revolutionary Army, which John Brown is said to have taken from Connecticut and placed against the side of the house; nor can I recall the great rock near the door, by the side of which lies his body,

"mouldering in the ground,

While his soul is marching on."

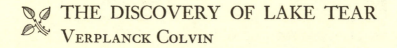

THE DISCOVERY OF LAKE TEAR
Verplanck Colvin

Down we plunged, down through the dense thickets of dwarfed balsam, whose dead limbs, clawlike spikes, clutched our clothing as though determined to resist all exploration. Our rubber

coats were speedily torn in ribbons, our other clothing ripped and
torn, and the icy drizzle of the clouds penetrated everything and
chilled us despite our labor. Suddenly, precipitous ledges barred
our way; the fog prevented our availing ourselves even of the best
route; the dwarf trees we grasped to aid us to descend pierced our
hands with their sharp spines. Here, as we hung halfway down, the
whimper of the hound above called us to aid him also, and frequently, poor thing, since he would come, he learned that tails will
serve for handles. Once, in some ravine, the next labor was to climb
from it again, and finally, when the side of Marcy seemed to lose its
downward slope and rose up in all sorts of rock masses, separated
by rifts and walled ravines and holes, we found ourselves quite lost
in the dense fog and all uncertain which way to go to find our
Gray Mountain.

The hound here commenced to sniff the ground fiercely, gave
tongue, and was off in pursuit of some wild creature, in high excitement. Hark! What sound was that? Are we called? Or is it the
echo of the hound's deep tongue? We shout, and quickly after
three mountains answer from the fog in echo . . . the deep near
answer of old Marcy; the southward voice is Skylight; the faintest
westward echo Colden. . . . The answers of the mountains shall tell
us where to go. Point toward Marcy's echo. The Gray Peak lies
the other way towards the dull, no-echo way. Laughing at this
strange assistance that the mighty mountains give us, we forgot the
cold and wet and scaled the rocks and fought the thickets with new
ardour till chill ooze or splintered branch provoked some fresh
displeasure.

Now a mountain ridge gathered high before us, lost in cloud, and
Marcy was behind. Fearful was the denseness of the balsam chaparral. This mountain crest appeared almost impregnable, so strangely
dense its pigmy forest, whose outer surface of dead boughs like
bayonets, as weathered and gray as was the frequent outcropping
rock, showed to what the mountain owed its colour. At length we
reached a summit. All around, the cloud hid everything, and we
shouted once again to our mountains for their aid. Irregularly they
responded, and Marcy now was distant. But what was this sharp
echo close ahead? Another peak. Then down we climbed from this

first pinnacle and up and at it went. More labour, more furious work, more chaparral. . . . At length we reach a crest of rock. The echoes only come to our halloos from distant mountains. We measure the direction of the echoes and determine by trilinear estimate method that we are on the summit of Gray Mountain. The barometer is brought from its case and observations taken. The readings show great altitude and prove that we are right in our conjecture. It grows bitter cold, and gladly we put up the instrument, the observations finished. The shivering guide shows his pleasure at the proposal to descend, and the dog leaps around with delight to see us moving once again.

And now from Gray Peak we have a downward work and must search for and reach that remote, unvisited lake which we have so long hoped to see. But which way does it lie? The clouds enwrapping us limit our view to a short radius. We have no compass bearings. "Call to the mountains once again." How strangely those dulled and fog-voiced echoes sound! This way southward the valley lies which we must enter and explore, and plunging from the crest, we fight another and descending battle with bristling chaparral. So steep the mountain side descends that the dwarfed timber of the crest, thus taken in flank, is soon pierced and left behind, above, but ledges now and slippery rocks make every footstep dangerous. Hanging by roots, slipping, sliding, and leaping, down we go. Now occasionally we reach a pleasant glade, deep with the thickest, richest velvety green moss, such as may be seen in Labrador. It rises to our boot tops and we stride through it as through snow. The trees, though no longer dwarfed, are but pigmy trees ten or twelve feet in height, all gray and lichen grown and ancient. . . .

At length we emerge on the edge of a little cliff, at the foot of which runs a stream amid black mossy rocks, the bottom of the valley. Descending, we hasten to drink of the gurgling water. But scarcely have we sipped when we start back and gaze at each other with astonishment. . . . This stream tells a strange story, and surely it flows westward to the Hudson. . . . We can see the shoulders of a pass opening westward. Surely this must be one of the many branches of the upper Opalescent, the Hudson's highest springs. But it is the water of this stream that excites our wonder. The water is warm or tepid and has not the usual icy temperature of the mountain brooks. It must come from a pond or lake, and this lake cannot flow to the Ausable and the St. Lawrence, but to the Hudson! ...

But the guide looks doubtful— "Perhaps this does not come from the little lake," he says, "but from some marsh, or perhaps there are two ponds"—for all the guides avowed that the lake from the top of Marcy "must go to the Ausable," though they never took the trouble to explore that valley, visit the lake, and be sure. Yet there might be a marsh; there might be another pond hidden from the view of Marcy; and interested, and excited, by the hope of discovery, we commenced to ascend the stream, hurrying along on the slippery boulders, leaping from rock to rock and at times diverging from the stream's bed into the woods. . . . Suddenly, before us, through the trees gleamed a sheet of water, and we shouted our "hurrah": for there were Marcy's slopes beyond, while the water of the lake was studded with those rocks which we had looked at with our telescopes from Marcy. It was the lake, and flowed, not to the Ausable and St. Lawrence, but to the Hudson, the loftiest lake spring of our haughty river!

But how wild and desolate this spot! It is possible that not even an Indian ever stood upon these shores. There is no mark of ax, no barked tree, nor blackened remnants of fire; not a severed twig nor a human footprint; and we follow the usual rule in this region and cut a broad blaze upon a tree and make it the register and proof of our visit. I saw it there but a few months since, already looking dark and gum-covered with the exudation of the tree. And now, skirting the shores, we seek the inlet and find that the numerous subterranean streams from different directions feed its waters. The meadow at the eastern, upper end is full of wide-winding openings, in which deep streams are gliding, and it is remarkable that, while the water of the lake is warm, the water of these subterranean streams is delicious, icy cold. The spring rills which feed these streams come from far up on the sides of the surrounding mountains, the water dripping from the crest of Marcy. First seen as we then saw it, dark and dripping with the moisture of the heavens, it seemed, in its minuteness and its prettiness, a veritable Tear-of-the-Clouds, the summit water as I named it.

THE ELUSIVE CORNER
VERPLANCK COLVIN

Despite a severe storm we reached South Branch at a point about thirty-five miles from Lowville. A depot of supplies was made, and on the 11th [July 1878] we took the field to commence the search for the *true* division line between the Brown tract and the Totten and Crossfield purchase [the latter had been surveyed a century earlier, in 1772].

The aged forest surveyor who more than twenty years before had seen the marks and had followed a portion of the line was now to verify its accurate restoration, and commenced his search under my direction, while the baggage of the party was conveyed down the Beaver to a trail leading northward to the Red Horse chain, near which the line was supposed to be located. Landing at the carry, the guides and packmen proceeded to transport the supplies over the portage, and passing Burnt Lake and Deep Pond, we reached Salmon Lake the same afternoon.

Here we were rejoined by the aged surveyor, who, greatly fatigued, alarmed us by the statement that, notwithstanding the most anxious search, he had been unable to find the line. Fire had years since swept over the section where he had hoped to discover it, and the old marked trees were gone—a dense second growth of maples and aspen now covering the rocky soil, having grown since the fire. . . .

The morning of the 12th was pleasant, and after the old surveyor had with great earnestness—though fruitlessly—searched the old timber of a tamarack swamp for the line, I resolved to adopt another course and see whether matters could not be expedited. Examining the old field-notes, it was found that the line was recorded to have crossed a lake—marked as "Hawk Lake"—somewhere, as I judged, over the mountains to the westward. As the old forest fires had not, probably, penetrated there, it seemed to me that on or near the shores of that lake the old trees might be found, still carrying the marks of the first compass surveyors.

Computing the bearing of the lake, I assembled the party, and cutting down the baggage to a minimum, each man carrying a knapsack, we set out in search of the lake. We immediately commenced to ascend a mountain, where in the dense thickets the summer heat was intense, and reaching the crest, looked out through the timber on the bright surface of Salmon Lake. Then turning, we descended, and through windslashes, dense timber and open forests, ascending and descending, we reached, at noon, the summit of a mountain where from a fallen tree lodged so as to serve as a projecting platform, I was able to look out over an extremely wild country. In the sea of woods before us sparkled the waters of two lakes with which neither myself nor any of the guides were acquainted. This was not surprising, as this was to a great extent unexplored territory; and we might reasonably expect many more discoveries of such waters.

Descending this mountain, a deep valley was seen to the left, and leading the party in that direction, I soon had the pleasure of standing upon the shores of a charming lake, whose bright green bordering of forest was reflected in the placid surface. The stately evergreens descended to its shores and gave grace and dignity to the scenery; while rocky points projecting into the clear water and marshy bays, rich with lilies and soft herbage, offered luxuriant feeding ground for deer, whose delicate footprints were seen along the shores. Above rose undulating hills, the dark slopes of which found partial reflection in the forest pool.

Satisfied from the form and the peculiar projecting points that this was the Hawk Lake of the ancient survey, we unslung knapsacks near a spring on the southern shore and partook of lunch. This finished, we commenced the search for the ancient line, which to our delight was at length discovered on the northern shore, on dead and crumbling timber. . . .

July 13th. I resolved to march the party to the northern terminus of the line to find, verify and monument the important corner whence the line originated, and see the party regularly started working southward toward their base of supplies. Found the region obstructed with much fallen timber. This and the retracing of the line made progress slow and difficult; but at four o'clock in the afternoon we struck one of the smaller affluents of the Oswegatchie, a still stream flowing northward through a vast forest swamp. Here we were surprised and interested by finding the remains of a very ancient city of the beavers. This forest swamp had evidently once been the pond of a settlement of these intelligent creatures, but at an extremely remote period. The beaver houses were most singularly preserved as to form—though themselves decayed and gone—by the tree roots. In one spot I noticed a tree apparently growing upon the top of a well-formed beaver house. An inspection showed that it was simply a dome of the tree's roots, which preserved as a *cast* the figure of the ancient habitation of the animal. Anxious to get on, we crossed the stream and made our way along its northern bank, traversing a deep swamp where dead trees with rocks and alder brush together made the march toilsome. . . .

Some idea of the roughness of the ground may be had from the fact that in going less than two miles of direct distance my pedometer recorded eight and three-fourth miles. For men carrying heavy packs of provisions this fallen timber makes each day's march an exhausting climb. At Hawk Lake I had foreseen this difficulty and had ordered the aids and guides to throw aside all baggage. Blankets, ponchoes, coats, and everything almost, except the instruments, axes and provisions, were left, and yet it was a weary company.

July 14th. We continued our march northward toward the great corner which we had hoped to reach at night, but made slow progress over the fearful windslashes. The land is broken into ridges with few swamps. At 2:20 p.m. we reached Wolf Lake [now Rock Lake, not to be confused with the Wolf Pond two miles to the northeast], a strange body of water, of which the broad branch of the Oswegatchie that we here struck was claimed by our old surveyor to be the outlet. Searching up along the wide, marshy shores of the river for a place to cross, I found a rapid where we were enabled to pass, and leaving the party to go forward on the line, with orders to build a camp near the west end of Wolf Lake, I proceeded with one assistant along a sand ridge on the southern shore to make a reconnaissance. The further I proceeded along this ridge the more I became interested in the odd form of the lake, which seemed to be made of two great bays, almost separated by the ridge on which I advanced. This ridge, by the way, was one of those singular long narrow dunes which had so interested and perplexed me in the Bog River section. It was most singular. Open and picturesque with superb white pine trees here and there upon it, with numerous deer paths deeply stamped, leading through its carpeting of moss and whortleberry bushes, the beautiful lake on the one side and the shallow winding river on the other, made it far more entrancing than the choicest ramble of guarded park. Now I began to surmise that there were *two lakes*, and hurrying forward found that it was true—the waters barely separated by the narrow ridge—and that the river passed was not the outlet of Wolf Lake at all, but came from a broad nameless sheet with low sandy shores [the "nameless" lake is Sand, a twin to Rock Lake].

This was an interesting discovery; and passing around the head of Wolf Lake, I undertook to return along its opposite shore to where in the distance the faint smoke rising from the forest told that my party was encamped. This was soon found to be vastly different from the easy deer paths on the sand ridge; and wading along the shore, rather than traverse the fearful tangles of the fallen timber, a slow advance was made. In one of the wadings I suddenly entered a cold, heavy quicksand and descended so suddenly that I had barely time to grasp some laurel bushes (*Kalmia angusti folia*) at the shore, and with difficulty escaped entire submergence and drowning. Got ashore at length and made my way to camp, rather late in the afternoon. Secured map sketches and some barometrical observations, and in attempting to get a station to observe the sun for time, was caught in a severe thunder storm. . . .

Proceeding northward [July 15], we reached at length a broad branch of the little Oswegatchie, flowing through a large swamp [Alder Bed Flow]; the stream abounded with speckled trout, and a handsome string was easily caught with coarse tackle from where we forded it. Passing this swamp, we ascended and descended along ridges and occasional moist swales, still following the old line, sometimes only discernible under the moss on mouldering trunks of fallen trees. At 5 p.m. the men called a halt, being fairly unable to travel farther that day, and could not be persuaded to go on, though I now estimated that we were within a mile of the sought-for corner. Built a camp, and at dark retired to profound slumber.

July 16th, making an early start and leaving our packs at the camp —for I judged that we should reach the corner today—we traced the line northward still but with great difficulty; for many of the marks were not only a century old, but the trees themselves prostrate and decayed. We now came out on the banks of a large branch of the Oswegatchie [Middle Branch north of Alder Bed Flow]; a rapid stream flowing amid huge boulders of a reddish quartzite. Here the line was obscure, and we crept through a dense windslash. Now it crossed a brook, then ascended a hill, and I hurried in advance, as the corner must be near. Entering a level, partly swampy, the line ceased, and as I looked again, some singular hollows, sunken places, and contortions in the bark of the surrounding trees caught my eyes. They were evidently ancient witness trees, blazed on one side only, each blaze pointing toward the centre of the glade in which I stood. A glance showed a crumbling stake, having three small stones, moss-covered, at its foot. It was the long sought-for corner, the great pivotal point on which all the land titles of nearly five millions of acres depended. In a few moments the rest of the party had joined me, and the old surveyor recognized the stake by which he had replaced the mouldering fragments of the original corner post!

The shouts of the party showed their joy at reaching the end of an exhausting journey. . . . A ponderous boulder of brownish quartzite, of regular form, was selected as the monument with which to mark the corner. . . . The nickel-plated copper bolt, being heated red hot, was run in with melted lead, and the great southern corner of the largest county of the state, St. Lawrence (and of all the great land patents of the north), was for the first time marked with a stone monument.

❧ LOST POND
HENRY ABBOTT

"Lost Pond" was a tradition, a myth. It had never been seen by any living person. Two dead men, it was alleged, had visited it on several occasions while they were yet living.

Wonderful tales were told about that pond for which many persons had hunted, but which no one of the present generation had ever been able to find. Every guide in Long Lake township talked about Lost Pond and repeated the legends, which through the passing years had probably lost none of their original enticements. Many of these guides had even got the stories at first hand from Captain Parker and Mitchel Sabattis. . . .

Now, all of the natives knew that Lost Pond was somewhere on Seward Mountain, and they apparently believed that the best fishing place in the state was right in that pond. "By Mighty! that pond was just alive with speckled trout—big ones. You could catch all you wanted there in a few minutes. The water fairly boiled with the jumping fish. Now, if we could only find it," etc. . . .

The mountain was covered with forest, and there was not a human habitation on it or within many miles of it in any direction. Some lumbering had been done along Cold River and several of its tributary creeks, but the higher portions were untouched and the heavy spruce and hemlock cover looked black from up the lake.

Giving proper consideration to these facts and knowing the Long Lake guides as well as I did, I could readily understand that it might be less strenuous to tell the marvelous stories about Lost Pond than it would be to go up in the Seward country and search out the pond. Then there was always the possibility that too much investigation might spoil a good story.

Ever since childhood I have possessed that very human characteristic of wanting that which is forbidden, longing for what is just out of reach; and when a thing is said to be impossible, I at once have an intense desire to undertake to do that thing.

Now, there was good trout fishing in many of the ponds and streams tributary to Long Lake which were comparatively easy to reach, but this lost pond which I had heard so much about was so "impossible to find" that I was possessed with an irresistible longing to find it, to see what it looked like, to fish in it. So I discussed the matter with Bige, who, with some show of reluctance, agreed to assist. . . .

With our two packs stowed amidships, Bige in the bow with a pair of oars and I in the stern wielding a paddle, we got away in the morning just as the sun broke over East Inlet Mountain and gilded the summit of Sugar Loaf on the opposite side of the lake.

The early birds greeted us with a chorus of song, seeming to wish us luck as we made good speed down the lake, passing Owls Head Mountain on the left, Sabattis on the right, and farther down Blueberry, Kempshall and Buck mountains, while Santanoni and Seward loomed up in the distance.

It is about fourteen miles to the foot of the lake and five miles farther down the outlet, through "Lost Channel," to the place on Calkins Creek where we left our boat in the shade of some balsams.

We now shouldered our packs and started on the strenuous and interesting part of our undertaking. Following up Calkins Valley about six miles, we passed, at intervals of two or three miles, three abandoned lumber camps, the log buildings being in all stages of decay from long disuse, many of them with roofs caved in and overgrown with weeds and bushes.

A few rods beyond the last log camp, while pushing my way through the high grass and bushes in a log-road, I almost stepped upon a spotted fawn which jumped up under my nose and turned to stare at me with his solemn-looking eyes, which seemed much too large for his head. The little fellow was apparently about a month old and was as frisky and awkward in his movements as a young puppy. He had no doubt been hidden there by his mother, who had warned him to lie low till she returned, to look out for enemies, and especially to beware of any animal that walks upon two legs. He was now uncertainly wavering between fear and curiosity, and with his head turned and his eyes fastened upon me, he stumbled clumsily away through the high grass directly into Bige's outstretched arms.

Here was now a situation not down on our programme. We had

captured a live deer. We were not intending to start a menagerie or to stock a zoological park. We were out in search of a pond that had been mislaid on a mountain. We could not very well carry the deer up the mountain while pursuing our explorations, and we had no idea that he could be made to walk in our company so far as we should have to go. Moreover, neither Bige nor I was properly equipped to feed an infant; so we put him back in his grassy bed, patted him on the head, advised him to stay there until his mother returned, and proceeded upon our journey.

Half a mile farther on we left the log-road, turned sharply to the right, and climbed up the steep slope of one of the foothills. Passing the ridge, we now came into a section of the forest which had never been visited by the lumberman's axe. The tall spruces and hemlocks interspersed here and there with yellow birch and maples cast deep shadows, and the forest floor was as free from underbrush as if cleared by a landscape gardener. This was what poets and nature writers call the "primeval forest." Also, traveling with a pack on one's back was much easier here than in the lumbered country.

A spring of cold clear water with a rivulet flowing from it down the slope reminded us that it was lunch time, and that this was an ideal place to eat it. After lunch we took up our burdens and continued our journey eastward until about two o'clock, when we had crossed the fourth high ridge from Calkins Valley and dropped into a deep basin. This was the valley Bige and I had located when we surveyed the country from over on Santanoni. This was the place where Lost Pond ought to be; but there was no pond here, lost or otherwise.

We sat down to talk it over. Bige said "Le's go home." But I outvoted him and we continued on, taking a northeasterly course, which we followed for what seemed about five miles. When we had passed through a valley between two high peaks we made a sort of oxbow curve around the one to the right, and there laid a straight course with our compass back in the direction from which we had come but a mile or more south of our outward route.

During the afternoon we encountered about all the different kinds of forest travel that it is possible to find anywhere. There were steep rocky ledges which had to be climbed; cedar swamps which must be negotiated; several acres of burnt ground now covered with a dense growth of poplar and wild-cherry saplings; blackberry bushes as high as one's head—oceans of them; balsam groves with deep beds of moss for a carpet; "witchhopple," which tangles one's feet and gives one a hard fall at unexpected moments; there were steep climbs up and steep slides down; and there were delightful stretches of "big woods," but always the charm of variety.

We were too intent upon our quest and made too much noise in our travels to see much wild life; the animals always had ample notice of our approach and always had convenient hiding places.

About six o'clock we came upon a noisy brook which was tumbling down out of the mountains through a steep valley. The bed of the stream was filled with boulders, and there were numerous short falls and rapids. We heard the noise of the brook long before it came into view, and Bige promptly named it "Roaring Brook."

There was something suggestive about this brook, and we sat and discussed it while resting. It was a dry season; there had been no rain for two weeks. Surface drainage could not account for all the water coming down that brook. It might come from one of the swamps we had passed through earlier in the day. It would have to be a very large spring or a lot of small ones to keep up the flow of that volume of water. It might be the outlet of a pond. We decided to follow upstream and settle the question of its source.

About a half-mile up, we came upon a level stretch of quiet water, but there was a noise of splashing in the stream ahead. Cautiously we crept forward and peering through a clump of alders saw an old black bear and one cub, wallowing in the shallow water. Neither Bige nor I had lost any bear, old or young, and we had no intention of attacking with our only weapon—a fishing rod—an old mother bear in the presence of her child; so without a conference, but with a common thought, we carefully backed up a few rods and hid behind a clump of bushes through the branches of which we watched the performance.

We were reminded of an old sow and one pig wallowing in a mudhole. The old bear lay down in the water and rolled over in it while the cub climbed upon his mother and took headers off her back. They were evidently taking their weekly tub and were enjoying it immensely.

After some ten minutes of this moving-picture act, the old bear climbed out on the bank and shook herself; the cub followed, stood on his head and rolled and tumbled about on the grassy bank until his mother gave a commanding grunt and started off into the woods with the cub following at her heels.

About twenty rods farther up-stream we arrived at the source of Roaring Brook. It was a beautiful sheet of glassy water set in a bowl in the hills, with the bowl tilted on one side until the water spilled over its lower edge into the brook. The pond was about two hundred yards in diameter. Three deer were standing in the shallow water on the opposite edge. The water was clear and cold as ice. We both dropped our packs and shouted in chorus, "This is where we sleep!"

It was getting late, so we hurried our preparations for making camp. I undertook to set up the tent while Bige collected a quantity of dry moss for a bed. This he peeled off a ledge of rocks on the hillside in great slabs that were three to four inches thick. Over a double layer of moss he placed balsam boughs, sticking the butt end of each bough through the moss in a sloping position and making one course of boughs overlap another like shingles on a roof. The result was most satisfactory. Bige is a wonder in making a camp bed.

While hunting material for tent pegs and poles I noticed a curious rectangular-shaped hillock of green moss a short distance from the shore of the pond. Kicking the mossy covering away, there was disclosed the rotted logs of what had many years ago been a camp about twelve feet square. A dozen yards away was a moss-covered log which seemed flattened on top and tapered at both ends. Scraping away the moss and rolling over the log, I found a dugout canoe. This had been hewn from a pine log about thirty inches in diameter and sixteen feet long. The canoe was in fair condition, but heavy and somewhat decayed at one end. Having finished our tent and bed, we rolled the canoe down to the water's edge and undertook to put it in order for use. To insure its floating with two heavy men aboard, we cut and trimmed out two dry spruces about six inches in diameter and lashed them, one on either side of the canoe and against two smaller cross-pieces placed above to keep the string-pieces near the gunwale. The cross-pieces also served the purpose of seats.

For many years I have carried in the bottom of the pack, when on camping trips, a coil of small rope or heavy twine and have often found it very useful. It fitted in perfectly on this occasion.

The dusk of evening was now upon us, so we hurriedly pushed our pirogue-raft into the water and climbed aboard. . . . Then followed twenty minutes of the swiftest and most exciting bit of trout fishing that I have ever experienced. I could have hooked three or four at a time if I had put on that many flies, but one kept me busy. With every cast two or three trout would make a rush for the fly, and they would fight one another for possession of it. Even after one fish was securely hooked and was struggling for his freedom others would appear and try to take the fly away from him. Bige said, "The trout climbed out, stood on their tails, and reached for the fly long before it hit the water."

It was now quite dark and we were losing more fish than we saved. It was impossible to see the landing net, and we often knocked them off the hook when trying to scoop them up. We had enough fish for supper, so we decided to leave some of them for morning, went ashore, built a fire, cooked our trout and bacon, and ate supper by the light of the fire. . . .

The pond had no visible inlet, but a considerable quantity of water was flowing out of it every minute. This must be replenished through some subterranean passage, and the water doubtless filtered through an enormous field of ice that had been buried under millions of tons of rock and earth for countless ages—since the glacial period, when the mountain slid down from the arctic regions into its present position.

Bige and I discussed it at supper, and that is how we accounted for the peculiar conditions. We were also agreed that there could now be no doubt that this was the pond of Sabattis-Parker fame. The stories fitted well with the facts. Some one surely had been here before and a long time ago, else how could the ruins of the camp and the moss-covered dugout be satisfactorily explained?

That night Bige and I went to bed with clear consciences. We were at peace with the world. We had put in a long and strenuous day, had met and overcome many obstacles and difficulties, and had accomplished something worth while. We had recovered and put back on the map a pond which had been lost for more than thirty years. Incidentally, we had had a lot of fun in doing it. A pair of hermit thrushes holding converse with each other across the valley and high over our heads sang us to sleep.

We were awake in the morning before the sun and in our skiff out on the pond casting with great care our most alluring flies. We whipped every square inch of that pond. We spent two hours and a half on it, used every fly in the book, and never got a rise. We never even saw a trout big or little. We could have seen them had they been there. It was not more than three feet to the bottom in the deepest part, and we could see the bottom and everything, animate and inanimate, in the water. The shoals of trout we had seen and heard—some of which we had eaten—the night before had disappeared utterly and completely. Bige said, "They have gone back into the ice-chest." . . .

We knew that, generally speaking, home lay in a southwesterly direction from where we sat, but we were uncertain whether Lost Pond was on the northern or the southern side of the high points in the Seward group of mountains. However, one of the first principles of woodcraft which I learned while still in the primary class is that water always runs downhill, and that if one follows a brook down far enough it will surely lead to a larger stream, and it in turn will finally take one to a lake. It may be a long and circuitous route, but when one has lost his bearings in the forest, that is generally a safe rule to follow. . . . In due time and without incident worthy of mention, we reached Cold River and later Calkins Creek, found our boat, and late in the afternoon were pushing slowly up the lake [Long Lake].

THE YELLOW LADY-SLIPPERS
HUGH FOSBURGH

Lady-slippers, especially the yellow ones, are my favorite flower. Everything about them—their delicate soft shape; their demure fragility that makes me wonder how they survive; the secluded places where they grow; their extreme rarity hereabouts —everything about them is enchanting.

My mother, who was passionate about wild flowers, was constantly on the lookout for yellow lady-slippers, but never found one here. Many years ago an old woodsman named Fay Weller told her that he had seen them growing at a certain place on the south bank of the Boreas River, and although she went there several times she wasn't able to discover them.

A few years later, in May, 1938, my brother Pieter and I were luckier—we fished the Boreas one day (without success as I recall) and on the way home we looked for and found the lady-slippers, about forty of them, at the exact place Fay had described.

We have searched diligently elsewhere but we haven't seen a yellow lady-slipper here since that time, so this morning, twenty years later, we made another excursion down the Boreas to see if they were still there.

It was a muggy day and the black flies were pestilential.

We remembered that the place was just east of where a small stream emptied into the river so we thought we could walk to the spot without any trouble at all. We were wrong; there were more streams—all small and almost identical—than we remembered, and the distance was much greater.

We found a few pink lady-slippers and one lush Hooker's orchis —a lovely plant with pale yellow-green flowers on a tall stem and two flat-on-the-ground waxy leaves that are the size and shape of butterplates—but no yellow lady-slippers.

When we had gone about four miles—twice as far as we had anticipated—we concluded that they no longer existed; but we continued to the next stream, went east a short way, and suddenly, there they were. They were all over that little place—some in bud, some in full bloom, some past flowering; there were tall lush ones and small dainty ones—a great serene colony of lady-slippers living in peaceful obscurity.

Finding them was something akin to a revelation.

 DISCOVERY, 1960

PAUL SCHAEFER

There is little doubt that the most ardent and indefatigable "trail blazer" in Adirondack history was Verplanck Colvin of Albany.

At the age of eighteen in 1865 he started mapping the Adirondacks in the Speculator region and soon was espousing the creation of an Adirondack park. By 1872 he had convinced the legislature of this need and was appointed superintendent of a topographical survey of these mountains.

His very first year of survey yielded dramatic results. He found that the source of the Hudson was a lakelet on the state's highest mountain, Marcy. He described it as being like a "tear of the clouds," a name which still clings to this 4,300 foot source of our greatest river.

Other discoveries followed one upon the other. He documented his work with wonderful books, written in diary form, and illustrated with many fine drawings and photographs. Ten substantial volumes followed. . . . About 1878 [he described the Adirondacks as] "a region of mystery, over which none can gaze without a strange thrill of interest and of wonder at what might be hidden in that vast area of forest covering all things with its deep repose. It is not of the deer of which we think, treading the deep rich moss among the stately tamaracks; nor the bear, luxuriating in the berry patches on the mountain side; nor the panther or the wolf in their lonely and desolate wilds, seeking their feast of blood: We gaze downward from the mountain height on thousands and thousands of square miles of wilderness, which always was one—since forest it became—and which hides today as it has hidden for so many ages, the secrets of form, and soil, and rock, and history, on which we ponder.

"Huge are these almost undecipherable pages of the world's annals; enormous and difficult to read; yet there are marks and traces here and there which tell in a brief, irregular and fragmentary way—to those able to decipher such inscriptions—the prehistoric growth of continents; the origin of rivers; the spread of vegetable and animal life, and the approach of man.". . .

There still is the kind of mystery in these mountains Colvin described. For in 1960, on occasion of the seventy-fifth anniversary of the founding of the Forest Preserve, I actually "discovered" a glacial lake, deep and dark, in the east central Adirondacks. Owned by the state since 1880, state officials had no record of it; it was a blank on U. S. G. S. topographical sheets and also on county maps. Nestling in a bowl high in some small mountains, it is known only by a few natives. Spring fed, the outlet goes over a rocky ledge and almost disappears in a thick swamp before it emerges to run freely down an open mountain slope to a large, well-known trout stream in the valley below.

In these vast recesses of the Adirondacks are many unknown, little known, or forgotten natural wonders.

Even a lifetime will not suffice to thoroughly explore these North Woods. In forty-five years of such adventuring I find myself having a good understanding of this fact and little more—little more, that is, except a deep and abiding love for the Adirondacks, a devotion which increases as the years roll swiftly onward and it becomes apparent that there are many wonderful places that, for want of time, I shall never get to see.

And even in this thought there is a certain richness—!

WHITEOUT
Laura Viscome

A Department of Environmental Conservation helicopter plucked two young men off the side of Algonquin Mountain Saturday afternoon, saving them from certain death after spending a bone-chilling night exposed to minus forty degree temperatures.

"They would not have been able to walk out," Dr. Edward Hixson said later, noting the two men had removed their boots after stopping. "And, if the helicopter had been unable to fly, the result could have been fatal."

The two hikers, Michael Boxer, nineteen, and Steven Sygman, twenty-one, both of Brooklyn, spent twenty-four hours—Friday night, Jan. 2, and part of Saturday, Jan. 3 [1981]—lost on 5,114 foot Algonquin Peak. During the night both had removed their hiking boots and were suffering from frostbite.

Mr. Boxer's ten toes were deeply frostbitten. Mr. Sygman escaped with only two frostbitten toes.

They were rescued about 3 p.m. Saturday through the concerted efforts of Department of Environmental Conservation personnel, who launched an all-out search Saturday morning. . . .

The two, along with four other students from Brooklyn College, had been camping in a teepee on the Adirondak Loj property and making day hikes in the area for almost a week when they decided to climb Algonquin.

Their day hike, which began Friday about 8 a.m., was made to achieve Mr. Boxer's goal: the summit of Algonquin. The other four hikers in their party, two women and two men, tried to persuade the pair not to go because of Saturday's below-zero temperatures and high winds.

Their persuasion was not successful.

Dressed warmly for their day hike and carrying a two-day supply of food, a small stove, a roll of ensolite (insulating material used under sleeping bags) and crampons, the two Brooklyn College students succeeded in reaching the treeless, snow-capped summit in the early afternoon. They did not bring snowshoes, a tent or sleeping bags.

Part way up the trail they met one of three hikers known to be on Algonquin that day. Tony Ballato of Bronxville met them about 11 a.m. He told rangers Saturday morning that Mr. Boxer and Mr. Sygman appeared warmly dressed. He also said that the wind was so strong on Wright's Peak that it had blown him off his feet. The hikers had to cross Wright to reach Algonquin, the major peak in the MacIntyre Range.

It was on Algonquin that they ran into a "whiteout" which caused them to lose their tracks and sense of direction. A whiteout occurs when wind-driven snow completely obscures a hiker's vision.

Roaming around in the blustery winds on the summit of Algonquin, they found a stream bed which they decided to follow. Once they reached the treeline they found themselves struggling through brush and snow that was up to their armpits. Although they did not know it, the stream led to the Scotts Clearing lean-to.

The struggle through the deep snows left them exhausted. They found an opening and dug in.

They used their stove to heat some hot chocolate and jello. Then the fuel ran out. Their efforts to light a fire were unsuccessful, even though there was plenty of good, combustible material at hand.

While following the stream bed, Mr. Boxer had broken through the ice and gotten his feet wet. Foolishly, he removed his hiking boots. They froze immediately and he was unable to put them on again. He put the liners of mittens on his feet.

The two spent the thirty-five degree below zero night about 3,500 feet up the mountain without benefit of a tent or sleeping bags.

"First we stamped around in the snow to keep warm and awake," Steven Sygman said later in the emergency room of the General Hospital of Saranac Lake about twenty minutes after their evacuation from the summit. "Then we took turns lying on one another to keep warm."

They used the ensolite pad to lie on. It offered some protection from the cold ground.

"I kept Michael awake through most of the night," Mr. Sygman said. "He seemed drowsy and incoherent at times and he shivered a lot."

During the night the pair blew a whistle continuously and kept calling out. "That's why I'm so hoarse now," Mr. Sygman said.

Mr. Sygman had removed his hiking boots about 4 a.m. "At this point, you were trapped," Dr. Hixson told the two men after it was all over. "You could not have gotten out, and if help had not come when it did . . ." He left the sentence unfinished.

When the two hikers failed to return to Adirondak Loj, the four other members of their party became concerned and went to the Loj for help. They were fortunate to find that a group of former summer rangers for the Department of Conservation had picked that weekend to hold a reunion. John Wood, who is employed by the DEC as a wilderness ranger, was with the group. He immediately contacted Keene Forest Ranger Peter Fish.

Early Saturday morning, Lake Placid Forest Ranger Gary Hodgson was contacted and immediately began organizing a search and rescue operation for the overdue hikers. He contacted the DEC in Albany, requested helicopter assistance, and notified the New York State Police.

Rangers Joe Rupp of Lake Clear, Wes Hurd of Wilmington, Dave Ames of Keene Valley and Doug Bissonette of Lake Placid were also notified and began preparing for their roles in the search.

Meanwhile, Pete Fish, who carried a radio, and John Wood had already left the Loj about 8:30 a.m., leading separate rescue groups. The temperature was about twenty-five below zero. The day was clear with sunshine and no wind.

One group took the old trail to Wright's Peak and the other the new one. The two groups met four hikers, who continued the climb with Ranger Fish. . . .

Mr. Hodgson then proceeded to Adirondak Loj to gather information. When he arrived at the Loj's hikers building, a somber group greeted him. Most were experienced hikers who were aware of the consequences of being lost atop an Adirondack peak.

A cranberry and popcorn bedecked Christmas tree standing in the corner seemed inappropriate to the occasion. The many newspaper clippings pinned to the bulletin board told stories of a lost hiker who never returned and of the dangers of hypothermia, the killer of unprepared hikers.

Mr. Hodgson conferred briefly with the two women in the party to get as much information as possible. The two men in the college group had already left with the search parties.

After conferring with Tony Ballato and Richard and Paul Burns of Chappaqua, Hodgson theorized that the hikers would probably be found "on the west side of Algonquin, the Indian Pass side." He continued, "They probably started down my favorite stream. If they follow it, they'll come out near the Scotts Clearing lean-to on the Indian Pass trail.". . .

When Joe Rupp arrived, Mr. Hodgson gave him a radio and asked three of the summer rangers—Nancy Proctor, Jeff Brown and Bill Rudge—who were waiting quietly to help if they were needed, to go with Mr. Rupp. Equipped with food, snowshoes and winter hiking gear, they left within a few minutes.

Mr. Hodgson waited until Wes Hurd radioed in that he would arrive momentarily to take over the control center at the Loj. The ranger then left for the Lake Placid Airport. It was already well past noon, and the helicopter had radioed moments before that it was en route.

Rangers Doug Bissonette of Lake Placid and Dave Ames of Keene Valley were already at the airport when Mr. Hodgson arrived. Equipped with snowshoes, packs and winter hiking gear, the three men boarded the chopper shortly after 2:30 p.m.

On the Indian Pass trail, Joe Rupp and his team had begun the ascent of Algonquin at the base of the stream bed. . . .

Once airborne, the helicopter pilot headed for the west side of Algonquin at Ranger Hodgson's direction. The chopper came in low and followed the ravine formed by the stream bed up towards the summit. It actually passed over the hikers, who were in a small open patch well below treeline. They later said that they waved some yellow material, but they were not detected.

When the chopper reached treeline, tracks were visible in the snow. The tracks disappeared into the trees. The rangers decided to go down and follow them. Hodgson and Ames were dropped out, about eighty feet, on the end of the winch line. Mr. Bissonette operated the winch. Within minutes the hikers were found.

They were lifted into the helicopter. Mr. Hodgson and Mr. Ames followed. It was now 3 p.m. and the temperature was still well below zero. Ten minutes later the helicopter touched down on the pad next to Saranac Lake General Hospital.

Dr. Edward Hixson, who had been alerted by radio while working at the Lake Placid Ski Jump, was waiting with the emergency room personnel.

Following an examination in which Dr. Hixson found their body temperatures to be slightly below normal, in the 96 and 97 degree range, he ordered them to the whirlpool, where they soaked their feet in body temperature water for about half an hour.

Both were admitted to the hospital. Steven Sygman was released the next day to return to Brooklyn. Michael Boxer remains at the hospital taking whirlpool treatments. He is expected to return home in about a week.

The answer to his question as to whether he will lose any of his toes will not be known for several weeks, according to Dr. Hixson.

"Never take your boots off in situations like that," Dr. Hixson said as he left the hospital. "You can walk with your feet frozen in your boots. Once you take them off, you're trapped."

The two boys from Brooklyn can be thankful for their good fortune. "If they had to be found by a search party and had to be carried out, things could have been much worse," Dr. Hixson said as he headed for his truck.

In his hospital bed, Michael Boxer was already planning his next trip into the mountains.

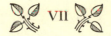 VII

Shelter for the Night

Oh for a lodge in some vast wilderness,
Some boundless contiguity of shade.
William Cowper

M AKE IT "camp" for short. In the Adirondacks this word covers nearly every variety of shelter for temporary lodging in the woods, from the hollow log to the castle with walls six feet thick. There are a few holdouts. The Lake Placid Club and the Whiteface Inn were not camps, though their outlying cabins were. That parvenu the motel, with its standardized comforts and hurry-let's-be-on-the-move air, is not yet assimilated. In time it too will probably go native and be honored by the name "camp." A set of deer horns over the office door and balsam pillows on the beds should be enough.

It is nearly inadmissible to go to the woods without camping. Camping is the essence of life in the woods. So there has been pressure on the word "camp" to encompass the needs and whims of ninety thousand summer residents and of several million annual visitors who come for overnight or longer stays. Some of them like nature but not wilderness. They expect a million-dollar beach, an eighteen-hole golf course, and hot and cold running water. Others go in for varying degrees of roughing it. The Adirondack Park is large enough and hospitable enough to cater to all these folk. When they go home they can say, in perfect conformity with established usage, "We have been camping in the Adirondacks."

"Camp" had proved its versatility by the early 1880s, but the real breakthrough came shortly after. " 'Camp' has come to mean," wrote Fred Mather in 1882, "a commodious log house used either as an occasional resort by a private person or a backwoods hotel." Structures of either purpose, he adds, cost from $500 to $1,500 to build. But even as he wrote William West Durant was evolving on Raquette Lake a luxurious summer residence called Camp Pine Knot, which combined the styles of the native log house and the Swiss chalet. An exterior facade of rusticity disguised city amenities such as efficient plumbing (and later wiring), powder room, and banquet hall. A family camp of this kind soon became a small village to accommodate staff and guests. When sold to Collis Huntington in 1895, Camp Pine Knot consisted of ten cottages and a dozen or so other buildings. It was the first of many show places in the woods. And these, too, whether of logs or not, whether of native or foreign style, were "camps."

Purists complain about the word. Donaldson says that it calls loudly and despondently for definition, as one lost in a wilderness of meanings. But this is a narrow view. We need such a word to express in a pregnant monosyllable the ever-fresh novelty of living in the woods, whether the shelter be a lean-to or a chateau. "Camp" is no semantic misfortune but a masterpiece of suggestion.

Thoreau explained the everlasting appeal of camping when he said of the Walden experiment that he went to the woods to front only the essential facts of life. Camping is a test and a refuge—a test of our worthiness of pioneer ancestors and a refuge from whatever bothers us in the settlements. Going to the woods once a year may avert weekly visits to the analyst. The art of the thing is to simplify as much as circumstances and temperament permit. At one end of the scale is the hiker who packs in thirty-five pounds of bare essentials for three nights in a lean-to. At the other is the going in of a New York family of the 1880s embarrassed by worldly possessions. Having chartered a "special parlor horse car" on the railway, the family rolls massively from Forty-second Street to Ausable Forks:

> Anson Phelps Stokes, wife, seven children, one niece, about ten servants, Miss Rondell, one coachman, three horses, two dogs, one carriage, five large boxes of tents, three cases of wine, two packages of stove pipe, two stoves, one bale china, one iron

pot, four washstands, one barrel of hardwood, four bundles of poles, seventeen cots and seventeen mattresses, four canvas packages, one buckboard, five barrels, one half barrel, two tubs of butter, one bag coffee, one chest tea, one crate china, twelve rugs, four milkcans, two drawing boards, twenty-five trunks, thirteen small boxes, one boat, one hamper.

But the logistics problem once solved and the family established in their island camp, their woods life—described by a daughter, Mrs. Mildred P. Stokes Hooker, in *Camp Chronicles*—is a real simplification. They live in tents until cabins are built, eschew evening dress, and complain that camp is not so "campy" after the telephone comes in. Surveying the colony of which they were a part, on Upper St. Regis Lake in the domain of the hotel proprietor Paul Smith, that genial host once exclaimed: "I never saw anything like it! There's not a foot of land on that lake for sale this minute, and there's not a man in it but what's a millionaire, and some of them ten times over. . . . I tell you if there's a spot on the face of the earth where millionaires go to play at house keeping in log cabins and tents as they do here, I have yet to hear about it."

Since that day other gadgets besides the telephone have reduced the campiness of the summer camps. A funicular railway drew guests up from the boat landing to Marjorie Merriweather Post's camp village atop an esker on Upper St. Regis Lake. A private turboprop plane whisked thirty guests to Boston for a seafood dinner and returned them for a cool night under the pines at Camp Topridge. Thoreau and his philosophy are frustrated in such a camp. The wise dreamer, looking about for the best time, place, and circumstance to be young in, would fix on the Adirondack family camp of the 1880s and 90s. There, if anywhere, was realized Lord Bryce's vision of American life as "pleasanter, easier, simpler" than life in Europe, floating "in a sense of happiness like that of a radiant summer morning."

The luxury camps of the Durants, Morgans, Vanderbilts, and Huntingtons have today passed into the hands of foundations, universities, or, in the case of Camp Topridge, the state itself. They are being preserved more or less intact as historical monuments of a distinctive architecture and way of life.

Less subject to the whims of the wealthy and of time is the three-sided open camp or lean-to. It has a long tradition. Pioneers and trappers developed it and passed it on to the Adirondack guide; the guide in turn passed it on to the sportsman, tourist, and summer resident (often it was one of the outbuildings of a family camp), and finally to the state Conservation Department. Before its adoption by summer residents and the state, it was constructed wherever needed of materials—saplings, trunks of windfalls, bark, boughs, moss for chinking—drawn entirely, as an admiring sportsman put it, from the closet of the woods. A handy trapper or guide could build one in two hours. Called a "shanty" or "bark shanty" by Headley and other early writers, it later became the "open camp" and finally, in the present century, the "lean-to." Its functional design changed little. After the cutting and barking of trees were prohibited in the Forest Preserve, the state took over the construction of lean-tos, now built to last, of standard materials and design, and spaced them along the trails at convenient intervals or in clusters at such base camps as Lake Colden. The fame of the Adirondack lean-to has spread throughout the country. People have forgotten the three-sided structures open to a fire that in pioneering days were indigenous to many states of the union. In Kentucky, for instance, where Daniel Boone left a trail of "shanties" along his hunting lines, wherever lean-tos are reproduced today they are known as Adirondack-style shelters.

The Adirondack lean-to is aesthetically pleasing. Favorably located, it seems almost an emanation of the forest floor. As a shelter, its marginal protection against wind, rain, and cold enables you to revel in all the minor inconveniences and discomforts of camp life. You front, in the precise meaning of that verb, the essential facts of life, more truly than Thoreau did in his Walden hut. The open front invites big thoughts. Out there, unscreened after the fire dies down, is the untamed wilderness of our ancestors on the continent. No wonder that a night of "spiritual alertness" in a lean-to above Panther Gorge marked William James's completest union with his native land.

REDUCING LIFE TO ESSENTIALS
Joel T. Headley

It is a little after noon, and a most lovely day, and there, at the foot of the lake, back a few rods in the forest, is burning a camp fire. On a stick that is thrust into the ground and leans over a log hangs a small kettle of potatoes—a little to one side is suspended to a tree a noble buck just dressed, some of the nicest bits of which are already roasting in a pan over the fire. In a low shantee, made of hemlock bark, entirely open in front, lazily recline the young clergyman and the doctor, watching with most satisfied looks the cooking of the savory venison. On the other side are stretched the weary hounds in profound slumber. An old hunter is watching, with knife in hand, the progress of a johnny-cake he is baking in the ashes, giving every now and then a most comical hitch to his waistbands while, as if to keep up the balance, one whole side of his face twitches at the same time. Close by him is my Indian guide whom I obtained yesterday, coldly scrutinizing my new-modeled rifle. Taciturn and emotionless as his race always are, he neither smiles nor speaks.

Knowing that his curiosity was excited, I remarked, "Mitchell, I wish you would try my rifle, for I have some doubts whether it is perfectly correct." Without saying a word, he took up an axe and, going to a distant tree, struck out a chip, leaving a white spot. Returning as silent as he went, he raised my gun to his face, where

[295]

it rested for a moment immovable as stone, then spoke sharp and quick through the forest. The bullet struck the white spot in the centre. He handed back the rifle without uttering a word—that shot was a better comment on its correctness than anything he could say.

Our venison and johnny-cake and potatoes were at length done; and each of us peeling off a bit of clean hemlock bark for a plate, we sat down on the leaves and, placing our bark dishes across our legs with a sharp stick in one hand for a fork and our pocket knives in the other, commenced our repast. I have dined in palaces, hotels, and amid ancient ruins, but never so right royally before. We were kings here, with our rifles by our side and no one to dispute our sway; and then such a palace of countless columns encompassing us, while the gentle murmur of the tiny wave as it laid its cheek on the smooth pebbles below made harmony with the refreshing breeze that rustled in the treetops and lifted the ashes of our already smouldering camp fire. I thought last winter, at the Carlton House, that the venison made a dish that might please a gourmet, but it was tasteless, savorless, compared to *this* venison, cut off from the freshly killed carcass and roasted in the open forest. A clear stream near by furnished us with a richer beverage than wine, while the fresh air and gleaming lake and sweet island sleeping on its bosom gave to the spirits a healthier excitement than society.

After the repast was finished, we stretched ourselves along the ground and smoked our cigars and talked awhile of trout and deer and bears and wolves and moose. At length the Indian arose and made preparations for departure. Taking our rifles and fishing tackle, we pushed our boats into the lake and made for Raquette River, the outlet of the lake, and thence into Cold River. . . .

When the sun at length totally disappeared behind the mountains and the surface of Cold River, overshadowed by an impenetrable forest, became black as ink, the trout left their retreats; and in a short time the water was in a foam with their constant leaping. Where but a short time before we had passed, looking down through the clear depths without seeing a single finny rover, now there seemed an innumerable multitude. . . . I never saw anything like it in my life—it was a constant leap, roll, and plunge there around our lines—and some of them such immense fellows for brook trout. In a half an hour we took at least a half a bushel, many of them weighing three pounds and few less than a pound.

At length, however, it became too dark to fish, and a single rifle shot of the Indian recalling our scattered boats, we started for the camp.

Turning the head of our boat, we drifted down to Raquette River and then pulled for the lake. This was a mile of hard rowing, and it was late before we reached the outlet. One skiff having started sooner than we was already at the camp—the cheerful fire of which burst on us through the trees as we rounded a point of the outlet and shot upon the bosom of the quiet lake. "Look, R——ffe," I exclaimed, "yonder is the camp fire, and now another light moves down to the beach, where they are dressing the trout for supper." He sprang to the oars, and the light boat fled like a wild deer toward that cheerful flame. Islands and rocks flew by, and under a cloudless sky and myriads of bright and glorious stars, we sped gaily on till at length the boat grated on the pebbly beach, and a joyous shout that made the solemn old forest ring went up from the camp and shore. In a moment all was bustle and preparation for supper, and the noblest dish of trout I ever ate I took there by fire light in the woods. . . .

After supper we lay around in every variety of attitude upon the dry earth, lazily snuffing up the fragrance of the woods and looking off on the still surface of the lake, in whose clear depths the stars of heaven stood trembling, and listening to wild hunting stories, interspersed now and then with flashes of broad humor, till at length the deep breathing of the Indian admonished us that we, too, needed repose to prepare us for the toils of the next day. We did not retire to our rooms and blow out the lights, but spreading a blanket on the earth and leaves, stretched ourselves upon it in a row and with our feet to the blazing fire composed ourselves to rest.

FROM BUCKINGHAM PALACE TO THE BACKWOODS THE HON. AMELIA M. MURRAY

This zestful narrative of a camping trip in 1855 is the first recorded traverse of the Adirondacks by a woman tourist—a spinster of sixty and maid of honor to Queen Victoria. Others in the party are Horatio Seymour, governor of New York State, his niece, a "Mr. H.," and three guides.

September 12. We reached the Saranac Lake [from Elizabethtown] about an hour after dark, conveyed by buckboards and wagons—much too civilized a mode of proceeding; but we go on in boats or on foot and hope to travel more than a hundred miles with packs on our backs and staffs in our hands—this will be delightful! On our way yesterday we passed through fine passes and grand mountains. I made one sketch in which Tahawus, "the cloud splitter," was included. We thought ourselves unhappy at sleeping in the little Saranac hotel last night, though it was three in a room, constructed of rough boards and laths; still this will be the last time for some days we shall have any other canopy than heaven and the small tent which is to be carried with us. Our drive from Elizabeth Town to this place was about thirty-two miles; the road rough, but practicable by walking up the steepest parts. On our way we picked a variety of wild fruits, blackberries, huckleberries, cherries, and above all, a little red plum, which, though rather hard and acid, I thought would make a good pudding at our first camp in the woods; so I got enough for that purpose. It was quite dark for an hour before we reached Baker's—the name by which this last house of reception on the Saranac River is known. . . .

Mr. Moody, the head guide, rowed the boat, in which I had a comfortable seat of cloaks and cushions, with the Governor. Miss M——, his niece, and Mr. H—— were conducted by a fine youth of nineteen, who goes by the name of "Prince Albert," and it is believed he was so christened at two years old, though he looked shy and annoyed when asked about it and said he believed it was *"Pliny* Albert." The weather was perfect as we rowed along the

beautiful Saranac Lake. For the first time I saw the Loon and heard
it utter its wild cry, more resembling a mocking laugh than anything else. I could have fancied it saying, "You intruders, you—you
will have enough of this before you have done." A fine eagle next
soared over our heads and ravens also. . . .

Upon landing, we chose a pretty spot; the guides hastily built
up a great log fire. I gathered up some brush and fir cones to help
the blaze, and we broke off small branches (or "feathers") of the
hemlock spruce, which makes the sweetest and best foundation
for an Alpine couch in this country—sweeter than, if not so pretty
as, our heather. Over this the Governor spread a thin oilskin. My
air-cushions were most valuable; we puffed them up, and with
these, my leather bag as a bolster, large plaids and felt coverings,
and Mary M——'s black and scarlet shawl as a curtain of division,
we, two ladies, and two gentlemen, slept soundly, after making a
hearty supper off trout and potatoes. I had provided a dozen lemons, aware that when no milk can be had, the juice is an excellent
addition to tea, and this plan was unanimously approved. To our
guides the idea was quite new; and, as all forest fare is common
potluck, they were quite pleased. "It isn't bad,"—"Right fine, I'll
assure you"; but the first sentence implies almost as high praise as
"It won't hurt you," and that is the *acme*. I concocted my pudding
with the wild plums, deprived of their stones, biscuit, brown sugar,
a little butter, and some water; but as some hours' stewing was
necessary, this dish was not produced before our breakfast. One
of the boats was turned upside down for a table; our candlestick,
a large potato placed upon a tin pail inverted. The guides bivouacked close around the little tent. About half-past two o'clock,
according to a common habit in the forests, we all roused up for
half-an-hour, replenished the fire, and I removed my stew to a little
fire of its own, that it might not get quite stewed away before
morning. We then again composed ourselves to sleep again and had
comfortable naps till daylight. During the night I heard a horrible
noise once or twice, and, imagining it might be the howl of a wolf,
I called to Moody, who assured me it was nothing but a screech
owl. At five o'clock began preparations for breakfast—frying pork,
boiling trout and potatoes, and water for the kettle of tea; at last,

trout were broiled in the same pan with the pork gravy, an excellent dish. We two ladies went down to the lake to make our
toilet and balanced ourselves in one of the empty boats to use
tooth-brushes, etc. While the rest of the party were packing up
and preparing to undertake the portage to Story [Stony] Creek,
I made a sketch before the tent was struck and caught one of the
men in the act of carrying the boat, with his head concealed underneath, like some nondescript shellfish. . . .

Upon landing below the Raquette Falls, we had a mile and a
half of difficult portage. The signs of a trail were at times hardly
visible; gigantic timber felled by storms, or by time, crossed the
obscure path, sometimes every twenty yards; deep bogs and slippery rocks impeded it, and we had often to retrace our steps or
seek a blazed tree before we could find our way; each individual
of the party straggled on as he or she could, with their load. When
Mr. S—— had conveyed his to the edge of the river above the falls,
he kindly returned to relieve me of whatever basket or bundle I
had been able to carry; and so we all at last reached our intended
camping place, a beautiful spot. Our tent was soon pitched, a
bright fire in front of it was lit just at the edge of the water, and
another blaze for cooking made near to our boat-table. The largest
trout was boiled, the smaller ones broiled, with excellent potatoes,
for our supper; tea-lemonade our beverage. As an awakening
amusement for an hour afterwards we played a game of whist, with
a not very white pack of cards procured from one of the guides;
and then after arranging our couch as before, we slept very soundly
till after one o'clock, when the fires were made up, and then we
slept till again morning; not a sound disturbed the forest, except
that of the rippling waters at our feet; but when we awoke at six,
a gentle rain pattered upon the surrounding trees. However, it was
no more than "the pride of the morning," just enough to make us
more sensible of the blessing of fine weather. M. M—— selected a
sheltered rocky nook a little way back for our dressing-room;
there we bathed and adjusted our toilet with brushes, combs, tooth-
brushes, a luxury of towels, and even a tiny mirror hung upon
the lowest branch of a fine hemlock spruce; this smartening up
of the individual woman marked our Sunday morning, for no

Sabbath-day's rest can be set apart for travellers in the bush, who must get to their journey's end by a certain day or go without the common necessaries of existence. We came forth again arrayed in cleanliness; its opposite is at times picturesque but certainly not comfortable. On the whole, I was impressed by the tidy habits of our three guides; they omitted no opportunity for using the fresh pure water to wash away impurities, either on their hands or upon our culinary matters, and never left cup or platter in a soiled state if they could help it. . . .

After the violent rain of last night and today we found our hemlock spruce beds rather damp, although the guides had turned the tent so as to face a large fire and accommodate it to a change of wind. In spite of all the wet, however, no colds were caught, and early the 20th of September we embarked again on the lake in high spirits. The guides had stowed themselves under one of the boats during the night, which perhaps sheltered them even more completely than our tent did us.

During this last pause in our wanderings we could not help being struck by the wild, careless, picturesque appearance inside that tent. Seated upon the floor, where we were taking our meals, with pans of tea and plates of tin, air-cushions, and variously coloured plaids and felts scattered around; sketch-books and presses, books and maps; a large tin case containing our store of grocery, a huge basket full of biscuits, a hammer ensconced among bunches of berries; tallow candles under protection from the damp, towels, hats, bonnets, and other articles of attire impartially scattered; accidentally bestowed touches of scarlet and blue upon the interior, lit up as it was by the warm glow of a blazing wood fire—this would have formed a picture for Gerard Dow.

I forgot to say we ate Mr. Moody's partridge for breakfast, and it proved excellent. I did not omit to sketch this encampment before we left it. As we rowed up the Raquette Lake, a slight snow storm overtook us, but it was soon over. Even during that early morning, with its fog and snow, the lake was beautiful, with numerous bays and islands, and blue mountains rising in the distance. . . .

The seventh lake [of the Fulton Chain] is quite encircled by hills. We observed a tempting rocky promontory, and as the sun was getting low, we decided upon landing upon a pretty sheltered beach behind it.

Our tent was pitched behind a gigantic fallen tree, against which the fire was made: it served as a convenient table for our cooking operations, as well as a good back for the blaze. I made a can of excellent portable soup, a provision we had before tried with success; but now I added a little arrowroot, an onion, potatoes, two or three spoonsful of sweet wine, and several biscuits. It was generally agreed that this mixture "would not hurt anybody"; indeed it might anywhere have been considered an excellent soup.

I found a quarter of a pound of portable soup or a quarter of a pound of arrowroot necessary to make the quantity sufficient for seven hungry bodies. Although I brought these things with me from England more than a year ago, they were in good preservation; and I recommend London portable soup to all travellers in the bush, and advise them also to add lemons and a good store of sugar, brown and white, to their other preparations. We had a bright moon this evening. Some hunters and fishers were upon the lake, and from the latter our people procured trout, and all enjoyed this camp particularly, even though no deer were attained. . . .

At this place [Arnold's farm] we expected to find horses, but owing to our twenty-four hours' detention on Raquette Lake, they had been sent off to bring up some gentlemen from Brown's Tract; pedestrianism was therefore our only resource. . . . Mrs. Arnold was furious—she did all but try to detain us by force—declared we could not get on, and that she should soon see us back again; but necessity has no law: we felt the importance of determination, and we had become too experienced gipsies to fear camping out. For one mile we had a pleasant path, then commenced the series of bog-holes which, with few and short intervals, were to be scrambled through for sixteen miles. The worst was that as night closed in we could not find a dry spot upon which to pitch our tent. At last we sent Jamie on, and he brought us the news that, at a short distance, he had found a little knoll above the bogs.

Dark as it was, we reached this spot without any other mishap than an occasional flounder in the mud; but all the lumber around was soaking wet. No fire could be made till our guide had cut down a tree—for he had not forgotten his axe; and his experienced arm soon felled a birch of considerable size, cut it in logs about two yards long, and so built up a fire, which we assisted in lighting by breaking off dry brush from the surrounding bush. Jamie worked hard; and before Mr. Seymour and the other guides joined us with exclamations of astonishment how we had ever got through the places which had nearly swamped them, the tent was raised, hemlock branches gathered, and a good fire blazed all ready for cooking operations. The young moon occasionally peeped through the foliage above our heads; but it was too thick for much light to be visible. Our only misfortune at that moment was the sufferings of poor young Prince Albert, who lay upon the ground agonized and quite useless. We gave him what comfort we could; and I administered camphor, which soothed the pain, and enabled him to get asleep. Our head guide told me he knew the value of that substance in most cases of slight illness; and that he seldom went into the forest unprovided with some of it.

Before daylight next morning we again aroused ourselves. Fortunately sufficient portable soup and arrowroot was still left to make a good warm mess for breakfast; and this nourishment is so lasting that, with the exception of half a biscuit and some water, I got on upon it till we reached our resting place at Bonville [Boonville], after nine in the evening. . . .

Mr. Seymour must always be considered a brave man for having undertaken alone to take us that day's walk; but having never passed through this track before, he was happily not fully aware of what he undertook, or he confesses he should have been afraid. The path we had to follow was a road cut through the forest fifty years ago; planks had been laid down and corduroy bridges made; but, as no settlement followed, left to entire neglect, the rotten timbers only made bad worse; and I imagine that it would be impossible to find anywhere a track so difficult to get over as that through which we patiently laboured for ten consecutive hours. Mr. Seymour's patience and good humour never gave way. Putting off the packages on his back, he now extricated one companion, now another, from a boggy "fix." I never shall forget the astonishment of Mr. Stephens, of yacht celebrity, when, on horseback with another gentleman and guides, he met us emerging from the bush! They had four horses; and our *avant-courier*, Mr. Wood, had secured one of them, upon which I mounted; and although it was not easy to keep my seat upon a man's saddle in getting over such ground, I soon found the benefit of being carried on the last few miles by some other agency than my own feet. Mr. Seymour and his niece walked on; in one mile more we again reached the Moose River and crossed it in a boat; and another two hours brought us to the clearing, where a small wagon was procured—rough enough, but still a wagon—which took us to a comfortable hotel, at the small town of Bonville, from whence, after a good night's rest, we got on by coach and cars to Utica. . . .

Three days at Utica were necessary to recruit and repose myself.

MOTHER JOHNSON'S
William H. H. Murray

This is a "half-way house." It is at the lower end of the carry, below Long Lake. Never pass it without dropping in. Here it is that you find such pancakes as are rarely met with. Here, in a log house, hospitality can be found such as might shame many a city mansion. Never shall I forget the meal that John [Plumley, his guide] and I ate one night at that pine table. We broke camp at 8 a.m. and reached Mother Johnson's at 11:45 p.m., having eaten nothing but a hasty lunch on the way. Stumbling up to the door amid a chorus of noises, such as only a kennel of hounds can send forth, we aroused the venerable couple, and at 1 a.m. sat down to a meal whose quantity and quality are worthy of tradition. Now, most housekeepers would have grumbled at being summoned to entertain travellers at such an unseasonable hour. Not so with

Mother Johnson. Bless her soul, how her fat, good-natured face glowed with delight as she saw us empty those dishes! How her countenance shone and sides shook with laughter as she passed the smoking, russet-colored cakes from her griddle to our only half-emptied plates. For some time it was a close race, and victory trembled in the balance; but at last John and I surrendered, and, dropping our knives and forks and shoving back our chairs, we cried, in the language of another on the eve of a direr conflict, "Hold, enough!" and the good old lady, still happy and radiant, laid down her ladle and retired from her benevolent labor to her slumbers. Never go by Mother Johnson's without tasting her pancakes, and when you leave, leave with her an extra dollar.

🌿 PAUL SMITH'S IN THE SEVENTIES
CHARLES HALLOCK

Paul Smith's has been very appropriately styled the "St. James of the Wilderness." It has all the "modern improvements" except gas. A telegraph wire connects it with the outer world. It has commodious lodgings for nearly one hundred guests, and in the height of the season will accommodate many more than it will hold. Sofas and tables are occupied, tents are pitched upon the lawn in front, and blankets are spread on the floor of the immense Guide House, itself capable of lodging some sixty or more guides. And each guide has his boat. Beautiful crafts they are, weighing from sixty to eighty pounds and drawing but three inches of water. Most of them carry two persons, some of them three. A guide will sling one of them upon his back and carry it mile after mile as easily as a tortoise carries his shell. When the carries are long, wagons and sleds are in readiness to haul them from landing to landing; but few are the guides that will refuse to back them over for the price of the carriage.

Great is the stir at these caravansaries on the long summer eve-nings—ribbons fluttering on the piazzas; silks rustling in dress promenade; ladies in short mountain suits, fresh from an afternoon picnic; embryo sportsmen in velveteen and corduroys of approved cut, descanting learnedly of backwoods experience; excursion parties returning, laden with trophies of trout and pond lilies; stages arriving top-heavy with trunks, rifle-cases, and hampers; guides intermingling, proffering services, or arranging trips for the mor-row; pistols shooting at random; dogs on the *qui vive;* invalids, bundled in blankets, propped up in chairs; old gents distracted, vainly perusing their papers; fond lovers strolling; dowagers schem-ing; mosquitoes devouring; the supper-bell ringing, and general commotion confusing mine host. Anon some millionaire Nimrod or piscator of marked renown drags in from a weary day with a basket of unusual weight, or perchance a fawn cut down before its time. Fulsome are the congratulations given, manifold the ac-knowledgments of his prowess. He receives his honors with that becoming dignity which reticence impresses, and magnificently tips a twenty-dollar note to his trusty guide. The crowd look on in admiration and vow to emulate the hero. After supper there is a generous flow of champagne to a selected few upon the western piazza, and the exploits of the day are recounted and compared. The parlors grow noisy with music and dancing; silence and smoke prevail in the cardroom. This is the daily evening routine.

At early dawn of morning camping parties are astir. With much careful stowage and trimming of ship, the impedimenta of the voyage are placed in the boats. Tents, blankets, cooking utensils, provision hampers, rods, guns, demijohns, satchels, and overcoats are piled up amidships. A backboard is nicely adjusted in the stern for the tourist, who takes his seat and hoists his umbrella. The guide deftly ships his oars, cuts a fresh piece of tobacco, and awaits orders to start. Singly and by twos or threes, the boats get away; cambric adieus are waved by the few receding friends on shore, and the household of St. James is left to finish its slumbers till summoned to breakfast at eight o'clock. Delicious and vivifying is the pure morning air; grateful as a mother's lullaby the long sweep of the oars; enchanting the shifting scenery and ever-changing outline of shore. In a dreamland of listless and "sweet do-nothing" the hours lapse away. Cigar after cigar melts into smoke. Lunch is leisurely eaten meanwhile. Through the outlet of one lake into the next, winding through many a tortuous stream, gliding past many an islet, with one boat ahead and another astern, and the mechanical oars dripping diamonds of spray that flash in the sun—what can be more deliciously pleasant—what freedom from anxiety and business cares so complete!

"Hallo, guide, what's that? Struck something? Good gracious, you ain't going to stop here in this sedge-grass! Why, the pesky mosquitoes are thicker than lightning. Whew! I can't stand this! They'll eat us alive."

"Got to carry over here, mister. It's only a mile and a half!"

A mile and a half to tramp through woods, mud and mosquitoes!

Ah! the lake once more! This is bliss. What a relief to get on the water again and away from the mosquitoes. How clear it is! What beautiful shores! Anon into the noble Raquette, with trees overarching, current sluggishly flowing, still waters running deep. Just here the current is swifter. Toss your fly in where it breaks over that rock. A trout! Play him well—a large fellow, too! Well landed —no time to stop long—we'll pick them out as we proceed. The trout always lie among the rocks, in the quick water, at this season. A fortnight later they will be at the mouth of the cold brooks that flow into the main stream. Look! boats coming up— So-and-so's party—been camping down at Long Lake. What luck? Report us, please. . . . Bartlett's at last! We tarry here tonight. What a place for trout! Two years ago, just in there, above the dam, where you see that rock in midstream, I hooked a lake-trout on the tail-fly of an extraordinary long cast; they say a lake-trout won't rise to a fly. *He* did, though, and took it handsomely. I never had better sport in my life. . . .

Pleasant is the voyage around the route. Each day's experience differs from the last. New scenery constantly opens to view. Friendly parties and familiar faces are constantly met. And one need not camp out at all, if indisposed. The guide will arrange to stop at a hotel each night. And what rousing fun there is in these wayside hostelries when parties meet! What blazing fires, what steaming venison, what pungent odor of fried pork and bacon, what friendly aroma of hot coffee!

Here I would fain indulge my wayward pen and in fancy go over the ground once more. Perhaps, however, it is better to leave something to the anticipation of those who may seek a new experience in this enchanting region.

NESSMUK VISITS CHIEF BERO
NESSMUK (GEORGE W. SEARS)

William Bero, chief of the St. Regis tribe, heads a gang of twenty young braves whose tomahawk is the axe of the backwoodsman, whose scalping knife is the spud of the barkpeeler. Luckily, in going in, I met William on the trail, who, with a companion, was going in to the tannery on business.

He went no further. He had promised that if I came out to his camp he would "take care of me," and he did it.

Relegating his business to his partner, he took my blanket roll and rifle away from me. He even insisted on carrying my nine-ounce rod. From the moment I met him on the trail he took possession of me, so to speak, and I followed his lead implicitly.

What a grand woodsman the fellow is!

I wanted to go to the Indian camp the first thing. Not a bit of it. He knew of a spring hole that he wanted me to fish, and I surrendered. He led me by trails and across swamps until I lost all notion of compass points, and at last brought me out on the banks of the Moose at the mouth of a cold trout stream; and then he explained that trout had been taken there the present season weighing over three pounds. I dare say he was right. But as they had been taken, of course they were not there.

I whipped the water in my best style for half an hour without a rise, while Chief William, with tamarack pole, coarse cotton line and large bass hook baited with a chunk of shiner, stood on a log below me and hauled out trout after trout in the most business-like and unartistic manner. . . .

I succeeded in drawing Bill off and we started for the Indian camp. He said it was "a mile 'n half." I think it was. It took an hour and a half of rapid marching to reach it. The camp was simply two bark-roofed log shanties standing among and underneath large spruce and hemlock trees. One of the whirlwinds so common in these woods would make a bad tangle of that camp.

The inmates of the shanties consisted of the fifteen choppers and peelers, with Bill's family of seven—Mrs. Bill, a portly, comely squaw; the daughter, a pretty-featured, plump young squaw with a voice like a silver bell; and four young Indians, the smallest being the inevitable papoose, on his ornately carved and painted board.

That papoose is and always has been to me a Sybilline mystery. I first made his acquaintance many years ago among the Nessmuks [an Indian tribe from which Sears derived his pen name] of Massachusetts. He was on his board, swathed, strapped and swaddled from chin to toes, immovable save that his head and neck were left free to wiggle. I next saw him among the Senecas of New York State. Then in Michigan, in Wisconsin, on the upper waters of the Mississippi; and now I meet him again in the North Woods. The same mysterious, inscrutable eyes, the same placid, patient, silent baby, varying in nothing save the board, which in Wisconsin was simply a piece of bark. In this case the board is a neat bit of handicraft. When Bill assures me that the carving was "'done with a jack-knife" I can hardly believe him. And when he says that the bright vermilion, blue and yellow have not been retouched in thirty-five years, I don't believe him at all. The painting is as bright as though it was put on the present season. Commend me to the papoose board. We judge men, actions and things by ultimate results.

After a royal supper of trout, cooked in a manner worthy of Delmonico's, I watched Bill's young barkpeelers as they got red around a rousing fire which they had the good sense to build under a huge hemlock. There was not a pair of round shoulders or a protruding shoulder-blade in the camp. Straight, strong, stalwart fellows, one and all. And every man of them spent the first year of his life on a papoose board.

It has been said a thousand times that Indians will not work, or only in a fitful, desultory way that amounts to nothing; and this is true of the plains Indian; also of the Cree and Chippewa, with other nomadic tribes; but not of the St. Regis or Mohawk and only in part of the Senecas and Oneidas.

As an instance of what Indian muscle can do, let me state that the day before I reached the St. Regis camp ten of Bill's barkpeelers felled and peeled 138 large hemlocks, yielding over thirty cords of bark. In most white camps a cord of bark per day is accounted fair work.

I think the papoose is glad when darkness settles down on the forest and they let up on him. He throws his arms and legs about for all the world like a white baby and crows like mad; then of a sudden his head lops over; he is asleep. I, too, turn in, but not to sleep. Three of the young Indians, including the sweet-voiced maiden, gather around the fire and sing in a low minor key and with soft pleasant voices, the Indian songs of their tribe. And at last I drop into slumber and waken five minutes later, as it seems to me. But it is daylight, and Mrs. Bill has the breakfast nearly ready. I have slept the sleep of the just man and am fresh for the day.

The maiden has got that inscrutable papoose out and is strapping him to his board for the day. When they get him fixed they will pull out from under the roots of a huge hemlock the inevitable jug of tar oil and anoint every visible part of his tawny pelt. The tar oil, well applied, will last some two hours, when it begins to fail, and venomous insects begin to wire in on you.

That papoose understands it. So long as the tar oil lasts he spends his time peering with deep, curious eyes into the gloomy depths of the forest, or, when the wind rises, watching the swaying tree tops. But at the first decided mosquito or punkie bite he gives tongue in a straight, steady yell, without any ups or downs; and Mrs. Bill comes to his relief, takes him between her knees, anoints him from neck to crown, takes him by the basket handle of his board, as one might a peck of potatoes, and stands him up against a hemlock, a log, or the shady side of the shanty. He resumes his eternal occupation of gazing at the mysteries of the forest and is placidly content.

An Indian baby is not expensive in the way of playthings. . . .

I took the papoose by his basket handle and carried him off into the woods. I stood him up against a spruce and made him a speech in mixed Chippewa, Portuguese and English. I explained to him the brutal manner in which his ancestors had roasted and scalped my forefathers and foremothers. I brandished a big knife above his baby head, sang a snatch of Chippewa war song and gave a war whoop. A white baby would have gone into convulsions. He looked at me calmly with those dark, fathomless eyes and when I gave a final whoop, broke into a placid smile that covered his face all over like a burst of sunlight.

An Indian baby doesn't scare much.

WILLIAM WEST DURANT AND THE LUXURY CAMP Harold K. Hochschild

Adirondack residents of today, who enjoy the benefits of travel by airplane, fast train or smooth motor roads, the comforts of electric refrigeration, steam heat and up-to-date plumbing and the sometimes questionable advantage of the telephone, might not care to be whisked back through time to find themselves living at Pine Knot or Sagamore [private camps on Raquette Lake and Shedd Lake] in the 1880's and 1890's, but, for its period, that life represented all the luxury and enjoyment that could be contrived by lavish expenditure and by the ingenuity and good taste of W. W. Durant. He liked to entertain his friends from New York in the grand manner and to provide for them in the depths of the Adirondacks as good a cuisine and as fine wines as could be found at Sherry's or Delmonico's. Durant, who was an expert cook, had gathered many recipes in the course of his travels here and abroad. Much of this lore he imparted to the wife of his superintendent at Uncas [another of his camps, on Mohegan Lake], Mrs. John Callahan. She, in turn, acquired such culinary fame that when J.

Pierpont Morgan bought Camp Uncas the New York gossip writer Cholly Knickerbocker facetiously suggested, much to Mrs. Callahan's annoyance, that the buyer had insisted that the cook be included in the sale. "Mrs. John Callahan was an excellent cook," wrote her brother-in-law, the late Maurice Callahan. "I can testify to that. When she prepared a dinner for Mr. Durant and his guests, those of us who worked around the camp would have to wait until W. W. D. and his guests had finished, then we would be lined up at table. The only trouble was that sometimes they wouldn't finish until 7:30 or 8 P.M., and we would be darned hungry. I recall that Schuyl Kathan [the stonemason and guide-boat builder] complained very bitterly one evening about waiting—said he would rather eat beans than wait so long, even though it was damn good."

For a while, Durant had the locomotives on his Adirondack Railroad between Saratoga and North Creek burn wood instead of coal, at considerable extra expense, so that the smoke would not offend the nostrils of visitors to the Adirondacks. When his friends came in winter he had fresh relays of horses waiting every ten miles or so between North Creek and Raquette Lake. On one occasion Durant's mother, Mrs. T. C. Durant, arrived early in the spring at the Marion River Carry, en route to Pine Knot, to find that the river was open to its mouth but that Raquette Lake was still frozen. Durant sent men to break a passage for the steamboat through the ice across the two-mile stretch between the mouth of the river and Pine Knot, pushing the displaced ice under the unbroken ice, so that his mother could complete her journey on the steamboat without discomfort or delay.

The harmonious lines and the excellent state of preservation of Durant's buildings still standing at Pine Knot and Uncas, and of his houseboat, testify to his instinct for architectural fitness and his insistence on perfect construction. Durant had a sharp eye for anything wrong with a building. If a post was ever so faintly out of plumb, he could spot it immediately. He had the porch at Sagamore rebuilt twice. Nor would he allow deviations from the standards which his aesthetic sense demanded. . . .

One day while Durant was staying at Sagamore Lodge and his mother was due to arrive from New York at Big Moose station by the afternoon train, Durant sent Collins in a carriage to call for her. Durant, as related by Collins, calculated that the carriage should be back at Sagamore by five o'clock sharp and so instructed Collins. As Collins left Big Moose with Mrs. T. C. Durant, he whipped the horses to such a pace that she remonstrated. Collins related her son's orders. "You are driving for me now, not for William," replied Mrs. Durant; "slow down!" As the carriage, forty minutes late, rolled up the long driveway leading to Sagamore Lodge, Durant could be seen pacing angrily up and down in front of the Lodge. He upbraided Collins, ready to discharge him. Mrs. Durant explained what had happened and told her son that he was in the wrong. Durant at once apologized. It was rarely that he could be convinced that he had erred, but when he was, he acknowledged it without delay or qualification.

Durant's directives to his employees were drafted with military precision. . . . While a few of Durant's employees found his methods too autocratic for their tastes, most of them became warmly attached to him. His insistence that their work conform rigidly to his orders was tempered by a genuine concern for their welfare. He was generous with those who needed help. In several instances he paid the salaries, for long periods, of employees who had fallen ill from causes not connected with their work. If a family in the neighborhood was in distress he sent them money and food, whether or not they were in his employ. Every Christmas, to ensure that no Raquette laker would go without Christmas dinner, he sent each family on the lake a turkey and, if they were not teetotalers, a bottle of whiskey. . . .

On the *Utowana* [Durant's sea-going yacht], at Camp Pine Knot or at Sagamore, it was something more than creature comforts that attracted people to visit William West Durant. His cultural interests were wide and he was a fine conversationalist. As host, he had the rare ability to watch over the well-being of his guests and at the same time to make them feel at home by knowing when to leave them to their own devices. Above all, he had an unquenchable zest for life which made men and women want to be his friends.

THE FINEST TRIO
Craig Gilborn

On January 3, 1893, near the end of their holiday visit to Camp Pine Knot, a party of Durant and Stott family members accompanied William West Durant in sleighs over the ice and snow to Mohegan Lake where they enjoyed a picnic in the "snowy forest," walked in snow shoes on the lake and watched as William selected a site for Camp Uncas. This territory, south of Racquette Lake and encompassing all of Township 5 and part of Township 6, was untouched except for trails and two cabins which William built in the 1880s on Sumner and Shedd Lakes (later Kora and Sagamore Lakes) as retreats for friends and acquaintances, including Governor Black and other officials, who eagerly took advantage of William's invitation to hunt and fish there and in the fine grounds farther south, near the Moose River. Between 1893 and 1897 William would carve out three large preserves of 1,000 to 1,500 acres apiece, and at the edge of each would be built a camp, Uncas, Sagamore and Kill Kare, described in 1903 by an English writer as "the finest trio on the North American Continent." Already known for Pine Knot, William's later reputation as the creator of the "Camp Beautiful" was derived from these camps.

William set the pattern for these camps and their emulators elsewhere in the Adirondacks, but the fragmentary record indicates that they were smaller, more intimate and nearer to the wilds when he was running things, down to about 1902, than in later years. In 1901 William said that Sagamore could be staffed by a superintendent and wife, a teamster and two laborers, at a monthly cost of $260 including board. Two horses, two cows, incidentals and taxes brought the estimated monthly cost, "without entertaining," to a grand total of $450. By the time of the First World War, the camps, particularly Sagamore and Kill Kare, had grown considerably. . . .

In 1903 a writer and traveller from England, Henry Wellington Wack, had the opportunity of comparing the three camps. He concluded:

I suppose these three camps, thus situated on private lakes, connected with the rivers of the region by inlets and outlets; with trails carefully blazed in every direction; connecting each other by private roads and telephones, with driveways to Racquette Lake, to Old Forge and the Fulton Chain [of Lakes], with two hundred thousand acres of State forest preserve all around them . . . constitute in cost and comfort, in pleasurable appointments and luxury, the finest trio on the North American Continent. And I doubt if there is any forest villa in Europe to compare with either of them in any respect.

Elsewhere Wack said that seventy guests could be housed at Kill Kare, a plausible enough number after the reconstruction and enlargement of Kill Kare by the Garvan family about 1916, but possibly exceeding the camp's capacity in 1903.

Life at the camps was two-fold, divided between the staff and the owners and their guests. Crucial to the happiness and smooth running of a camp was the superintendent and his wife. Responsibility for the entire camp complex was in the hands of the superintendent, whose authority was exceeded only by the owner, his family or, when the family was in residence, perhaps by a personal secretary.

The camps were located within several miles of one another and there was an ongoing exchange of men among the three. John and Mary Callahan worked for Durant and then for the Morgans at Camp Uncas until about 1920, at which time their son, Thomas, replaced them until he assumed the superintendent's job at Sagamore in 1924. The Callahans were cooks, but Mary's culinary reputation, gained partly by Durant's instruction, was known far and wide. J. Pierpont Morgan asked William to let them remain at Uncas, and William, who had employed them since 1889, reluctantly complied. Morgan and his guests so seldom visited the camp during the first years that William, on April 30, 1900, inquired into Morgan's plans that summer: "John and Mary Callahan do not want to stay there another summer unless some of the family do occupy it. It seems too lonely for them, and besides, Mary gets out of practice in having no one to cook for except a laborer or so. . . ."

The Vanderbilts came to Sagamore with a retinue of their own, among which might be a secretary, valet, chef, assistant chef, butler, chamber maid, laundress, footman, horseman, governess and nurse. Kamp Kill Kare had a staff almost as large. An insurance report in 1930 reported that the Garvan place had ten to twelve employees in winter and thirty to forty in summer. . . .

The grand camps of the wealthy in the Adirondacks attracted a number of admiring journalists at the turn of the century, among them William Frederick Dix, editor of *Town and Country* magazine. Writing in *The Independent* in July, 1903, he said, "An Adirondack camp does not mean a canvas tent or a bark wigwam, but a permanent summer home where the fortunate owners assemble for several weeks each year and live in perfect comfort and even luxury, tho in the heart of the woods, with no very near neighbors, no roads and no danger of intrusion." The development of "the cottage idea" had, he noted, flourished for only a decade or so, but despite its newness, "it is an interesting phase of American social life and decidedly significant," by which he meant the turn toward "more simplicity for the vacation" and the united efforts of wealthy preserve owners and the state to protect the woods, waters and wildlife of the Adirondacks for future generations. The heyday of the grand camps is all but finished; Dix perhaps did not realize how brief their "significant phase" would be, about sixty years, and while it is difficult for us to see simplicity in woodland communities with a dozen or so employees, his remark about the camps as outposts guarding the Adirondack environment accurately describes the stewardship role their owners performed in later decades.

CAMP CHRONICLES
MILDRED P. STOKES HOOKER

It will be seventy years this summer since I first came to camp as a little girl of two, so I think I can fairly claim to be the longest, if not the oldest, inhabitant.

In 1876, five years before I was born, father brought his family to Paul Smith's and went into rough camp with them on what we later called "Birch Island." They slept on balsam branches and washed in the lake, and used their only pillow, so I have been told, as a bed for my sister Ethel, who was then a baby. But though they lived in such primitive fashion, and did without so many other things, they showed that they had the proper St. Regis spirit by immediately building, to quote my father, "what was said to be the first sailboat ever seen in this neighborhood—a catamaran made by fastening together two rowboats by a platform and placing a centerboard in the platform."

Father was so charmed by the beauty and peace of the Upper Lake [Upper St. Regis]—there were no camps at all on it then— that he bought the island from a Mr. Norton for $200. . . .

St. John's played an important part in camp life. We were always a church-going community, and it was a gay and lovely sight on sunny Sunday mornings to see the long line of rowboats with flags fluttering at bow and stern wending its way down through the "sleughs" to church. Gayest of all was a boat from the Livingstone camp with white paint and red cushions. Even sailboats joined in the parade. Father used to say that though he didn't, of course, approve of Sunday racing, it was quite another matter to take two boats and see who could get to church first! He was happiest when he had the minister on board for then he couldn't possibly be late for service, and this was a privilege he often enjoyed for Sunday morning preachers were usually our Saturday night guests. In fact, we used to call one of our cabins "The Rectory" or "The Prophet's Chamber" because our ministers used it so often.

In those days one minister ministered to a host of little missions in the neighborhood. Mr. Larom, who held services at St. John's for years, was known as "The Bishop of All Outdoors." He did a good deal of his traveling in a canoe with a two-bladed paddle, and when he arrived early enough on Saturdays he would hoist a little sail and join in the afternoon boat race. . . .

On July 23rd, 1883, although camp, to quote my mother, was "not near ready," the family moved to the island. By night they had six tents ready besides the cook house and dining tent. Five beds in the "parlor" (a fourteen by fourteen tent) accommodated the overflow.

No one delivered supplies in those early days, so mother took with her forty chickens and an old hen, "to kill as required." She describes buying the chickens from a farm woman who apologized for asking twenty cents apiece. The old hen cost twenty-five cents.

Father used to rent cows and keep them on "Cow Island" and later at the farm to provide his large family with milk. Cow Island was later known as "Hog Island" when the pigs moved in, and as "Pearl Island" when it achieved the distinction of housing humans.

The farm consisted of fifty acres of mainland which Father bought, for $1.50 an acre, very shortly after buying Birch Island. That same summer he bought Pearl Island, High Island and the two (now three) islands in front of our camp. They were listed on the deed as Chickencoop Island and 2 Tree Island.

Meat used to be sent up in barrels from New York; but this wasn't too satisfactory an arrangement for it often spoiled in transit. Sometimes a whole lamb or a side of beef could be bought from someone up here.

Supplies were kept in storerooms and in ice houses. The ice houses were regular cold storage plants with thick insulated walls. Every camp had one. These were filled yearly with ice from the lakes, although often some of the ice lasted for more than one season. I still remember the chill that one felt on entering them, and the feeling amounting almost to awe, with which we children gazed on the rows and rows of delectable delicacies, rising tier on tier to the roof. . . .

Alas, in spite of her well-stocked storerooms, mother wrote in 1884 that she didn't dare give a dinner party for "Charles" was "so poor and always thinking he has too much to do." Father came to the rescue and sent her up another chef from New York who had "been all winter in the White House." His cooking was pronounced "delicious," so I presume they made up for lost time and invited all the neighbors in to share in their good fortune. . . .

Although so much time was spent in hunting and fishing, social life was not neglected. Mother speaks of going with Father to call on Miss Reid and of "dressing" to call on Mrs. Trudeau and Mrs.

French, but evidently the "dressing" was not too formal, for she writes later: "I do like the freedom of this place in the way of dress. Even calls are made in flannel suits and gentlemen wear knicker-bockers and coarse stockings."

Speaking of dressing, the "freedom" Mother mentions went right on until I was grown up, and some of us took a firm stand against evening clothes. We always told our guests not to bring them, and I believe Dr. James, after due notice, even went so far as to throw a guest in the lake because he came all dressed up. However, eve-ning dress did finally creep in. I once saw one of our neighbors in full evening dress and bedecked with diamonds paddling in a canoe with a man in a "boiled" shirt en route to a dinner at the Vander-bilts!

It was the Vanderbilts, by the way, who put the Japanese touch to the Pratt camp. When they took it over from the Twombleys, they had just returned from a trip to Japan. They thought our lake very Japanese and Whiteface the image of Fujiyama so they sent for an army of little Japs, who had just completed the Japanese Vil-lage for the Buffalo World's Fair, to come and make their camp over. They not only had the cabins Japanized, they dressed all their maids in kimonas! They had taken over a stout English maid of Mother's and she nearly died of embarrassment when she had to appear before us in this odd new uniform.

Father was Commodore of the Yacht Club from its inception . . . and every year he gave a yacht club dinner to the men who belonged. The time came when he felt that in politeness to his guests, who most of them dressed in the evenings, he should wear a dinner coat too. We protested, but Father was firm and sent for his coat to Lenox. When the night of the party arrived Father sat at the head of the table in all his glory, but there wasn't another tuxedo to be seen. All the guests, in deference to what they knew was Father's preference in camp, had come in camp clothes. . . .

Another housekeeping help was the telephone which, believe it or not, was installed on Birch Island that same summer [1884]. On it they could talk to Paul Smith's, Saranac and Bloomingdale, the latter being at that time the shopping center; but mother complains that with it camp "doesn't feel so campy," the first sign of that conservation in everything to do with camp and camp life for which we "old timers" have always been noted. . . .

This is perhaps as good a place as any to explain how our camps took on their unusual form and grew up into little villages instead of developing into houses. At first we all lived in tents as you know, so they were naturally separate. Tents couldn't be left up over the winter, and Mother found it very inconvenient to move all the furniture into the cabin and back and hit upon the scheme of building little wooden "storerooms" behind the tents into which the furniture could be moved. When the tents wore out it was a natural transition to add to these storerooms by putting cabins instead of tents in front. Often the old tent floors were used. This transition shows very plainly in the two tent cabins on Birch Island and the row at the Earles'. Guide houses, carpenter shops, and ice houses all fitted well into this unit system, and pretty soon it became the accepted way to build, even if you had never had any tents. . . .

My own memories come thick and fast, memories of childhood days, of the old coach, of buckboard drives over corduroy roads, of fishing from the breakwater, and our disappointment when mother ruled that no cook could be asked to skin and cook a catfish, of happy swimming times, all too short for us, because Dr. Trudeau, who looked after us, thought it was bad to stay more than twenty minutes in fresh water and Mother or a nurse always hovered nearby, watch in hand—of the comfort of our dear Anna Valet's hand reaching for mine in a thunderstorm at night—of Fanny, our little fawn, and of playing house in the tangled roots of the one big pine which gave the name of "Pine Tree Side" to the south side of Birch Island. The thrill of leading people "around the Island" for the first time—and most thrilling of all the day when Mr. Drake didn't come to start the boat race, and I, at the age of six or so, was allowed to officiate, Father's watch tightly clutched in one hand and a handkerchief held high in the other to be dropped at the ordained moment.

Memories of girlhood days and adolescence—"puppy" love and jolly house parties—and of the happy summer when Ransom and I decided to "play house" together for the rest of our lives—and later memories of those early years on Spitfire, where, in our own camp, surrounded by good friends and with our children growing up happily in the old camp traditions, we spent what were perhaps the happiest summers of all.

"Pine Tree Side" was not the only part of Birch Island to have a special name. There was Horseshoe Bay, Birdie Hollow, Crystal Hollow, and Blueberry Hill, and the northwest end of the island was always known as the "Guide's Camp." When Father had our little log playhouse built as a surprise, it was "Goldilocks Hall" and when he first led us to it there was a bear looking out of the window. That same bear is old now, and tame, and Alice has taught him to stand in her living cabin and hold umbrellas.

"Fanny" was found swimming all alone in the lake and brought in to be a pet for Carrie and me. We kept her in a stockade between Newton's cabin and the lake. . . .

There is another animal story I like to remember. A man came to Paul's with a performing bear, and the bear got loose and strayed away. His owner was distressed, not only at losing the bear, but because he feared she would starve to death, as she had never learned to hunt for food, it just came as a reward for doing her tricks. All the men in the neighborhood were begged to join in a hunt, and this they did, spreading out through the woods so that they covered a considerable territory. Suddenly one man halted, almost unable to believe his eyes. There, in a clearing, was that hungry little bear trustfully going through her tricks so that food would be provided! . . .

One year camp had been rented to a family who looked upon frogs not as old friends but as table delicacies. Hardly a croak bade us welcome home; everyone was upset. My sister Carrie and I decided something must be done about it and set out for Chicadee Creek armed with red flannel, string and fish nets. Not for us the bows and arrows which the Conservation Department now claims you need a license for. We just tied a piece of the flannel to a string and threw it out near a frog, who would seize it in his teeth and hang on for dear life, making it simple to slide a net under him and haul him out. We went home with a boat load. Unfortunately we didn't just turn them loose in our own deserted frog haunts. We had what seemed to us the brilliant idea of having Mr. Hochard, the chef, bake a crust and put it over a big dishpan with all the frogs inside, and Barton, the butler, was told to pass it to Mother. Mother, thanks to our big family and countless guests, wasn't a bit daunted by the enormous size of the dish presented to her. She just opened it up with the spoon, and out hopped the frogs. She was quite cross with us, almost the only time that I ever knew her to be so. We said it wasn't fair, for only a short time before she had had the butler bring in a live pig on a platter and thought it funny, though the pig had jumped down from the platter, and the great dane had run after the pig, and we had all had to run after the great dane; quite a boar hunt that didn't end until we caught the great dane and rescued the pig out near "Goldilocks Hall." . . .

Houseparties had always been a feature of Birch Island life, and a stream of English people and foreigners kept turning up with letters of introduction. (Once one of Queen Victoria's granddaughters asked to come, but fortunately for our peace of mind she changed her plans.) Now we younger ones began to have houseparties of our own. What plans we made for them! The invitations were sent out months ahead, after much consultation, for not only must the guests be congenial as a group, but some, especially amongst the men, must be more congenial to one daughter and some to the others; and there was always great excitement after our guests arrived as to who would invite whom to go rowing after supper.

We had supper early so as not to interfere with the sunset, and then hurried down in couples to the boathouse. The men would row or paddle us while we sat in the stern facing them, ensconced in cushions.

When I was fifteen, Anson persuaded Mother that I was staying out too late with my best beau, so Mother ruled that *everyone* was to come in by ten o'clock, and she used to stand on the breakwater and ring the dinner bell for us as a signal to start for home. When we got in we all repaired to the dining room, where we regaled ourselves with milk and gingerbread bun-loaf and talk before going to bed. I soon learned to spend my evenings in the bay towards Keese Mills. It took longest to come home from there. . . .

The houseparties on Birch Island were not the only ones. The Reids always had a camp full of people, young and old, and other campers had guests too, so we young folks began to do much more visiting from camp to camp.

If . . . I tried to list a typical day's activities at that time, it would go something like this: breakfast, 8:30 to 9:30; tennis most of the morning; swimming before lunch; sailing in the afternoon; tea at 4:30 or 5:00; supper at 6:30; canoeing until 10:00; refreshments and talk in the dining room until about 11:00; then bed. . . .

Besides the racing there was lots of tennis always going on on the new en-tout-cas courts and golf at the St. Regis River Golf Club, and dinners and "lean-to" parties (at which Kitty Chace would sing delightfully even after innumerable pancakes), and charade parties, not to mention the annual tournaments and the fancy dress dance at the Reids' in the Labor Day week end.

A feature of these parties was that they were not segregated as to ages. Except for dinners everyone over fifteen played around together. A group of young people once came to me and asked if I couldn't "do something" about a party to which no elders had been invited. They felt that camp customs were in jeopardy. . . .

As a child when anything went wrong I would say to myself, "Never mind, we're going to the Adirondacks," and just the thought of this place would make me happy again.

I know that according to most authorities the word "Ad-i-ron-dacks" meant "tree eaters" and was used by the Mohawks as a term of derision suggesting that our predecessors were poor hunters. I prefer the definition once seen by Robert Garrett claiming that the word was better translated as "sissy" and that the appellation was given to the Iroquois in this neighborhood because, once they had taken to themselves the peace and beauty of our mountains, woods, and waters, they desired nothing better than to settle down here and live at peace themselves.

INSIDE—NOTHING
GERTRUDE ATHERTON

From the Lady Helen Pole to the Countess of Edge and Ross

Chipmunk Lake,
August 19th

Dearest Polly:

It is eleven o'clock p.m., and I have been in bed and asleep since half after seven. I foresee myself wide awake for two hours and giving you an account of the last two days. How flat that sounds—but wait! And otherwise you might never hear of them, for I return to Boulder Lake tomorrow, and in this country events are so quickly crowded into the past.

I wrote you—did I not?—that the subject of a camping expedition had been mooted more than once, but put off from time to time on account of threatening weather and various other causes. I longed to go; "camping out" in the "Adirondacks wilderness" being pitched upon a most adventurous and romantic note; and finally I begged Mr. Nugent to arrange it. He went "straight at it" in the energetic American way, and in two hours it was all arranged: Opp drove out in the buckboard for another guide, and Mrs. Opp was making so many good things at once that all the other cooks had to come over to help her. Then Mr. Nugent and Mr. Van Worden packed the big pack-baskets, and everybody was ready to start at nine o'clock the day before yesterday.

The original plan was that all of us should go, but the actual party were Mr. and Mrs. Meredith Jones, Miss Page, Myself, Mr. Nugent, Mr. Latimer, and Mr. Van Worden. The others "backed out" on one excuse or another, and happy it was for them and us that they did. . . .

I insisted that I wanted a genuine rough camping experience, and we all took Opp's word for it that he knew the very spot—where there was fishing, a clearing, and an "open camp," erected by other wood-loving spirits. It is true he grinned as he assured me that I would get a good taste of the "genuine article," but I suspected nothing. What imagination, indeed, would be equal to it! . . .

It was one of those crystal mornings when life seems the divine thing of those imaginings of ours when we have lost for a little the links that hold them to facts. I never felt happier, I was almost excited. It seemed such a delightful thing to float off into the unknown like that, to go in search of adventures, with the certainty that six strong men, one of them your devoted slave, would take the best care of you. It was all so undiscovered—that rough mountain world beyond the lake—so unimaginable—well, I know all about it now.

We were a very picturesque party, my dear. The men wore white sweaters, corduroy breeches, and top boots. I wore hunter's green, a short skirt of covert cloth just above my boot tops, a linen blouse the same shade and a little bolero to protect my back and arms from the mosquitoes. Miss Page, who is very dark, wore a bright red skirt and cap and a red and white striped "shirt waist" with a red tie. Mr. Nugent said she looked exactly like a "stick of peppermint candy," and I am sure I shall recognise that indigestible the first time I enter a "candy store." Mrs. Meredith Jones, who has golden hair and blue eyes, wore a dark blue skirt and cap and the inevitable "shirt waist"; but hers was striped with blue; and the jauntiest little cape hung from her shoulders. Of course we all wore canvas leggins as a further protection from the mosquitoes, which are the least of Adirondack charms.

Well, the moment we stepped on shore our troubles began. We were landed on to a big slippery stone, then handed across several others and a few rotten logs into a swamp. Before us was an impenetrable thicket as high as our heads and wet with dew. We stood staring at it until the guides had shouldered their packs and picked their way over rocks and logs to take the lead.

"That's all right," said Opp, "there ain't bin anyone in here for two years and the road's growed over, but it'll be all right in about a mile. Good trail then. We'll go first and break the road. Wimmin folks'd better bring up the rear."

So we started; crashing through the wet bushes over the wetter ground until we came to a narrow rocky trail sidling along the inlet. This is a gentle stream in a wild setting. Its rocks are so many and so big that the wonder is the water can crawl over them, and the mountain beside the path is as precipitous as a cliff. None of us paid much attention to the beauties of Nature; we did not dare take our eyes off the path, which had given way in places and was swampy in others. Where it was safe it was rocky. Nor could the men help us much; the trail was too narrow. Single file was a necessity, but Mr. Nugent was just behind me and gave me occasional directions, besides surrounding me, as usual, with an atmosphere of protection. So, slipping and bending and clutching at trees, we picked our way along until at last the trail turned up hill, and if no less rough was free of the worst element of danger. In another half hour we had passed a lumber camp and were on a level trail along the crest of the mountain. The forest was more open here, so much "lumbering" had been done, but only the spruce were gone—not all of those—and high on one side and down in a valley on the other was the beautiful leafy forest, full of the resinous odor of spruce gum, the spaces rather a welcome change after the forest densities of the last two months.

And our procession was very picturesque. The guides with their big pack-baskets strapped to their shoulders were in the lead, almost trotting, that they might outdistance us and have an occasional rest. All our men carried small packs and strode along looking very supple and free, with the exception of poor Mr. Van Worden, who is rather stout and must have felt the irksomeness of his pack. But he was enjoying himself, no doubt of that; and indeed, so were we all. Mr. Latimer, who had looked a little conscience-stricken as he said good-bye to Mrs. Van Worden, whistled as gaily as a schoolboy on a runaway lark. And it was so cool and fresh in the woods, who wouldn't be happy? Not that there was one minute of easy walking—nor an opportunity for sentiment. When we followed the narrow trail through the brush we had to stoop and overlook every inch before we put a foot down. When we were on the long stretches of corduroy, built by the lumbermen to haul their logs over, Mr. Nugent held my hand, but he might have been his ghost for all the impression he made on me, so many were the holes and so rotten some of the logs. Conversation was impossible.

We exchanged an occasional remark, but we were all too intent on avoiding sprained ankles and broken tendons—you can not imagine the painfulness of walking too long on log roads—to be interested in any one but ourselves.

There were four hours of this, and good a walker as I am I was beginning to feel tired, when Opp, who had gone far ahead, came in sight again, looking sheepish, rather.

"Be gosh!" he remarked to Mr. Van Worden as we met, "here's a fine lay out. One of the camps is burned. Them last campers done it, I reckon. I seen 'em go round by way of Spruce Lake."

I heard Mr. Van Worden swear softly under his breath and saw an expression of blank dismay on Mr. Nugent's face. Mr. Latimer burst into a peal of boyish laughter. But Mr. Meredith Jones said sharply:

"Well, let's go on and cook dinner. That is all that concerns us now. We can decide what to do later."

"Are we there?" I asked hopefully, for I longed to give my poor bruised feet a rest.

"Yes'm," said Opp, "we're there, all right."

And in a moment, Polly, we "were there."

Have you wasted any time, my dear, imagining what an "open camp" is like? I hope not, for it were a waste of good mental energy. The briefest description will fit it. Three sides and a sloping roof, all of bark. The front "open" in the exactest interpretation of the word. Inside—nothing. Twelve feet long and not quite the depth of Mr. Meredith Jones, who is six feet two.

This mansion stood on the edge of a clearing, across which lay a big felled tree. Against this we immediately all sat down in a row. Beyond was a charred ruin and near the log a rude table. Does that sound romantic? I wish you could have seen it. But we all laughed and were happy, and we women, even then, did not realise the true inwardness of the situation. The forest, the beautiful forest, rose on three sides of us; beyond a stream, concealed by alders, was a high sharp ridge of mountains; and we were hungry.

The guides immediately set about making a fire. There seemed to be plenty of logs and they soon had a roaring blaze. Opp found a limb with a forked top, which he drove into the ground just beyond the fire and in the fork transfixed a long curving branch which held a pail of water above the flames. Mr. Nugent and Mr. Van Worden unpacked the baskets, Mr. Meredith Jones set the table, and Mr. Latimer fought off the hornets which swarmed at the first breath of jam and ginger-nuts. When we finally sat about that board, on logs or "any old thing," we eat that excellent luncheon of fried ham and hard boiled eggs, mutton cutlets and fried potatoes, hot chocolate and cake, with a grateful appetite, I can assure you. Mr. Van Worden fried the ham and potatoes and made the chocolate, and we all coddled his culinary pride. All my fatigue vanished, and Mrs. Meredith Jones looked equally fresh and seemed prepared to take whatever might come, with the philosophy of the other sex. But poor Miss Page looked rather knocked up. She has never gone in for walking and her very cap had a dejected air; her fine colour was almost gone, but she looked very pretty and pathetic and all the men attempted to console her.

"I wouldn't mind it," she said with a sigh, "if we didn't have to go back." Then, as if fearing to dampen our spirits with the prospect of carrying her out, she added hopefully, "But it'll be two days hence. I reckon I'll be all right by that time. I'll just lie about and rest."

When luncheon was over Mr. Latimer made her a comfortable couch of shawls, with a small pack-basket for pillow, and she soon fell asleep. The guides washed the dishes, then immediately felled two young spruce-trees, and, with the help of Latimer and Mr. Meredith Jones, shaved off the branches and covered the floor of the cabin. This was our bed, my dear, and it was about a foot deep. When it was finished they covered it with carriage robes, and all preparations for nightly comforts were complete. By this time it had dawned on Mrs. Meredith Jones and myself that we were *all* going to sleep under that roof. Opp had examined the sky and predicted rain before morning, and Miss Page was not equal to a return journey—"doubling the road," as they say here—even if any of us had contemplated such a thing.

"Tom and I will sleep in the middle," said Mrs. Meredith Jones reassuringly to me, after an earnest conversation apart with her husband, but I was immensely amused at the whole situation. We

were as helpless against certain circumstances as if we did not
possess sixpence between us; for it would have taken nearly a day
to build another camp and the guides were too tired to think of
such a thing. We were all stranded out in space, and there was
nothing to do but make the best of it.

About two hours after luncheon I felt as if I had had no exercise
that day and Opp suggested that I go up the mountain to see a
gorge locally famous. So, accompanied by Mr. N. and Latimer, I
followed him up the steepest and roughest mountain of my experience. There was no trail. He trampled ahead through the brush
and we followed. Mr. Nugent preceded and literally pulled me up
more than one perpendicular place, but Opp insisted upon taking
charge of me through the slippery intricacies of a rocky stream. But
we were rewarded by the most beautiful spot I have yet seen. . . .

When we returned to the camp, we found Mrs. Meredith Jones
asleep and Miss Page keeping watch. The men had all gone fishing
and Mr. Nugent and Mr. Latimer hastened to join them. Miss
Page looked refreshed but turned to me a perturbed face.

"I cannot believe it is possible that we are all going to sleep in
there," she said. "Why, it is shocking! I begged Mr. Van Worden
to put up a partition, but he says it is quite impossible, that there
won't be room to turn over, as it is. I wish I hadn't come. Suppose
it should get out? Why, people would be horrified."

"Really," I said, "I think you take an exaggerated view. We
are all going to bed with our clothes on, the camp is open, there are
nine of us, and our chaperons will sleep in the middle. We may not
be comfortable, but I think the proprieties will take care of themselves."

"I think it is shocking," she said, "perfectly shocking. It seems so
coarse and horrid. I'll remember it as long as I live."

I felt like shaking her, but she looked so distressed that I said
soothingly: "Please don't worry. I will sleep next to Mrs. Meredith
Jones and you can tuck away in the corner where no one can see
you and you will be quite forgotten."

"Yes," she replied quickly, "I insist upon having the corner—
particularly as you don't mind," she added apologetically. "You

are quite different from my idea of English girls. I should have thought that you would be simply horrified."

"Perhaps we are more matter-of-fact than you are," I said drily. "Where a thing can't be helped it can't, and we are sensible about it. Now, I am surprised at you. I had always supposed that American girls—"

"Oh, don't!" she exclaimed. "You are going to judge us all by those horrid things you meet in Europe and in novels. I can assure you that Southern girls—*gentlewomen*—are as particular as English girls—more so, I reckon. Do you realise that we are going to sleep in the same room with six men?"

"I don't look at it in that way at all," I said tartly. "And for heaven's sake make up your mind to the inevitable and think no more about it."

The men returned soon after with a basket full of trout and Mr. Van Worden fried them for supper. I don't think I ever eat anything quite so good as those trout.

"He beats the cars, cookin'," observed our chief guide, and Mr. Van Worden looked as pleased as if he had made a million in Wall Street.

After supper the guides built a high fire of great logs, and we all sat about and the men "spun yarns" of the days when the panther and the bear roamed the woods, and finished with stories of the beautiful red deer that alone claims the forest today. Of course the men smoked, and we were all very happy and comfortable until we went to bed. Mr. N. sat as close to me as he decently could, and— I will confess to you, Polly—under the encouragement of the shadows which covered a part of me and all of him he held my hand. I could not struggle—well—

About ten the men all marched up the hill in single file, singing, and we had the camp to ourselves for a half hour. We took off our boots, corsets and blouses, put on dressing sacks, tied our heads up in silk handkerchiefs, and our night toilet was complete. Miss Page had evidently made up her mind to accept the situation, but she was so manifestly uncomfortable that I tied nearly all of her face up in her handkerchief and tucked her away in the corner with the blanket up to her nose. She turned her back upon us and regarded the chinks of the bark wall in silent misery. Mr. Van

Worden had brought three extra pairs of socks and these he had directed us to pull over our stockings as the night would grow very cold.

We had been in bed nearly twenty minutes and had already learned something of its hardness when the men returned.

"Now," said Opp, "you must all lie on the same side and when one of you wants to turn over be sure to sing out and then we'll all turn over together."

His was the only remark. The other men pulled off their boots and crawled into bed without a word, looking rather sheepish, and ostentatiously refraining from glancing in our direction. Men are certainly more modest than women in certain conditions, and Mrs. Meredith Jones and I almost laughed out loud, especially as the other guide went to bed with his hat on!

For about a half hour we were as quiet as the sardines we must have looked. Then my side—the one I was lying on—began to ache from my neck to my heel, and from the numerous sighs and restless jerks I inferred that we all were affected in the same way. At all events Opp "sang out," "Heave over, hey?" and we all turned like a well-regulated machine. I whispered to Miss Page, but she would not answer me.

It was just after that we became conscious that the temperature was about ninety. The fire was not three feet in front of us and blazing more violently every moment. I had been endeavouring to forget my discomfort in watching the black masses of the treetops thrown by the blaze into extraordinary relief against the dulled sky and tarnished stars, when I heard Mr. Van Worden whisper fiercely,

"What in heaven's name did you build that red hot fire for? It's hot enough for three camps and we won't sleep a wink."

Opp replied apologetically: "I thought it was goin' to rain and it was best to have things well het up, but I guess it hain't. It's hot and no mistake."

I saw Mr. Latimer fighting to get out of an extra sweater without attracting attention, and I, by the same herculean efforts, managed to reach down and get off my stockings and those socks. But still the heat was insupportable and the bed grew harder every moment. Our pillows, too, were logs under the spruce, and I am used to a baby pillow that I double under my neck and face. How I longed for it!

Finally Latimer slipped out of bed and went over to the edge of the clearing and lit his pipe. The guides followed immediately, then Mr. Meredith Jones, and they sat along the log in dejected silence. Mrs. Meredith Jones heaved a deep sigh. "I really can't stand it, girls," she whispered; and followed her husband. Of course we went too, and Mr. Van Worden was left alone.

For a half hour we sat about in an almost complete silence, waiting for that wretched fire to burn down. Opp separated the logs, and finally, as we were all too sleepy to hold our heads up, we crawled back to bed, one by one, all except Mr. Latimer, who stretched out on the table, and Mr. Nugent, who made a bed for himself on the ground. That gave us a trifle more room in the camp, and we could turn without "singing out." In a few minutes, hot as it still was, I fell asleep.

I suppose it was two hours later that I awoke. The fire had taken a fresh start and was blazing more merrily than ever. I felt as if I were in a Turkish bath, and as Miss Page was no longer in front of me I inferred that she had been driven forth again. Then it occurred to me that she would not have budged without Mrs. Meredith Jones, and I turned about quite suddenly. Mrs. M. J. was not there! Nor Mr. M. J. Nor the guides. Oh, Agatha! Agatha! I was alone in bed with Mr. Van Worden.

The situation was humorous, but somewhat embarrassing. I hardly knew whether to pretend sleep or not, for I did not feel like going out and sitting on that log again. I could see the dark figures in various dejected attitudes. Mrs. M. J. and Miss Page were sitting back to back with their heads hanging, while Mr. M. J. stood with his hands in his pockets glowering at the fire. Latimer was sitting on the table smoking his pipe, and Mr. N. was digging his heels viciously into the earth. As for the guides they lay flat in the distance, tired out, poor things. Only Mr. Van Worden looked serene. He, too, lay on his back, his hands clasped over the greater part of him. I supposed he was asleep, but he remarked genially:

"Hot, isn't it, Lady Helen? I'm afraid one camping experience will do you for the rest of your natural life."

I assured him that I never had been so much entertained, and we conversed as naturally as if it had been noon-day until I was reminded of the irregularities of the situation by a gasp from Miss Page. She nudged Mrs. M. J., whispered hurriedly, and in another moment I was chaperoned on either side.

It was at least another hour before the fire burned down and the temperature cooled. Then the men crawled back to bed, one by one, and in a few moments they were all sleeping—and as quietly as kittens. It really was quite remarkable.

But one could not sleep long at a time on that bed, and once I was glad to be awake. High up on the highest tree of the mountain a hoot owl broke the petrified stillness of that lonely forest.

"Too wit, too wit, too wooo!" he called loudly, and then he added with impatient emphasis, "Too wit, too wit, *too woo*," as if to say, "Do you understand that?" He was a bit of a scold, but he had all the grey dome and all the forest depths to talk into. No comrade answered him, and nothing ever gave me such an impression of the solitude of a mountain forest.

By six o'clock we had endured all that the human frame is capable of in the way of sleeping on hard and prickly spruce, and the men rose as by one impulse and went down to the spring to wash. We dressed as hurriedly as possible and, I must say, looked surprisingly fresh. And the morning was so deliciously cool, and Mr. Van Worden's coffee so fragrant and bracing, his trout so crisp and Mrs. Opp's "johnnie cake" so excellent that we sat about Mr. Latimer's bed in the highest spirits and congratulated each other that we were "camping out." Even Miss Page, having weathered the worst of it, announced herself ready to stay another night, and talked continually in her pretty Southern brogue. She was looking like a beautiful gypsy, too, and I think our one small mirror had consoled her for many things. She flashed her eyes about with the impartiality of the kind-hearted coquette, and was quite the life of the uncomfortable group about the table.

After breakfast Mrs. M. J., Latimer, Mr. Nugent and myself, led by Opp, with an axe over his shoulder, started off to see some famous falls. The rest went fishing. . . .

Well, we spent all of that day very pleasantly, and the night promised to be rather more comfortable, for Mr. Nugent, Mr. Latimer, and the guides all made beds for themselves under the stars, and the fire was left to go out after supper. But, alas! about midnight it began to rain, they all came crawling under shelter, and there was little more sleep that night.

The rain stopped long enough for us to breakfast comfortably, and then we held a consultation. The plan had been to "stay out" three nights, but we were all a little tired of it, and the skies looked very forbidding.

"If you want my opinion," remarked Opp, "I say go and be quick about it. It's set in for all day, and if we git back to the lake without a soakin' we'll be luckier'n I think we will."

That settled it. We had no desire to sit on our bed all day and then sleep on it another night. The guides began to pack at once, and within an hour we were on our way.

We had hardly started when it began to pour, and it has not stopped yet. What a walk it was! However we reached home without pneumonia and broken ankles heaven only knows, but not one of us has a cold; and although my feet feel as if they had been pounded with a hammer they are quite whole. When we were not picking our way over the narrow trail through the brush—dripping and as high as our heads—we were on those horrible corduroy roads, made so slippery by the rain that every step was a danger. Once I fell, and I twisted my foot three times and wrenched myself up to my waist. My feet were swimming in my boots, and it was an effort to lift them. I felt sorry for Miss Page, who is a pampered creature, but she never uttered a complaint, although she told me afterward that every time we came to one of those interminable stretches of corduroy she wanted to sit down and cry. She certainly is a fine creature, with all her little foibles.

When we got to the lumber camp we all sat down in the rain and rested before climbing the corduroy hill beyond. Mr. N. explained to me the use of the curious objects piled under a shed. They were huge boxes on runners with four round holes in each end. When the snow is on the ground, covering corduroy and rocks, these boxes are filled with water and dragged by horses over the road to be used for drawing the lumber to the streams. From the front holes the water spouts continuously, and as it strikes the ground it freezes, making a solid smooth surface over which the log sledges can travel with ease. But what a life! No wonder these mountaineers look old; but Mr. N. told me that lumbermen become so fascinated with the life that they cannot be tempted into the valleys.

You can imagine the difficulties of that narrow sidling swampy trail by the inlet. It was just twice as bad as in dry weather, and I almost was discouraged once or twice. Perhaps I should have been, had it not been for a very reassuring and helpful presence; but it was bad enough.

Latimer had hastened on to the lake to fire his revolver, the signal that we were coming. When the rest of us arrived, the boats were almost there, but as we were all hot and wet, and a cold wind played upon us as we stood on the stones again, it is a wonder we are not all wrecks. As soon as I reached home, Mrs. Van Worden made me drink hot whiskey, while Mrs. Opp and Henriette undressed and rubbed me down. I am none the worse for wear, but felt quite done up by half-after seven and went to bed. Hence this great letter. . . .

Helen

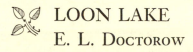

LOON LAKE
E. L. Doctorow

I didn't know what would happen in my life but I knew whatever it was it would have to do with her, with Clara. I thought even having her name was an enormous inroad of intelligence. . . .

Of course I couldn't express to Libby even the most idly curious question about this princess living on the grounds. But she had loved showing me the guest book and I thought from her same peasant identification with Bennett wealth she would enjoy the wonder on my face as she secretly showed me the main house, where they lived and had their lives and Charlie Chaplin and the one-named kings sat down to dinner.

The Bennetts not at home there was a bending of the rules: on Saturday night two Loon Lake station wagons pulled out leaving a skeleton staff.

On Sunday afternoon with the sun coming through the trees at low angles to light the rooms, through rectangles of sun along dark corridors, Libby and I tiptoed about the vast upstairs with its hall alcoves of casement windows and window seats and bookshelves and its suites of rooms, each with its generous shade porch, and Adirondacks chairs and sofas.

Whatever empty room I saw led my mind to the next room, the next turn in the corridor, everywhere the light off the lake cast its silvery shimmer on the walls or in my eyes as we passed open doorways.

One wing was closed off. "We can't go there," Libby said.

"Why not?" I asked, casual as I could be.

"It's the Bennetts' wing, where they stay."

"Is someone there?"

"No. But I wouldn't feel right about it. Rose and Mary take care of it," she said.

She led me down a back stair through a kitchen with two black steel ranges and pantries of provisions and several iceboxes each crowned with its humming cylindrical motor.

Through a room of glass cabinets filled with sets of china and drawers of silver service.

Through the hexagonal dining room, three walls of glass and a table hexagonal in shape to seat thirty people.

To the huge living room, the grandest room of all, with tan leather couches built into the walls, the walls hung with the heads of trophy. There were two different levels of game tables and racks of magazines and clusters of stuffed chairs all looking out enormous windows to the lake.

I found myself tiptoeing, with a sense of intrusion, my chest

constricted—and something else—the thinnest possibility of destructive intent, some very fine denial on my part to submit to awe.
"Of course this is just one of their places," Libby said. "Can you
imagine?"

One or two steps up and we were in the entrance hall. The walls
were of dark rough wood. We stood under a chandelier made from
antlers. I gazed up a wide curved staircase of halved logs polished
to a high shine, with balusters of saplings. I gazed at this as at the
gnarled and swirling access to a kingdom of trolls.

"Don't you love roughing it?" I said to Libby, running her up
the staircase. "What!" she cried, but laughing too, entirely subject
to my mood. In the long upstairs corridor I placed her hand on my
arm and strolled with her as if we were master and mistress. I led
her into one of the suites and flinging open the glass doors of the
porch, I extended my arm and said, "Let us enjoy the view that
God in his wisdom has arranged for us, my deah." She swept past
me giggling in the game and we stood in the sun side by side looking over the kingdom.

"Do you mind if I smoke, old girl?" I said in my best imitation of
wealthy speech. "No? Why, thank you, I think I'll light up one of
these monogrammed cigs with my initials on them."

She was animated with pleasure, how easily she could be made
to live! I kissed her to show her how the wealthy kissed, their noses
so high in the air that their lips never met, only their chins. Then
of course I kissed her properly. She was confused, she drew back
blushing, she had thought it her secret that she was sweet on me.

Whatever I wanted from poor Libby I couldn't explain what I
was doing solely to gain it. We had the run of the house and pre-
tended to be masters. For those few minutes the upstairs maid and
the hobo boy were the Bennetts of Loon Lake.

Libby took my hand and showed me a storage room where F. W.
Bennett kept his stock of outfits that he provided his guests as gifts:
riding habits and boots, tennis flannels, bathing suits, a goddamn
haberdashery.

I stood in front of a full-length mirror and took off my greens
and put on a pair of tan tweed knickers with pleats, ribbed socks,
brown-and-white saddle shoes, my size, a soft white shirt, and a

white sweater with an argyle design of large gold and brown diamonds across my chest.

I was stunned by the magnificent youth that looked back at me from the mirror. All the scars and deeper marks of hard life were covered in fine fashion. The face, a bit gaunt but unlined, the hair I combed back hastily with my fingers. He made a passing aristocrat! Well, I thought, so a lot of the effect comes from the outside, doesn't it? I might be a Bennett son!

And then I felt again my child's pretense that those two gray sticks in Paterson were not really my parents but my kidnappers! Who knew whose child I was!

I dreamed of recognition from her from Clara. It was her nearness that made me so crazy, and bold with Libby. So feverish so happy.

And as for Bennett I thought, He is no more aware of me than of some unfortunate prowler mauled by the wild dogs. But here I am, wearing his clothes, wandering freely through his house. Here I am, Mr. Muck-a-muck, and you don't even know it!

Then Libby came back from the female supply store and she was wearing jodhpurs and a silk blouse and a riding helmet perched none too securely on her thick hair and she wobbled in a pair of shiny boots too wide in the shank for her thin legs.

"You look swell, Libby," I said. She turned around with little shaky steps and gave me all the dimensions. Her gray eyes shone, her mouth stretched in her tremulous overbitten smile. I danced her out of there down the corridor doing a fast fox trot full of swirls while I hummed the tune I had heard the night I came, "Exactly Like You," Libby laughing and worrying at the same time, telling me to hush, looking back over her shoulder, giggling, falling against me every other step, brushing my cheek with her lips. And the light lay like a track along the carpet and shone in golden stations of the open doors.

VIII

Year-Round Folk

=====

*The people have long since become accustomed to living
with nature....It is their institution, their civilization,
their art.*

Burton Bernstein

THE 1980 CENSUS COUNTED 119,578 permanent residents of the Adirondack Park. These people own 25 percent of the total acreage within the Blue Line, mostly in small holdings of less than 500 acres (37 percent consists of large holdings owned by about 625 corporations, clubs, and wealthy individuals based outside the park, and the balance of 38 percent is state Forest Preserve).* Although the population has grown by over seven percent since 1970 while that of the state as a whole has declined, there is still plenty of elbow room. Fifty acres apiece on average. Elbow room is the great attraction. It explains why, when some young people are leaving, a greater number of middle-aged and retired folk are coming in. It may explain too why so few natives have felt the itch to write. There is too much to do in the woods. Besides, who needs another low-paid calling in this region—an Appalachia of the North—that has little else?

"Literature," John Burroughs admitted, "does not grow wild in the woods." No Thomas Hardy, William Faulkner, or Robert Frost has yet appeared to interpret this country as a real insider.

---

*Statistics from the Temporary Study Commission's *The Future of the Adirondack Park*, 1970.

The material is rich, and someday this void may be filled. Until the moment arrives, we must rely primarily on the outsider as interpreter or on that hybrid, the outsider who settles here or the native who goes out to make a living.

Earning a living is the problem. The heroine of a recent novel about an Adirondack village, Sloan Wilson's *Small Town*, attributes her hesitation to marry to her fear of joining the Twenty-three Club. Whether or not they are pregnant, most girls in the neighborhood marry at eighteen. The couples live in trailers and have children while the husband tries to find work. After five years of trying to live on practically nothing, the husband gets discouraged and takes off. The abandoned wife, now with three or four kids, is just twenty-three and a full-fledged member of the Twenty-three Club.

Pioneers from northern New England hoped to find more fertile land west of Lake Champlain. Those who settled in the lowlands of central and northern New York found what they were looking for. But the few who were lured into the foothills and mountain valleys of the Adirondacks found only a shorter growing season and thin soils soon depleted. Discouraged as farmers, they turned successively to other employment such as trapping, logging, seining fish for market, mining, milling, guiding, taking boarders, hotel or motel keeping, small merchandising, building camps, caretaking and so forth. Most of these jobs were seasonal and some terminal. Mines gave out; paper mills became unprofitable and closed down; bulldozers, chain saws, and trucks replaced lumberjacks; hotels failed or burned down; and sportsmen ceased to hire guides. With logging far down in second place, recreation has been the one enduring and expanding source of income, but it too is seasonal and volatile. Most available jobs are related to catering to sportsmen and tourists and to the ninety thousand summer residents.

Nimble shifts of occupation have made the Adirondack workman versatile. In the nineteenth century the pattern was guiding and farming in summer; trapping, logging, and boat-building in winter. Today the Adirondacker often has a greater variety of occupations and skills. In the course of a long life a resident of Indian Carry I knew was trapper, guide, fire warden, caretaker, postmaster, carpenter, cabinet-maker, electrician, plumber, boat liveryman, and builder, owner and renter of summer camps. After putting a daughter through a liberal arts college and a son through a college of forestry, he applied the accumulated skills of a lifetime to building a new home for his wife and himself on a knoll of one of the Stony Creek Ponds overlooking Seward Mountain. This man was among the more fortunate. Initiative, energy, and versatility are often not enough in a region where opportunities are limited and seasonal. Rates of unemployment in the Adirondacks are usually among the highest in the state and relief rolls the heaviest.

There is a fundamental contradiction in the life of the native Adirondacker. Background and training equip him for independence; circumstances tighten a noose of dependency about him. On the one hand is a family heritage of rugged independence, whether ancestors are the transplanted subsistence farmers of Vermont or the roving Irish and French-Canadian lumberjacks who chose to settle in northern New York. The freedom of the woods also fosters a spirit of independence. Ready adaptability to shifting employment fosters self-reliance. On the other hand, economic, social, political, and bureaucratic constraints limit freedom of choice. Important decisions affecting the life and livelihood of the native are made elsewhere, in the state legislature, by state agencies, or in the offices of corporations based outside the park. Alvah Dunning was among the first natives to chafe under the imposition of game laws he had no part in devising. Since then other constraints have been imposed on permanent residents—dependency on a fickle tourist trade, poverty amidst the affluence of summer residents, and, climax of indignities, passage of the Land Use and Development Plan in 1973 with its restrictive zoning of private land, giving the Park Agency control of all environmentally significant projects. State control in the interest of environmental management now supersedes personal choice and local option.

The reaction of a majority of native Adirondackers to Park Agency controls has ranged from discouragement to defiance. According to a state Assemblyman representing an Adirondack district, the Park Agency "places a knife at the heart of the North Country's economy. It doesn't bring a ray of hope to the area."

Other typical comments are: "Under the guise of environmental-ism the average grass roots citizen is being herded back into feu-dalism." "You should not destroy a person's economy and tell him it is for the benefit of future generations and that he must pay the penalty for posterity." "[Regionalism] is government of the people, but not by and for the people—government by bureaucrats we did not elect and over whom we have no control." And over and over again: "Nobody is going to tell me what I can do with my land!" One town in St. Lawrence County threatened to "secede" from the Adirondack Park.

Perhaps the way out of dependency is to take the third step on the ladder of moral evolution, responsibility to the land, which Warder Cadbury speaks of in the last selection here, "The Land Ethic." A significant minority of Adirondackers have taken that step. They believe that in a state park the greatest good of the greatest number—including the community of plant and animal life—is the preservation of open space. Some of the strongest sup-porters of the Park Agency Act are newcomers who have adopted homes in the Adirondacks after fleeing conditions elsewhere that environmentalism seeks to avert. Among them is the forty-year old owner of a sugarbush farm. With a modest reserve of capital he is content to take odd jobs paying five dollars an hour, such as assisting a surveyor, instead of the fifty dollars he customarily earned on the outside. The woods and open space mean more to him than a thriving economy. Newcomers of this sort, who volun-tarily choose residence in the park, have made important contri-butions to Adirondack life and literature over the last century.

The compensation for a depressed economy, long harsh winters, and subjection to control from the outside is the ever-present woods. The woods provide an informal education, a livelihood for some, and recreation for all. Adirondackers love the woods. A home at Coreys, woodsy enough for the city people who summer there, is not so for its native family, which owns besides "a camp in the woods." Adirondackers are skilled in woodcraft. Nearly every home has an array of camping equipment, a boat, guns, skis and snowshoes, all kept in prime condition. A recent addition is the snowmobile. Much as it is resented by some outsiders, it has transformed winter life for natives. "Winter today is free and fun," writes Anne LaBastille. "Snowmobiles bring fresh faces, conviviality, enthusiasm, and excitement to winter-weary hamlets."

The city man escapes to the woods only at wide intervals. The native has only to step outside his back door to shake off the constraints of village or hamlet and of a region governed largely from outside. A tramp of an hour or two inducts him into the freedom and expansiveness of the woods.

PIONEERS
REV. JOHN TODD

The colony [on Long Lake in 1844] now consists of eighteen families and about one hundred souls. In some respects their situation and circumstances drew more deeply upon our sympathy than ever before. The road which the state is making in to them from Lake Champlain advances very slow, and it made our faces grow long when they talked as if it would be two years more before it is done. We have strong hopes that it will not take so long. The post office is still half a hundred miles off, the nearest physician is sixty miles, and the nearest mill that deserves the name of a mill is not much nearer. The same long, weary way lies between them and the nearest store. The sawmill had not yet been put up; and in addition to all the rest, the winter preceding had been long and severe, their cattle had died of starvation in many cases, and the annual income of a few hundred dollars which they . . . calculate to receive for working on the road had been cut off. They had done the work, but by a process of which I am ignorant, they had no income.

It is very easy for us, surrounded by all manner of appliances, to think how we would do this or that to mend our condition were we placed in certain situations. But it is not so easy to work when you have no handles to your tools, and no tools to your handles; when your arms must be fifty miles long in order to reach anything that will aid you. If there is nothing but wild land to be bought and you have nothing to buy with and nothing to sell, no outlet and no inlet, you find yourself shut up to narrow quarters. Suppose you are a settler in the wilderness. You may find that in the winter when you wish to be clearing up your land, you are compelled to leave all and catch what furs will procure the year's clothing for your family. In the spring when you wish to be making your maple sugar, you are taking the last harvest of furs; and when you ought to be planting and getting your seed in the earth, the spring having come all at once, you are compelled to go off to sell your furs and buy the necessaries of life for your family, and perhaps you must stop to fish and hunt to keep from starving. To surmount the point which lies between poverty and thrift in these circumstances requires a perseverance and a resolution which few possess. How hard must it be for a poor man with a family to get along when his axe must cut down every tree that is cleared, and his hoe must put in every kernel of grain he raises, because he has neither a horse nor an ox. I never so fully realized the difficulties of the situation of those who dwell in a new, cold, Alpine region as I did during this visit.

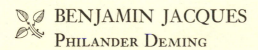

BENJAMIN JACQUES
PHILANDER DEMING

In an iron-bound valley of the Adirondacks Ben Jacques was financially ruined in the summer of 1842 by a mining speculation. His ruin did not mean so very much in dollars and cents, perhaps less than his previous failures in the same barren field; but somehow this last failure seemed to mean a great deal to him personally. His open, honest face revealed keen suffering.

Jacques had been very temperate and industrious. He would

have gained success if there had been half a chance. But mining in the Adirondack Mountains was hard. So long as a man was young and new at the business, he could endure the disappointments, after a fashion; but when he was turned of forty years of age and had learned that mining in the Adirondacks was contending against great commercial odds, if not natural laws, he was apt to think that he needed a change. One's best strength for "fighting the rocks" was likely to be impaired before middle life. Jacques, however, was still strong. It was the check upon earnest purposes and honest hopes that wrung his heart. He had tried so many times, he said, and so fair, and every time a failure.

On this last occasion Jacques's brown locks were turning to silver as the assets of his venture were made over to "the company," leaving him without a dollar; and he explained to his friends in his simple, direct way, with tears in his frank gray eyes, that he was tired.

"More than twelve years ago," he said, "I brought a little money and a hopeful heart to these mountains, and you all know whether I have worked faithful. I own I am down now, and my heart is sore. It ain't no use, boys," he added. "It is a hard country. Them few black holes over there in the hill is all I have to show for my work. And them ain't mine any longer," he added, struggling with a sob. He said to a friend, privately and with tears, "It's all right, George, to talk of settling down; but when a man has had his hopes and sees it's too late, and he has nothing to offer, what can he say?"

Three days after the failure, Ben Jacques started away from the mining settlement alone for a walk among the mountains. He was trying to get a mental view of what else there might be in the world beside iron ore and speculation and heartache. It was a July morning, all brightness; and, cheered by the birds, he walked along a little road up by a cabin where his newly-married friend Nellie and her husband lived. The little home was a sweet picture. Beyond it were the woods and the dark mountains. To the toiler whose existence had been for so many years a struggle to wrench a fortune from these rocky hills, they seemed implacable and pitiless. What was the serenity of their heights but contempt for his feeble struggles?

He passed on from the settlement into the woods. There was an old mining road that he knew of. It led many miles into the wilderness. It had been cut out and speedily abandoned in a mining speculation years ago. He followed this track five miles to Cherry Lake. The lake was very solitary. A dark, rugged hill, clothed with black spruce, rose beyond it. Where Jacques was, there was a plain covered with maple and beech trees. He noticed how fine the prospect was and how wonderfully the blue waters sparkled in the July noon. Then he sat down upon the shore and smoked his pipe and thought it all over again. When he returned to the settlement that evening, he remarked that he had considered the matter fully and was sure that he had done with mining forever.

A week later the news was circulated that Ben Jacques had put up a log cabin away off in the woods at Cherry Lake and was going to turn hermit. There were diverse comments upon this intelligence. Some reckoned that he had found a new mine out there; others were "afeard" that Ben had a soft spot in his head. His own statement of the case to Nellie was plain. He said he was tired. He declared, also, that it was pleasant at the lake and that he loved to dream there in the silence. "I remember a world outside of these mountains, Nellie," said Jacques, "that you have not seen." When Nellie said anxiously that she feared he was giving way to some secret sorrow, he did not reply.

Jacques's cabin at the lake was a pleasant place. During the autumn he cleared a little ground that he might have a garden in the spring; and he improved the old road, so that a team could be driven over it. A few weeks' labor at "The Works" supplied him with means to procure the necessaries he required. Then a little furniture and a few books were taken to the cabin, and the toiler settled down to rest.

Jacques was a sensitive man. The isolation of his hermit-life soon had its natural effect upon him. That unseen world that surrounds the living, both when they wake and when they sleep, seemed to him to come nearer and nearer. The strange spirits that woo and win the solitary found him in the wilderness. It was observed that he was becoming quiet and shy and that the little he saw of society when he visited the settlement oppressed him.

The seasons came and went with much feverish anxiety, and

many baffled enterprises, at the mining-settlement. Amid the worry and the failures Ben Jacques the hermit was little cared for and rarely remembered.

The little settlement did not encroach very rapidly upon the woods. Jacques's cabin was still miles away in the forest. His acre of garden was a rose in the vast wilderness. In spring the flowers bloomed around his doorway, and the bees from his hives hummed around the tiny clearing. Remote as it was, the robins and the bluebirds found this lonely home. It was one of the picnic journeys in summer for the young folks to travel the long, unfrequented road through the woods and visit Jacques the hermit. These visits were received as a great honor by the venerable man, and he always gave the visitors honey and flowers. But only Nellie and her husband and children knew "old Mr. Jacques" as something more than a strange man or a curiosity. Twice, at least, every summer, a horse and rude wagon were driven by Nellie's husband or by her own hands over the rough road to Mr. Jacques's. Almost every month in the year Jacques came to see Nellie and her family: it was the tie that bound him to the outward world.

AMAZONS OR MIRANDAS?
Joel T. Headley, Dickey Jones, Amelia M. Murray, and Thomas B. Thorpe

After Foster left, Herreshoff Manor was occupied by Otis Arnold, who raised a large family on Brown's Tract and ran a backwoods hotel. Visitors in the eighteen forties and fifties were much impressed by Arnold's daughters.

He [Otis Arnold] lives contented, year after year, with his family of thirteen children—twelve girls and one boy—by turns trapping, shooting, and cultivating his fields. The agricultural part, however, is performed mostly by the females, who plow, sow, rake, bind, etc., equal to any farmer. Two of the girls threshed alone, with common flails, *five hundred* bushels of oats in one winter, while their father and brother were away trapping for marten. Occupying such a large tract of land and cultivating as much as he chooses, he is able to keep a great many cattle and has some excellent horses, which these girls of his ride with a wildness and recklessness that makes one tremble for their safety. You will often see five or six of them, each on her own horse, some astraddle and some sideways, yet all . . . without any saddle, racing it like mad creatures over the huge common. They sit (I was going to say their saddles) their horses beautifully; and with their hair streaming in the wind and dresses flying about their white limbs and bare feet, careering across the plains, they look wild and spirited enough for Amazons. They frequently ride without a bridle or even halter, guiding the horse by a motion or stroke of the hand. What think you of a dozen fearless girls mounted on fleet horses, without a saddle, on a dead run? I should like to see them going down Broadway. Yet they are modest and retiring in their manners and mild and timid as fawns among strangers.

There was a lad about nineteen years of age with my friend B——n, whom one of these girls challenged to a race. He accepted it, and they whipped their horses to the top of their speed. The barn, nearly a mile distant, was to be the goal. Away they went, pell-mell—the girl without a saddle, across the field. The boy plied the whip lustily, ashamed to be beaten by a woman, yet he fell behind, full a hundred yards. Mortified at his discomfiture and the peal of laughter that went up, he hung his head, saying it was no fault of his, for she had the best horse. She then offered to exchange with him and try the race over. This was fair, and he was compelled to accept the second challenge. Taking their old station, they started again. It would have done a jockey good to have seen that stout frontier youth use his whip and beat his horse's ribs with his heels and heard him yell. But all would not do—that girl sat quietly leaning over her steed's neck; and with her low, clear chirrup and her sharp, well-planted blows inspired the beaten animal with such courage and speed that he seemed to fly over the ground, and she came out full as far ahead as before. The poor fellow had to give up beaten, humiliating as it was, and the girl with a smile of triumph slipped the bridle from her nag's head and turned him loose in the fields to graze.—*Joel T. Headley, c. 1846*

As I approached the house [Arnold's], about a dozen little flax-haired urchins met me, some stupidly staring, others blushing and laughing, with their bright blue eyes and chubby cheeks, and others scampering away over the hills toward the house. As I entered the door, to my left sat a beautiful girl, gazing on us with a hazel eye, wild as her native mountains, and with blushing cheeks, half hid in a flood of soft chestnut curls.

Dickey Jones.—Good evening, Miss!

Miss.—Good evening, sir.

Dickey Jones.—Fine day!

Miss.—Lovely!

Dickey Jones.—Delightful occupation!

Miss.—I loves to churn.

Dickey Jones.—Do you not feel very lonesome in these mountains?

Miss.—No, sir; I sometimes visit Mister Woods, on Raquette!

Dickey Jones.—What! so far?

Miss.—Why, yes! La, you don't call that far, do you! It's only forty miles (very softly).

Dickey Jones.—But the rocks, the forests, the briars, and your delicate beauty, Miss!

Miss.—Why, look here, Mister, you puny town folks hain't no 'count. Do you see that? (hauling out a thick blacksmith-looking arm)—now, if you insult this chicken by saying I'm a delicate beauty agin, I'll just box your ears. . . .

We walked in, S. following behind and soliloquising, "Pity so much beauty was born to blush unseen!"—*Dickey Jones, c. 1852*

Mr. Seymour remained to make arrangements with the guides while his niece and I walked on to Arnold's Farm. There we found Mrs. Arnold and six daughters. These girls, aged from twelve to twenty, were placed in a row against one wall of the shanty, with looks so expressive of astonishment that I felt puzzled to account for their manner till their mother informed us they had never before seen any other woman than herself! I could not elicit a word from them; but, at last, when I begged for a little milk, the eldest went and brought me a glass. I then remembered that we had met a single hunter rowing himself in a skiff on the Moose River who called out, "Where on the 'arth do they women come from?" And our after-experience [hardships of the walk from Arnold's to Boonville] fully explained why ladies are rare birds in that locality.—*Amelia M. Murray, 1855*

Mrs. Arnold received us cordially and with a dignity becoming to her station as the lady of an old feudal castle. Engaged in the active duties of her household, she never ceased them for a moment, but continued her work, merely interlining her remarks, acting on the good sense rule that the most complimentary thing in her power was to hasten dinner, for our appetite and that of our fellow-travelers was sharp-set, and the steaming coffee and fragrant venison which were by the fire, and the large wheaten loaf on the table, and the busy attentions of three blooming daughters promised that we should soon be gratified with a most substantial meal. A little rest, some unimportant change in our toilet, and we sallied out to enjoy the few moments which still remained of sunshine. While I was gazing about, Mrs. Arnold's twin daughters, now seventeen, and who have *never been out of the woods*, passed near me on horseback. They used no saddles or bridles, but the confident equestrians held such a firm seat that I involuntarily expressed my admiration aloud. When they came to the bars which inclosed the yard about the house, they beckoned to their mother and a few words passed, and the girls continued down the hill and were soon lost in the woods. While I was still gazing, the old lady remarked that "if I would keep my place, I would soon see a fine race on the bottom land." And sure enough a moment afterward the girls came rushing along at a speed that seemed almost dangerous, yet they displayed the most perfect skill, and sat so gallantly, and enjoyed the excitement so much that it filled me with positive enthusiasm. The mother was justly proud of her children—twelve she had reared in her solitary home. Not a physician had ever crossed her threshold, and yet they were pictures of health. The elder daughters had married and were excellent wives and mothers, and the three now grown to woman's estate, who had never seen a house except the humble one in which they were born, would compare favorably in address with those who possessed every possible advantage of city education. All this was the result of a mother's care.— *Thomas B. Thorpe, c. 1858*

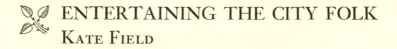

ENTERTAINING THE CITY FOLK
KATE FIELD

Revolutionary Plattsburgh, with its interesting past and most excellent present, welcomes us with flowers, trout, and salmon, lulls us to sleep with the lapping of the lake, and rouses us in the early morning for the labors of the day. Twenty miles of railroad, over trestlework and through the heart of many a hill bring us to Point of Rocks, where steam ends and staging begins. Where are we to go? There is a driver who takes our measure, finds that we answer the written description of his employer, and off we start for Martin's. The wagons of the Adirondacks are similar to the covered wagons of all mountainous regions, and the road to the Lower Saranac is as good as such roads usually are. The scenery by the stage route which leads through Franklin Falls is uninteresting, saving for the first hour, when you are attracted by the chattering of Ausable River, and the silent eloquence of Old Whiteface looming up five thousand feet in the air. Soon after, nature ceases to be entertaining, and for relief I turn to human nature arrayed in the garb of our driver, who bearded like a pard, looks like a retired pirate.

"What is the best product of the soil?" I ask.

"Well, I reckon the human family can't be beat," replies the driver, suddenly waking up. "If you keep your eyes open tight you'll see that there's more of 'em than you can shake a stick at."

"What is the next best crop?"

"Well, on the whole, I guess nothin' in particular."

Again subsiding, he again wakes up with the question:—

"You wouldn't like to be buried here, would you?"

"Why not?"

"Because the soil's so poor you'd never rise agin."

I am inclined to believe that my friend the driver has said this at least once before, if not oftener, for there is a consciousness in his eye not unlike that noticeable in after-dinner wits immediately subsequent to an impromptu *bon mot* over which sleepless nights and anxious days have been passed. Laughing with the heartiness of an *ingénue* in modern comedy, and being nodded to approvingly in consequence (such is the world's farce, even among the Adirondacks), I make inquiries concerning the climate.

"The climate can't be got ahead on nohow. Nobody ever dies here, except by accident. Sometimes people do kinder give out, but they are strangers, and generally come from New York. We what stay here all the year round dry up and blow away when we get tired of living. I'm gettin' sparser nor I used to be."

At this stage of the journey Mr. Driver seems to entertain fears of drying up before his time. Jumping out of the wagon, and proceeding to a spring, he empties the remains of a bottle labelled "Castor-Oil" into a glass containing very little water. It is very peculiar looking castor-oil, so peculiar that I venture to ask whether there is any prohibitory law among the mountains.

"Guess not," answers Mr. Driver, who offers to share his dose of castor-oil, and is rewarded for his virtue by a refusal. "We're a law unto ourselves. When there's no laws, there's no transgressors. Ain't that the best way? What's the use of makin' laws just for the fun of standin' round and seein' 'em broke? I don't call prohibition temperance nohow, do you? And I tell you what, them folks that come up here and go into epileptic fits whenever they see a fellow warming himself with a drop of somethin' that ain't tea, are jest the awfullest critters on tobacco and coffee that ever you sot your eyes on. They beat a smudge at smoking, and they drink coffee as often as them emigrants vote in New York on 'lection day. My eyes, ain't it strong though! blacker nor any nigger! Ef they go in for temperance, why on airth don't they peg away on it all round?"

Expecting a reply, Mr. Driver pauses to listen, but I inhumanly forbear to argue, mainly because I cannot. Silence is supposed to imply profundity; consequently I preserve it until the putting of another question.

"How do you people behave?"

"Pretty well, on the whole. We've only one church up here. The more churches the more backslidin' I find."

"Are you married, Mr. Driver?"

"No, I'm lookin' round for a rich wife. When I can find a woman worth thirty thousand dollars I reckon I'll marry her. I think considerable of women. I think they've got to save the country. Men have got to be so corrupt that ef somethin' don't step in, we'll go to pieces as slick as maple sirup."

"Then you would have women vote?"

"No I wouldn't neither. Here you galang, you Sal," interpolates the driver with a cut of the whip at the off mare. "I don't go women's rights no how. When I say I think considerable of women, I mean I think considerable of 'em in *their* way, but I don't want 'em in *my* way. Home's the place for 'em."

❧ AN INVALID LOOKS AT THE NATIVES
MARC COOK

To the year-round resident of the wilderness the world is bounded by Canada on the north, Plattsburg on the east, Boonville on the south, and Malone on the west. All that lies beyond this clearly defined territory is dim, shadowy, and uncertain. The end and aim of life is to "guide" in summer and "log" in winter. Nowhere else on the face of the earth is it so easy to divide all people into classes at once so distinct and comprehensive. Every man must come under one of the two heads—he must be either a guide or a sportsman. For the qualifications of the latter, anything like previous training is unnecessary. The writer freely confesses that before he came into the St. Regis country he had never to his knowledge shot off a gun in his life, except possibly the air-guns that are sometimes made a tributary means of revenue in church affairs; he had never cast a fly, nor jointed a rod, nor told a fish story—intentionally, at any rate—he had never seen a deer save those in Central Park, while the few "strikes" he ever made on speckled trout were confined exclusively to Fulton Market. And yet—the assertion is made with a full sense of the responsibility that may hereafter attach thereto—and yet he was not fairly in the wilderness before he made the startling discovery that he was a "sportsman." So much for one of the grand divisions of mankind as found in the St. Regis country. The other is far more unique and interesting.

To begin with, the nationality of these backwoodsmen is a mixed problem. French blood mingles in at least equal proportions with American, and probably nine-tenths of all the people are descended more or less directly from Canadian ancestors. The French of Canada is not exactly the French of Paris, but it may be said to bear about the same relation to the latter that the sardine does to the herring. Ichthyologists classify these fishes under the same family head, but it is not very difficult to distinguish between them. Here in the immediate St. Regis Lake region a large proportion of the inhabitants speak Canadian French with at least as much facility as they speak English. The vastness of the country, as compared with the population, has led to such a complex intermarrying that pretty nearly everybody is either the aunt or uncle or cousin of everybody else. If the soil yields but a sorry harvest of grain, it seems at least adapted to the production of large families. A dozen children and sometimes a score grow to robust maturity in spite of all hardship and privation.

That the life of these people is a hard one—that the privations they are called upon to endure are such as would drive away a less hardy or stubborn race—is not to be denied. The few acres of land that have been cleared and cultivated return at best but a meagre harvest for the most unremitting toil. Through the long winter the one industry which offers employment is the chopping and drawing of logs. Many a man is glad to swing an axe ten hours out of the twenty-four for seventy-five cents wages [1880]. Ready money is always scarce and always hoarded. Young and old live principally on pork and potatoes, with now and then a soup of dry beans or peas. Sheep thrive here fairly well, but the mutton is, as a rule, regarded too valuable a product to be used for food. The wife of the backwoodsman works even more untiringly than her husband, and in the absence of the latter often does unaided the drudgery which should be assigned only to men.

But there comes a genial ray of sunlight into the wilderness with the advent of the sportsmen. It is then that every man and boy is ready to offer his services as a guide. The guide does not grow. He bears a striking resemblance to the city barber in that he never serves an apprenticeship. . . . He rolls, so to speak, out of his log cradle into a pair of top boots, discards the bottle for a plug of tobacco, possesses himself of a boat and a jackknife, and becomes forthwith an experienced guide. His duties are multifarious. He pulls a steady if not exactly scientific oar; he carries his boat on his shoulders from one mountain pond to another, often a distance of two or three miles; he conducts you to the spot where deer ought to be, and where sometimes they are; he fishes for you if you don't know how to fish for yourself, and breaks your new fly-rod with perfect good humor; if in camp, he cooks and chops wood and forecasts the weather with an unvarying inaccuracy which would discourage the most hopeful of meteorological prophets. It would never do to assert that the Adirondack guide is constitutionally lazy after thus particularizing his labors. True, he is forced to drag through seven or eight months of the year in waiting for the other four or five months to come around; but that is not his fault. Nor is this period of waiting by any means one of idle ease. The winter work is far more laborious and much less profitable than the summer guiding. Many of the men spend a good part of the cold season in a logger's camp, as it is called, and that is a kind of camp which offers very few attractions. It implies steady chopping from sunrise to sunset, exposure to the coldest weather, coarse fare, small wages, and no pleasanter recreation than a pipeful of tobacco in the evening. Harder even than the cutting, "skidding" (which means piling), or drawing of logs, is the driving of them down the rivers in the spring. The drivers are often drenched with water or half frozen by cold; and they run no inconsiderable risk of losing life or limb. The work pays better, however, than any other branch of the lumberman's calling.

Besides the severity of the winter work here, there is frequently no job to be had even at the small wages demanded. Last winter, for example, the lack of sleighing, without which the drawing of logs cannot be undertaken, shut out many men from the chance of earning a few needed dollars. Were it not that the cost of living is reduced to its minimum, the less thrifty inhabitants would be driven to sorry straits. Many of them are poor enough as it is; but there is none of that acute suffering from poverty which is to be found in the cities. Oddly enough, the want of money here, while it may enhance its value as a personal possession, seems to give to the native a supreme indifference for the wealth of others. This wealth may have its existence wholly in the imagination, as much of it indeed does; but that is of small matter so long as the stock of imagination holds out. The Adirondack guide, whose uncertain income seldom reaches five hundred dollars a year, will talk to you of millions with the refreshing assurance of Colonel Sellers. He sets every man down as rich who comes into the wilderness unpursued by a deputy-sheriff. He believes that every man is a sportsman because he is rich, and that he is rich because he is a sportsman, and that he is both because he is not a St. Regis guide. There you have the pith of backwoods logic in a nutshell.

The crossing of nationalities—the uncommon congenital mixture of a French peasant and a Yankee backwoodsman—gives rise to some curious combinations in names. You may find the thoroughly Anglo-Saxon James, John, and Henry flanked by such surnames as St. Germain, La Bountie, and Robal. You may have your faith in philology sadly shaken by the discovery that Mitchell Sweeney is a Frenchman, and that Mrs. Stephen Otis cannot speak English. It is a noteworthy fact that almost without exception the French residents give no hint of their nationality in speaking English. It may not be very pure English, but it is certainly freer from provincialisms and infinitely better in its pronunciation than is the speech of the average rural New Englander.

This wilderness must be set down as a spot which puts greatness to a terribly severe test and extinguishes notoriety with a beautiful simplicity. Edison's name is unknown, and the thrifty housewife who told me that she thought she remembered vaguely of having once heard of Henry Ward Beecher compelled an indescribable admiration. The late Vice-President of the United States [William A. Wheeler] secured his claim to recognition, not because of the office he held, but because he lived in Malone. John Brown is not here the martyr to a great cause, but the man who bought a big tract of land in North Elba. . . .

Under this surface of calm indifference to all that is passing in the great world outside, there is a solid basis of content. Without this the Adirondack backwoodsman would be impossible. His ignorance, after all, is superficial; his wisdom is deep-rooted and practical. He may not be able to write his name, but he can read with unerring accuracy the chirography of nature. He may not know his letters, but he never trips on the alphabet of forest lore. He finds himself born to a lot of privation and hardship. Instead of repining over this, or vainly coveting the fortune of the more prosperous, he sets to work manfully to make the best of his surroundings. In an exceptional degree he is thrifty, saving, and industrious. Not a few of the men in the St. Regis country have, by the dint of unflagging toil, amassed a competence. They recognize, apparently by some intuitive wisdom, that while the lines of their life here are not cast in easy places, still it is here that they can best fight the battle for bread. They have no desire to throw themselves into the vortex of city life, nor are they often led away by the *ignis fatuus* of the indefinite West. In this respect, and especially among the young men, the prevailing characteristic of the year-round inhabitant is peculiar. In almost every farming region, the dream of the younger generation is to break loose from home moorings and cast their fortune upon the untried sea of the world outside. Here, on the contrary, this ambition for a larger field of action—this craving to see and know something of the busy world we inhabit—seems to be utterly lacking. If content be indeed another name for happiness, the dwellers in the wilderness ought to be supremely happy. . . .

Hard-working, truthful, sober, book-ignorant, nature-wise—this is the general character of these backwoods dwellers.

NEIGHBORS OF YESTERDAY
Jeanne Robert Foster

When I go to see her, I look about the room
Where she sits placidly knitting—knitting.
It has the curious musty odor
Of our grandmother's parlors. The old things
One remembers are all there around her:
The hair-cloth furniture; the kaleidoscope
On the "What-not," the wax flowers under glass,
The cardboard motto on the walls, saying
"God Bless Our Home" with flourishes
And sprays of rosebuds in fine shaded wools;
The antimacassars on the rocking chairs,
The album on the marble-topped table,
The striped rag carpet hiding the rough floor,
In the corner a sheaf of cat-tails tied with a ribbon,
A box of sea-shells on the mantel,
And a souvenir of Niagara Falls,
And pink china dogs and gilded vases
Of dried Everlasting flowers dyed scarlet.

On the walls are the family portraits:
Large tintypes that look out from oval frames,
Daguerreotypes in velvet cases,
Edged with their faded crinkling gold.

The woman who sits here knitting—knitting
Is never lonely, she tells me, for *neighbors*
Of yesterday come and keep her company.
It does not trouble her delight in them
That to me they are but shifting shadows,
Projected into the world of reality
By her love for them.

They are called to her
By that longing for perpetuation
That lived once timidly in their bodies,
And now, shorn of the fleshly vehicles,
Gathers in cloistral dwellings, in old things,
Loving stone most of all, and gripping close fingers
Upon wood well seasoned with usage.

There is passion in their mute returning
To this eddy of cast-off mortality;
There is passion in the woman who calls them—
In her wilful insistence that nothing
Can escape the self-centered mind moving
Backward steadfastly, as it is pushed forward
By the onrushing force of time and change,
Until it joins the opposite arc of the circle
And is immortal in its own fulfillment.

THE COWARD
JEANNE ROBERT FOSTER

It is all right for a man to be kind,
But there's such a thing as being too soft
To get on well with your work and neighbors.
I've often wondered just where the line lay.
Now, I think death is a mercy sometimes,
And we have a right to take it, or give it,—
Only we must be sure that we are right.
There's something wrong in life as I see it:
You've got to fight for everything you have,
And Nature's not kindly 'bout ways and means.
She's a flighty, unreasonable person
And she don't respect a coward at all.
The only man who ever tames her in harness
Is the man who don't fear her devilments.

Dave Murdock was a coward and fond of cats,
Though I dunno as the two go together.
But he kept on feeding stray kittens,
And naturally more kept coming—and then
The milk from two cows wouldn't feed them
And make any butter for Dave to eat.
He couldn't make a living because of cats;
They lay all over him purring; he wallowed
In kittens, and like a dang soft coward
He ran away leaving the house open,
The cats in possession—there must 'a' been forty.
He didn't have the nerve to drown them;
He liked them too well to give them away
To homes where they'd been well taken care of;
So one day he just up and ran away.

I had to take a day off from harvesting
And shoot those beasts; they were starving.
And he heard of it and sneaked back in the night,

And went to farming again. After a while
I kind of forgot he was a "softy,"
(We don't like that kind here in this country);
But blast me, if I didn't pass his house
Last week, and see a cat on the doorstep!

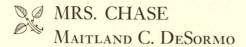

MRS. CHASE
MAITLAND C. DeSORMO

As had many other notable Adirondack hotel-keepers such as Paul Smith and the Stevens Brothers of Lake Placid, the Chases also migrated from Vermont: Mary Howe having been born in Jericho in 1843 and Ferd in Wheelock Hollow, a hamlet up in the northeastern corner, in 1840. Considered to be an accomplished musician as a young girl, she taught piano and voice; she rode her horse sidesaddle while making her rounds to the homes of her students. . . .

After their marriage in 1874 the young couple . . . , like many other restless Vermont people, listened intently to fascinating reports about the nearly unspoiled wilderness region whose alluring, serrated peaks beckoned irresistibly from beyond the western shore of Lake Champlain.

After several vacation trips to the Loon Lake vicinity they found exactly the spot they wanted: ten virtually untouched acres on a high knoll overlooking the upper lake. The decision having been reached the Chases went back to Vermont and made the necessary arrangements for the long-anticipated trip. They arrived at Loon Lake in October, 1878, and Ferd lost no time starting work on his own place. . . .

On May 19, 1879 the three story, thirty-one-room log structure was ready for guests. . . . Besides catering to hunters and fishermen during the early 1880s, people suffering from tuberculosis were also accommodated, and Mrs. Chase helped many of them to regain their health. She apparently had instinctive nursing skill and a genuine desire and ability to inspire courage and confidence. One of her patient-guests was the wife of President Benjamin Harrison, who made two trips from Washington to visit her. . . .

The Chases were not people who became easily discouraged. Within thirty years they had extended their original ten acres and one small hotel into an enterprise that eventually comprised 4,000 acres of forestlands, a hotel and two annexes, a golf course and numerous other service buildings and improvements—all of which were valued at well over a million dollars. The reputation of the Loon Lake House eventually reached a point where it accommodated nearly 800 guests in 1929, the last big season.

This compulsive urge to expand and then keep on expanding became a virtual obsession with "The Mrs." She used to the utmost her exceptional administrative ability and never ceased planning for an even bigger establishment. The profits from one season would be spent to add more annexes, cottages, barns, service buildings and other improvements which, besides the golf course, bowling alleys and tennis courts, also included a private acetylene lighting plant and a mile-long sewerage system that cost $5 for each foot dug through earth and $10 for the rocky sections, where the twin 12-inch tile lines had to be installed in a tunnel 92 feet deep at one point. A two-main water supply system was also a costly undertaking.

Development plans for the Loon Lake House also included the construction of many cottages; these finally totaled fifty-three. They ranged from small buildings which would accommodate only one family to far more elaborate log structures of the hunting lodge type. Since the hotel was operated under the American plan, the cottages were not equipped with kitchen facilities; therefore the guests were required to use the Main House dining room. This system of course proved very profitable for the management.

Another example of Mrs. Chase's business acumen was the arrangement for short-term leases which she made with several of her regular guests who were willing to pay a high price for the privacy of their own camps. Families such as the Mulfords, Jacksons, Demorests and Macdonalds were permitted to build their cottages on choice locations on her property. At the expiration of the lease, which sometimes ran for as short a time as ten years, the occupants could either renew or, after a fair appraisal had been made, sell the buildings to "The Mrs." In this way she acquired many additions to her holdings. . . .

"The Mrs." was a very astute business woman. She had no use for the blatant type of advertising used by many hotels. Convinced that third person or word of mouth testimonials and recommendations were enough in the early years, she usually just sent out a card each spring to former guests announcing the opening dates for the coming season. Later on, however, she made good use of well-illustrated brochures.

Although Ferd Chase was very active in the early management stages of the enterprise, his wife made all the major management decisions after the turn of the century. He then devoted most of his time to running the hotel farm and the outside operations. He had always felt more at ease with the guides and farm help than with the guests. . . .

For some reason Mrs. Chase seemed to have no desire to travel. She lived the year round at Loon Lake and left there only infrequently and then but for brief emergency trips to Plattsburgh or Burlington. Apparently, she was content to remain close to the place which her administrative skill and downright persistence had brought into being. Indeed the Loon Lake House was always her main interest in life and became a virtual obsession.

"The Mrs." never allowed herself to show outward indications of anger except for a reddening of her face. She never raised her voice when provoked. Sarcasm was her main resource against the relatively few people whom she instinctively and intensely disliked.

Typical of the way she handled objectionable guests is the encounter with the wealthy individual who arrived with a large party one Sunday. Since the Hotel had built up an enviable reputation for its delicious food, as many as a thousand people were often served in shifts in the huge dining room overlooking the lake. The regular guests were of course accommodated first, so the influential stranger started to get impatient and protested loudly and often that he was not accustomed to such treatment. The head waiter sent one of his assistants to report the incident to "The Mrs.," who took charge immediately. She explained the situation and assured him that he and his guests would be taken care of as soon as possible. They were finally served an excellent dinner which they enjoyed very much, so he stopped at the main desk on his way out to express his approval.

"Mrs. Chase," he said, in his most expansive manner, "that's the best dinner I've ever eaten! I shall come back often. How much do I owe you?"

"You owe me nothing," replied Mrs. Chase.

"Nothing! But I can't accept that. Why I..I..just couldn't possibly come here again if I didn't pay you now!"

"That's just exactly the way I had it figured out, mister," Mrs. Chase retorted. "Good day, sir!"...

Although she usually was seen in black silk dresses and sweaters, Mrs. Chase sometimes wore light green, her favorite color. This provided a strong contrast for her sand-colored wigs, of which she had four. Scarlet fever had left her nearly bald....

She slept only four or five hours per night (said that no one needed any more rest than that) and was up by five each morning to make her daily rounds of the kitchen and grounds. Although she was well up in her seventies at the time, she still had a keen mind and keener eyes. Nothing sloppy or half-heartedly done ever got by her sharp glance and sharper tongue. In fact about all anyone with any degree of management responsibility had to say to get prompt cooperation was—"I'll tell The Mrs.!"

She invariably read two New York papers each day not only to keep posted on world happenings but also to keep tabs on regular and prospective guests. If any of her summer people got involved in scandals, those individuals found it extremely difficult or even impossible to get reservations at Loon Lake the following season.

Apparently she had no strong religious convictions or, if she did, she never discussed them. As a girl she was a member of the Baptist Church but evidently something happened that soured her against ministers and religion. One soliciting clergyman was rocked back on his heels when Mrs. Chase told him that she would indeed make a donation to his worthy cause—but only after he had earned it at the woodpile out back. She declared that she wanted to know exactly where her money went, so her practical Christianity found expression in gifts of money to countless deserving or needy people. She often paid the funeral expenses of indigent former employees and several times paid the expenses for rebuilding homes of burned-out neighbors. Moreover, she sent several young people—mostly boys but also some girls—through medical and law courses.

Mrs. Chase was generous but not gullible, as one St. Lawrence University student found out. Since he came from a poor family and also had one of the less remunerative jobs at the famous summer resort, she told him that she would underwrite his college education at S.L.U. During the following years his written requests for money came frequently and his expense account showed indications of obvious padding. His benefactor became suspicious and finally insisted that the lad send itemized statements. This he did but he also senselessly included bills from his mother for doing her son's laundry. That did it! Mrs. Chase was understandably indignant to learn that the mother wasn't even willing to do that little bit to help out. So no more checks from Loon Lake for him. . . .

Mrs. Chase believed firmly in the transmigration of souls and that conviction probably helped explain her love for animals—particularly dogs and cats. She was especially solicitous of a donkey which had nearly lost its sight hauling cartloads of dirt and rocks when the sewerage system was being installed. "The Mrs." once declared to her secretary that dogs and cats came first in her affections, men came next, and women and children were welcome to whatever love she had left over.

One day in the kitchen she and Steve Leonard, one of her cooks, got into a conversation about her favorite topic—the souls of people inhabiting the bodies of animals.

"Stevie," she said, "when you die you're going to turn into a dog."

"If that's true," replied Steve, "I certainly hope that I don't turn into a pug dog!"

"Why not?" asked the Mrs.

"Because those dogs always have crooked tails," Steve complained. Both of them chuckled heartily over that bit of repartee.

Besides numerous dogs and cats "The Mrs." also had a parrot named Drexie, an ill-tempered, finger-biting creature that hated the narrow confines of a regular enclosure and was kept in a monkey cage instead. For several months after its acquisition the cooped-up carnivore was on display behind the main desk, near the bellhops' bench. Its location was changed shortly afterward when the bright-feathered bird was heard screaming raucously—"Tip the bell-boys! Tip the bell-boys!" A resourceful lad from Malone named Walter Mullarney was credited with that cadging endeavor.

The parrot's disposition did not mellow with age. She got even more ornery instead. Not wanting to see it cooped up all the time Mrs. Chase often let Drexie out of her big cage. The gaudy bird showed her perverted sense of gratitude by digging deep divots into the furniture and upholstery, shredding magazines and catalogs and not infrequently attempting—sometimes successfully—to take sizable chunks from the fingers of anyone who touched her, as I found out for myself.

She was certainly no prize as a pet but nevertheless her owner tolerated and even liked her. Therefore when Mrs. Chase was critically ill with pneumonia, she asked June if she would take care of Drexie. Although Miss Jarvis did not want to hurt her beloved employer's feelings she gently refused. Somewhat disappointed Mrs. Chase then added, "You are the only one I would give her to. But if you honestly don't want her, June, why that's all right. I want her to be with me." So after the death of "The Mrs.," the parrot was chloroformed and placed in the coffin beside her. . . .

The seasons of 1930-31 were critical for the Loon Lake Hotel Corporation and Mrs. Chase. By then the Depression was well underway and business was going from bad to worse. A receivership representing the creditors took over and finally, on one grim afternoon in late 1931, Mrs. Chase was called into a meeting and summarily told that while she would of course be welcome to remain at Loon Lake House as long as she wished, from that day on she would have nothing to do or say about its management. According to Henrietta Earle, her secretary, when "The Mrs." came out of the room, she burst into tears—the first such display of emotion the former had ever seen during the more than twenty years of her employment.

The bitter experience seemed to break her spirit because she never showed much interest in life or living thereafter, according to her maid, June Jarvis. Had she lived until the following October 7th she would have been ninety, but "The Mrs." died of pneumonia on Thursday, January 18, 1933. As she lay there four kittens played around and even on the deathbed. Her secretary watched but did not disturb them because she felt that their antics would have amused Mrs. Chase. . . .

Although the old Loon Lake has now become just another fascinating phase of Adirondack history, there are still a dwindling few of us who worked there and "knew it when." For us the very mention of the place evokes pleasant memories of it and the person who made it memorable—the unforgettable, unforgotten Mrs. Chase.

THE HERMIT OF COLD RIVER
NOAH JOHN RONDEAU

Noah John Rondeau chose one of the wildest and most remote parts of the Adirondacks for his hermitage, the Cold River. For several years he lived in the woods only during winter months when he could not do guiding, but in 1929 he began living there year round. His longest continuous stay was 381 days. He called himself the Mayor of Cold River City, population 1. (The tiny log hut he lived in is now on display at the Adirondack Museum.) He was forced to leave after the Big Blow of 1950 (he was then sixty-seven years old), when the Cold River was closed because of the danger of fire.

A colorful personality, Noah, who died in 1967, is by far the most celebrated of Adirondack hermits. Most of the others have been rather dour, but Noah was friendly and outgoing, as the two letters here quoted show. A visitor to his hermitage described him thus: "A pippin of a man with a face as smiley as the full moon....When he was speaking it seemed as if he was vocalizing the mystic spirit of the woods....I could plainly see that beneath his frolicking humor there lurked a soul of rare sincerity and worth. I once heard that nature is our oldest and best teacher, and after spending those few hours with Rondeau I believe it is true....Noah John had graduated from this unique school with a *magna cum laude* degree."

The following letters were addressed to Dr. and Mrs. Adolph C. Dittmar.

May 11th, 1944

Dear Old People—To start away back—Sept. 6th, 1943 I launched you for Calkin Creek from the Balsams and Spruces at High Bank Cold River. I took my Pack to Town Hall; on the way I watched a doe and a fawn slowly cross the River. The bride flowers stayed on the table in Mrs. Rondeau's Kitchenette for a week. About Oct. 20th Dr. Latimer and Attorney Gregory came to High Bank for ten days hunt. They brought in my supplies for winter and after many back loads I got the supplies to the Town Hall. In November I got a Raccoon and a 10-Point Buck and a 200-Pound Bear. And two days after I got the Bear I could have had another Bear; But you understand the law says "one bear." Now if anything makes me mad—it's to see a Bear and can't shoot. In fact I was so mad I bit the top off from a little Spruce. November 21st there was 6 inches of snow. By Christmas it was 4 feet. 1944 came along. I had no *Almanac* but I watched the stars and planets and kept tabs on the moon. By the time the Calendar said "Spring," at Cold River nights below zero still felt like Winter and hard packed snow was still 4 feet deep. It took all April to sweep the snow out of the Valley. Brooks are high and the swamps wet. Pussy Willows have Kittens an inch long. They look as if they might turn into Bumble Bees if they could grow wings. The leaves have peeked out just enough to speckle the borders with green. May 9th I left Cold River and I came through Ouluska Pass. The last mile of climb to Ouluska had snow all the way—up to 4 feet. I reached the main road in Ampersand Park and went to the Pond but found no one there except a Wild Rabbit on the Lawn. So I went back to the Guide's Camp and rocked myself in Avery Rockerfeller's Rocking Chair.

By the way I think you have a nice sweet young wife especially since She got her Eye Brows lifted at the Beauty Parlor in Cold River City [Rondeau had been a barber in civilian life]. Now I don't mean that Mary was not good looking before that. But every little bit helps and I tell you it pays to employ an Artist who has the equipment. My last stay at Town Hall was 374 days; the furtherest I got from Beauty Parlor was when I went to launch Newly Weds to Calkin Creek. On my last debut at Cold River I wrote four poems and a manuscript (119 pages) of prose—my recollections of 54 years ago, "A French Wedding in a Log House." It's an outstanding *Scream*. I will close.

Very Truly,
Noah John Rondeau

January 19, 1945

Addressing Dr. Ditt and our Mary that he stold.
Dear Old People—Now, Hmmmm! I was away from Cold River from June 1st to 12th the first time in 376 days. I saw no one from November 22 to March 14. And I had one woodfire that burned 138 days without relighting. That sounds like the Irishman on the subject of the clock that runs 8 days without winding, he said, "How long would it r-r-run if it was wound?" I got all the letters, cards and photographs. When I opened the Christmas cards (June 2nd) the snow-clad trees on the card did not know what to make of the Buttercups and Robins and the old farmer across the fence—planting potatoes. I just got the May-June issue of *The Cloud Splitter* and I note with interest your article on canoeing and observation of the trimmed cedar borders of lakes and ponds—that in itself is closer observation than most city guys. Of course—you're semi-citified. This six-foot trim is due 100% to Deer Brousing. An old Buck comes along to breakfast and he trims a cedar; but only as far as he can reach. Then he goes to another cedar and without knife and fork, napkin or prayer—he trims it likewise. And during the winter without spirit-level or measuring tape the deer establish a line. Further you'll observe such a border until you

find a spruce. You'll find the spruce like a woman of the gay nineties—wearing its skirts to the ground just because Deer don't eat Spruce. . . . So in the meantime Saint Peter might find out what a fine Harper I am and snatch me by the seat of the breeches over the renounced Pearly Gates.

Sincerely,
Noah John Rondeau

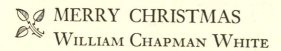

MERRY CHRISTMAS
WILLIAM CHAPMAN WHITE

John Roberts is a forest ranger. He is a grayed, gaunt man, as sturdy as one of the tall spruces in his care. For forty years he has watched over what he calls "his trees."

A few days before Christmas last year John came out of the woods, following a human trail. It had started at a freshly cut white spruce stump, then crossed the heavy snow in a clearing, and came out on a back road. The heavy footprints turned down toward an unpainted bleak house a quarter-mile away. As John plodded down the road following the footprints he knew what he was going to have to do. It was one part of his job he never cared for.

The trail led right into Joe Carson's ramshackle place, where Joe, wife and seven kids somehow lived. John had known Carson all his life. He had never amounted to much.

In the littered front yard small children were building a snow man. A pack of black puppies ran at their heels. John went by them to the old barn. On the floor inside was the fresh-cut white spruce. Kids and puppies followed John when he turned to the house. Carson opened the door before John could knock. He asked without much surprise: "Something you want, John?"

The ranger nodded as he went into the house, along with the kids and dogs. In its one big, steamy, downstairs room were more children, more puppies. A faded woman in a faded dress stood by a littered dining table. Behind it were three ill-made beds.

John nodded to Mrs. Carson. He said to Joe: "You cut a tree off state land, Joe. You know there's a fine of ten dollars a tree for that. I didn't make the law. If we didn't have it, soon we wouldn't have any trees left, particularly at Christmas."

Joe nodded. "Yeah, I know. We can't have much for Christmas this year, but I figured I'd get the nicest tree I could and I didn't expect you'd see it. My wife even made some paper chains for it. Well, what do I do now?"

"You can pay me the fine, on stipulation, as we call it," John said bluntly. "Or you can come to justice court and stand trial."

"No use," Joe shook his head. "I just about got $10."

"How much money have you altogether?"

"I got $11.58 in all this world. We were going into town to-night to get some things for the kids' Christmas, but we won't go now."

"I guess not." John hoped he did not sound as miserable as he felt. He saw Mrs. Carson and the circle of children 'round about staring at him. "Law's law, Joe. Give me the $10 and I'll give you a receipt." He stooped down for a moment to brush away two puppies that were chewing at his shoelaces.

The ranger took a dirty crumpled bill from Joe and gave him a receipt. He felt angrier at the man for having put him in this spot. "Okay," he said. "That's all, Joe."

"Thanks," Joe answered. "Well, Merry Christmas!"

John just nodded at that as he hurried to the door to get away. At the door he had to stoop again and push puppies away. Then he turned back. "Joe," he said, "would you sell me one of these puppies? I have a nephew who wants a dog for Christmas."

"I'd sell most of 'em if I could."

Joe picked up one puppy. "How about $10 for this one?"

Joe stared at the ranger, then grinned. "That's a high price."

"It's worth that to me." John took a dirty crumpled bill from his pocket, handed it over and hurried out with a puppy squirming under his arm.

Two nights later the ranger was in town finishing his Christmas shopping. He ran into the Carsons on the main street.

"Glad I met you," Joe told him. "The darndest thing happened after you left the other day. People started coming to buy those puppies. I musta sold seven."

"That's fine," John said. "News sure gets around fast up here in the backwoods. Well, Merry Christmas, Joe!"

"I'll say," Joe answered. "Merry Christmas!"

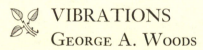

VIBRATIONS
George A. Woods

I can hear a train whistle way off in the distance. It's a diesel. That's different from what Corky and I used to hear. There's no heart, no soul to the diesel's horn; it's a mechanical thing. What we heard was a steam locomotive's call, a cry of sadness that came from way down deep in its iron belly.

Corky went away in one of those trains. I didn't. I never thought about climbing those steps, sitting down, having my head snap backwards as the train lurched ahead. The Delaware, Lackawanna, that was it. Pullman cars with names—Ticonderoga, Saranac, Lake Champlain—in neat letters on the sides, club cars, put a penny on the track and try to find it in the gravel bed after the train's gone by, whistle once for the crossing by the station, whistle again going through the valley, red lights blinking, white gate arms folded over the road, cyclops eye shining down the track.

I grew to hate the sound of that whistle, because I lived in a

resort town. We lived for the busy seasons, starved in the off-
seasons. Oh, we didn't really starve, but we waited through the
long months of March and April, through the wet and dreary
spring, through May when the Public Works Department got
around to sweeping up the sand and cinders they had been spreading on the ice and snow. I mean that was the scene, go downtown
and watch them sweep up sand. When the sand and grit goes can
summer be far behind?

Summer meant people, change, faces you hadn't seen for a year.
People opening up their summer homes and camps, people pale but
with smooth skin, not the leathery, beaten-down, lined expressions
of the year-round residents who had to live through the wind and
weather. It was the summer people who pumped blood into us and
money and a new life.

Every day in June you'd see someone you knew, someone you
hadn't seen since the previous summer. People shook hands and
smiled again and we threw ourselves into the job of making money,
knowing full well that the summer wouldn't last, that there'd be
another fall, another winter, that one morning you'd get up and it
would be cold out, a warning that made us count the few days left
to September.

Those summers were good. The streets were crowded. There
were girls with light dresses, sweaters just draped over their shoulders, girls with their hair tied neatly with a ribbon or their hair
piled on top of their heads. They were new and exciting, lean and
lithe. They were different from the freckled, pig-tailed, horn-
rimmed glasses types we went with all year.

The town was alive. Merchants went to bed tired from work
and not just boredom. Lights were on in the stores and each night
stretched out and didn't end at nine P.M. There was laughter and
music and voices in the dark. . . .

When I got a little older I used to go down to the station and see
some girl off, say good-bye, and maybe get a chance to kiss her just
once.

Sure, it was always a kind of puppy love and everybody, adults
especially, make fun of you for it, but how do they know how
deeply you feel it, how much it hurts? You can't even explain to

them, because they'd tell you you are too young to know about such things. How old do you have to be, for crying out loud, to miss somebody?

I missed a Jewish girl once, an awful lot. Her name was Betty Friedlander and I didn't get to meet her until the summer was almost gone. There isn't much to tell about her. We never did anything momentous together except she was the one who made me kiss her. No, she didn't make me kiss her; she kissed me a couple of times one night. I guess she was the first aggressive girl I've ever known—the only one, I think. She wasn't bold or brazen. It was just I was kind of slow and if she hadn't taken the initiative I'd still be standing there scuffing my toes in the dirt.

She was a nice girl, don't think the wrong thing about her. We enjoyed talking to each other and we spent a lot of time sitting on park benches in the daytime and at night, sitting in drug stores, sometimes just walking around, going no place. She didn't mind. We used to talk about life, about growing up and what we were going to do, about school and people and God. She told me about her life in New York City. She was smarter than I was; I could see that and I tried to keep up with her as best I could and still not reveal my ignorance so she wouldn't discover all the things I didn't know. But she'd listen to me patiently and never laugh or make fun of me even if I was slow and awkward.

I don't know how it happened. I walked her home like I had been doing for several weeks, standing in front of her door with her, trying to think how I should go about kissing her good-night. I tried to think of all the ways I'd seen it done in the movies, read about in books, or remembered from what the other guys had told me about how you kiss a girl.

I was trying hard to come up with an approach when she put her arms around my neck and kissed me. And not once but twice. Oh, hell, maybe it was three or four times. I was too stunned to keep count and I was scared too. I mean, I didn't think girls did that; I thought it was supposed to be my responsibility. But I liked it, which is an understatement. And you know after she kissed me once she kept her arms around my neck, pulled her face back a little, and smiled at me saying, "You know you're an awful dope."

It was the way she said it that was nice. It seemed to be kind of affectionate.

The breaks after that were that we couldn't get together very often. Either I was working or else her parents made her go with them to plays or stay home to meet some visiting relatives. Besides there was only another week left before Labor Day. And then the week was gone.

I went down to the station to say good-bye the night she left. I asked her if it would be okay and she even told me that she wanted me to be there. I found her in spite of all the people standing around in groups, in spite of all the taxis and piles of luggage. She was standing by herself, sort of looking for someone; I guess it was for me. Her parents were already on the train, even though it was fifteen minutes before it was supposed to leave. We walked a little, along the platform, down to the end where there weren't so many people. Neither of us said much other than we'd write to one another, that she was sorry she had to leave, and I was sorry she had to go.

There was a chill wind moving through the leaves and I thought about how lonely I was going to feel tomorrow. Hell, it was going to be a long time until next summer and there was no certainty that she'd be back or that she'd even remember me if she did return.

And the whistle blew a warning and we hurried back to her car and just before she stepped up to get on, she turned around and let me kiss her and then she was gone. No, not really gone; she was behind a thick glass window saying something I couldn't hear or read on her lips and then she was smiling and blowing a kiss and then the whistle blew louder, sort of shaking me inside, and the window with the girl behind it began to edge away. I walked a little with it and then it began to go faster and I was afraid I'd bump into someone on the platform and I let it go. There were a lot of windows going past; I could count them and then they were going too fast to count and everything was a blur of windows, light and dark.

Then there was nothing, just a patch of light moving off down the tracks, the last car with its gate and swaying chains getting smaller and smaller. The whistle blew for the crossing, mournful, miserable, hateful whistle.

So now maybe you can see why I'm not fond of trains, why when I hear those whistles, something sweeps me up, shrinks time and me and for a moment I'm back there feeling the car vibrating under my feet and people pressing in on me to keep me from going where I want, and I feel the hurt all over again of having said good-bye to someone who touched me, someone who'd maybe understand why I walked home tonight. Betty Friedlander? Maybe. I never did see her again. She never came back. We wrote a couple of times to each other but the letters sort of trailed off.

Somebody sent me a copy of the old hometown newspaper last month. I read that the train doesn't go there, not to Paradox, not anymore. I imagine weeds are growing all over the roadbed now.

DECLARATION OF INDEPENDENCE, SPIRIT OF 1976   SLOAN WILSON

The occasion of Howie Hewat's speech is a Fourth of July celebration in the not-so-mythical "Livingston" of the novel *Small Town*, which might have been any Adirondack village in the bicentennial year 1976.

Howie Hewat had just begun his speech when Ben and Ebon entered the crowded, bunting-draped gymnasium of the high school where the Legion picnic had been moved to escape the rain and muddy fields. His bulky figure draped in a dark blue business suit with a star-spangled tie in the colors of the flag, Howie was a surprisingly effective speaker. His evocation of the glories of the past and his celebration of the spirit of independence down through the years in the mountain valley did not, however, last long.

"All this history is glorious indeed," he continued after taking a deep breath, "but let us be frank: we can't eat it. In the midst of national plenty and state plenty, Livingston County is starving!

Even with the mill going full blast, we have an unemployment rate of twenty-eight percent, higher even than Essex County, which is chronically the capital of depression in New York State. Our children are leaving as soon as they finish school because there's no work for them here. Good men are on relief year after year. Business of almost every kind shrinks every year and nearly everybody but Eddie Pace is going broke!"

Old Ed Pace, the undertaker, was sitting at the speakers' table near Howie. Accustomed to being the butt of jokes, he grinned tolerantly. The crowd laughed.

"Don't think I'm not serious," Howie continued. "We must ask ourselves, why are we broke? And we all know the reason, the Adirondack Park Agency, the most vicious kind of dictatorship ever to be spawned by our fair democracy—"

This accusation was greeted by loud cheers. A man beside Ben jumped on a chair and yelled, "You tell 'em, Howie! Tell it like it is!"

"I will," Howie said, holding up his hand for quiet. "Now you all know what the Adirondack Park Agency is. It was created by the Rockefellers and other great nature lovers who want the Adirondacks, including our valley, to be 'forever wild.' They love the beauty of the forest. They love chipmunks and deer, raccoons and even skunks! The one living thing they don't love is people, the people who live in these mountains. You see, the trouble with people is, they're not scenic. If we could learn to be cute and kind of sit up on our hind legs and beg for peanuts, why, hell, the Rockefellers might love us!"

The hall exploded with laughter, and many in the audience beat plastic plates on the tables to show their approval.

"Because people ain't as cute as bears, the Adirondack Park Agency is trying to keep them out of this whole region, including our valley," Howie went on. "Now, they don't drive us out with guns or poison, like rats. They just do the next best thing: they confiscate our land. And I say *confiscate!* They like to call it zoning, but when you tell a man he can't sell less than forty-three acres of land, you have reduced the value of his land enormously and you probably have made it impossible for him to sell it at all.

Telling him he can't sell a lot less than eight acres is better, like having an arm cut off is better than being killed. This whole crazy patchwork of zoning they've imposed on us drains our life blood. It's hated by everyone but the city people, who like to have a park up here they can use without paying for it—"

After more cheers and table-pounding, Howie continued, "Now let me tell you a little story. Not so long ago my wife and I were sitting on the porch of a little camp we have up at Lost Lake. We have an outdoor fireplace down near the water, but it don't draw too good and we hardly ever use it. Anyway, on this morning I smell meat cooking. I walked to the end of the house and saw smoke pouring out of that chimney. Some people in bathing suits which left very little to the imagination had set up a picnic table in my backyard, and believe it or not, they were prying boards from the bottom of my old garage for firewood. When I told them to get the hell off my property, they were very indignant.

" 'What the hell!' one of them said. 'We're in the Adirondack Park, ain't we? This is as much our land as yours!' "

The crowd roared.

"These people really do think they own the Adirondacks," Howie said. "And with this forty-three-acre zoning, they're not far wrong. A lot of folks can't afford to pay taxes on land they can't sell. A lot of those forty-three-acre tracts are reverting to wilderness. We're going to be 'forever wild,' all right, if we don't do something about it."

"What, Howie?" a bald man shouted. "What should we do?"

"First of all, we have to bust that zoning like a rotten egg. With that, we can bring some industry in here, businesses of many kinds. So there will be jobs for people and money enough to live like other Americans."

"But how are you going to bust the zoning?" the bald man shouted.

"I don't pretend I know all the answers to that one," Howie replied, wiping his forehead with a handkerchief. "The Adirondack Park Agency is nothing but an appointive bureaucratic committee. It's backed by the Rockefellers and their successors. In fact, it's backed by just about everybody in the world who loves nature without having to pay for it. The only people who hate it are the people who live here, the people whose land is being zoned, not bought by the State to make a park. We suffer great losses without compensation. Still, I think the Agency can be licked. The only place to do it is in Albany, where all the strings are being pulled. You have to be one of the power boys to have any chance in this kind of battle."

Howie paused and took a deep breath.

"Which is why, ladies and gentlemen, I am running for the State Senate, starting right now! I am running as an independent candidate because I do not want any political party to impose its views about the Park Agency on me. If you will send me to Albany, I will break the chains that Agency has wrapped around us or damn well die trying! Guarantee it . . ."

While the audience stood to applaud, Ben and Ebon made their way through the crowd to the fresh air outside.

"I always thought he was such a bastard," Ebon said. "Is he really all that sincere, or does he just want to get elected?"

"The truth is, I don't know for sure," Ben said. "In a lot of ways, Howie for sure is an SOB and a thief, but I suppose that doesn't mean he can't help this town, even if it is for his private reasons. I haven't made my own mind up about the whole Park Agency issue. Is it better for us all to starve here among scenic wonders, or to put up a huge smoky factory that will enable everyone to buy new cars and trailers?"

"Is that the only choice?"

"No. Like most towns everywhere, we can contrive to get the huge smoky factory and starve to death anyhow."

Ebon laughed. "You don't believe in happy endings?"

"I never knew a government that made one. Individuals, sometimes, if you can stop the story with the wedding."

THE LAND ETHIC
WARDER CADBURY

The following talk on prospects for the Adirondacks in the year 2000 and after was given at St. Lawrence University's fifth annual conference on the Adirondack Park, in 1975.

One of the things that is sometimes forgotten in the battles and struggles we have been involved in is that history determines the future not only by economic and technological changes, some of which we can predict and some of which we can't (and the track record isn't too good right now), but by ideas as well. In the last analysis these are moral ideas because it is on our moral beliefs that our ultimate political and legal policy decisions are made.

One of the pioneers in the conservation movement was a man named Aldo Leopold. In 1933 he wrote an essay called "The Conservation Ethic." This was reprinted later in a book, *A Sand County Almanac*. Now, I am a philosopher as well as a dealer in antiquarian miscellaneous irrelevancies of Adirondack history, and I want to summarize Leopold's theory, because even if it isn't original with him, it is very interesting. He pointed out, as he saw history from the long range, not just the next twenty-five years, that our moral thinking goes through three stages of development. The first and earliest of these stages is working out the way individuals deal with individuals. Historically, and perhaps logically, the most pressing problems are the moral ones on a man-to-man, one-to-one basis. He tells the story that when Odysseus returned from the wars at Troy he heard rumors that some of his slave girls had been misbehaving, and with absolutely no moral compunctions he hung them all from the same rope. Incidentally, he didn't hang his wife, who busied herself with weaving. There are moral problems between individuals and these we have to settle first.

The second stage in our moral development focuses on the relationships between the individual and his community. (I am grossly over-simplifying this second stage.) This presents a whole new set of problems before man can begin to organize into communities or into societies. Over the centuries, and it is a matter of centuries, we get clearer about who we are as moral beings when the distinctions between slave and freeman, Greek and barbarian, etc., begin to vanish. I might remind you that in 1954, there was a constitutional amendment to begin the integration of schooling. Once we got clear as to who was to count as a moral being, we naturally had to focus on the problem of rights and duties because they are correlative. They are interdependent between the individual and society. This is particularly true in a democratic political society. We are more factitious, more fussy about moral issues than those in some other kinds of political systems.

Leopold said there is still a third stage that we have not yet fully developed. This is the ethics, if you will, regarding man's relationship to his natural environment, to its non-human plants and animals. I have been looking at some material written by philosophers (I don't recommend it) on some esoteric questions as to whether trees have rights. Do the redwoods in California have moral rights? Do lakes and rivers have moral and legal rights? Leopold's point was that we still treat land as property. We still treat it in the same way as Odysseus treated his slave girls—with no rights of their own and no correlative duties to the property owner. Many people today still tend to think of man's relationship to man in terms of the property rights of the owner, entailing economic privileges, but with no correlative obligations or duties.

As a non-professional observer of the extraordinarily complex controversies about the Adirondacks and their future, I will say right now that I have no expertise on the topics that this conference has been focusing on—I leave them to the experts. It seems to me that in the last analysis they have had their root—and this is not news to anybody—in a basic disagreement about the legitimacy of the rights of property owners and industry to do what they please with their land, whether it be subdivision of ancestral acreage or use by industry of the free air, the free water, the free land, the free timber. In more current terms this is what we call home rule vs. public welfare for the future.

We are missing, and I am not sorry to be missing it, a cavalcade to Albany. I read the newspapers urging people to assemble with full cars with a flag flying on each car and a full tank of gasoline. "To all concerned citizens of the Adirondack Park: If you feel that the Adirondack Park Agency has restricted and zoned out any opportunity for growth in the Adirondacks for you and your children, has ignored your economic future and has taken away your rights as a citizen to free property, now is the time to get in the cavalcade and head on down the Thruway." What I am saying is that in the last analysis we are down to Leopold's third ethic— what he roughly called a land ethic. The term is a kind of misnomer. It really is this fundamental moral struggle between what we have called for centuries the rights of individuals to property versus a moral obligation to what is not human and to what we had always thought had no rights—trees, rivers, mountains, birds, endangered species. . . .

My own hunch is that if we are going to try to solve these problems (and by "solve," I put myself on the side of the environmentalists), we cannot count, in spite of our victories in the past, on solving them on economic grounds or on legal grounds as we have been fighting them in the past. What we really need is some public education on the underlying moral issues, and this is not an easy job. I have friends who regard Leopold as an optimist in the sense that he regarded the land ethic as an inevitable evolutionary stage in man's moral thinking. What he couldn't anticipate in the 1930s was the rapidity with which this ecological crisis has come upon us. I have friends who are pessimists about preserving the wilderness, and their theory is that in the last analysis property rights and money and the energy crisis and unemployment and all these other very difficult problems with which we are now dealing are going to win. If it comes down to a showdown and times are tough, the wilderness is going to lose.

There is another alternative, and that is that the land ethic will come to be accepted. We are going to have to abandon some of our cherished notions about property rights. Unless we do abandon them, however slowly, all the progress we have made in the earlier two stages of our moral development will become meaningless. Unless we can put moral and legal teeth into an ecology act, we will have lost everything. Without a quality environment there can be no organized society, and without a quality environment there can be no quality in the lives of individuals.

I said I wanted to urge us to do more public education about the

moral dimensions of this problem. I do not say this to the exclusion
of legal and technical issues, but the thing that has bothered me all
along is that the only argument, except for some hardnosed ecological or economic arguments, is all this talk about the spiritual
values of the wilderness. When we ask why we should preserve
the wilderness, why we should have zoning and the banning of
closed cottages and pure rivers and all the rest, apart from all the
utilitarian arguments that we have used and will continue to use,
some of my "forever wild" friends say that the important thing we
are talking about is spiritual values. If we could have a little dia-
logue with those citizens of the Adirondacks driving down to
Albany today and tried to talk to them about the spiritual values
of the wilderness, it wouldn't go over very well. To them it would
sound like elite snobbism. It would be meaningless and I think
unconvincing. In spite of the difficulty, I think we should try to do
it. I would like to be optimistic and think that we can actually do
it. We have a new generation—what I call the post-Woodstock
generation—and they are not quite as locked into the value system
as previous generations. . . .

Recreation, I remind you, means "to re-create," and recreation
is more than just hunting, fishing, and trapping or just sitting in the
sun probably hurting your health by absorbing too much ultra-
violet rays. Recreation is spiritual recreation and a re-creating of
the human spirit, and it seems to me, at least for most of us, that
this is really what the land ethic is all about. . . .

My conclusion is not a prediction, but a plea that in addition to
all the other things that we are doing it is most urgent and most
important that we try to articulate why a wilderness experience is
so important, why it is that we need it for our identity, for our sanity. This is not the British notion, a "because-it-is-there" kind of
thing. We need to educate people to this kind of experience. We
have no illusions that we can educate every American. I feel this
because the only argument we have (apart from the economic and
scientific arguments) is that the preservation of the wilderness is
essential for our sanity and our health.

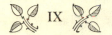

IX

Woods-Peaks-Waters

The Forest Preserve . . . is one of our great natural re-
sources. It is a whole complex of nature: trees and rocks
and ferns and flowers and wildlife. It is clean water and
clean air. It is the beauty of nature as nature evolves. It is
solitude and the music of stillness. It invites man to adven-
ture, to refreshment, and to wonder.

Sharon Mauhs

FOR THE SOCIOLOGIST the Adirondacks are a northern extension of Appalachia. For the geologist they are a
southeastern lobe of the Canadian Shield, connected by a narrow
isthmus at the Thousand Islands called the Frontenac Axis. The
basement rock of the Adirondacks is the crystalline Precambrian
rock of Canada. Though not so old as the oldest of the Shield, its
age of one billion one hundred million years is a quarter of the
estimated planet itself. Successively upthrust and downworn, the
Adirondack mountains are now rising again at two or three milli-
meters a year, a rate faster than that of the Alps.

"The rocks are old, but the landscape is new," remarks geologist
Yngvar Isachsen. Ancient events shaped the mountains, but a
comparatively recent one, the last ice sheet, retreating only ten
thousand years ago, sculptured the intricate bas-relief of the landscape. It gouged U-shaped valleys. It scoured glacial drift, including
huge boulders, from one region and moved it to others, dammed
the streams and deflected their courses into new channels, mounded
kames and eskers, and hollowed the depressions of bogs and lakes.

Innumerable lakes and waterfalls are evidence that the rivers in their altered courses have not been long at work. The topography left by that gigantic plough, the glacier, was varied, youthful, receptive to a new era of highly diversified plant life.

Values are accented by contrast. When I settled in northern New York a half century ago after an underprivileged youth in the flatlands of Iowa, the uneven ground of the Adirondacks was a revelation. This country of ancient bedrock and youthful landscape, of woods and waters upthrust by lateral and subterranean forces, split in fault zones, gouged, grooved and molded by the glacier into a treasure trove of kettle holes, drumlins, kames, valley trains and eskers, seemed admirably designed for outdoor recreation that engages the whole person, body, mind, and spirit.

So it seemed to Ebenezer Emmons while engaged in the first systematic survey. Other voices grew so insistent that in 1885 New York became the first state to preserve wilderness by law in a fledgling Forest Preserve. Today's Forest Preserve of 2,300,000 acres, designated in 1964 as a national historical monument, is a link with America's past and a vast playground for the fifty-five million people who live within a day's drive.

Several generations have found recreation and renewal here. In colonial and early national times when only the perimeters were known, Trenton Falls in the southwest and Lake George on the eastern fringe were tourist attractions. Reports of the first ascent of Mount Marcy in 1837 brought a thin stream of tourists to the Tahawus area of the interior. Mountaineering, however, did not become widely popular till several decades later.

The Lake Belt of the central and western Adirondacks was the principal center of attraction in the mid-nineteenth century, as sections II and III of this anthology attest. From hotels of the Saranacs parties embarked on camping trips to near and distant parts of the wilderness with a guide who rowed a light wooden craft, known as a guide-boat, of native design and build. While the more active "sports" engaged in fishing and hunting, others were content with exploring the intricate system of waterways. "The novel and romantic peculiarity of this wilderness," wrote W. H .H. Murray in 1869, "is its marvelous water communication. . . . One can travel in a canoe or light boat for hundreds of miles in all directions through the forest." A chorus of praise arose for travel in that "faery craft," the guide-boat. "We are afloat. . . two in a boat, rowed at the bow by a guide. . . . I want to lounge in an attitude half lying and half sitting and 'invite my soul.' Newspapers, letters, steam, dust, noise are left behind, and I am nothing but a waif. Day after day we float along with only woods and waters for companions [Kate Field]." "[Guide-boats] are indeed the most fascinating of little barques—so easy to guide, so delicate, so graceful in their movements. To lie in their stern, on a couch of fragrant balsam, to be swiftly paddled along in the most gentle gliding manner, while the waves ripple against the sides, and lapse away again with a softly murmuring cadence, illustrates the very poetry of motion [M. H. G.]." "There is a feeling of rest and happiness in being swiftly pulled through the Adirondack waters which I have felt in no other place [Martin Burke]."

Through most of the nineteenth century the guide was an essential aid to travel. In the last quarter, however, his importance lessened as other aids became available—reliable maps, the reports of Colvin's Adirondack survey, and the annual guidebooks of S. R. Stoddard and E. R. Wallace. A little shoemaker and sports writer, George Washington Sears ("Nessmuk"), pointed the way for the independent tourist when he made three long cruises in lightweight, one-man Rushton canoes in the early 1880s, demonstrating that a loner could dispense with guide services. Gradually the canoe replaced the guide-boat in popularity. It was all very well for a native guide, who knew the country, to back into it as rower. The visiting explorer preferred to front the unknown as paddler.

In 1880, the year of Nessmuk's first Adirondack cruise, a journal of which appeared in *Forest and Stream*, the American Canoe Association was founded. Its first three annual meets were held on Lake George, a fact bearing witness to the popularity of the Adirondacks for small-boat recreation in the last century.

A split has long existed in Adirondack recreation between the people of the waterways and the mountain people. The former group has the larger realm to roam in, though many prefer to settle down in summer camps on cherished lake shores. The mountain people favor the comparatively limited area of the northeast sector, where all of the so-called High Peaks are located.

Adirondack mountaineering has limitations. Heights are modest, seldom more than 3,500 feet above the level of the surrounding plateau. Though cliffs of up to a thousand feet attract rock climbers, the same heights can be ascended by mountain hikers on other routes. There are compensations, however. The mountaineer is not likely to exhaust opportunities in a lifetime. Besides the High Peaks, culminating in Mount Marcy's 5,344 feet, there are hundreds of lesser ones which offer remoteness and solitude. The greatest attraction is probably the forest that all of these mountains bear on their backs. The interest of a ramble through the woods is heightened on mountain slopes where in two hours one passes through three zones of vegetation. In the view from the summit the forest is again dominant, dropping away and spreading out to the horizon in green-blue billows accented by shining lakes and outcroppings of gray rock.

By the first quarter of this century mountaineering had a past rich enough to impel Russell Carson to write a history of it. In *Peaks and People of the Adirondacks* (1927) he defines four periods up to that time. The Emmons period, named for Ebenezer Emmons, who led a party of explorers and scientists in the first ascent of Mount Marcy, brought tourists into the Adirondacks but induced only a hardy few to climb mountains that had no trails. In the Phelps period, approximately 1849-1869, Orson Phelps, popular guide of Keene Valley, stirred an interest in climbing as a recreation and blazed a trail up Marcy from the east. During the next period, 1870-1900, the outstanding name was Verplanck Colvin, mountain measurer.

Colvin's vocation and avocation met in mountaineering. The consciousness of a still largely unexplored and unsurveyed wilderness to the northwest haunted his youth in a well-to-do Albany home. At eighteen he was making maps on his tramps in the Adirondacks, and for the next thirty-five years, first on his own and then as state surveyor from 1872 to 1900, he crisscrossed the Adirondacks, beginning by measuring mountain heights and discovering ponds and settling down later to the more routine work of establishing boundaries of state-owned land. As mountaineer he had a gift for timing. He was present on summits for rare phenomena like Ulloa's rings and particularly brilliant displays of the aurora borealis. His best stroke of timing was to forget time in the absorption of his observations until daylight was used up and maximum hazard assured for the descent of a pathless mountain in darkness. Night descents were his specialty. But mountaineers prize his writing for other qualities. He evokes the sensations of motion over the uneven, encumbered ground of Adirondack forests and mountain slopes. He imparts to the ascent of four-thousand footers a zest worthy of the Alps and the Himalayas. His reports to the state legislature—especially the early ones of the 1870s—read like an Odyssey of adventure.

The fourth period Carson defines, the first quarter of the twentieth century, ended with two landmark events besides Carson's own book. The Adirondack Mountain Club, with its twin goals of recreation and conservation, was founded in 1922. In 1924 two young brothers, Robert and George Marshall, and their family's guide, Herbert Clark, completed the ascent of the forty-six peaks then measured at 4,000 feet or higher. The period since Carson's book might be called the Marshall period.

In the 1930s a few others repeated the Marshall feat of climbing all forty-six High Peaks, and in 1937 a club called the Adirondack Forty-Sixers was founded. Prior to World War II only thirty qualified for membership. Today the number is rapidly approaching two thousand. Aspiring Forty-Sixers now feel that to strengthen their standing vis-à-vis the pioneers of the club, whose ascents were made when half or more of the peaks were without trails, they need some prestigious winter climbs, with a blizzard or two thrown in. Winter climbing, as well as cross-country skiing, has paralleled the development of organized winter sports in Lake Placid, site of the Winter Olympics of 1932 and 1980.

The best part of qualifying as a Forty-Sixer is, ambition fulfilled, the freedom of mind to range Adirondack woods, peaks, and waters just for the fun of it. Today seekers of a wilderness experience are learning to shun the overcrowded trails of the High

Peaks in favor of still untrammeled areas of the Forest Preserve. Often this means using as avenues the clean, free-flowing rivers of the park. Except for a few mountain fastnesses and scattered other spots in the northeastern states, says John Kauffmann, "waterways remain our only avenues into the dimensions of wilderness experience." Canoeing waters lead the hiker into areas where foot trails are little eroded and bushranging on mountain slopes is a solitary act of discovery.

The future of wilderness recreation in the park, during the seasons of open waters, may lie with amphibious travel. This would bridge the old gap between waterways and mountain people. Each side has much to gain.

FIRST ASCENT OF MOUNT MARCY

EBENEZER EMMONS

During the month of August last [1837], I visited the mountains of Essex with a view of determining the position and height of some of the most conspicuous elevations at the source of the Hudson.

This tour of exploration was made in company with a party devoted more or less to scientific pursuits, a part of whom were also personally interested in the survey.

In the prosecution of our objects, it is but justice to notice in this place, the aid we received of the Hon. A. McIntyre, of this city [Albany], and D. Henderson, Esq. of New-York, inasmuch as they liberally supplied every thing necessary to secure the success of our enterprize. Indeed, the party were but their guests, whether at the little village of McIntyre or on the mountain summit: an instance of liberality I take the liberty thus publicly to acknowledge. . . .

The points of greatest interest to us were, to determine the height of three or four peaks in the neighborhood of the source of the Hudson, and also the height of one of its sources at its extreme point or origin. To accomplish these objects, we ascended the east branch of the Hudson [Opalescent] to its source, which we found to be in a small mountain meadow, ten or twelve miles N.E. from the iron works at McIntyre, and at the base of the summit of what finally proved to be the highest point in the group of mountains. In the same meadow, one of the branches of the Ausable takes its rise; so that it constitutes the pass, and probably the highest, between the waters which flow into the Atlantic on the south, and those which flow into the Gulph of St. Lawrence on the north. The height of this meadow is 4,747 feet.

Our route up the east branch was one which furnished many interesting facts in a geological point of view, one in particular, the effect of attrition on the boulders which are in their course down to the lower levels. It seems that although at the commencement of their journey they are huge and unwieldy, yet before they reach their final resting place, they are reduced to the size of what we call stones and even in many instances to gravel. As the rock is peculiar, and well characterized through the whole region of the upper Hudson, it is very easy to recognize it. It is, however, rare that we meet with it far down the main branch of the Hudson; in fact, I doubt whether it is possible to find a pebble of this rock in the course of this river below Glen's Falls. The fact is, before they reach the wide and deeper portions of it, they are ground to powder. If this is not true, we should frequently find masses of this rock along the shores of the Hudson, which have been transported either by the force of spring freshets, or by ice at the breaking up of the streams.

The region in which the east branch of this river rises, it seems, had never been explored previous to our visit; and it is not unreasonable to suppose this, for all our writers on geography have uniformly underrated its height, have made incorrect statements in relation to the origin and course of the principal branches of the Hudson, and also in relation to the character of the whole mountain group in which they rise.

This being the case, it is not surprising that names have not been given to the highest points of land in the state. This privilege belongs by common consent to the first explorers. This, to be sure, is of but little consequence; still, as things must have a name, the party saw fit to confer upon a few of the highest summits designations by which they may in future be known. As this tour of exploration was made by gentlemen who were in the discharge of their duties to the state, and under the direction of the present Executive, whose interest in the survey has been expressed both by public recommendation and private counsel and advice, it was thought that a more appropriate name could not be conferred on the highest summit of this group than Mount Marcy. . . .

Another remarkable mountain, bearing N.47°W., was named Mount McIntyre. It was supposed to rank next in height to Mount Marcy. . . . An isolated mountain, situated between Mount Marcy and Mount McIntyre, has been named Mount McMartin [Colden], in honor of one now deceased, whose enterprize and spirit, in conjunction with two others, whose names it is unnecessary to mention, has contributed much to the establishment of a settlement at the great ore beds, as well as to other improvements, advantageous to the prosperity of this section of the state.

A distant view of this mountain is given from Lake Henderson. It is particularly remarkable for its trap dyke, which is about eighty feet wide, and which has apparently divided it into two parts near its centre. A portion of this dyke is visible from Lake Henderson, a distance of about five miles. A fine and spirited view of it has been furnished me by Mr. Ingham of New-York, who was one of the exploring party. It was taken near the base of the mountain, at Avalanche Lake, and is merely an exhibition of the termination of the gorge which has been formed by the breaking up of the dyke by a small stream of water, assisted by frost and other agents.

The cluster of mountains in the neighborhood of the Upper Hudson and Ausable rivers, I proposed to call the *Adirondack Group*, a name by which a well known tribe of Indians who once hunted here may be commemorated.

MOUNTAIN MEASURING
VERPLANCK COLVIN

1. Seward

The main object of the expedition was the barometric measurement of Mt. Seward, a lofty peak, of the ascent of which there is no record and the height of which remained in doubt. Prof. Emmons, while engaged in the survey of the second geological district of the state, estimated the elevation at 5,100 feet above tide. . . .

October 14th.—The camp was about thirty feet above Cold River, the banks of the stream being very steep. When we awoke, clouds and fog enveloped everything, and a drizzling rain was falling. Before 9 a.m. the fog lifted, the rain ceased, and finally the clouds broke a little, though the mountains were still obscured. There was no wind. This was the first station where observations were made, four readings being taken. . . .

I had previously determined the compass direction of the mountain, and notwithstanding the dubious state of the weather, set out immediately to commence the ascent. . . . Taking a northeasterly course, we struck directly into the forest toward a small mountain, whence we might be able better to select the way. Our progress was slow, for, as there was no trail, my guide [Alvah Dunning] took the precaution to blaze the path by chopping upon the trees every fifty or a hundred feet, and continued so to do, with great labor, throughout the day.

At length, reaching the height we had in view, we were disappointed to find it overlooked by another crest, more lofty than the one which we had climbed and separated from us by a slight depression. Believing that from its top we would be able to discover Mt. Seward, we addressed ourselves to the task and laboriously climbed it, only to discover two loftier peaks towering opposite, beyond and above which the clouds, as they drifted, at times opened to view a misty summit higher than all. It was evident that we were already upon the slopes of the mountain. A narrow valley was between us and the opposite peaks; descending into it, we found the forest carpeted with deep, wet, sphagnous moss. Again ascending, the slope became all but precipitous; yet, by means of small trees, mainly silver birches, we drew ourselves up. . . .

With much labor we at length climbed a ridge and saw no more peaks above us; the valley we had left was far down, and the surrounding country, wherever the eye could reach, spangled with lakes. Now the forest began to show that we had attained an altitude where vegetable life recoiled; the trees, principally Canada balsam, spruce and white birch, were dwarfed and stunted, being barely fifteen or twenty feet high. The abundant, deep moss was a sponge of icy water, so cold as to make our feet ache as we stood. In clambering upon hands and knees, as we were often compelled to do, we were wetted to the skin, waist high. Our breath was visible in the cold air, which chilled us through our wet clothing; yet the day, though windy, was now bright and clear.

After a hasty repast we hurried along the ridge to gain the highest point upon it, being anxious to accomplish our work and descend part-way the same afternoon; not wishing to camp in that wet, cold region, where sleep, if possible, would be extremely hazardous.

About 3 p.m. we seemed to have gained the highest point on the ridge, though the thick, miniature forest obscured the view, telling by its presence—before I had glanced at the instruments—that we were still far beneath the height ascribed to the mountain. . . .

My guide, who had wandered off, returned to announce a still higher point in view. The barometer was returned to its case, and we hurried on. The balsam trees continued to dwindle in height until we stood upon an open crest. The world seemed all below us; but northward, half a mile away, a lofty summit reared itself, grizzly with dead and withered balsams, struggling to keep their hold upon the rock that here and there looked out gloomily; it was Mt. Seward. Between us and it was an abyss through which clouds floated.

It was a grand though disheartening spectacle, so near yet seemingly inaccessible. The afternoon was nearly spent; it was evident that we would now be compelled to camp amid the clouds. However, evening and twilight continue upon the mountains long after the valleys are dark with shadows, and we determined to improve the time by attempting the passage of the gorge. At length, as the clouds parted, we noticed a narrow ridge, or "horse-back," far below, which crossed the deep valley and on which it seemed that one might pass over.

Starting to descend, we discovered snow in small quantity, the remains of a last winter's drift, lying exposed to the air, discolored and icy. Its preservation thus must be exceptional. Descending amidst precipitous rocks, we reached the "horse-back" and, by hastening, were able at nightfall to cross the deep valley. With the last rays of the sun upon us, we formed a camp just below the true summit of the mountain, on the edge of the impenetrable thicket of dwarf balsams.

There was no spring, but water was easily procured by pulling up moss; the space thus made being soon filled with excellent cold water which, when settled, was sufficiently clear for use. The night came down dark and chill, and a strong westerly wind made the camp fire burn fiercely. The rubber blanket, spread upon a thick bed of balsam boughs, kept me from the wet moss, and some of the small trees, piled bodily to windward, tempered the blast, the rear of the camp being a large rock.

At about eight o'clock in the evening the sky was lightened by that brilliant aurora borealis which excited such attention throughout the northern hemisphere by its wonderful iridescence and brought the inhabitants of beleaguered Paris upon their ramparts [the siege of Paris, 1870, in the Franco-Prussian War], to gaze with awe at a manifestation by many deemed of dire import. It shot up from the northwest and, passing over to the east, formed a broad crimson belt overhead, while the whole dome of the heavens was lit with silvery glory, which flashed and swayed in seeming concord with the eddies of a gale then whirling round the mountain. With every wave and brightening of the aurora a sighing, whispering sound was heard, like the rustling of great folds of silk, which my guide assured me was the "noise of the northern light." At the northwestern horizon pencils of blue darted up toward the zenith, but I was in doubt whether the color was not that of the

sky seen through intervals in the auroral cloud. The rays seemed to
center a few degrees south of the zenith. The display lasted long
into the night. The guide, who was without coat or blanket, kept
himself warm by chopping firewood, and we hailed the day with
pleasure.

October 15th.—We had not far to ascend from our camp before
we reached a dense growth of dwarf balsam trees which form a
barrier to the summit. They were at first about seven or eight feet
high; with much labor we pushed or chopped our way through
them, their branches being stiff and numberless and intricately
locked. At 8 a.m. we walked upon the trees, which had dwindled
to great shrubs, flattened to the ground, with long, spreading,
lateral branches, and stood at last upon the summit.

The view hence was magnificent, yet differing from other of the
loftier Adirondacks in that no clearings were discernible; wilderness everywhere; lake on lake, river on river, mountain on mountain, numberless. . . .

The height of the mountain had indeed been over-estimated. Of
the 5,100 feet attributed to it, it lacked 638 feet; the elevation as
measured being 4,462 feet above tide-level, or the sea [4,361 by the
survey of 1953]. . . .

Of the provisions carried with us, there now remained only sufficient for one light meal. Since leaving the boat, it had taken us
two days and a portion of a third to make the ascent, and we were
now in the depths of the wilderness.

About 10 a.m. we commenced the descent, taking a new course
west of south, and, under powerful incentives, by dint of rapid and
hazardous traveling, at nightfall reached the boat, where our extra
provisions and baggage were found undisturbed.

2. Dix, Nippletop, Colvin

The morning of August 17th [1873] opened brilliantly. The
golden sunshine glimmered around the mountain crests; and anxious
to avail myself of so favorable a day, after breakfast the heavy baggage was left in charge of one who remained at the camp, and we
immediately commenced to climb the slopes of Mount Dix [from
Hunter's Pass], which was to be the next trigonometrical station.

This was an entirely different route from that by which I ascended this mountain in 1870, where we marked a line and cut a path through the timber. Here there was no sign, but instead, paths stamped by the footprints of deer, panther and bear showed us where these creatures had found spots amid the cliffs which they could climb, and availing ourselves of these runways, we slowly toiled upward. By 9:30 a.m. we had reached a height as great as that of Camel's Hump Mountain [in Vermont], and carefully finding its level, we took its height by barometer, which when computed and corrected for curvature and refraction, gives for its altitude above tide 3,548 feet. It was after 11 a.m. when we reached the level of Nipple Top, and looking across the depths of the Hunter's Pass, we could search the opposite rugged mountain for some path by which to climb it. The exact level of Nipple Top was carefully determined, and the station being favorable, a base was measured with steel tape along the mountain side, and the angular distance of that mountain from this station found by measurement with sextant from each end of the base. This would admit of an exact application of my method of leveling with barometer and hand-level, and a careful computation, based upon this work, showed Nipple Top to have a height of 4,656 feet above the sea.

After struggling through dense thickets of spruce and balsam, at half-past one in the afternoon we reached the summit of Mount Dix. It was wonderfully clear, not a cloud to be seen, and the atmosphere comfortably warm. No signal was at first visible upon Bald Peak [their signal station on the west shore of Lake Champlain], which from this height appeared as a rocky mound, yet the unaided eye could distinguish near the shore of Lake Champlain the glimmer of the automatic stanhelio-signal upon Crown Point. Setting one man to helio-signal Bald Peak, in order, if possible, to obtain a response from the assistants stationed there, we set up theodolite and barometer and entered on our work. Northward Mount Hurricane was seen, and the theodolite telescope was hardly directed upon it before the flash of the automatic signal I had placed there was visible and proved the wonderful success of the invention. The angular measurements were rapidly progressed, and with the aid of the telescope the Bald Peak stanhelio automatic signal was seen, and its angular place found with precision. At a quarter to four in the afternoon our signal was answered by a flash from Bald Peak, the first intimation that we had of the presence of the assistants at their station. It was needless, for the stanhelio signal had served all our purposes.

As the afternoon shadows lengthened, we pushed our work without rest or conversation, and Crown Point lighthouse being visible, formed a third zero and established point, with which the other measurements were joined. Clear Pond, Mud or Elk Lake, the Boreas range, Haystack, Marcy, and a multitude of other points were reached, twelve pages in the large theodolite book being occupied with the records of measurement. Four reconnaissance maps of topography were made, and forty-six barometrical observations upon the summit gave a mean that enabled us to determine the height of the mountain with greater accuracy than ever before attainable; my computation showing Mount Dix to be 4,916 feet above tide level [4,857 by the 1953 survey]. The height of this mountain, according to Prof. Emmons in 1837, was 5,200 feet. It is unfortunate that without climbing or measuring it by barometer, he should have been led to record such an erroneous approximation.

Absorbed in our work, we were startled by sunset to the consciousness that night had already settled in the chasm valleys below. It would be impossible to descend in the dark amid the cliffs and ledges, where only the footprints of the catamount had guided us by daylight to places which could be scaled; and our camp and camp-guard and provisions were miles away. There was no time for discussion, and I ordered a descent into the Hunter's Pass so far down as it would be necessary to find water and a resting place. Water, unfortunately, was not to be readily found, and soon we became entangled amid ledges, slides and cavernous rocks that rendered the previous night-descent of the Giant inferior in danger. In the darkness, clinging by roots, aiding each other from ledge to ledge, and guiding with special care the footsteps of those carrying the theodolite, etc., we finally found ourselves slipping on the edge of rocks draped in cold, wet, sphagnous moss, and a little lower we found water. A moment's rest and we descended further only to find that we were in a cul-de-sac—with walls of air—turn which

way we would save toward the mountain top; and we reached the
verge of an overhanging cliff, so high that even the treetops below
were not distinguishable. The slender stream leapt the edge and was
lost in the depths. Here we were compelled to halt and, reclining
at the edge of the precipice, passed the night; the feeble fire, by its
suggestions of supper—which we had no means of gratifying—
only giving edge to our hunger.

Daylight, August 18th, showed us the wildness of our situation
and the means of extrication; and, breakfastless, after dangers unnecessary to relate, we descended to the south portal of the Hunter's Pass upon a stream which, flowing southward out of the pass,
formed one of the sources of the Hudson River. Turning northward, we entered the portals of the Hunter's Pass (the Gorge of the
Dial), which so many have longed to explore and endeavored in
vain to reach, and ascended betwixt its walls of rock to its summit.
Here barometrical observations were taken. They indicate the
height of the pass above tide to be 3,247 [3,234, 1953 survey]. The
inclosing mountains rise over a thousand feet above on either side,
and the spectacle is grand and imposing. Descending northward,
we were once more on the St. Lawrence River side of the mountain range. We had left camp for the ascent of Mount Dix with the
intention of returning that night, and now, fearing lest our friend
left there should become alarmed at this continued absence, we
marched as rapidly toward where we thought the camp might be
as our exhaustion permitted, firing occasionally revolver shot signals
to acquaint him with our approach, but more, perhaps, with the
hope that he might prepare us a breakfast. We at length found
camp and man all right. A heavy storm in the afternoon tried the
value of our bark roof and gave us opportunity for rest. Barometrical observations this day give the height of this station at 2,788
feet above tide.

August 19th. Raining slightly and very threatening. Determined,
nevertheless, to set out upon the ascent of Nipple Top Mountain,
on the eastern slopes of which we were encamped; followed up a
stream till its course diverged from what (so far as we could judge
in the fog and storm surrounding us) would be our way; climbed
steadily, and at one p.m. thought we were upon the summit, but

having chopped down trees, and the clouds rolling away, we saw another summit further south, which we reached at 2 p.m., which proved to be the true crest. Dense white cloud enveloped us, but it was in rapid motion and at intervals opened and showed glimpses of chasms and mountains. Suddenly it was swept away at the east and Mount Dix, scarred and savage rock, rose before us; beyond it the rolling country near Lake Champlain, with our Bald Peak like a little hillock beside the distant gleaming lake. The gorgeous sunshine streaming on the distant cirro-cumulus clouds below produced a rare effect. Suddenly, starting with surprise, our mingled shouts arose, for on the breast of the cloud each saw his own form, the head surrounded by a rich *anthelia*, a circular glory of prismatic colors, the renowned "Ulloa's rings," which that philosopher beheld from the summit of the Pambamarca. Not one of the mountain guides had ever seen or heard of such sight before. It was gone all too quickly, yet it seemed as though nature today were reveling in splendors, for the clouds vanishing in the west, a sierra of mountain crags was uncurtained, torn, rugged and wild, above all which rose Ta-ha-wus, "Cleaver of the Clouds" [name for Marcy suggested by C. F. Hoffman soon after the peak was christened by Emmons]. Topographical maps were executed and in our barometrical work we had the first record of measurement made on this summit. From these *direct* observations the height of Nipple Top has been computed at 4,684 [4,600, 1953 survey] feet above tide level. It will be remembered that the height of this mountain had been taken two days before by combined barometer and spirit level from Mount Dix and computed at 4,656 feet. The difference is twenty-seven [sic] feet, far within the limit given by Humboldt for Mountain measurement.

Not designing another night climb (as we carried now all our camp equipage), we left the summit at 5:30 p.m. and, descending rapidly, reached the bottom of Elk Pass in time to erect a shanty of boughs.

The camp was in an open grove fronting an unknown waterfall, which from its silvery spray and step-like form I named the *Fairy Ladder Falls*, the height of the foot of which I found to be 3,111 feet above tide.

Rousing the men early on the 20th, the last ration of flour baked and breakfast over, leaving at this camp all our impediments, we commenced our climb to the summit of the next mountain eastward, which the guides had named Mount Colvin. The knowledge that it was a mountain heretofore unascended, unmeasured and—prominent as it was—unknown to any map made the ascent the more interesting. The indications of game were naturally abundant; the rocks and ledges geologically interesting, and, judging by the outlook from inferior summits, the view from the top could not fail to be superior. A trap or *sienite* dyke was discovered, but there was no time for its examination, and reaching at length the height, its last approach a cliff almost impregnable, we drew ourselves up over the verge to find a seat upon a throne that seemed the central seat of the mountain amphitheatre. Deep in the chasm at our feet was the lower Ausable Lake, each indentation of its shore sharply marked as on a map; beyond it the Gothic mountains rose, carved with wild and fantastic forms on the white rock, swept clear by avalanches and decked with scanty patches of stunted evergreens. Everywhere below were lakes and mountains so different from all maps yet so immovably true. There was too little time to satisfy us. Here was golden sunshine, a balmy air and a wealth of work before us, but an empty larder. It was the sixth day, the evening of which I had before set as the termination of this branch expedition. Topographical reconnaissance was therefore pushed forward, and a careful measurement made, from which the height of Mount Colvin is found to be 4,142 feet [4,057] above tide level.

It was after 4 p.m. when we left the summit and hurried down into the Elk Pass again, and reaching a point further south than our camp, on the Hudson River waters, we came upon a beautiful meadow and further, on a shallow pond which we called "Lycopodium," from the occurrence of that plant near its shores. The height of the summit of Elk Pass was found to be 3,302 feet. The sun sinking fast, we hastened on, reached our camp, slung on the knapsacks we had left there, and on a run struck northward down the rugged unknown pass, yet hardly hoping to accomplish that night the miles of wilderness between us and the first settlement of Keene. Still, we strained every nerve, pressing onward without resting, seldom glancing at the compass, guided better by the sun upon the peaks, of which now and then some opening in the thick foliage of the trees would give us view.

Twilight, and still marching, despite the wish of wearied men to camp. Dark, and still marching. Night, marching; and our goal gained. We were partaking of a late supper at Keene Flats when the team drove to the door with the assistant returning from New York, barometer, etc., repaired, and every duty well discharged. In all things we had met with uninterrupted success, and every mountain and pass which we intended to visit had been reached and measured, and the work accomplished exactly within the six days set.

3. Gothics

[October 11, 1875] Reaching at last a level space just under the highest peak and benumbed by the cold, we hurried to build a fire before venturing further. After a hasty lunch in the snow, we resumed the climb and soon reached the timber line and at length beheld the crest of the Gothics.

Before us an irregular cone of granite, capped with ice and snow, arose against a wintry sky. The dwarf timber crept timidly upward upon it in a few places, not too steep for root to find a foothold, and on either side the icy slopes leaped at once down into gloomy valleys. Beyond, irregularly grouped, the great peaks, grizzly with frost and snow, were gathered in grand magnificence, all strange and new—in wild sublimity. No sound save the shuddering hiss of the chilly blast as it swept over the fearful ridge of ice that must now be our pathway. With fingers benumbed with cold I hastily sketched the wild landscape—the shivering guide holding the broad sheet on which I drew. Then with spikeless boots and no alpenstock save the tripod of the instrument, we essayed the last ascent; the glary slopes of ice on either side descending a thousand feet or more threatened death as the penalty for a single slip.

At length the summit was attained, a small flat space on the solid rock, and the instrument quickly placed in position and a circle of observations taken. Deep in the basin to the eastward lay a dark, narrow pool—black as ebony between its even darker walls of rock—the lower Au Sable Lake; further south the Upper Lake, like a bright jewel set in the gorgeous autumnal forest; and southward, still other ponds and lakes; while to the westward and northward a portion of the Saranac waters and the bright surface of Lake Placid showed themselves, and above or beyond them, all the black, frost-crested mountain billows—revealed from this new station in strangely different contour—with new passes, new gorges and new chasms. It was nearly 4 p.m. when we attained the summit, and the angular measurements and topographical work required every moment; so that darkness was upon us when, shivering and almost frozen by the cold wind having a temperature of 22° Fahr. . . . we started on along the icy ridge to seek some means of descending. We were struck with horror. On every side yawned icy precipices, showing more grim and dreadful in the fast increasing darkness; and the elder guide attempting to pass along below the crest, where some ice-clad stems of the Labrador tea (*Ledum latifolium*) alone offered assistance to the hand, was suddenly suspended over the edge of a cliff—where a thousand feet below the clouds were drifting—and rescued himself by the sheer strength of his muscular arms.

Down a sharp ridge into a sag between the peaks we made our way southward till at length, following the sunken dyke or gorge worn in this angle of the mountains, we reached precipitous rocks barely descendible in safety. Down these the guides dropped or lowered their packs and knapsacks, step by step, ourselves following as best we might, till at length, reaching a little shelf on the face of the mountain, further descent appeared, in the gathering darkness, impossible, and we determined to camp in the little cluster of trees this oasis afforded. A rough shelter of evergreen boughs was quickly improvised, and the ledge made home-like by the warmth and light of the camp fire; a scanty repast was soon finished, and wearied with the labors of the day, wrapped in blankets, we dropped into profound slumber. In the midst of the night a crash like some strange thunder awakened us. The moon now shone bright, and we started up to see a vast mass of ice, detached from the cliffs above, go dashing down into the abyss below. Again and again these dread disturbers of our slumbers swept down with sudden and fearful noise. At length the warm breath of the

south wind thawed the ice and snow upon the trees around us—
and we slept again.

October 12th. Awoke this morning overheated by the combined
influence of a fierce fire and heavy blanket. It has turned cold again,
however, and the frost crystals float in the air. Water taken from a
little fall near our camp became congealed in a few moments beside the fire! Recommencing the descent as soon as our frugal
breakfast was finished, we found a route which, though difficult,
enabled us slowly to make our way down into the great circular
gorge—a mountain-walled amphitheatre—from which Basin Mountain takes its name. Rejoicing that we had not attempted to descend
further the preceding evening, we toiled downward—for our camp
seemed to have been the only spot available upon the mountain's
side. Descending an icy ravine, we at length lost sight of the grizzly
front of Basin Mountain and the Saddleback and reached an upland
forest glade where the ground was covered with the fresh tracks
of deer, while in one spot the recent signs of bear were noticed.
Hurrying on our journey—being short of provisions and anxious to
reach the Upper Au Sable Lake that evening—our march was between a walk and a run until a sudden and dangerous fall of one of
the party admonished us to go more carefully. From this upper
basin a steep descent led down, and obliged by a cliff to diverge, we
took to the bed of the stream and found a difficult descent. Now
we began to leave the dark spruce forest behind us, and more fresh
signs of bear and deer were seen, the hardwood or deciduous forest
was reached, and a little later we struck a brook flowing to the Au
Sable in many a sparkling cascade and rapid. Here we came suddenly upon a high fall where the whole body of the stream leaped
down in foam. Another branch of the stream now joined, and we
hurried on, and at length, thoroughly wearied, reached our old
trail over Bartlett Mountain now disused—the first trail which we
had seen since starting for the Gothic—and soon reached the shores
of the Upper Au Sable.

4. Seven Years of Progress

The Adirondack Survey has now been in progress under the authority of the state government for seven years. Beginning in 1872
with the smallest of appropriations, its work has been steadily ad-

vanced as far as the means admitted, from year to year, until at length the great mass of the highest mountains of the state—the immovable landmarks of the past and of the future—have been covered with an intricate network of triangles, and thousands of miles of distances measured, so that from the astronomical and trigonometrical work, we now find for the first time the true positions of thousands of places within our state that were not known before. . . .

During the years that have passed, I have been enabled not only to extend the survey but to study the growth of settlements throughout the region, so as to obtain an insight into the probable ultimate character of the development of the country; to which attention must be paid by our state administration in order to properly aid and forward this growth where it has found a place in natural channels leading toward permanent results. . . .

To the lover of nature and of the wilderness, the progress of settlement, and the extension of civilization into the primeval forests, is recognized only with regret. To the explorer, also, it is pleasanter to imagine the wild mountain crest or mirrored lake which he was first to reach remaining as unvisited, in all its aspects as unchanged as when he first beheld it.

Viewed from the standpoint of my own explorations, the rapidity with which certain changes take place in the opening up to travel of the wild corners of the wilderness has about it something almost startling.

A few summers since, I stood for the first time on the cool, mossy shore of the mountain springlet lake, Tear-of-the-Clouds. Almost hidden between the gigantic mountain domes of Marcy, Skylight, and the Gray Peak, this lovely pool lifted on its granite pedestal toward heaven the loftiest water-mirror of the stars. . . .

It is still almost as wild and quite as beautiful. But close behind our exploring footsteps came the blazed line, marked with axe upon the trees; the trail, soon trodden into mire; the bark shanty, picturesque enough but soon surrounded by a grove of stumps; while Skylight, so recently the untrodden summit, with its barrier of dwarf forest, is now from this new pass by a new trail an ascent of only so many minutes. . . . The first romance is gone forever. . . . The woods are thronged; bark and log huts prove insufficient; hotels spring up as though by magic, and the air resounds with laughter, song, and jollity. The wild trails, once jammed with logs, are cut clear by the axes of the guides, and ladies clamber to the summits of those once untrodden peaks. The genius of change has possession of the land. . . .

But while these changes have opened to travel many of the most interesting nooks among our mountains, they have only rendered more marked, by contrast, the wildness of the remainder, and the unvisited wilderness centres or cores are still left in all their sylvan purity. . . . No unselfish person will for a moment regret that his once solitary pleasures are now shared in by the many. The sportsman has still a thousand unfrequented recesses—if he will seek them—where he may travel unmolested. . . .

The region is already the summer home of untold thousands—a public pleasure ground—a wilderness park to all intents and purposes.

AMPERSAND
Henry J. van Dyke

It is a mountain. It is a lake. It is a stream. The mountain stands in the heart of the Adirondack country, just near enough to the thoroughfare of travel for thousands of people to see it every year and just far enough away from the beaten track to be unvisited except by a very few of the wise ones who love to digress. Behind the mountain is the lake, which no lazy man has ever seen. Out of the lake flows the stream, winding down a long untrodden forest valley until at length it joins the Stony Creek waters and empties into the Raquette River. Which of the three Ampersands has the prior claim to the name I cannot tell. Philosophically speaking, the mountain ought to be regarded as the father of the family, because it was undoubtedly there before the others existed. And the lake was probably the next on the ground, because the stream is its child. But man is not strictly just in his nomenclature; and I conjecture that the little river, the last-born of the three, was the first to be called Ampersand and then gave its name to its parent and grandparent. It is such a crooked stream, so bent and curved and twisted upon itself, so fond of turning around unexpected corners and sweeping away in great circles from its direct course, that its first explorers christened it after the eccentric supernumerary of the alphabet which appears in the old spelling books as &.

But in spite of this apparent subordination to the stream in the matter of a name, the mountain clearly asserts its natural superiority. It stands up boldly and dominates not only its own lake but at least three others. The Lower Saranac, Round Lake [Middle Saranac], and Lonesome Pond [now Kiwassa Lake] are all stretched at its foot and acknowledge its lordship. When the cloud is on its brow, they are dark. When the sunlight strikes it, they smile. Wherever you may go over the waters of these lakes you shall see Ampersand looking down at you and saying, quietly, "This is my domain."

Now I never see a mountain which asserts itself in this fashion without desiring to stand on the top of it. If one can reach the summit, one becomes a sharer in the dominion. The difficulties in the way only add to the zest of the victory. Every mountain is, rightly considered, an invitation to climb. . . .

The right day came for the ascent. Cool, clean, and bright, the crystal morning promised a glorious noon, and the mountain almost seemed to beckon us to come up higher. . . .

As we walked onward the woods were very quiet. It seemed as if all living creatures had deserted them. Indeed, if you have spent much time in our Northern forests you must have often wondered at the absence of life and felt a sense of pity for the apparent loneliness of the solitary squirrel that chatters at you as you pass or the little bird that hops noiselessly about in the thickets. The middle of the day is an especially silent and deserted time. The deer are asleep in some leafy covert. The partridge has gathered her brood in a quiet nook for their noonday nap. The squirrels are perhaps counting over their store of nuts in a hollow tree, and the wood thrush spares her sweet voice until the evening. The woods are close—not cool and fragrant as the foolish romances describe them —but warm and still; for the breeze which sweeps across the hill-top and ruffles the surface of the lake does not penetrate into these shady recesses, and therefore all the inhabitants take the noontide as their hour of rest. Only the big woodpecker—he of the scarlet head and mighty bill—is indefatigable, and somewhere unseen is "tapping the hollow beech-tree," while a wakeful little bird, invisible though near at hand, pierces the air with his long-drawn "chick-a-dee-dee-dee-dee-ee!"

After about an hour of this easy walking our trail began to ascend more sharply. We passed over the shoulder of a ridge and around the edge of a fire slash, and then we had the mountain fairly before us. Not that we could see anything of it, for the woods still shut us in, but the path became very steep, and we knew that it was a straight climb; not up and down and round about did this most uncompromising trail proceed, but right up, in a direct line for the summit. Now this side of Ampersand is steeper than any Gothic roof I have ever seen, and withal very much encumbered with rocks and ledges and fallen trees. There were places where we had to haul ourselves up by roots and branches, and places where we had to go down on our hands and knees to crawl under logs. It was breathless work, but not at all dangerous or difficult. Every step forward was also a step upward; and as we stopped to rest for a moment, we could see already glimpses of the lake below us. . . .

It is with mountains, as perhaps with men, a mark of superior dignity to be naturally bald. Ampersand, falling short by a thousand feet of the needful height, can not claim this distinction. But what Nature has denied, human labor has supplied. Under the direction of Mr. Verplanck Colvin, of the Adirondack Survey, several acres of trees were cut away from the summit, and when we emerged, after the last sharp scramble, upon the very crest of the mountain, we were not shut in by a dense thicket, but stood upon a bare ridge of granite in the center of a little clearing.

I shut my eyes for a moment, drew a few long breaths of the glorious breeze, and then looked out upon a wonder and delight beyond description.

A soft, dazzling splendor filled the air. Snowy banks and drifts of cloud were floating slowly over a wide and wondrous land. Vast sweeps of forest, shining waters, mountains near and far, the deepest green and the faintest, palest blue, changing colors and glancing lights, and all so silent, so strange, so far away that it seemed like the landscape of a dream. One almost feared to speak lest it should vanish.

Right below us the Lower Saranac and Lonesome Pond, Round Lake and the Weller Ponds, were spread out like a map. Every point and island was clearly marked. We could follow the course of the Saranac River in all its curves and windings and see the white tent of the hay-makers on the wild meadows. Far away to the northeast stretched the level fields of Bloomingdale. But westward from that all was unbroken wilderness, a great sea of woods as far as the eye could reach. And how far it can reach from a height like this! What a revelation it gives to us of the power of sight! That faint blue outline far in the north was Lyon Mountain, nearly thirty miles away as the crow flies. Those silver gleams a little nearer were the waters of St. Regis. The Upper Saranac was displayed in all its length and breadth, and beyond it the innumerable waters of Fish Creek were glistening among the dark woods. The long ranges of the hills about the Jordan bounded the western horizon, and on the southwest Big Tupper Lake was sleeping at the base of Mount Morris. Looking past the peak of Stony Creek Mountain, which rose sharp and distinct in a line with Ampersand, we could trace the path of the Raquette River from the distant waters of Long Lake down through its far-stretched valley and catch here and there a silvery link of its current.

But when we turned to the south and east, how wonderful and how different was the view! Here was no wide-spread and smiling landscape with gleams of silver scattered through it and soft blue haze resting upon its fading verge, but a wild land of mountains, stern, rugged, tumultuous, rising one beyond another like the waves of a story ocean—Ossa piled above Pelion—McIntyre's sharp peak and the ragged crest of the Gothics and, above all, Marcy's dome-like head, raised just far enough above the others to assert his royal right as monarch of the Adirondacks.

But grandest of all, as seen from this height, was Mount Seward —a solemn giant of a mountain standing apart from the others and looking us full in the face. He was clothed from base to summit in a dark unbroken robe of forest. *Ou-kor-lah*, the Indians called him—the Great Eye; and he seemed almost to frown upon us in defiance. At his feet, so straight below us that it seemed almost as if we could cast a stone into its clear brown depths, lay the wildest and most beautiful of all the Adirondack waters—Ampersand Pond.

On its shore, some five-and-twenty years ago, the now almost forgotten Adirondack Club had their shanty—the successor of "the Philosophers' Camp" on Follensbee Pond. . . . They had bought a tract of forest land completely encircling the pond, cut a rough road in to it through the woods, and built a comfortable log cabin, to which they purposed to return from summer to summer. But the Civil War broke out, with all its terrible excitement and confusion of hurrying hosts; the club existed but for two years, and the little house in the wilderness was abandoned. Ten years ago, when I spent three weeks at Ampersand, the cabin was in ruins, tenanted only by an interesting family of what the guides quaintly call "quill pigs" and surrounded by an almost impenetrable growth of bushes and saplings, among which a brood of partridges were in hiding. The roof had fallen to the ground; raspberry bushes thrust themselves through the yawning crevices between the logs; and in front of the sunken door sill lay a rusty, broken iron stove, like a dismantled altar on which the fire had gone out forever. . . .

It has been my good fortune to climb many of the famous peaks of the Adirondacks—Dix, the Dial, Hurricane, the Giant of the Valley, Marcy, and Whiteface—but I do not think the outlook from any of them is so wonderful and so lovely as that from little Ampersand.

HERBERT CLARK, MOUNTAINEER
ROBERT MARSHALL

In the spring of 1906 . . . Herb came to work for Father. At this time my brothers, my sister, and I were all under ten years of age. I can not speak authoritatively of what Herb meant to the others, although I have strong suspicions. I do know positively that to me Herb has been not only the greatest teacher that I have ever had, but also the most kindly and considerate friend a person could even dream about, a constantly refreshing and stimulating companion with whom to discuss both passing events and the more permanent philosophical relationships, and to top it all, the happy possessor of the keenest of humor I have known. . . .

For my brothers and myself Herb would make up the most amazing fables. A rock on Lower Saranac with a peculiar dent was where Captain Kidd had bumped his head. The Ausable River below the present Olympic ski jump was where the *Monitor* and *Merrimac* had fought their famous battle, and an old lady who came limping along as he told us this tale was used as a circumstantial evidence, for her shinbone had been taken off by a stray shell at the time of this great conflict. There were those great heroes of our youth: Sliny Slott, a sort of reverse Paul Bunyan, who did everything inconceivably poorer than you would imagine it could be done; Jacob Whistletricker, a man with many marvelous drugs; Joe McGinnis, who got the fantod, a disease in which one shrinks to the size of a baseball; Susie Soothing-syrup, a gay young lass of many virtues; and of course the grandfather pickerel, which we would some day catch, with gold teeth and spectacles.

Herb is full of songs. Almost every year he adds to his repertoire, which consists either of garbled versions of ancient popular ditties, fitted to suit his needs, or of jingles which he makes up expressly for the occasion. I recall once, while we were battling our way through the clumps of mountain balsam on Colden, hearing Herb's cheerful voice far above us booming out:

"Don't let the golden moments go,
Like sunbeams passing by;

You'll never miss the cripplebrush
            Till ten years after you die."

"Cripplebrush" was the name which Herb gave to mountain balsam, and anyone who has had his shins and arms battered by half
an hour's tussle with it will appreciate the appropriateness of the
nomenclature. . . .

Although Herb's greatest fame has come as a mountain climber,
strangely enough he had never scaled a peak in the four-thousand-
foot class until he, George Marshall, Carl Poser, and I ascended
Whiteface in 1918. Thereafter, for the next six years, Herb,
George, and I found Adirondack mountain climbing our greatest
joy in life. We spent from twenty to thirty days during each of
these summers on the woodland trails and in the later years, even
more delightfully, where there was no sign of pathway.

When we first commenced our climbing, there were few sign-
boards and no trail markers at all. Neither was there the present
heavy travel which really makes markers superfluous. It took some
skill in those days to find your way about, particularly with the
numerous fresh lumber roads which forked off from the similar
lumber roads which constituted many of the trails. It was often
quite a problem to decide which fork would bring you to your
destination and which might end at some loading deck in a
jungle of second growth. In solving these problems we all took a
part, but Herb's interpretations showed the greatest frequency of
correctness.

In our later adventures on trailless peaks—and back in 1921
only twelve of the forty-six high peaks had trails to their summits
—Herb was really a marvel. At the age of fifty-one he was the
fastest man I have ever known in the pathless woods. Furthermore, he could take one glance at a mountain from some distant
point, then not be able to see anything two hundred feet from
where he was walking for several hours, and emerge on the summit by what would almost always be the fastest and easiest route.
Just as examples, I recall how perfectly he hit the dike which leads
to the top of Calamity, travelling from Adams; how he found just
the right slide which cut off a long battle with aspen and cherry
thickets on Cascade; how he led the way straight to the top of

Panther Peak, which we didn't see for nearly five hours after we left the dam on Cold River.

I spent the early part of this summer [1933] at our home on Lower Saranac, living alone with Herb. Every morning he would wake me up with some different song or quotation. On July 10th he came in shouting: "Sixty-three years ago this morning there was wild rejoicing in the Clark household. Let's celebrate by taking that trip into the Wallface Ponds." So it was arranged that to celebrate Herb's sixty-third birthday we would take the jaunt which he had been urging on me for several weeks.

We started from Adirondack Lodge and followed the Indian Pass trail for eight miles, past the stupendous grandeur of the rock mass of Wallface. We left the trail to follow up the Wallface Pond outlet, a turbulent brook which tumbles over great boulders and smooth granite slides to meet the stream from Indian Pass. About half way up to the pond there were bad beaver slashings and beyond a steep climb over the slippery rocks of the creekbed. Soon, however, we stood at the outlet of Lower Wallface, which we had not seen for eight years, and though it had been seriously marred by beavers, its remoteness from the paths of men was a cause of genuine exultation. Around the Wallface Ponds we delighted in the shady freshness of one of the most beautiful virgin spruce forests on the continent. Leaving the Upper Pond, we dropped steeply through another splendid stand of virgin spruce to that glorious series of cascades which is known as Roaring Brook. This seldom visited stream cut its way through canyons, tumbled over waterfalls, brushed by thickets of lush, green herbage, and reflected the primeval forest of spruce and birch and hemlock. We followed along in silence and elation until we came to where the creek took a sharp bend to the left. Then we realized that we must cut across a narrow range of hills which separated us from the Moose Pond trail. Once this was reached, when the spell of the primeval was lost, Herb suddenly became his most jocular self. He invented gay songs to tease me and reminisced pleasantly of the days before the trails were so heavily marked, travelled, and covered with orange peels. On the last lap into Averyville Herb set a jaunty four-mile-an-hour pace, and when we emerged on the meadows after twenty-five miles, ten of them without a trail, he was virtually as fresh as when he started.

This makes as appropriate an ending as I can conceive for the biography of this clear-headed, strenuous, exultant climber of mountains, this kindly, humorous, sensitive lover of the wilderness, Herb Clark.

━━━━━━━

 # FOURTEEN IN ONE
ROBERT MARSHALL

· July 16, 1932

Yesterday I ascended fourteen Adirondack peaks. The details of my climbing are shown in the following table:

Peak or Place	Time	Ascended Feet
Lv. Johns Brook Lodge	3:30	
1. Big Slide	4:52	1900
Johns Brook Lodge (breakfast)	5:39—6:00	—
2. Lower Wolf Jaw	7:30	1900
3. Upper Wolf Jaw	8:16	600
4. Armstrong	8:48	500
5. Gothics	9:18	400
6. Saddleback	10:04	500
7. Basin	10:48	700
8. Haystack	12:07	1000
9. Marcy (lunch)	1:30—1:54	1200
10. Skylight	2:40	600
Lake Colden	4:04—4:10	—
11. Iroquois	6:07	2100
12. MacIntyre	6:39	400

13. Wright _____ 7:32   400
    Adirondak Loj _____9:15—9:30   —
14. Jo _____10:00—10:10   700
    Adirondak Loj (supper) _____10:35
    Additional elevation gained on minor peaks, in-
        cluding Boundary, Little Haystack, and the
        subsidiary summits of Upper Wolf Jaw, Arm-
        strong, Gothics, Saddleback, Basin _____   700
    Total _____   13,600

Thus I have carried a little farther the fantastic pastime of record climbing, adding three to Malcolm's total of eleven. Perhaps within a few weeks, surely as soon as a few more mountains in the vicinity of Mount Marcy have trails cut on to them, somebody will readily enough overtop my record. Certainly it is a mark which any reasonably vigorous person in good physical condition can equal if he tries it when there are long daylight hours. In fact, it would fit perfectly in a class with flagpole sitting and marathon dancing as an entirely useless type of record, made only to be broken, were it not that I had such a thoroughly glorious time out of the entire day.

To begin with, the weather was absolutely perfect, one of those crystal clear days such as only occurs occasionally in an entire Adirondack summer. Furthermore, although I had already climbed each mountain from two to twelve times, the views seemed almost as fresh and exciting as on the first ascent, so splendid in fact, that any one peak was worthy of a long and tedious journey. Finally, seeing the view from fourteen different mountains all in one day gave me an excellent opportunity to appreciate the distinctive character of these Adirondack mountains, which made each summit leave an entirely different effect of delight.

From Big Slide I was chiefly impressed by the rising sun playing on the summits of the great range across Johns Brook, and then by the joy of running down hill at 5:00 in the morning through the dewy raspberry bushes, and feeling how good it was to be young and able to feel sure you could climb fourteen mountains in a day.

The Lower Wolf Jaw showed the entire Johns Brook Valley bathed in the still early morning sunlight, looking so bright and cheerful that I couldn't help feeling a triumphant happiness.

On Upper Wolf Jaw I recall especially the trail which violates almost every proper trail standard and is delightful for this very quality. It shoots straight up cliffs, stumbles over all sorts of tree roots, and skirts through narrow crevices among the rocks. All the time it shows the flora which at normal elevations is blooming a month earlier—goldthread, wood sorrel, twinflower, saxifrage— and the shady freshness of the mountaintop forest of spruce and balsam and paper birch.

On Armstrong it was pleasant to walk out on the same ledge Herb and George and I had found eleven years ago before there was any trail on this mountain and see the same splendid horseshoe of high mountains which has remained in my mind ever since, with Armstrong and Big Slide at the two ends and the rocky cone of Marcy at the apex.

From Gothics I was particularly impressed yesterday by the two mountain masses, one of Giant and Rocky Peak Ridge, the other of the four successive tiers of Sawteeth, Colvin, Nippletop and Dix, which frame a vista of the Champlain Valley, while the Green Mountains beyond appeared so close that I had the feeling that I ought to be able to skip over in a couple of hours.

From Saddleback, as always, there was the breath-taking sight of the overtowering rock needle of Gothics across Storrow Pass, with an almost sheer wall nearly a thousand feet high tumbling off on the south face of the peak.

The views of the three undefiled valleys of Shanty Brook, Haystack Brook and Upper Johns Brook, all lying directly below me, gave the greatest exhilarations from Basin.

I had wondered whether, after three summers and a winter of exploration in Arctic Alaska, I could still recapture any of the sense of wilderness I had always gotten from Haystack. Gloriously enough, I did. It was still possible to forget the automobiles and machinery of the present in the vista from this rocky summit, from which only in the extreme distance could any signs of man's meddlesome ways be observed.

Marcy as always impressed me with the breadth of vision, encompassing as it does in its panorama practically the entire expanse of the Adirondacks except the extreme southern and western portions and being the only mountain from which all 46 of the 4,000 foot peaks are visible. But if this familiar delight was pleasant, it was exceedingly disconcerting to find the nearby slope of Mount Adams all scarred by logging operations, which I had supposed were ended in the high mountain region, while a great fire streak extended up the slope of North River Mountain.

From Skylight a wall of virgin summits, extending from Iroquois to Dix and including all twelve of the highest peaks in the Adirondacks, filled the entire northern half of the panorama. It gave me an impression of massiveness which I do not recall from any other Adirondack mountain.

After Skylight there followed three splendid hours down Feldspar Brook and the Opalescent, around Lake Colden, and up the steep grade to the height-of-land of the MacIntyre range. All but half an hour of this journey was through the most inspiring sort of virgin spruce slope forests.

Then came Iroquois, from which the magnificently wild country north of Wallface seemed even darker and less explored than usual when backed by the late afternoon sun. In the middle of these black mountains the waters of Scott Pond and Upper Wallface were sparkling in the sunlight.

MacIntyre showed the rolling mountains which culminate in the Marcy-Skylight divide all light and cheerful as the setting sun shone directly on their western flanks. The usually dark streaks on Colden between the rock slides were just as bright as could be.

After a strenuous tussle with windfall and mountain balsam, the trailless summit of Wright was reached just as the sun was dipping behind the distant mountains north of Street, and the entire panorama, including the nearby slope of MacIntyre, the Marcy Range, the mountains back of South Meadows, and the fields of North Elba, was tinted by a reddish purple glow.

Mount Jo, ascended with the aid of flashlights, made an ideal climax. Northward Lake Placid was a host of lights twinkling beyond an extensive plain. Southward and westward towered the pitch black mass of Marcy, Colden, MacIntyre, Wallface and Street, while right at our feet the almost full moon was reflected in the waters of Heart Lake. All around a heavy mist was rising from the streams and meadows, giving everything an appearance as unreal as this entire perfect day had been to the normal world of twentieth century mechanization.

In concluding this account of a great day, I want to mention that Herb Clark met me on top of Marcy with luncheon and his usual uproarious humor. In addition to Marcy Herb also went over MacIntyre and Wright with me, which was quite a day's activity for a man of sixty-two. Eugene Untermyer accompanied me on the flashlight ascent of Mount Jo. When I got down from this last peak Jed Rossman gave me the kindest sort of reception, and Elise Untermyer had a most delicious supper awaiting, which tasted doubly excellent after nearly seventeen hours since my last warm food, which Mrs. Hanmer had served that morning at Johns Brook Lodge.

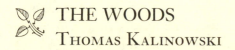

THE WOODS
THOMAS KALINOWSKI

"The stern depths of immemorial forests, dim and silent as a cavern, columned with innumerable trunks, each like an Atlas upholding its world of leaves, and sweating perpetual moisture down its dark channeled rind . . ." This was the description given by Francis Parkman after journeying through the thick, primeval forests of the Adirondacks in the early 1840s. The impenetrable character of these forests, along with the rugged terrain and harsh climate, discouraged many an early traveler who ventured into the region. Therefore it was not until the early to middle part of the nineteenth century that the region was extensively explored and settlement began—exploration and settlement often aimed at exploiting those selfsame forests. The virgin forests at that time were quite different from the forest cover today, for thick evergreen woodlands covered a much greater portion of the land than they do now. The Adirondacks and the vast coniferous forests closely resembled the great wilderness of northern Quebec, which earned this area its reputation as part of the "Great North Woods."

Because of its elevation, the Adirondack region possesses a climate more like that of the subarctic taiga than the surrounding area's milder, more temperate weather. The harsher growing conditions, therefore, favor plants like the conifers, which are better adapted for surviving in such an environment. Of the dozen species of conifers that grow in the Far North, all find favorable conditions at some location in the Adirondacks. These trees, either by themselves or in various combinations, form a number of different types of coniferous forests, which give the Adirondacks a true North Woods character.

In some areas, the growing conditions are ideally suited to a particular species of conifer, which often results in the exclusion of all other trees from that forest type. Pure stands of hemlock, for instance, are common at lower elevations on rich, moist soils. Hemlocks grow to be extremely tall and are more tolerant of shade than any other conifer. Because of this, in areas left undisturbed for long periods of time, these trees can become established under the stifling shade of a closed canopy. After many years they will eventually tower over surrounding trees, causing them to be shaded out of existence. Large groves of magnificent hemlocks were at one time extremely common across much of the Adirondack landscape. Most of these forests, though, were destroyed in the late 1800s when hemlock bark was in great demand for the tanning industry. In areas left undisturbed since then, however, some of these great trees have again become established, forming beautiful evergreen groves.

White pine, red pine, and scotch pine may also be found growing in pure stands in various places within the Adirondacks. Many such forests exist on sites where severe forest fires scorched the land, rendering the soil dry and nearly sterile. Because the pines can tolerate poor, sandy soils, they either naturally sprouted in such areas or were planted as part of reforestation programs.

Most coniferous forests, though, are composed of a combination of two or more types of softwood trees. On the upper slopes of most Adirondack mountains, for instance, balsam fir and red spruce grow together to form the dominant growth. Because of their tolerance to subarctic weather and their ability to grow in shallow soils, both of these trees thrive at the higher elevations. Because these trees also grow well in wet areas, they commonly intrude in the thick stands of cedar which cover most lowland areas in the Adirondacks. Cedar grows best in places where the soil is totally saturated with water, which is why cedars also grow in abundance along many sections of Adirondack shoreline. In areas of poor drainage, such as bogs, black spruce is generally the dominant tree of the surrounding forest. This species is the conifer most tolerant of the harsh, acidic conditions which characterize such areas.

While each of these types of coniferous forest possesses its own distinct character and ecology, they also have many important similarities. The soil on which conifers grow, for instance, is generally quite poor when compared with the soils found in most other ecological settings. Conifers contain large amounts of tannic acid, a reddish-tan chemical that was formerly used in tanning animal hides. The dead needles and bark of fallen trunks and branches which accumulate on the forest floor gradually release this acid to the soil, creating a very harsh environment for the many microorganisms which live in the soil. Bacteria of decay, for instance, are seriously affected by acids, causing a decrease in the rate at which organic plant litter is decomposed. As a result, only a limited amount of plant nutrients is recycled into the soil from decaying plant matter. Although there may be a seemingly rich deposit of dead, humus-like material covering the forest floor, the actual amount of compounds available to growing plants is quite slight, making the quality of the soil poor.

As rain water filters down through this soil, it usually washes some of the acid into the small streams and brooks which flow through these thick conifer areas. Adirondack streams fed by this type of runoff often possess the distinctive, reddish-tan color of this natural acid. These streams seem to favor more northern species of aquatic life, as they are better able to tolerate these conditions. For example, blackflies, which spend their larval stage in streams or brooks, are quite tolerant of such acid settings, so they thrive in these Adirondack waterways.

While many microorganisms and various other plants and animals are adapted for surviving in fairly acidic places, few can exist if the acidity exceeds its natural levels. Currently the precipitation which falls in the Adirondacks carries potent industrial acids which have their origin in the large urban areas around the Great Lakes. As this acid rain falls, it adds to the already acidic conditions of the soil and water. This abnormally high level of acidity is slowly building and reaching the point beyond which many things in the environment will be unable to survive.

Another similarity among all coniferous forests is, of course, that they are evergreen, for all conifers except the larch and the cypress retain most of their needle-like leaves for a year or more. Because the soil is often critically low in the nutrients required to produce new leaves, most of the plants which grow here are forced to keep their leaves for more than one growing season. By keeping their leaves these plants are also able to resume the all-important process of photosynthesis as soon as conditions become favorable in the spring. These adaptations fit evergreen trees for surviving in places with poor, acid soils and a short growing season.

In the spring, with the dense canopy of needles overhead, only a small amount of sunlight reaches the ground plants growing under the conifers. In deciduous forests, however, the trees minimize the chances of being damaged by a late frost by waiting well into the spring before putting out their tender new leaves. Thus, before their leaves emerge in the spring, sunlight is readily available to the small ground plants in hardwood stands. During these first weeks of the growing season, while they are in sunlight, many of the wildflowers in deciduous forests bloom. In softwood forests, however, most of the wildflowers do not bloom until much later in the spring; some wait until early summer. Another difference between the wildflowers of these two forest types is that those which grow in coniferous areas are generally evergreen. The leaves of such plants as bunchberry, wintergreen, goldthread, wood sorrel, partridgeberry, twinflower, trailing arbutus and dewdrop can be seen under the conifers right up to the time snow covers the ground. In the spring, new leaves sprout from the well-established roots of these plants to add to those few leaves which last through the winter.

Because of the lack of light available to these and other species of woodland wildflowers, only a limited amount of the plants' energy goes into seed formation. The root systems of these plants help in their propagation and keep them alive from year to year. The underground network of roots is occasionally quite extensive and produces thick, lush patches of surface vegetation. In the late spring, when they are in bloom, these dense mats of plants can create a truly beautiful spectacle. Wild lily-of-the-valley is one wildflower which grows in such dense patches, and its spikes of fragile white flowers are a common sight.

During the late spring, the male cones of conifers, located at the tips of their branches, release vast quantities of yellow pollen into the air. As it settles, this pollen often forms a thin, yellowish coating on everything in the area. This yellowish powder is particularly noticeable on the surface of the lakes and ponds in the Adirondacks for a week or so during mid-June.

As summer arrives, new needles grow on the twigs to fill in the already thick canopy spread by the closely spaced trees. Little light is able to penetrate such a dense covering of needles, so the light below remains dim. This lack of direct sunlight kills the lower branches of the trees, leaving an entangled maze of dead sticks and twigs—excellent, dry tinder for the campfire even in wet weather. The dim light also severely limits or may totally prevent the growth of small trees or shrubs in thick softwood forests. Consequently, the ground in these areas is usually covered by little vegetation except for small but often dense patches of shade loving and acid-tolerant wildflowers. There are also scattered clumps of moss and occasional bouquets of ferns growing from the vast spongy carpet of dead needles.

Besides filtering out most of the light, the dense canopy of a softwood forest also drastically reduces the effect of the wind. Because the air near the ground is shielded from summer breezes, heat builds to a greater level in these thick boreal forests than in most deciduous forests. As the temperature rises, so does the humidity,

and the quiet, heavy air often takes on a beautiful and unforgettable fragrance.

In autumn, as the leaves of deciduous trees turn color and die,
many of the older conifer needles also discolor, die, and fall to the
ground. As this new layer of organic matter is added to the soil,
many of the mushrooms which thrive in softwood areas begin to
appear. Fungi are an important group of plants to the conifers, for
most softwood trees rely on various types of fungi for water. The
roots of conifers are quite poorly adapted for absorbing water and
dissolved minerals from the soil. Most fungi, however, are well
adapted for such purposes, yet are unable to use this water to man-
ufacture their own food because they lack chlorophyll. As a result,
these two organisms enter into a partnership. The conifers exchange food stored in their roots for the water absorbed through
the threadlike bodies of the fungi. This is why the softwood trees
are much more difficult to transplant than are the hardwood trees.
If the fungi attached to the roots of a conifer are unable to exist in
the soil of its new location, the conifer will not be able to get all
the water it needs and will also die.

The roots of conifers are also poorly developed for sending up
shoots, as are the roots of many species of hardwoods. After logging occurs in deciduous forests, new growth quickly sprouts from
the stumps or roots of the cut trees, or from the roots of nearby
trees that were left standing. After a coniferous forest is cut, however, conifers can be reestablished in an area only through seeding
or the planting of seedlings. Compared to the seeds of conifers, the
seeds of most species of hardwoods are hardier, more successful in
germinating, and better adapted for traveling long distances, all of
which enables them to reach the cleared sites first. Thus when a
mixed hardwood-softwood forest, or a pure coniferous area is cut,
deciduous trees are usually the first to sprout in the clearing. This
frequently results in the broad-leaf trees becoming dominant in
areas previously occupied by conifers. As a consequence, the forest composition in the Adirondacks is somewhat different now
than it was 120 years ago, before the great logging operations of
the late 1800s, which focused mainly on the conifers. Because conifers are better adapted for the climate and soil conditions of the

Adirondacks, they will inevitably dominate again many of the sites they formerly covered, especially in areas that are free of man's influence; but it may take them a long time to recover territory conquered by beech, maple, yellow birch, and aspen.

Although deciduous forests harbor a greater abundance and diversity of life, nowhere is the presence of wildlife so evident as beneath the conifers in winter. Although thinned during autumn, the canopy of needles helps to shelter these areas from the severe effects of winter. The force of the wind, for instance, is drastically reduced in thick evergreen stands, which makes the chill factor much less severe. Snow conditions are usually more favorable for animals to travel, thus making it easier for them to move about in search of food and in their efforts to escape from natural enemies. Various studies have also shown that on very cold and calm nights, the temperature is slightly higher in thick evergreen areas than in those of surrounding hardwood forests. Small evergreen trees, the many dead branches and twigs near the ground, and the closely spaced trees provide ample cover for ground-dwelling animals. In the upper branches, needles give cover to arboreal creatures.

The tremendous abundance of tracks in the snow in coniferous forests is evidence of the attractiveness of these areas in winter. The crisscrossing patterns and well-traveled runways of the varying hare, or "snowshoe rabbit," are a common sight in most types of evergreen woods. Red squirrels also dot the snow with their tracks as they scamper about on the ground searching for cones they missed the previous summer or fall.

In large, lowland coniferous swamps, deer tracks are often abundant, for it is here that they congregate, or "yard-up," for the winter. Despite the lack of food for them here, the restrictive snow conditions and icy winds of the open hardwoods force deer to seek shelter in coniferous settings. Occasionally, during harsh winters, the deer may exhaust food supplies in the hardwood stands near their yards, so many die of starvation. The resulting carrion attracts such mammals as coyotes, fisher, and fox.

The ruffed grouse is another creature whose tracks are often seen in the snow of such thick evergreen woodlands. Small birds such as chickadees and nuthatches, though, are perhaps the most common and conspicuous of the birds in this habitat. These birds feed on various types of seed and on tiny eggs and larvae of invertebrates which winter under the loose bark of evergreen trees. Woodpeckers feed almost entirely on the invertebrate organisms concealed in trees, and their tapping on insect-infested wood is a familiar sound in boreal settings. The chorus of high shrills echoed by flocks of evening grosbeaks is another sound that helps to fill the air in coniferous forests during winter. And as the name suggests, the pine grosbeak is also a creature of the evergreen forests. The crossbills, although never very numerous, are perhaps more perfectly adapted for life in the conifers than any other bird. These birds are so named because their upper and lower mandibles cross rather than meeting flush, as in other birds. This peculiar adaptation enables them to pry open the cones of the evergreen trees, exposing the seeds for easy extraction.

Throughout the seasons, then, conditions in coniferous forests, while similar in some instances, are generally quite different from those in other woodland settings. Despite various differences among the many types of softwood forests, there are basic features which all of them have in common. And it is this unique character of the evergreens which gives Adirondack ecology the true flavor of the Great North Woods.

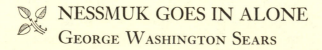

NESSMUK GOES IN ALONE
George Washington Sears

Wellsboro, Tioga County, Pa.
June 9, 1880

Editor *Forest and Stream*:

Many months ago some old admirer of my weak pen sent an inquiry to you asking about "Nessmuk," erst of *Porter's Spirit*. I did not respond. I dropped the pen in '71. It was pleasure, but, like

Mr. Micawber's "coals," "not remunerative." I found that there were several thousand aspirants for literary honors and emoluments who were constantly boring publishers without ever getting a show on any respectable journal—or deserving it—and I stepped aside. For nine years I have attended to business, and that is not very remunerative, either. Editors, I will just remark here, have always treated me fairly. The *Atlantic, Aldine, Lippincott,* and the old "pea-green" [*Porter's Spirit*] recognized—and paid—the nameless backwoods writer handsomely.

My best hold is the rod, rifle, canoe, camp, and in short the entire list of forest lore and backwoods knowledge comprised in the one word, woodcraft. And I am going back to my first love. My fishing kit is revised and corrected. The nail-driving, muzzle-loading, hair-trigger rifle is ready at hand.

My canoe is ready for launching. She is clinker built, of white cedar, and the lightest that ever went through the Adirondacks. Weight, seventeen pounds, thirteen and three-quarters ounces. If I live a month longer, there will be another "fool i' the forest." The "melancholy Jacques" may find him somewhere between the Fulton Chain and the lower waters of the West St. Regis, drowned, with a capsized cockleshell nearby.

For I am going through alone.

The faithful guide and the festive landlord of the woodland hotel will not work me to any extent.

There are five thousand pleasant, shady nooks in the Northern Wilderness on which a camp was never raised. Colvin's Report shows that the heart-cores of the Wilderness are as yet unexplored. His final map will show not less than three hundred new lakes and ponds never before mapped.

I have traveled in foreign lands; have been twice to the Amazon Valley; and I rise to remark that there is but one Adirondack Wilderness on the face of the earth. And, if the great State of New York fails to see and preserve its glorious gifts, future generations will have cause to curse and despise the petty, narrow greed that converts into saw-logs and mill-dams the best gifts of wood and water, forest and stream, mountains and crystal springs in deep wooded valleys that the sun shines on at this day.

Nessmuk

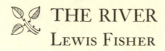

THE RIVER
Lewis Fisher

> Since no two rivers are alike, paddlers tend to become explorers, sampling many rivers. But there is something to be said for long, intimate association with one river corridor. Lewis Fisher, member of the Jordan Club at the confluence of the Jordan and Raquette rivers, writes here of a four-mile stretch of the Raquette as it was before 1953, when a great dam at Carry Falls turned it into a lake.

When we "go down river," we descend the hill and cross the bridge with armloads of pillows plus twelve feet of stair carpeting. We make the canoe elegant enough for the likes of Cleopatra. Mother had a wonderful old soft wool cape with hood for the cool return trip. Also to wrap around the breadmixer on the hearth before retiring—no easy-way, one-day yeast then. Of course, as youngest, I rode the front seat and to keep track of what went on behind me my head became as turnaroundable as a ventriloquist's dummy's. . . .

For evening paddling we are apt to go among the islands. These are done up in thick ruffs of alder, honey-ball, and a red-barked shrub in front of high elms and water maples. We go by or through fields of pond lily, whether white floaters or the yellow cow lilies that stick their necks out. Pickerelweed and such, but never (I wonder why) any cattails. A few islands have only grass covering, and these often shelve off deeply so that one can, pillowed in civil luxury, ride intimately beside their soddy profusion. Only two channels and two islands have names. Worm Island was an unstable character that at least once moved to another place as its population shifted. Pie Island, which describes itself, was out in the open near Cranes' and was nameworthy because on dark nights a rower now and again tried to go right over it, which felt like plowing into a soft snow drift. Steamboat Channel, behind an island out from Jordan Landing, was of course where the prehistoric steamboat lay at rest. Secret Channel was the darling, a cul de sac in one of the largest islands. A canoe could push and twist its way perhaps an eighth of a mile before the passage closed. It was otherworldly and beloved of turtles; its deep muck bottom answered the rude paddle with great rude belches of gas that went pop when you touched a match to them.

Heading all the way down, we tend to go by the east channel. The high bank dips at the mouth of Jordan Road, where were a small sulphur spring and something of an open field that in the nineteen twenties we used for coeducational softball matches. Beyond, the bank rises again until the bend at the swimming hole, when it swerves in east around the Great Bog. If closer wood gave out for the swimming hole fire (we always had a big one to dry by and pull heavenly black potatoes out of), we pursued it up the heights on what are now shoals back toward Pisgah from Irene's Beach. . . .

At the foot of the islands, just this side of Cold Brook (up whose aldery curves you can paddle a way before you hear the tinkle of its tiny rapids) is Indian Burying Ground. If you landed and walked into those young woods, for instance after balsam with the Cranes, you found tufts the size of big sarcophaguses which had evidently suggested burial mounds to some poetical imagination. I believe no one ever dug in search of prose and realism. Nature in one of her real-estate-agent moods had even equipped these mortuary grounds with a monumental white-birch entrance gate.

From here we enter the long uneventful straightaway (rockless for once) toward the mountains. We cross the heart of the Great Bog: that wonderful place, as it turned out, to put a big pile of water. Not floating land like the banks of Twin Ponds, it nevertheless looks like it, with moss plants, cranberries, and such. It is sparsely decorated with tamaracks and pointed firs, including branchless spars that stand for decades. . . .

In this straightaway (unless you were my older brother, Bob, that famous oar breaker) you succumb to space and paddle more and more slowly, close to shore, watching the shallows for whatnot, including the entrance to muskrat holes with the crumbs of clam feasts, little black swarms of baby bullheads, and all kinds of water bugs and water weeds. In coves a deer may be approached even closely enough to splash you when he jumps. Near the end is the Cow Pens, a short channel straight off to the right through which the canoe squeezes into a half acre of quiet pond. Like many places where you are sure to see deer, the Cow Pens never exhibited to me anything more stupendous than a hell-diver. A guest of mine once shot one of these ducks. It dove to the bottom and never came up. We were later told we should have probed with an oar to loosen it from what it died clinging to. Why our hell-divers were replaced by American mergansers, I can't think unless the shift was to display patriotism after the [Joseph] McCarthy epoch, if you remember that, God forbid. Or perhaps we ought to— indeed, it was to keep his name fragrant that I christened a certain building the Senator McCarthy. Must a john foster dullness? . . .

The Carry was more a couple of hundred yards dash of rapids than a falls. Nevertheless, west of the island there was one straight drop of almost twelve inches—complete with a cave of the winds and as pretty as Niagara if with your chin right beside it you lay on the long, red-granite, water-molded beach that ran out to where the current gradually puckered toward its exciting moment. One could swim in smooth water above the drop, or choose one or another of the little rocky pools that had white water along one edge. Cedar trees grew plentifully in clumps or odd single shapes out of crevices, especially above the dark deeps with foamy surface where we got back in the boat after the carry. The shoot was too rocky and tortuous to ride, but Carol and Alice often let their canoe down through by rope in preference to toting it.

By and large our favorite picnicking spot came to be in the east bank, where a commodious area of flattish rock was formed into benches, long chairs and fireplaces. Those nice people, as Carol called cedar waxwings, played and fluttered there as they always did on Jordan bridge. It was decorated also with an immense and quite cubic boulder carefully abandoned there on the flat table by whatever large force had been toying with it, covered with lichen and sporting a few optimistic baby cedars. Behind, the bank rose very high above the sluice and had in one place a sheer granite face, a smooth slope just off the vertical that you were tempted to slide down but would only if that was the last thing you ever did.

After dinner I preferred to be back at the straightaway while still some rose lingered from the sunset. The flat top of Bog [Mountain] curved down toward the lowlands in such a line that it and its perfect reflection made a great jet black bottle lying there. As you cut behind the little island at the bend, alders the red sky shone through gradually fitted over the bottle's mouth to give it the oversized cork that identified the contents as champagne. And at this hour you would be just right if the full moon was rising over the Great Bog, its perfect setting.

If not, darkness deepens. Among the islands ghost figures of mist rise and brush past and vanish around the canoe. At the end we navigate by sound, coming in for the landing by the Jordan. Over the bridge on the way up, even cold and damp, you always take a cup from the spring.

It was because we are on yonder side the Jordan that Pop named us Camp Eden.

WHITE WATER DERBY
HOMER DODGE

Expanded version of a telephone conversation between Miriam Underhill, questioner, and Homer Dodge, answerer, March 15, 1968:

Question.—I am in need of some material to fill out the next issue of *Appalachia* and, failing to find anything better, am having to ask you for help. Can I count on you?

Answer.—There is no one to whose wiles I would rather succumb, but my obligations are like the dog's tail that is never caught up with.

Q.—I don't want a history of your life, but only to know what you have been up to in the very last of your fourscore years. You are now eighty, are you not?

A.—Yes, I reluctantly admit to having reached eighty last October. And I resent it very much, for in the last two or three years I seem to have been falling apart.

Q.—Not from what I have heard. In your Christmas card you mentioned something about races on the Hudson River at North Creek, N.Y., in the Adirondacks. What about that?

A.—Now that they have a "mature" class at the Hudson River White Water Derby at North Creek early in May each year, with handicaps planned to encourage paddlers to keep on trying until they can't help winning, I have somehow managed to win first prizes in the giant slalom and downriver race each year.

Q.—And will you get an additional handicap this year now that you are over eighty?

A.—Yes, that is true, and at the same time false. I have always admired the girls who never admit by their appearance or actions that they are over twenty-nine. I cannot match that, but I have already sent word to the North Creek management that, no matter what the calendar says, I am never going to be classified as over seventy-nine at the Hudson River Derby. As a matter of fact, I could just as well have said seventy, since I shall have to race on even terms with those from seventy to seventy-nine. If I can't do that successfully, I will insist on moving down the line.

Q.—What is the nature of the Hudson River races?

A.—There are two days of racing. On Saturday there is a giant slalom held upriver from the village of North Creek, consisting of about twenty-four gates. First there are several in a rapid; these are followed by some tricky gates which involve difficult maneuvering among both visible and invisible boulders above and below. The last gates are in a rapid with some very heavy water.

On Sunday there is a seven and one-half mile downriver race from North Creek to Riparius through several rapids, the last of which is a half-mile long steep rapid consisting of a wide boulder field extending from shore to shore. There is no main channel; the boulders are the size of hogsheads: the water finds its way among them as best it can, so do the paddlers, but with less success. I have never gone through without expecting to turn over and without seeing several canoes capsized, with their crews in the river. The worst that has happened to me is to get caught on the rocks and for a few moments be certain that I would capsize. I have always somehow managed to work my way off into running water again—

often having to run stern first for awhile before finding room to turn. I always have to save a little energy for the last lap to the finish line at the bridge, for there are inevitably a couple of young bucks behind me trying their best to pass—and that is just what must not happen.

Q.—What's this about having to store up energy? I thought you had an infinite supply.

A.—Why, I supposed that you understood that. For years I have never *really* raced except on one occasion. Twenty years ago the doctors told me "never to run another rapid, never to climb another hill." On Memorial Day I had paddled the Ammonoosuc River, which comes off the slopes of Mt. Washington, with an A.M.C. group from Boston. Normally my eyes are able to take in all the river ahead, looking back and forth, up and down the stream, so that every action may be taken with a view to what lies ahead as far as one can see. On this day the run was one continuous stretch of boulders and I found myself busy solving serious problems right at the bow of the canoe, with no chance to look ahead. Muscle had to take the place of planning. When at last we ran up on the bank I felt distinctly different from any way I had ever felt before. In fact, I sat in the canoe for what seemed many minutes before I moved at all. Result, cardiograms when I got home, consultations with Boston experts, and the verdict that I must quit such foolishness.

That did not make sense to me. Besides, I had run all the White River except the very worst part. After a night's sleep, I decided to match against the doctors' verdict the application of a principle I had long believed in, which is to let the current do the work. In this case, to play doubly safe, I also put my son in the bow to work with or against the current as might be necessary, and three days later made the run on the White River without difficulty.

I promptly learned what it took the heart specialists several years more to learn and announce, which is that the heart should be kept working up to capacity but not beyond. If one does that, the heart's capacity increases indefinitely.

Q.—Doesn't that mean that you should not be engaging in white water racing, even though you may run rapids?

A.—Yes, it does, and I really don't race in the usual sense. I find the races a grand opportunity to see old friends all over the East and to make believe that I am taking the competition seriously. But I know the pace I can maintain and also that at any moment there may be extra demands upon one's energy. Accordingly, whenever I feel the least bit out of breath or see the possibility of needing a little extra energy at some tricky place ahead, I simply rest until I feel the urge to go on.

One thing that has amused me greatly is that the last two years I have planned to do more than that and really to hold back and use up my handicap so that someone will push me out of the first place. This has not worked, for, when I get out on the water, I can't bring myself to apply greater brakes than nature itself imposes. I guess that must be a character defect. So this year I am taking care of that by refusing, well in advance, to accept the additional handicap due at age eighty.

Q.—I can understand your resting in a slalom, but how can you manage it in a downriver race?

A.—It is merely a matter of knowing what pace one can maintain for an hour and a half and starting out at that pace and maintaining it. When one approaches a rapid one holds back a bit, so as to have a little stored energy and an eagerness to use it if required. Even in a rapid I find that I take every opportunity to let the current do more of the work. It has surprised me to see that often pictures taken of me in rapids show my double paddle resting across the gunwales, because the current is taking me exactly where I want to go and I can give my attention and energy to the next problem, where the current may suddenly shift from friend to foe.

Q.—You recognize then that you can't always make the current your friend?

A.—You can't in slalom races, where the gates are usually quite unnatural obstacles. Nor in downriver races where one must do a great many abnormal things in order to gain time. But when running rapids for fun, with other paddlers out for a day of pleasure, one of the satisfactions is to make the trip with a minimum of effort.

By giving undivided attention to picking the course ahead and continually revising one's decisions, one can follow the main current with very little effort. Here and there may be found critical points where for a moment one may need to use considerable effort before letting the current take over again.

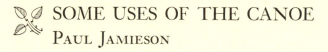

SOME USES OF THE CANOE
Paul Jamieson

People in my home town of Canton know what canoes are good for. Frank White, florist, has a fleet of them to cover his hobbies of fishing, exploring, running rapids, racing, and leading scout groups. Atwood Manley, retired newspaper editor, recovers his youth with a double-bladed paddle and satisfies his pride in a Rushton canoe seventy years old but tight and gallant. Dwight Church, photographer and father of a son in Olympic canoeing, takes his canoe off his car top only to put it in water. While the North Country is icebound, he paddles in Florida. For three years in a row Mike Maroney, postal clerk, and Ernie Locke, carpenter, have won firsts in the Rushton Memorial Canoe Race on the Grass River. They promise to withdraw so that John Green, biology professor, and Charlie Nevin, forester, can move into first place next May. John also uses his fiberglass for duck-hunting on the St. Lawrence. College students on our campus, where two woodsy rivers join, use canoes for "girling," as paddlers of the 1890s called that popular sport. Girling in slow motion is a revelation to this fast generation. It is half the secret of our quiet campus in this decade of student riots. The SDS bites its nails as revolutionary ardor dissipates upriver. The administration orders more canoes for the boathouse and winks at the coughs and sniffles that come in as ice goes out. Spring colds are more acceptable than spring riots.

Both geography and tradition account for Canton's partiality to the canoe. On the northwest watershed of the Adirondacks, St. Lawrence County funnels fifteen scenic rivers to the St. Lawrence. Most of them flow down from the wild uplands of the southern half of the county into a broad valley of dairy farms and woodlots. The paddler has a choice of whitetail or holstein country, swift or still water. Inside our southern boundary lie three great attractions: the Raquette River from Piercefield Falls to Jamestown Falls; Massawepie Park, with its kame and kettle topography and its chain of lake and ponds strung like beads along both sides of the central esker; and great Cranberry Lake, its satellite ponds, and its inlet, the Oswegatchie, which in twenty meandering miles leads into a virgin forest of noble pines and northern hardwoods.

As for tradition, Canton was the home of J. Henry Rushton, canoe builder. From his shop on Water Street, canoes went to all parts of the country and abroad. He was the Stradivarius of the all-wood canoe. Canton honors this master craftsman in several ways, but most of all in fidelity to the canoe through all such passing temptations as the bicycle, the motorcycle, and the speedboat. The motorcar must be excepted because it is handy in transporting canoes.

As a newcomer to Canton many years ago, I had my initiation on the ten-mile float that begins in Harrison Creek, comes down the Grass River, and ends on the Little River at the Park Street bridge. I saw a muskrat, a great horned owl, two great blue herons, and a herd of cows plashing through a hollow of marsh marigolds. I picnicked on a knoll of violets and bluets. This upriver pastoral made me a canoe bum for life.

As you work south from home waters toward the central Adirondacks, canoe bumming gets more strenuous. The tilt of the land adds a third dimension. You must carry if you would go any distance. Clarence Petty has a story about his father, an Adirondack guide, who, as a regular service to fishing sports, carried an eighty-pound guide-boat from Middle Saranac Lake five miles over a shoulder of Ampersand Mountain to Ampersand Lake. Even in better years I was never up to that. But I like amphibious operations. And because the lovely all-cedar *Sairy Gamp*, weighing just

10½ pounds, is locked up in the Adirondack Museum, with no craftsman capable of duplicating her since Rushton passed away, I have fallen back on substitutes, an aluminum canoe and an ABS plastic. They are embarrassing to own in this village of traditionalists but the lightest things this generation seems able to make.

Atwood Manley in his cedar *Vayu*—long, slim, and every inch a Rushton, though one of the heavyweights—looks down his nose at me. He floats in a Stradivarius. But he has to treat it like one too. My canoes take a good deal of banging on rocks and in the bush. He looks better on water, I on land. I toss my craft overhead and strike off with barely a stagger. Atwood needs a tandem to get his *Vayu* over the carries. . . .

When I run out of ideas for a knockabout land-and-water jaunt, there is the almost inexhaustible source of E. R. Wallace's *Descriptive Guide to the Adirondacks*. I have the edition of 1887. Wallace was a bug for the waterways, which he described in persuasive and florid detail. Any stream with a three-inch draft seemed to him eminently navigable. He loved carries, possibly because his guide did all the work. Some tours he didn't know firsthand he got from wicked guides or from letting his imagination run wild over the map. The object of the Wallace game is to take those 1887 tours and see how they work today. After much toil and sweat, you finally reach the "gorge" of Round Lake Outlet and find it, contrary to Wallace's purple rhetoric, less stupendous than the Grand Canyon. You run aground in shoals. You float into an ambush of deadfalls and alder branches. You find an impenetrable spruce thicket where Wallace says there is a carry trail. On the other hand, you make some discoveries you would not have missed—the little rivers and creeks that wind through specimen gardens of the North Woods. . . .

As a pocket-sized wilderness for an aging canoe bum, I like the headwaters of the Saranac and St. Regis rivers, some distance of course from all the commotion around the Fish Creek Ponds. The 15-minute *Saint Regis* map shows over 150 lakes and ponds ranging in size from a stone's throw to eight-mile long Upper Saranac Lake. To paddlers this generous display of blue nudity is the centerfold of topographic maps. With a little ingenuity you can chart a number of circular tours. Each pond and carry trail has a distinctive character and atmosphere. Most of the carries are short or moderate. Even the few long ones have compensations. . . .

Pond-hopping is not the only kind of amphibious travel possible in this area, which has a top as well as a bottom. The canoe deserves a place in mountain climbing too. Though modest in height, the peaks of the St. Regis quad are better endowed with canoeable waters than the High Peak region. They are also more generous in revealing their charms. On the approach over winding waters that alternately narrow and widen, revealing the mountain flank by flank, framing it in profile or full face, moody under a cloud or glowing in full sun, you get a matchless psychological conditioning to the climb that lies ahead.

St. Regis, Jenkins, Floodwood, a nameless 2,180-foot peak northwest of Ledge Pond, Boot Bay, and Long Pond mountains offer partial to full circle views from their summits. All have seductive water approaches. Only the first two have trails. The others test your timber cruising accuracy, especially in the descent, when locating your beached canoe in no more than three minutes of scouting is a matter of pride. True, on its northeast face St. Regis Mountain has a popular trail accessible by road. But one ascent by that route is enough. Thereafter you will prefer the irregular, solitary, tall-timbered southern face, rising abruptly from the shore of St. Regis Pond.

Long Pond Mountain is definitely a canoeist's peak. Many visitors to the Saranac-St. Regis country never see it at all. Yet it is strategically located for the best possible view of the great oval Saranac basin and of the ring of mountains enclosing it, with the blue serrated ridge of the High Peaks in the distance. The south face is a propped-up natural park.

There is a short approach from the canoe landing at the southwest tip of Long Pond. But the approach I prefer is the long, winding one from Hoel through Turtle, Slang, and the north end of Long Pond to the Mountain Pond carry trail. The climb from the east end of Mountain Pond is an hour's scramble from one choice nook to another. The summit is an elongated flat of grass and bedrock. Ponds of St. Regis, Saranac, and Raquette drainage radiate outward in sparkling lanes through the forest; one lane terminates in the big glitter of Upper Saranac Lake.

Interstellar imagination used to appall us with Earth's insignificance. But now that space travel has begun, a still more staggering thought opens up. Three men recently sent back word of the void loneliness of outer space and the bleak, dead landscape of the moon. From lunar orbit Captain Lovell called Earth "a grand oasis in the big vastness of space." What if this oasis is the only planet in the universe with just the right conditions to produce a wilderness garden such as one sees from Long Pond Mountain?

It is too early to draw firm conclusions, but until something better turns up out there, I intend to make-do with the woods, peaks, and waters of the St. Regis quad as "grand oasis" and a fifty-pound canoe as spacecraft. (Adapted from the March-April 1969 *Adirondac*)

HEAVY WATER
CLYDE H. SMITH

"What would you consider the most horrendous canoeable river in the Adirondacks?" I've often been asked that question but there's no clear-cut answer. A river's "canoeable" rating depends upon a number of variables. Generally, horrendousness is a product of the water level combined with the river's gradient and width. Accessibility is another psychological factor: heavy rapids in a remote region seem more frightening than paddling in a similar situation beside a highway.

More recently another variable, one I never used to consider, is age—and I don't mean the river's. As each year goes by, familiar rapids seem just a bit tougher, and I approach each new experience more apprehensively.

But to the original question: taking into consideration all the optimum conditions—high water, steep gradient, narrow width and remoteness—my choice would be the Boreas. During spring runoff, or even at other seasons after several days of rain, its last few miles before entering the Hudson offer as wild a ride as any stream in the country. Here the Boreas drops at nearly one hundred feet a mile, over ledges, around huge boulders and into foaming souse holes. It is a white water paddler's dream—or nightmare.

I've tried canoeing the Boreas a number of times and succeeded in doing it only once without a swamping. On that particular occasion, I was with my friend Ed Hixson, and we were each running single in open canoes. The river was high and we pulled out to scout a section where the rapids disappeared around a twisting curve in a gorge that was getting progressively deeper. The roaring noise was so deafening we had to shout at the top of our voice to be heard.

From our vantage point high on a bank we had just about decided to try it in short spurts of running and lining when Ed shouted to me and pointed upstream. A lone kayaker appeared and without a moment's hesitation pointed his craft confidently down the cataract. We watched as his boat disappeared nose first into the first big souse hole and he was catapulted into the swirling foam. Then, like a wet muskrat, he swam for shore while his kayak bobbed a few times and plunged downstream, never to be seen again.

Ed and I climbed down from our perch, picked up our canoes and portaged the last two miles to the Hudson. And that is how we got through without swamping. . . .

The width of a river is certainly a big factor in its canoeability. Broader pieces of water offer more choices, whereas tiny steep streams have only one route, right down the middle. The West Branch of the Ausable is a "one choice" stream. Bounding over and around huge boulders the size of VW's, from the bridge a mile or so below Heart Lake all the way to the Olympic ski jumps, the Ausable is as difficult as any stream going.

Other rivers that certainly qualify as toughies in heavy water are the Cedar, upper and lower sections; the Indian, a real rough-house when the Lake Abanakee dam is open; the Rock, an obscure but exciting route to the Hudson; the Bog, a rollercoaster to Tupper Lake; and the Moose. There are many others, too, with portions that certainly fit the "heavy water" category.

But our all-time favorite for all-round adventure is the Upper Hudson. It could quite possibly be the finest wilderness white water stretch in the East.

THE UPPER HUDSON
JOHN M. KAUFFMANN

Eighty miles long from its source in Lake Tear of the Clouds to the town of Luzerne, the upper Hudson is New York's premier wild river. . . . Its tributary Cedar, Indian, and Boreas rivers add to this wildwater resource. No, it is not wilderness in the purest sense of that term. A road and a railway run along parts of its lower section, and an occasional camp stands on its banks. Civilization visits it briefly at the hamlets of Newcomb, North River, North Creek, Riparius, and The Glen. But in secluded, brawling rugged beauty it is wild, offering probably the most exhilarating river adventure in the Empire State and one of the finest in the East.

Once the Hudson's beguiling current takes you downriver from the bridge at Newcomb, the wilderness spirit of the Adirondacks claims your entire consciousness. It is as if you stepped into one of Winslow Homer's watercolors, or had been magically transported into some Canadian north woods fastness. The white throated sparrow pipes his clear call for "Old Sam Peabody, Peabody, Peabody," and the bordering conifers roll out their clean fragrance with the clean calm current of water. Only old traces of log driving days remind you of man, and the not-so-far away Northway is leagues out of mind. If you look behind, Santanoni

Mountain and its neighbors lend a far blue backdrop to the river scene. Rumbling ahead promises action. It comes first at Long Falls; then Ord Falls. If the water is high, the ride is a wild one. But relaxation comes again along Blackwell Stillwater. The wilderness mood is broken where a timber company has permitted a scattering of cabins to be built along the stillwater, and has bulldozed a spiky dam and former road crossing necessitating a portage. Wilderness soon reasserts itself in atmosphere and current, however, and the Cedar River adds its own wild flow to the Hudson's. A beautiful campsite invites you to stop at the junction, but the day is early yet and the Hudson rushes on. Below the Gooley Club, perched on its bluff, the river turns abruptly left, the Indian River brawls in, and the Hudson drops ominously deeper between its dark forested shores. The gorge begins to yawn, and the cold, damp breeze, like the breath from a cave, sends a tingle along your spine.

May's high water roars and spumes through this canyon in drop after drop, tumultuous in giant waves and gushing chutes, dazzling, awesome in the somber cleft. Only decked boats and rubber rafts can then navigate this grandest of all whitewater runs in the East. Highwater time is not the occasion to enjoy the details of natural beauty in the Hudson Gorge; attention is totally preoccupied with surviving the monstrous rapids. In June, however, when the water has subsided and an open canoe can, with care, run down, the camping is delightful. Then you can examine the water worn rocks, undercut into weird grottoes. Each niche at river's edge seems a Japanese garden of gnarled trees, shrubs, creeping vines and winking flowers. Blue Ledge, its beetling precipice long an eagle's eyrie, overlooks a favorite fishing place, where a father may bring his boy, backpacking in to taste wilderness and catch a fat rainbow in the misty morning. Mink Pond Brook, draining one of the score of ponds set in the plateaus that flank the gorge, flashes white through the trees, tempting you to stop and explore. O.K. Slip leads to a gossamer cataract higher than Niagara.

Typical of many glacier-gouged rivers of the north, the Hudson drops in steps, each pitch spewing into a welcome pool or stretch of quieter water. Below its confluence with another beautiful wild tributary, the Boreas, the Hudson seems to brawl along continuously, however. After passing the settlements of North River and North Creek, its rush of white rapids disappears into rock-studded, forest-flanked seclusion. Civilization touches it again at the hamlet and cottage colony of Riparius eight miles downstream, and once more at The Glen. Then roads tag along, and by the time it nears Warrensburg and its confluence with the Schroon River, the Hudson's character begins to change. It becomes placid at last, though still moving steadily. Mountains—the Three Sisters, Number Seven, Deer Leap, and others—guard a channel now divided by islands and edged by occasional pasturelands. This last fourteen miles to the waterfall at Luzerne marking the end of the upper river is in many ways the most beautiful reach of all. It is one still surprisingly little used, but offering an idyllic journey, a hope for bass and a campout or lunch hour long and pleasant to remember.

It makes no difference to New Yorkers that the Hudson's white water is too tough for any but experts in spring, and often too low to be navigable in summer, or that its trout fishing, while fairly good, is not widely enjoyed because access is difficult. The Hudson is the shining, roaring gateway to Adirondack wilderness. "It's unique," explained a state forest ranger. "There's nothing else like it. It's part of the soul of the Adirondacks." . . .

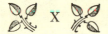

Imperishable Freshness

As a man tramps the woods to the lake he knows he will find pines and lilies, blue heron and golden shiners, shadows on the rocks and the glint of light on the wavelets, just as they were in the summer of 1354, as they will be in 2054 and beyond. He can stand on a rock by the shore and be in a past he could not have known, in a future he will never see. He can be part of time that was and time yet to come.

William Chapman White in *Adirondack Country*

"IF EVERY CHURCH would make up a purse and pack its worn and weary pastor off to the North Woods for a four weeks' jaunt in the hot months of July and August, it would do a very sensible as well as pleasant act. For when the good dominie came back swarth and tough as an Indian, elasticity in his step, fire in his eye, depth and clearness in his reinvigorated voice, wouldn't there be some preaching!" This was the Reverend "Adirondack" Murray's rejoinder to critics in and out of his congregation. His annual flight to the woods was not mere self-indulgence or sentimental nostalgia. It was escape, to be sure—escape from the tormenting round of "Sabbath-school festivals and pastoral tea-parties." But the escape was temporary and bracing. The good dominie returned, refreshed, to the work of bettering his congregation and advancing civilization.

America's speedy progress from Plymouth Rock to Wall Street and Fifth Avenue has outstripped our inner adjustment to it. We have not had leisure to assimilate civilization fully. Settled urbanity eludes us. We are like the American expatriates in Henry James's novels, a little blundering and awkward in European society, try as hard as they do. We all try, and some are able to manage on their nerves. But for most of us the effort reaches, at least once a year, a crisis of exhaustion. We have to escape the grip of rushing time. So it is back to Plymouth Rock; or to some available approximation such as the Adirondacks.

Escape-and-return is an American way of life. Most of the writers assembled in this book are addicted to it. Years after leading the camping trip of Boston intellectuals to the Adirondacks in 1858 and while living in over-civilized London, William J. Stillman voiced his need of escape in a letter to an American friend: "I must go back to America. . . . It is of no use trying to live under these conditions—I cant fire a shot from my rifle—I cant catch a trout —I cant indulge for one instant in any of my savage propensities or escape decorum, & my very life is made gloomy by the want of a healthy day in a savage state—I must go back."* This cry of pain came from an artist, a friend of Emerson and Lowell, an international journalist who knew the value of both the gregarious city and the lonesome woods. Both were necessary to him, as they are today to Anne LaBastille in her double life as woodswoman and world-roving ecologist.

The two lives support each other. From the woods come relaxation and renewal; from the city, enhanced appreciation of the wilds through books, music, art as well as the need to escape. Even our popular culture celebrates wilderness and the frontier. The true lover of wilderness is not likely to be the pioneer, who must subdue it, but the city man, who takes it in small installments with insights he has garnered from libraries, art museums, or simply from Western movies. "To the modern man in the Adirondacks," said Henry Beers, "the roar of the rapids, the gaunt dead trees around the lake, the wet carry, the big rotten trunks that impede his steps, even the punkies that defy his smudge, are sources of joy and refreshment unspeakable."

A guide, a surveyor, a young mountaineer who was later to

---

*Quoted with the permission of Cornell University Library.

explore Alaska and found the Wilderness Society, a story writer recalling his boyhood, an English Shakespearean actor, a naturalist strayed from his home in the Catskills, another schooled from his twelfth year in the North Woods, a teen-age hunter who later became President as he made a hurried descent from Mount Marcy to North Creek and Buffalo, a president of Yale University, a Harvard philosopher, a health seeker and sensitive observer of wildlife, a great artist whose "Adirondack phase was a new departure in American watercolor painting," a father exploring a wilderness pond with his son, an ecologist returning to her cabin in the wilds after an assignment in the abrasive city—these make up a diverse group. But in the pieces that follow they have one thing in common. All have the knack of reverting periodically to the natural rhythms of woods life. All are members in spirit of the Sunday Rock Association, knowing that on the outside of Sunday Rock our days are named and chartered, and that time rules over space. On the inside, clocks relax their hold on us, Sunday is no different from any other day, and we enjoy the freedom of a world of space.

Space is ample in the Adirondacks, but love is limited. Adirondackers are likely to fasten on one or two places which for them are most secure against the shifting values of time. For William James those places were Keene Valley and the Great Range. In 1877 James and his Harvard companions were staying at Smith Beede's Old House in the pasture where Roaring Brook joins the East Branch of the Ausable at the foot of Giant Mountain. Four Yale men were also there, obviously enamored with the place. The Harvard men were cool and reserved. They suspected Yale of a secret design to buy the place and tried to conceal their own hankering for it. Secretly they raised the few hundred dollars necessary for purchase. They turned the house into a summer camp to be shared in common with their families and friends. James was there the following year on his honeymoon and continued to return nearly every summer for the rest of his life.

His favorite recreation was tramps on mountain trails, alone or with guide or friends. One of his trail companions, first met when he was fifty-three and she was a Bryn Mawr senior of twenty-one, was Pauline Goldmark, "an up-at-sunrise, out-of-door, and moun-taintop kind of girl." She was in the party that he joined on Mount Marcy in 1898 for a night of camping and next day's descent over the Range into Keene Valley, the trip he describes in the letter to his wife included here. "That summer," he wrote to Pauline several years later, "when we walked over the 'Range' and I went to California to talk to teachers, marked my completest union with my native land."

The timelessness James associated with Keene Valley is phrased in a letter four years before his death to his brother Henry, the Europeanized American who seems never to have experienced a complete union with his native land, but to have remained aloof and critical: "You missed it, when here, in not going to Keene Valley, where I have just been, and of which the sylvan beauty, especially by moonlight, is probably unlike aught that Europe has to show. Imperishable freshness!"

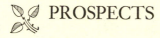 # PROSPECTS

From Mount Marcy

It makes a man feel what it is to have all creation under his feet. There are woods there which it would take a lifetime to hunt over, mountains that seem shouldering each other to boost the one whereon you stand, up and away Heaven knows where. Thousands of little lakes are let in among them so light and clean. Old Champlain, though fifty miles away, glistens below you like a strip of white birch when slicked up by the moon on a frosty night, and the Green Mountains of Vermont beyond it fade and fade away until they disappear as gradually as a cold scent when the dew rises.

John Cheney as quoted by C. F. Hoffman

From Mount Haystack

Everyone has his favorite mountain. My favorite is Haystack. Primarily because in the whole vast panorama visible from the mountain there is virtually not a sign of civilization. Whichever way you look, save toward a small burned section near the Giant, there are the forests, the mountains, the ponds, just as they were before white man had ever set foot on America. It's a great thing these days to leave civilization for a while and return to nature. From Haystack you can look over thousands and thousands of acres, unblemished by the works of man, perfect as made by nature.

Robert Marshall

Mountaintops of the Central Adirondacks

Elsewhere are mountains more stupendous, more icy and more drear, but none look upon a grander landscape, in rich autumn time; more brightly gemmed or jeweled with innumerable lakes, or crystal pools, or wild with savage chasms, or dread passes, none show a denser or more vast appearance of primeval forest stretched over range on range to the far horizon, where the sea of mountains fades into a dim, vaporous uncertainty.

Verplanck Colvin

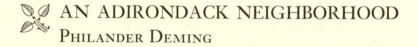

AN ADIRONDACK NEIGHBORHOOD
Philander Deming

There was a freedom in the neighborhood that I have never found anywhere else. The mountains and a hundred miles of woods shut us out from the busy life of "the States." The vast dim landscape below to the northward was "only Canada." The isolation was considerable.

The neighborhood was not a small place: we knew literally everybody for a dozen miles around. It made it very much of a home indeed, and very pleasant, to have so wide an acquaintance and to never meet strange faces. There was an utter lack of formality.

I am telling about the neighborhood as it was many years ago; but, so far as a mere description of the place is concerned, I might just as well tell how it is now. For the place does not change. It is as wild and free as ever. Only last summer, when I went home, my brothers and relatives who reside there, and the neighbors, were telling me all about that bear that had eaten the corn last fall until the men caught him at it and chased him across the lots, and down the road, and killed him. The women said they were all out looking at the sport, and one woman drove him away from her dooryard with a piece of a board. The accounts which were given of the transaction were as fresh and picturesque as the stories that used to thrill me when we first went there to live many years ago. . . .

We three brothers were boys when our family moved into this neighborhood. The place and the people interested us very much. There were some queer characters. There was the man down the river who had heard of a runaway pond which destroyed a good deal of property, and who therefore lived in constant fear that the lake at the head of our river would get away and come down upon us. He slept in the garret of his house, with a small boat hanging out of the window, ready for the emergency. There was also the nervous, timid man, who was always excited for three days after leaving his quiet home and visiting "The Corners" and the store and the mill. Our nearest neighbor was a famous fisherman —in his own little brook, but he had never in all his life ventured into the deep woods. He astonished us by his almost superstitious respect for the wilderness. In all his younger days he had desired to visit the wonderful places in the famous South Woods, as men in other localities desire to visit Europe; but the cares of home had prevented him until he had become too old to make the journey. He told us, in all confidence and good faith, that a far-off mountain, called Whiteface, was too precipitous for any human foot to climb. It was known, however, that the top was composed of silver ore. That was what made it so white. The Indians knocked off pieces of the silver with their arrows. So he had understood, and he regarded it as a probable story.

The general tendency in the neighborhood was to exaggerate the marvels of the forest. It happened late one evening that our neighbor Ralph and his two daughters, returning home from a visit, saw by the light of their lantern a panther right in the road before them. As the light struck his face, the creature turned and dashed off into the woods. It was a great scare to the little party and produced a wonderful excitement in the neighborhood. The incident afforded opportunity to exaggerate, and some queer reminiscences were narrated. One story was that a painter (so they called it) away off somewhere in the mountains had jumped down from a tree and seized a boy sixteen years old. The story ran that this pussy of the woods had taken the boy alive to the top of a lofty pine and there played with him as if he were a mouse, throwing him into the air in a lively manner and catching him as he came down. The gradual weakening of the young man in the paws of the panther until he became "limpsy," so that his agonized mother, who stood at the foot of the tree, gazing upward and watching the operation, could see that her son was at last dead, was a very thrilling part of the grim recital. Preposterous as the story seemed, it was narrated, not to say trembled over, with an air of deep conviction by some of the storytellers of the neighborhood.

Another incident will illustrate the feeling which existed, among those who were not hunters by occupation, in regard to the dangers of the forest. A sturdy neighbor went with a party into a very wild, unfrequented section to hunt and fish. He accidentally strayed away from his comrades. Finding himself alone, he began to run and fire his gun. His comrades pursued him. It was difficult to catch him. He seemed wild or insane. He avoided his pursuers as if he had been a wild beast. When they caught him, he was very pale and beside himself. And yet he was within a day's journey of his home, and following any water-course down the northward incline for ten or fifteen hours would have brought him to the cleared country.

There was, however, some excuse in this locality for regarding the wilderness with such profound consideration. Several persons had been lost in it, and some had perished. It required a journey of about a hundred miles through the long, narrow lane of arable land between the wilderness and Canada, and so around the mountains, to get fairly out of the shadow of the forest.

To us boys, who were newcomers and had read much of the Adirondacks, the woods were full of interest. We passed many days in the trackless solitudes with only a pocket compass as guide. There is no other loneliness so deep and solemn, or that so haunts the imagination, and is so full of joy and fear to the boyish spirit as the far-away loneliness that is felt in the gloomy, trackless wilderness. With a party, or upon well-known routes, this is not experienced. But it will be understood that this feeling of loneliness may be very strong in young and inexperienced persons, whose travels are to them adventurous explorations.

Some of our first adventures in the forest left a deep impression upon our minds. Jule, the eldest, was the first of our youthful trio who sought to gratify the curiosity we felt in reference to the deep woods. It was the summer of our arrival at our new home. It was in August. He went alone a day's journey into the forest and camped a dozen miles away from even a hunter's cabin. He did not burden himself with a gun. His outfit consisted of some bread and butter, a pocket compass, and a bunch of matches. The only serious adventure he met with was in the night. It was merely a few sudden footsteps near him, and the whistle of a deer enlivening his reflections, as he sat nodding over his little fire of bark and dried branches. It should be added that he was a thorough sceptic in regard to the alleged dangers of the forest and cared nothing for mere hunting and fishing. He was a lover of nature and an enthusiastic disciple of Wilson and Audubon. . . .

[One] trip [I recall] was made very soon after Jule's solitary excursion. It was his excursion that gave rise to this second one a week later. I recall it the more vividly because it was the only occasion upon which any of us were driven out of the woods. It had been resolved to reach, if possible, two lonely ponds called twin lakes, said to be hidden between mountains and not easily found. Two of our youthful trio started on this quest and had made the best part of a day's journey into the forest wilds when it began to rain. They undertook to camp; but suddenly there sprang up a sound of voices so unearthly and terrific that it seemed to freeze the very marrow in their bones. In the deep stillness the sounds were fearful. A very sincere desire to get out of the woods as quickly as possible was felt and acted upon. A desperate rush was made. By the aid of the compass a watercourse which led to the clearings was fortunately found. A good stretch was made before dark; and, stumbling along through the night, home was reached before morning. It turned out that the awful voices which had been heard came from a pack of wolves howling in the lone dreariness of the rainy afternoon. One of the adventurers who retreated from this wild music was only fourteen years of age. Since that time he has seen life in the wilds of California, and among the Sierras, and has faced death upon the field of battle; but he still refers to that scare among the Adirondacks, when he was so young and so easily impressed, as his most thrilling experience.

EXPLORING INDIAN PASS
WILLIAM CHARLES MACREADY

While on a theatrical tour of the United States in 1844, the English actor Macready and his American friend David C. Colden were guests of David Henderson at the Adirondack Iron Works. These three, with two guides, went into Indian Pass. Macready, according to Henderson, showed a fine taste for wild scenery and was "enraptured with the Notch."

To his wife. Auburn, New York, June 20, 1844. I went with Henderson and Colden, and two attendants, on our excursion to one of the grand passes of this wild region—called the Notch:—I took the precaution of arming myself with the hunter's bowie-knife, and this put me completely at my ease.—We made our way along the length of a wild lake—resembling, in its fringe of blasted and withered firs, those on Mt. Catskill, but this was five miles in extent.—We then struck into the wood and, starting three deer at our outset, pushed, climbed, scrambled and tore our way through and over this wild and grand labyrinth. An European can have no idea of an American forest—indeed many Americans are as much abroad in forming any idea of its savage grandeur. I constantly pause to look around, above and all about me to *feel* the depth of loneliness that it impresses on one. The pass, or glen, we went to see exceeds in beauty and grandeur any other that

I have chanced to look upon, considered in regard to its own distinguishing features. Its peculiar characteristic is that along and over its whole extent it may be said to be formed entirely of boulders, varying in size from the stone that a single hand could raise to masses of rock, tumbled one upon another, of an immensity that one hesitates to state in measurement. The side of the mountain has tumbled down at various times and thus produced this wild scene of terrible beauty. Most of these rocks are grasped by enormous roots of trees that send their huge trunks high into the air. They form varieties of pictures beyond all power of numbering. Some stand sharply erect in the midst of the ravine. Some piled in the wildest confusion upon others form deep and extensive caverns beneath, with long and intricate passages, capable of holding several hundred men, whilst between the clefts and in the depths of their interstices lie masses of ice and snow beyond the reach of sunlight.

The river, or rather torrent, the infant Hudson, rushes among and over the rocks, forming cascades and rapids, or deepening in its swift course through closely pent-up channels. Enormous trees, uptorn and broken, are thrown across or into the stream in the most furious disorder. Over these—except on the more recent victims of the tempest, is spread a growth of mosses, varying from one to two feet in depth, and frequently it happens that in placing one's foot upon some giant trunk laid prostrate, it yields to the pressure, and the traveller has to draw his leg out of a mass of decomposed vegetable matter of all depths.

On the right side of the pass the mountain rises in a rapid slope, covered with trees of all dimensions, from the pine just bursting from its seed up to the loftiest forms of the giants of the wilderness. On the left, rugged and bare, except where on its ledges the birch and pine have enrooted themselves, the mountain of rock rears its naked front abrupt and perpendicularly from the tumbled heaps of its own ruins and forms a perpendicular wall to the height of above twelve hundred feet. It is not easy to imagine a scene inspiring profounder awe or more sublime emotions than this. . . .

Ever your most affectionate husband, lover and friend,
William Charles John Anderson Macready.

NATE'S POND
JOHN BURROUGHS

Our guide proposed to conduct us to a lake in the mountains where we could float for deer.

Our journey commenced in a steep and rugged ascent, which brought us, after an hour's heavy climbing, to an elevated region of pine forest, years before ravished by lumbermen and presenting all manner of obstacles to our awkward and incumbered pedestrianism. The woods were largely pine, though yellow birch, beech, and maple were common. The satisfaction of having a gun, should any game show itself, was the chief compensation to those of us who were thus burdened. A partridge would occasionally whir up before us, or a red squirrel snicker and hasten to his den; else the woods appeared quite tenantless. The most noted object was a mammoth pine, apparently the last of a great race, which presided over a cluster of yellow birches on the side of the mountain.

About noon we came out upon a long, shallow sheet of water which the guide called Bloody-Moose Pond, from the tradition that a moose had been slaughtered there many years before. Looking out over the silent and lonely scene, his eye was the first to detect an object, apparently feeding upon lily pads, which our willing fancies readily shaped into a deer. As we were eagerly waiting some movement to confirm this impression, it lifted up its head, and lo! a great blue heron. Seeing us approach, it spread its long wings and flew solemnly across to a dead tree on the other side of the lake, enhancing rather than relieving the loneliness and desolation that brooded over the scene. As we proceeded, it flew from tree to tree in advance of us, apparently loth to be disturbed in its ancient and solitary domain. In the margin of the pond we found the pitcher-plant growing, and here and there in the sand the closed gentian lifted up its blue head.

In traversing the shores of this wild, desolate lake, I was conscious of a slight thrill of expectation, as if some secret of Nature might here be revealed, or some rare and unheard-of game disturbed. There is ever a lurking suspicion that the beginning of things is in some way associated with water, and one may notice that in his private walks he is led by a curious attraction to fetch all the springs and ponds in his route, as if by them was the place for wonders and miracles to happen. Once, while in advance of my companions, I saw, from a high rock, a commotion in the water near the shore, but on reaching the point found only the marks of a musquash.

Pressing on through the forest, after many adventures with the pine-knots, we reached, about the middle of the afternoon, our destination, Nate's Pond—a pretty sheet of water, lying like a silver mirror in the lap of the mountain, about a mile long and half a mile wide, surrounded by dark forests of balsam, hemlock, and pine, and, like the one we had just passed, a very picture of unbroken solitude.

It is not in the woods alone to give one this impression of utter loneliness. In the woods are sounds and voices and a dumb kind of companionship; one is little more than a walking tree himself; but come upon one of these mountain lakes, and the wildness stands revealed and meets you face to face. Water is thus facile and adaptive, that it makes the wild more wild, while it enhances culture and art.

The end of the pond which we approached was quite shoal, the stones rising above the surface as in a summer brook, and everywhere showing marks of the noble game we were in quest of—footprints, dung, and cropped and uprooted lily pads. After resting for a half hour and replenishing our game-pouches at the expense of the most respectable frogs of the locality, we filed on through the soft, resinous pine-woods, intending to camp near the other end of the lake, where, the guide assured us, we should find a hunter's cabin ready built. A half-hour's march brought us to the locality, and a most delightful one it was—so hospitable and inviting that all the kindly and beneficent influences of the woods must have abided there. In a slight depression in the woods, about one hundred yards from the lake, though hidden from it for a hunter's reasons, surrounded by a heavy growth of birch, hemlock, and pine, with a lining of balsam and fir, the rude cabin welcomed us. It was of the approved style, three sides inclosed, with a roof of bark and a bed of boughs and a rock in front that afforded a permanent backlog to all fires. A faint voice of running water was heard near by, and, following the sound, a delicious spring rivulet was disclosed, hidden by the moss and débris as by a new fall of snow, but here and there rising in little well-like openings, as if for our special convenience. On smooth places on the logs I noticed female names inscribed in a female hand; and the guide told us of an English lady, an artist, who had traversed this region with a single guide, making sketches.

Our packs unslung and the kettle over, our first move was to ascertain in what state of preservation a certain dug-out might be, which, the guide averred, he had left moored in the vicinity the summer before—for upon this hypothetical dug-out our hopes of venison rested. After a little searching, it was found under the top of a fallen hemlock, but in a sorry condition. A large piece had been split out of one end, and a fearful chink was visible nearly to the water line. Freed from the treetop, however, and calked with a little moss, it floated with two aboard, which was quite enough for our purpose. A jack and an oar were necessary to complete the arrangement, and before the sun had set our professor of woodcraft had both in readiness. From a young yellow birch an oar took shape with marvelous rapidity—trimmed and smoothed with a neatness almost fastidious—no makeshift, but an instrument fitted for the delicate work it was to perform.

A jack was made with equal skill and speed. A stout staff about three feet long was placed upright in the bow of the boat and held to its place by a horizontal bar, through a hole in which it turned easily; a half wheel eight or ten inches in diameter, cut from a large chip, was placed at the top, around which was bent a new section of birch bark, thus forming a rude semicircular reflector. Three candles placed within the circle completed the jack. With moss and boughs seats were arranged—one in the bow for the marksman and one in the stern for the oarsman. A meal of frogs and squirrels was a good preparation, and when darkness came, all were keenly alive to the opportunity it brought. Though by no means an expert in the use of the gun—adding the superlative degree of enthusiasm to only the positive degree of skill—yet it seemed tacitly agreed that I should act as marksman and kill the deer, if such was to be our luck.

After it was thoroughly dark, we went down to make a short trial trip. Everything working to satisfaction, about ten o'clock we pushed out in earnest. For the twentieth time I felt in the pocket that contained the matches, ran over the part I was to perform, and pressed my gun firmly, to be sure there was no mistake. My position was that of kneeling directly under the jack, which I was to light at the word. The night was clear, moonless, and still. Nearing the middle of the lake, a breeze from the west was barely perceptible, and noiselessly we glided before it. The guide handled his oar with great dexterity; without lifting it from the water or breaking the surface, he imparted the steady, uniform motion desired. How silent it was! The ear seemed the only sense, and to hold dominion over lake and forest. Occasionally a lily pad would brush along the bottom, and stooping low I could hear a faint murmuring of the water under the bow: else all was still. Then, almost as by magic, we were encompassed by a huge black ring. The surface of the lake, when we had reached the center, was slightly luminous from the starlight, and the dark, even forestline that surrounded us, doubled by reflection in the water, presented a broad, unbroken belt of utter blackness. The effect was quite startling, like some huge conjurer's trick. It seemed as if we had crossed the boundary-line between the real and the imaginary, and this was indeed the land of shadows and of spectres. What magic oar was that the guide wielded that it could transport me to such a realm! Indeed, had I not committed some fatal mistake and left that trusty servant behind, and had not some wizard of the night stepped into his place? A slight splashing in-shore broke the spell and caused me to turn nervously to the oarsman: "Musquash," said he, and kept straight on.

Nearing the extreme end of the pond, the boat gently headed around, and silently we glided back into the clasp of that strange orbit. Slight sounds were heard as before, but nothing that indicated the presence of the game we were waiting for; and we reached the point of departure as innocent of venison as we had set out.

After an hour's delay, and near midnight, we pushed out again. My vigilance and susceptibility were rather sharpened than dulled by the waiting; and the features of the night had also deepened and intensified. Night was at its meridian. The sky had that soft luminousness which may often be observed near midnight at this season, and the "large few stars" beamed mildly down. We floated out into that spectral shadow-land and moved slowly on as before. The silence was most impressive. Now and then the faint *yeap* of some traveling bird would come from the air overhead, or the wings of a bat *whisp* quickly by, or an owl hoot off in the mountains, giving to the silence and loneliness a tongue. At short intervals some noise in-shore would startle me and cause me to turn inquiringly to the silent figure in the stern.

The end of the lake was reached, and we turned back. The novelty and the excitement began to flag; tired nature began to assert her claims; the movement was soothing, and the gunner slumbered fitfully at his post. Presently something aroused me. "There's a deer," whispered the guide. The gun heard and fairly jumped in my hand. Listening, there came the cracking of a limb, followed by a sound as of something walking in shallow water. It proceeded from the other end of the lake, over against our camp. On we sped, noiselessly as ever, but with increased velocity. Presently, with a thrill of new intensity, I saw the boat was gradually heading in that direction. Now, to a sportsman who gets excited over a gray squirrel and forgets that he has a gun on the sudden appearance of a fox, this was a severe trial. I felt suddenly cramped for room, and trimming the boat was out of the question. It seemed that I must make some noise in spite of myself. "Light the jack," said a soft whisper behind me. I fumbled nervously for a match and dropped the first one. Another was drawn briskly across my knee and broke. A third lighted, but went out prematurely in my haste to get it up to the jack. What would I not have given to see those wicks blaze! We were fast nearing the shore—already the lily pads began to brush along the bottom. Another attempt, and the light took. The gentle motion fanned the blaze, and in a moment a broad glare of light fell upon the water in front of us, while the boat remained in utter darkness.

By this time I had got beyond the nervous point and had come round to perfect coolness and composure again, but preternaturally vigilant and keen. I was ready for any disclosures; not a sound was heard. In a few moments the trees alongshore were faintly visible. Every object put on the shape of a gigantic deer. A large rock looked just ready to bound away. The dry limbs of a prostrate tree were surely his antlers.

But what are those two luminous spots? Need the reader be told what they were? In a moment the head of a real deer became outlined; then his neck and foreshoulders; then his whole body. There he stood, up to his knees in the water, gazing fixedly at us, apparently arrested in the movement of putting his head down for a lily pad and evidently thinking it was some new-fangled moon sporting about there. "Let him have it," said my prompter—and the crash came. There was a scuffle in the water and a plunge in the woods. "He's gone," said I. "Wait a moment," said the guide, "and I will show you." Rapidly running the canoe ashore, we sprang out and, holding the jack aloft, explored the vicinity by its light. There over the logs and brush, I caught the glimmer of those luminous spots again. But, poor thing! there was little need of the second shot, which was the unkindest cut of all, for the deer had already fallen to the ground and was fast expiring. The success was but a very indifferent one, after all, as the victim turned out to be only an old doe, upon whom maternal cares had evidently worn heavily during the summer.

This mode of taking deer is very novel and strange. The animal is evidently fascinated or bewildered. It does not appear to be frightened, but as if overwhelmed with amazement or under the influence of some spell. It is not sufficiently master of the situation to be sensible of fear or to think of escape by flight; and the experiment, to be successful, must be tried quickly, before the first feeling of bewilderment passes.

Witnessing the spectacle from the shore, I can conceive of nothing more sudden or astounding. You see no movement and hear no noise, but the light *grows* upon you and stares and stares like a huge eye from the infernal regions.

According to the guide, when a deer has been played upon

in this manner and escaped, he is not to be fooled a second time. Mounting the shore, he gives a long signal snort, which alarms every animal within hearing, and dashes away.

The sequel to the deer-shooting was a little sharp practice with a revolver upon a rabbit, or properly a hare, which was so taken with the spectacle of the camp fire and the sleeping figures lying about that it ventured quite up in our midst; but while testing the quality of some condensed milk that sat uncovered at the foot of a large tree, poor Lepus had his spine injured by a bullet.

Those who lodge with Nature find early rising quite in order. It is our voluptuous beds and isolation from the earth and the air that prevent us from emulating the birds and beasts in this respect. With the citizen in his chamber, it is not morning but breakfast time. The camper-out, however, feels morning in the air, he smells it, sees it, hears it, and springs up with the general awakening. None were tardy at the row of white chips arranged on the trunk of a prostrate tree when breakfast was hallooed; for we were all anxious to try the venison. Few of us, however, took a second piece. It was black and strong.

The day was warm and calm, and we loafed at leisure. The woods were Nature's own. It was a luxury to ramble through them—rank and shaggy and venerable, but with an aspect singularly ripe and mellow. No fire had consumed and no lumberman plundered. Every trunk and limb and leaf lay where it had fallen. At every step the foot sank into the moss, which, like a soft green snow, covered everything, making every stone a cushion and every rock a bed—a grand old Norse parlor; adorned beyond art and upholstered beyond skill.

Indulging in a brief nap on a rug of club-moss carelessly dropped at the foot of a pine tree, I woke up to find myself the subject of a discussion of a troop of chickadees. Presently three or four shy wood warblers came to look upon this strange creature that had wandered into their haunts; else I passed quite unnoticed.

By the lake I met that orchard beauty, the cedar waxwing, spending his vacation in the assumed character of a flycatcher, whose part he performed with great accuracy and deliberation. Only a month before I had seen him regaling himself upon cherries in the garden and orchard; but as the dog-days approached he set out for the streams and lakes, to divert himself with the more exciting pursuits of the chase. From the tops of the dead trees along the border of the lake, he would sally out in all directions, sweeping through long curves, alternately mounting and descending, now reaching up for a fly high in air, now sinking low for one near the surface and returning to his perch in a few moments for a fresh start.

The pine finch was also here, though as usual never appearing at home, but with a waiting, expectant air. Here also I met my beautiful singer, the hermit thrush, but with no song in his throat now. A week or two later and he was on his journey southward. This was the only species of thrush I saw in the Adirondacks. Near Lake Sandford, where were large tracts of raspberry and wild cherry, I saw numbers of them. A boy whom we met, driving home some stray cows, said it was the "partridge-bird," no doubt from the resemblance of its note, when disturbed, to the cluck of the partridge.

Nate's Pond contained perch and sunfish but no trout. Its water was not pure enough for trout. Was there ever any other fish so fastidious as this, requiring such sweet harmony and perfection of the elements for its production and sustenance? On higher ground about a mile distant was a trout pond, the shores of which were steep and rocky. . . .

Of wild animals such as bears, panthers, wolves, wildcats, etc., we neither saw nor heard any in the Adirondacks. "A howling wilderness," Thoreau says, "seldom ever howls. The howling is chiefly done by the imagination of the traveler." Hunter said he often saw bear-tracks in the snow, but had never yet met Bruin. Deer are more or less abundant everywhere, and one old sportsman declares there is yet a single moose in these mountains [1863]. On our return a pioneer settler at whose house we stayed overnight told us a long adventure he had had with a panther. He related how it screamed, how it followed him in the brush, how he took to his boat, how its eyes gleamed from the shore, and how he fired his rifle at them with fatal effect. His wife in the mean time took something from a drawer, and, as her husband finished his recital, she produced a toenail of the identical animal with marked dramatic effect.

But better than fish or game or grand scenery, or any adventure by night or day, is the wordless intercourse with rude Nature one has on these expeditions. It is something to press the pulse of our old mother by mountain lakes and streams and know what health and vigor are in her veins and how regardless of observation she deports herself.

<hr />

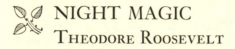

NIGHT MAGIC
THEODORE ROOSEVELT

Fire-hunting from a boat, or jacking, as it is called, though it entails absolutely no skill in the hunter, and though it is, and ought to be, forbidden, as it can best be carried on at the season when nursing does are particularly apt to be the victims, nevertheless has a certain charm of its own. The first deer I ever killed, when a boy, was obtained in this way, and I have always been glad to have had the experience, though I have never been willing to repeat it. I was at the time camped out in the Adirondacks.

Two or three of us, all boys of fifteen or sixteen, had been enjoying what was practically our first experience in camping out, having gone out with two guides, Hank Martin and Mose Sawyer, from Paul Smith's, on Lake St. Regis. My brother and cousin were fond of fishing and I was not, so I was deputed to try to bring in a deer. I had a double-barrelled twelve-bore gun, French pin-fire, with which I had industriously collected "specimens" on a trip to Egypt and Palestine and on Long Island; except for three or four enthralling but not oversuccessful days after woodcock and quail, I had done no game-shooting. As to every healthy boy with a taste for outdoor life, the Northern forests were to me a veritable land of enchantment. We were encamped by a stream among the tall pines, and I had enjoyed everything; poling and paddling the boat, tramping through the woods, the cries of chickaree and chipmunk, of jay, woodpecker, chickadee, nuthatch, and crossbill, which broke the forest stillness; and, above all, the great reaches of sombre woodlands themselves. The heart-shaped footprints which showed where the deer had come down to drink and feed on the marshy edges of the water made my veins thrill; and the nights around the flickering campfire seemed filled with romance.

My first experiment in jacking was a failure. The jack, a bark lantern, was placed upon a stick in the bow of the boat, and I sat in a cramped huddle behind it, while Mose Sawyer plied the paddle with noiseless strength and skill in the stern. I proved unable to respond even to the very small demand made upon me, for when we actually did come upon a deer I failed to see it until it ran, when I missed it; and on the way back capped my misfortune by shooting a large owl which perched on a log projecting into the water, looking at the lantern with two glaring eyes.

All next day I was miserably conscious of the smothered disfavor of my associates, and when night fell was told I would have another chance to redeem myself. This time we started across a carry, the guide carrying the light boat, and launched it in a quiet little pond about a mile off. Dusk was just turning into darkness when we reached the edge of the little lake, which was perhaps a mile long by three-quarters of a mile across, with indented shores. We did not push off for half an hour or so, until it was entirely dark; and then for a couple of hours we saw no deer. Nevertheless, I thoroughly enjoyed the ghostly, mysterious, absolutely silent night ride over the water. Not the faintest splash betrayed the work of the paddler. The boat glided stealthily alongshore, the glare of the lantern bringing out for one moment every detail of the forest growth on the banks, which the next second vanished into absolute blackness. Several times we saw muskrats swimming across the lane of light cut by the lantern through the darkness, and two or three times their sudden plunging and splashing caused my heart to leap. Once when we crossed the lake we came upon a loon floating buoyantly right out in the middle of it. It stayed until we were within ten yards, so that I could see the minute outlines of the feathers and every movement of the eye. Then it swam off, but made no cry. At last, while crossing the mouth of a bay we heard a splashing sound among the lilies inshore, which even my untrained ears recognized as different from any of the other noises we had yet heard, and a jarring motion of the paddle showed that the paddler wished me to be on the alert. Without any warning, the course of the boat was suddenly changed, and I was aware that we were moving stern foremost. Then we swung around, and I could soon make out that we were going down the little bay. The forest-covered banks narrowed; then the marsh at the end was lighted up, and on its hither edge, knee-deep among the water lilies, appeared the figure of a yearling buck still in the red. It stood motionless, gazing at the light with a curiosity wholly unmixed with alarm, and at the shot wheeled and fell at the water's edge. We made up our mind to return to camp that night, as it was before midnight. I carried the buck and the torch, and the guide the boat, and the mile walk over the dim trail, occasionally pitching forward across a stump or root, was a thing to be remembered. It was my first deer, and I was very glad to get it; but although only a boy, I had sense enough to realize that it was not an experience worth repeating. The paddler in such a case deserves considerable credit, but the shooter not a particle, even aside from the fact to which I have already alluded, that in too many cases such shooting results in the killing of nursing does. No matter how young a sportsman is, if he has a healthy mind, he will not long take pleasure in any method of hunting in which somebody else shows the skill and does the work so that his share is only nominal.

THE CHICKAREE
Clinton Hart Merriam

The Red Squirrel . . . is the most hilarious of the preeminently merry and frolicsome family to which he belongs, and his joyous and jubilant nature enables him to triumph over the sense of gloom that pervades the sombre coniferous forests of the North, rendering him cheerful and contented in the darkest and most impenetrable of our evergreen thickets. Indeed, it is this happy faculty of adapting himself and his modes of life to a diversity of surroundings that has permitted his wide dispersion, the present boundaries of his habitat being coextensive with those of the wooded portions of the northern part of our continent.

The Chickaree combines qualities so wholly at variance, so unique, so incomprehensible, and so characteristic withal, that one scarcely knows in what light to regard him. His inquisitiveness, audacity, inordinate assurance, and exasperating insolence, together with his insatiable love of mischief and shameless disregard of all the ordinary customs and civilities of life, would lead one to suppose that he was little entitled to respect; and yet his intelligence, his untiring perseverance, and genuine industry, the cunning cleverness displayed in many of his actions, and the irresistible humor with which he does everything, command for him a certain degree of admiration. He is arrogant, impetuous, and conceited to an extreme degree, his confidence in his own superior capabilities not infrequently costing him his life. In fact, these contradictions in character and idiosyncrasies in disposition render him a psychological problem of no easy solution.

From earliest dawn till the setting sun has disappeared behind the distant hills, the Red Squirrel enlivens the silent solitude of the forest with his merry ways and saucy chatterings; and he may sometimes be discovered in the darkest hours of the night, stealing softly over the ground—bent, doubtless, on some errand of dubious propriety. Moonlight evenings he is often as active, though not so noisy, as during the day, and in early autumn he vies with the flying squirrel in nocturnal nut-husking exploits. Though an expert climber, delighting in long leaps from bough to bough, which he executes with grace and precision, he spends far more time on the ground than the other arboreal squirrels, sometimes even making his home in holes in the earth. . . .

He is the least wary of the squirrels, rarely taking the trouble to hide himself at the approach of man. In fact, on such occasions he usually assumes an aggressive attitude, chippers, shakes his tail in an impudent and wholly uncalled-for manner, but takes care to keep just out of reach. . . .

His curiosity is almost as striking as his impudence, and more than once when I have been standing or sitting motionless in the forest he has approached nearer and nearer, eyeing me inquisitively, chippering, and shaking his tail, till finally he has jumped upon my person, to be off again in a trice. When sleeping on the ground in July, 1878, I was awakened, just at daybreak, by a noisy and excited chippering close at hand, but before my eyes were fairly open one of these mischievous imps alighted in my face. The surprise was common, and I must have started rather unceremoniously, for he sprang so suddenly to the nearest tree that the prints of his claws were visible for sometime after upon my forehead and nose.

Of all the annoyances that beset the trapper in this region, none compare with the Red Squirrel. Not only is he the most vexatious of all the animals that roam the Adirondack wilds, but he often proves a source of disaster to the fur dealer. From an overhanging limb he looks on with unfeigned interest while the trapper arranges the bait for the marten or fisher; but a moment later he has sprung the trap and is chippering with exulting derision at the result. He is often caught, it is true, but half a dozen others are always ready to take his place, and it affords little satisfaction to the hunter, on his lonely rounds through the snow-clad forest, to find a worthless Squirrel in his trap, instead of the valuable fur for which it was set. But if, instead of consulting the hunter's interests, we take another view of the case, it is easy to see that the Chickaree is a good friend to the marten. He furnishes the latter with food of an exceptionally agreeable kind, and though it cost him his life, takes great pains to discover and spring the traps set for the marten's destruction.

He is not always to be found in equal numbers, but is influenced in a marked degree by the beechnut crop. In seasons when mast is plentiful there seems to be a Squirrel for every tree, bush, stump, and log in the entire Wilderness, besides a number left over to fill possible vacancies. When, on the other hand, the nut crop has been a failure, a corresponding diminution in the numbers of Squirrels is observable, and they are sometimes actually scarce. Hence it is clear that while the diet of the Red Squirrel is varied, his staple commodity is the beechnut, the yield of which in any year determines his abundance in the succeeding winter and spring. That he migrates, on a small scale at least, is a fact concerning which there can be no reasonable doubt: on any other hypothesis we are at a loss to account for the suddenness of his increase and decrease over certain areas of large extent, and find it difficult to explain why he is sometimes met with in numbers swimming our lakes and rivers, always in one direction.

As might be inferred from the boreal distribution of this animal, he is the hardiest of our squirrels. Not only does he inhabit regions where the rigors of Arctic winter are keenly felt, but, refusing to hibernate, he remains active throughout the continuance of excessive cold. When fierce storms sweep over the land he retires to his nest, to appear again with the first lull of the wind, be the temperature never so low. I have many times observed him when the thermometer ranged from thirty to forty degrees below zero Centigrade (-22 to -40 F.), but could never see that he was inconvenienced by the cold. When running upon the snow he often plunges down out of sight, tunnels a little distance, and, reappearing, shakes the snow from his head and body, whisks his tail, and skips along as lightly and with as much apparent pleasure as if returning from a bath in some rippling brook during the heat of a summer's afternoon.

He possesses the rare and philosophical accomplishment of combining work with recreation, and sets about the performance of his self-imposed tasks with such roguish humor that it is a pleasure to watch him. In marked contrast to these free and happy habits is the stealth and sullenness that characterize the actions of some of the Carnivores, notably of the family Mustelidae.

The Red Squirrel enjoys a game of "tag" even more than the average schoolboy, and one is often startled by a couple of them as they rush madly through the leaves, chasing each other hither and thither over the ground, up and down and around the trunks of trees, and in and out of hollow logs and stumps with a degree of recklessness that is astonishing to behold.

However frivolous the Red Squirrel may appear to the casual observer, he is, nevertheless, a most industrious animal. Unlike most of his associates, and many of our own species, he is not content with the enjoyment of present plenty, but takes pains to provide against a time of future need. When the summer has grown old, and the mellow days of early autumn cast a glow of color over the sumac and woodbine, the prudent Squirrel has commenced to gather the provisions for his winter's use. Impatient to make sure his store, he does not wait for the nuts to ripen and fall, but cuts the stems by which they hang, till many lie scattered on the ground below. He then descends and collects them in a heap between, or near, the roots of the trees; or, if he thinks them here too exposed, carries them directly to some hollow log or stump. Later in the season, when the mast is fully ripe and the danger from mould is past, he fills the hollows of the limbs and trees about his nest, and often secretes reserve hoards in his burrows in the earth. In the evergreen forests he lays up large supplies of cones. I have seen him, even before the middle of September, engaged in gathering those of the white pine (*Pinus strobus*). At this early date he cuts the yet green cones from the branches, and, when a sufficient number have fallen, takes them to some hiding-place to ripen for his winter's fare. He eats the little buds that may be found scattered sparingly along the small branches of the spruce, and, in order to obtain them easily, bites off the terminal twigs and drags them back where the limb is large enough to allow him to sit comfortably on his haunches while feeding. Under single trees, both in the great forest and on our own lawn, I have found enough twigs to fill a bushel basket. The injury thus done is sometimes very extensive.

He is fond of a variety of fruits and sometimes commits great havoc in the apple orchard. From his liking for mushrooms some would consider him an epicure, but in whatever light we regard this taste, it is a droll spectacle to see him drag a large "toadstool" to one of his storehouses. If the "umbrella" happens to catch on some stick or log and is broken from the stem, as is frequently the case, he is pretty sure to scold and sputter for a while, and then take the pieces separately to their destination. . . .

The Red Squirrel is a good swimmer, swimming rapidly and with much of the head, back, and tail out of water. . . . June 28th, 1878, while rowing on Brantingham Lake, in Lewis County, I saw a Red Squirrel swimming about midway between "the Point" and the main shore opposite. He was moving toward the Point, and, as I reached him, climbed up on the oar, ran over my back and legs, then along the gunwale, jumping ahead from the bow in the direction toward which he was swimming when first seen. On overtaking him he again came aboard and jumped ahead as before. This was done a number of times, the Squirrel gaining each time two or three boat's lengths, till finally he succeeded in reaching the shore. I have repeatedly been told by hunters and guides that they occasionally meet these Squirrels swimming various lakes and rivers in the Wilderness, and James Higby tells me that in June, 1877, he saw as many as fifty crossing Big Moose Lake, and that they were all headed the same way—to the north.

A FAREWELL ON UPPER AUSABLE LAKE   J. H. TwicHELL

Among my treasured memorabilia is the photograph of a group of which President Porter [Noah Porter, president of Yale University] is the central figure. The date of the picture is 1875; the scene, a camp on the Upper Ausable, loveliest of the Adirondack lakes. The party of fifteen that appear with him in it is com-

posed of men, women, young children, and guides—all his friends.
He stands forward in the midst, dressed for the woods, flannel-
shirted, without a coat, holding a gun sportively put into his hand
by one of us while the camera was being adjusted, the amused smile
with which he had permitted such an absurd misrepresentation of
his taste and practice still lingering on his scholarly, benignant
face. . . .

His pedestrian powers, in the period of his summerings in the
Adirondacks, were extraordinary for one of his age. Year after
year he explored the wilderness into which Keene Valley projects,
with an ever fresh ardor. One of his luxuries was to conduct a party
of friends to see some attraction—view, or rock, or cascade, or
tree—which he had discovered. With what zest and youthful exhilaration would he lead such an expedition! Not an angler himself,
he would follow another who was fishing a mountain brook, all
day long, occupied with the endless succession of objects of interest
and delight that his progress would bring in his way. A mountain
lake afforded him inexhaustible resources of enjoyment. . . .

I have heard Melville Trumbull, the guide who was most with
him in the woods, and whom I name in accordance with what I am
sure would be Dr. Porter's wish, relate the manner of his farewell
to the Upper Ausable Lake, already mentioned, his favorite haunt,
on which he had spent many a happy week, with which, one might
say, he was on terms of the tenderest living sympathy. It was in the
course of the vacation which his consciousness of declining strength
had warned him would probably be his last in the Adirondacks. He
had gone with Trumbull to the lake to pass two or three days there
in camp and have one more look at a place so dear. The morning
he was to return to the Valley, when everything was made ready
to start, he bade Trumbull leave the luggage where it was for a
while and row him out into the lake. Midway between the shores
he caused the boat to stop. A long time he sat there, turning this
way and that, bending his eyes earnestly, steadfastly, but without
speaking, on the views around—the Gothic Range, the cone of
Haystack, the encircling forest. Then he directed the guide to take
him near and along the shore. As they moved slowly on, by one
and another familiar spot, Trumbull saw that the Doctor's eyes

were filled with tears and perceived that it was a leave-taking. "I never in my life had anything make me feel so bad," he said in telling the story. So they passed around the circuit of the lake, the silence between them hardly broken by a word, the Doctor parting with all as one would part with a friend he might never see again, the guide stealing furtive glances of sympathy at him.

PHILOSOPHER'S HOLIDAY
WILLIAM JAMES

To his wife. Keene Valley, July 9, 1898. I have had an eventful 24 hours, and my hands are so stiff after it that my fingers can hardly hold the pen. I left, as I informed you by postcard, the Lodge [Adirondak Loj at Heart Lake] at seven, and five hours of walking brought us to the top of Marcy—I carrying 18 lbs. of weight in my pack. As usual, I met two Cambridge acquaintances on the mountain top—"Appalachians" from Beede's. At four, hearing an axe below, I went down (an hour's walk) to Panther Lodge Camp, and there found Charles and Pauline Goldmark, Waldo Adler and another schoolboy, and two Bryn Mawr girls—the girls all dressed in boys' breeches, and cutaneously desecrated in the extreme from seven of them having been camping without a male on Loon Lake to the north of this. My guide had to serve for the party, and quite unexpectedly to me the night turned out one of the most memorable of all my memorable experiences. I was in a wakeful mood before starting, having been awake since three, and I may have slept a little during this night; but I was not aware of sleeping at all. My companions, except Waldo Adler, were all motionless. The guide had got a magnificent provision of firewood, the sky swept itself clear of every trace of cloud or vapor, the wind entirely ceased, so that the fire-smoke rose straight up to heaven.

The temperature was perfect either inside or outside the cabin, the moon rose and hung above the scene before midnight, leaving only a few of the larger stars visible, and I got into a state of spiritual alertness of the most vital description. The influences of Nature, the wholesomeness of the people round me, especially the good Pauline, the thought of you and the children, dear Harry on the wave, the problem of the Edinburgh lectures, all fermented within me till it became a regular Walpurgis Nacht. I spent a good deal of it in the woods, where the streaming moonlight lit up things in a magical checkered play, and it seemed as if the Gods of all the na-ture-mythologies were holding an indescribable meeting in my breast with the moral Gods of the inner life. The two kinds of Gods have nothing in common—the Edinburgh lectures made quite a hitch ahead. The intense significance of some sort, of the whole scene, if one could only *tell* the significance; the intense inhuman remoteness of its inner life, and yet the intense *appeal* of it; its ever-lasting freshness and its immemorial antiquity and decay; its utter Americanism, and every sort of patriotic suggestiveness, and you, and my relation to you part and parcel of it all, and beaten up with it, so that memory and sensation all whirled inexplicably together; it was indeed worth coming for, and worth repeating year by year, if repetition could only procure what in its nature I suppose must be all unplanned for and unexpected. It was one of the happiest lonesome nights of my existence, and I understand now what a poet is. He is a person who can feel the immense complexity of in-fluences that I felt, and make some partial tracks in them for verbal statement. In point of fact, I can't find a single word for all that significance, and don't know what it was significant of, so there it remains, a mere boulder of *impression*. Doubtless in more ways than one, though, things in the Edinburgh lectures will be traceable to it.

In the morning at six, I shouldered my undiminished pack and went up Marcy, ahead of the party, who arrived half an hour later, and we got in here at eight [p.m.] after 10½ hours of the solidest walking I ever made, and I, I think, more fatigued than I have been after any walk. We plunged down Marcy, and up Bason Mountain [Basin], led by C. Goldmark, who had, with Mr. White, blazed a trail the year before; then down again, away down, and up the Gothics, not counting a third down-and-up over an intermediate spur. It was the steepest sort of work, and, as one looked from the summits, seemed sheer impossible, but the girls kept up splendidly, and were all fresher than I. It was true that they had slept like logs all night, whereas I was "on my nerves." I lost my Norfolk jacket at the last third of the course—high time to say good-bye to that possession—and staggered up to the Putnams [the camp in Keene Valley bought from Smith Beede by Charles and James Putnam, Henry Bowditch, and James in 1877] to find Hatty Shaw taking me for a tramp. Not a soul was there, but everything spotless and ready for the arrival today. I got a bath at Bowditch's bath-house, slept in my old room, and slept soundly and well, and save for the unwashable staining of my hands and a certain stiffness of my thighs, am entirely rested and well.

WINSLOW HOMER IN THE ADIRONDACKS JAMES FOSBURGH

When Homer first went to the Adirondacks, the land was a wilderness which suited well the then popular concept of the "forest primeval." At that time, he was still doing illustrations for *Harper's Weekly,* and his earliest Adirondack pictures were for such periodicals, reflecting his years of training and experience as a reporter—notably, of course, of Civil War scenes. His earliest Adirondack paintings are the literal reports of a trained and highly competent reporter. Homer's journalistic training was to serve him well and he made good use of it all his life. Even in his mature work, in which mood and selection take charge, the acuteness of the reporter's eye almost certainly accounts for the selection of the precise fact which would both validate and enhance the mood.

In his own day, this quality in his work was called "originality"; perhaps "freshness" or "acuteness of vision" would be more accurate.

Nonetheless, the first aspect of his work that comes to mind is its extraordinary originality. This is easy to overlook now that time has made us very familiar with his pictures, although it was noted during his lifetime, and by present-day critics as well. Kenyon Cox once wrote: "Homer was always making the most unexpected observations and painting things that were not only not painted till then but apparently unseen by anyone else."

"Homer's Adirondack phase was a new departure in American water-color painting," Lloyd Goodrich points out. "Up to this time most work in this medium had been in the old style of finished representation, even in the hands of progressive artists, like Inness, Martin, LaFarge and Eakins. Nothing like the freedom and brilliancy of these works has been seen before in this country."

It is perhaps possible to attribute these qualities to outside influences, but I am inclined to think they were more the product of an original and extremely personal approach to his subjects.

Winslow Homer was not, of course, the first to paint the Adirondacks. Artists of the Hudson River School had been there before and others were to follow. Such men as Jasper Cropsey, J. F. Kensett, Asher B. Durand and Homer Martin had all painted in the Adirondacks. The works of these men, almost without exception, have qualities in common. They painted panoramic pictures. Kensett's view, *Lake George*, is an excellent example. All these artists were *painters of views*, and they sought these out, making expeditions to the Catskills, the White Mountains and the Adirondacks, in search of suitable material to illustrate their commonly held romantic vision of nature.

The vision itself was based on a number of things. Primarily, they were all part of an international romantic movement, and their attitude toward nature was that of the American Transcendentalist poets and writers. The influence of Emerson is apparent in all their works. . . .

This certainly was not true of Homer. To the best of my knowledge, he never painted a "panoramic" landscape, and when he did paint views, they were specific and endowed with a special mood and meaning peculiarly their own. He painted details of the Adirondacks and peopled his pictures with figures that emphasize the special relationship of man to nature that moved him and motivated his work. Not only did he notice, as Kenyon Cox pointed out, details of landscape that never had been seen before, but he chose to depict details that illustrated the specific qualities of landscape that were meaningful to him: moods of climate, weather, time of day, atmospheric effect. He would wait days for the precise light he wanted to paint, in order to make his very personal statement. The dominant mood in the Adirondack pictures is one of quiet, of stillness, remoteness and solitude. He seems to have been preoccupied with the loneliness of the human spirit, particularly in natural surroundings, and this gives even his most realistic paintings a larger meaning. He felt this solitude strongly; he was a lonely man and probably by choice, and his observations were characterized by objectivity and impersonality. Certainly his concept of the natural world was a far cry from the romanticized and benevolent one of Emerson and the Transcendentalists.

Some account of life in the Adirondacks, from the 1870s until Winslow Homer's last visit in 1908, will suggest the attraction this landscape and this life must have held for him. I have been unable to ascertain the dates and lengths of his stays in Keene Valley, the first place there he visited, except that he was surely there in 1876, when the large oil *The Two Guides*, now in the Clark Institute in Williamstown, Mass., was painted. It is even possible to identify the figures. A fellow painter, Roswell Shurtleff, has written that the older man was a locally famous character known as "Old Mountain" Phelps and the younger, one Monroe Holt.

Fortunately, there is much more information about his life in what is still the North Woods Club, near Minerva, New York, of which Homer was a charter member, and where he painted most of his Adirondack watercolors. Homer first went to this remote spot in 1870, with two fellow painters, Eliphalet Terry and John Fitch. At that time it was still no more than a clearing in the wilderness, with one farm on it belonging to a family named Baker, who had settled there in 1854. In 1859 Terry painted a picture of the clearing. The two main sources of information about the place and Homer's visits there are Terry's letters to the Bakers' daughter, Juliette, and the diary that Juliette kept from 1865 until 1886 (all still preserved). After 1886—the year land was officially purchased to found the North Woods Club—the entries of Homer's visits in the Club register, all in his own handwriting, provide a record of the times he spent there. The last one, dated June 25, 1908, and written in a quavering hand—he had suffered a stroke earlier that year—mentions that he had shot a bear. Two Homer drawings (both, apparently, done with a steady hand) in possession of the North Woods Club commemorate this exploit. These are probably the last pictures Homer did in the Adirondacks. He died two years later, on September 29, 1910, in Prout's Neck, Maine.

From a letter of Terry's, we know that Homer first visited the Baker farm in September, 1870. In that year he published the woodcut *Trapping in the Adirondacks* in the magazine *Every Saturday*. Terry wrote Juliette a letter about this, referring to the picture of Rufus Wallace and "Charlie" (who was probably Charlie Lancashire, a friend of the Bakers), and said that Homer would send her a copy. Wallace figures in a number of Homer's later pictures along with a younger man, Mike "Farmer" Flynn.

So began the artist's life in the Adirondacks, which was to go on intermittently for the next thirty-eight years. For an account of this life, the sources are again Terry's letters and Juliette's diary. Terry wrote an itinerary of the trip from New York City. They first took the Hudson River night boat to Albany; then the train to the "stop," which was apparently Saratoga; then, the Lake George stagecoach as far as Chestertown. . . .

The life that greeted him when he arrived is vividly described in Juliette's diary. It was one of extraordinary hardship. These people lived off virtually nothing but their rugged land; spring came late and winter early, as they still do, and in the short summer season they worked from dawn until dusk. Everything was utilized. Hay fed the livestock and provided stuffing for bed ticks. Wool was spun, woven and made into clothing; socks and mittens were knitted for sale to obtain the tiny amounts of cash needed to purchase those items they could not provide for themselves. The sugar they used was boiled down from the sap of forest maples.

Every berry was picked and most were preserved. Finally of course, there were the fish and game, the main supply of sustenance.

This way of life that Homer sought out for so many years is important to an understanding of his work. Many writers have emphasized that Homer was a sportsman. No doubt he was to an extent, but it is important to remember that the hunters and fishermen in his pictures are not sportsmen, but men who lived in this wilderness, and who hunted and fished to provide themselves with enough to eat. Their lives, in short, depended on their skill. . . . This Homer understood. He shared their lives. His relationship with them, and feeling for them, was very much the same as his understanding of and concern for the Maine fishermen with whom he associated—virtually to the exclusion of everyone else—at Prout's Neck, in the 1880s and 1890s.

Throughout Homer's life, the subject of his paintings is man in his environment: the relationship between man and nature. But there is an easily recognizable development in his understanding and vision. His early work is far more literal than that of the later years. . . .

Well before the 1890s, Homer's vision had gained in depth. Through his participation in the life of the wilderness and association with its people, and the hardships and the beauties of both, he seems to have become increasingly preoccupied with the world of nature itself, its moods, benign and threatening, sinister and beautiful. As this happened, the figures in his pictures became increasingly anonymous. They are focal points in the paintings, employed to emphasize a mood. Later, they disappear altogether and the landscape, once so literally represented, is altered and rearranged imaginatively to the same end. However, it would be wrong to think that these alterations and rearrangements were dictated solely by the exigencies of pictorial composition. Homer was first and last preoccupied with the world about him.

This world was to him both mysterious and beautiful, and could as well be cruel and, at times, incomprehensible. He observed it closely and set down on paper or canvas his observations with the accuracy and truth of an artist—that is, the accuracy and truth of the imagination. His powers of observations were at once extraordinary and direct, but not especially intellectual. He does not seem to have read very much, and his infrequent pronouncements on his art tend to be inarticulate and confused. He seems to have lived in a solitary world of feeling, observing and setting-down.

I have said earlier that the dominant mood of Homer's pictures is one of quiet, of stillness, remoteness and solitude. Even a picture of the leap of a trout seems only to accentuate the enveloping silence: the tumult of a waterfall seems muted by the hush of the forest through which it tumbles.

Great art is sometimes said to be the expression of the universal in terms of the particular. The particulars Homer loved and painted so well are in all these pictures. He captured perfectly the movement of wild things, the arabesque of a fly cast, the awkward posture of a hunting dog balanced on a log or a deer straddled across a fallen tree trunk, drinking. This latter, a watercolor, is one of his most striking achievements. Homer could scarcely have come very close to this shy creature, but the watercolor is almost a close-up, and captures all the nervous tension of the animal. There is the backward glance of the eye always on the alert for danger, even while the animal is intent on quenching its thirst, the ears that seem almost to twitch as they listen and the ungainly but characteristic posture, here somehow made graceful—and for those who deplore Homer's realism, there are strokes of pure cerulean blue in the animal's coat.

Homer could paint equally well and endow with mood—often one of prevailing sadness—the dark waters of the Adirondack pond broken by the silvery wake of a canoe, the torrent of a swollen brook in spring flood, the overcast skies of a fisherman's perfect day, the fisherman himself, and the hunter pausing to rest, silhouetted against the blue distance of receding hills. . . . This vision developed and deepened as his observation gained in intensity and acuteness. Since this vision was novel and personal, it also determined his technical methods, which were the result of personal necessity, rather than of artistic or philosophical doctrine, or outside influence. His response to life in the Adirondacks created within him this necessity, just as did his response to life in Maine or the Bahamas. His stylistic development was the result of his maturing responses to the different worlds in which he moved.

TO A WATERFOWL
Martha Reben

One still morning toward the middle of July when the shores were mirrored in the most magical and delicate and illusory blending of foliage and water, a slight distortion in the reflection over near the far shore brought the loons to my attention. What I saw sent me hurrying for the binocular.

When I focused the glass I found that the two dots on the water beside the older birds were baby loons. The new additions to the family looked so unbelievably tiny, that when I thought of the turtles, coons, minks, otters, hawks, and other enemies by which they were surrounded, I wouldn't have given a nickel for their chances of living long enough to become the size of their parents.

Almost from the day they were hatched, the babies would dive and stay under water a disturbingly long time. While I stood on shore and worried for fear they had been eaten by a big fish or turtle, their mother sat on the water as complacently as a young matron sitting on a park bench with her children romping about her.

Insofar as I knew, except when they were nesting, these waddlers, with their short legs set far back on their bodies to act as propellers, spent practically all their lives on the water, and when they did fly, they hurled themselves through the air on their narrow wings (they have been clocked at sixty miles an hour) intent only on finding another body of water to light on. If, in bad judgment, they choose one that is too small for them to take off from (loons must run a long distance on the water before they can get into the air), they are trapped, and freeze or starve to death when cold weather sets in.

They even slept on the water, and I was curious, therefore, to know how the mother brooded her young (which left the nest soon after they were hatched), since all young birds need lots of warmth and rest.

One day, to my delight, I found out. I was watching the old loon through the binocular, and I saw that she was carrying both chicks on her back, one cuddled under each wing. Now and then a tiny head would rise above the upper side of her wing to look around. Patiently the mother sat on the water, barely moving her feet, glancing back over her shoulder from time to time to make sure the youngsters were taking their naps, apparently completely at peace with the disordered world around her. Loons are gentle and solicitous, if unsentimental parents, brooding, feeding, and defending their young with zest and devotion.

I saw one chick leave the protection of her wing, walk down her back and lean out over her tail and get himself a drink. His thirst quenched, he hurried back to bed, where it was warm.

Both parents shared in feeding their young, and in this, as in everything else they did, they seemed to take an almost frivolous enjoyment. All wild animals experience a joy in living that civilized man can only envy.

Whenever the old birds caught a fish, the young would paddle with anticipatory speed toward them, calling in tiny, bell-like voices, a sound so subtle and wild it required a keen ear to hear it. Often they came in so close I could see the glistening fish passed from one bill to the other, a ritual that was accomplished so smoothly that one had to have a sharp eye to see it. Sometimes they crippled small fish with their strong, serrated bills, then released them so the young ones could have the fun of catching them, an effective way of teaching them to capture their own food.

I don't know how much untaught wisdom these young, web-footed creatures were born with, but their schooling started early and was both ancient and progressive. My impression was that the parents, besides teaching them to fish, drilled them frequently to respond to warning signals. Even our boat leaving the landing (harmless though they knew it to be) was sometimes used as an excuse to send the young loons into hiding, where they were expected to remain until the parents gave the "all clear" signal. These drills operated on the honor system (the parents followed our boat and called directions to the young, which were out of sight), and the young waterfowl learned to obey promptly. They had to, if they wanted to stay alive. It is the duckling that stops to look behind it that never grows up. The reason almost all wild things panic so easily is that they have to move first and consider afterward. With them flight takes the place of thought.

One afternoon I heard the loons crying havoc again. I went out and called to them, and their shrill replies confirmed that another of the welter of workaday disasters was befalling them.

When I hurried down to the water's edge I saw an eagle fly out of a big pine. It circled the pond, flying low over the loons, helplessly exposed out in the middle. They dived, every time it went over them, then popped right back up to call warnings to the babies, which were nowhere in sight.

I got in the canoe and quickly paddled out to them, because if the babies were trying to avoid the eagle by diving, too, I thought they would soon be exhausted. As soon as it saw me, the eagle hid among the branches of a pine farther down the pond. . . .

One morning a delegation of visiting loons appeared on the pond, and this caused a lot of excitement among the local residents. They enjoyed a regular beanfeast, running on the water as if competing with each other, dipping bills convivially one minute, mocking and jeering each other the next. The parents lured the strangers well away from their young, but whether they constituted a real threat or were being used for drill purposes, I couldn't decide, as the parents called out almost continually to their offspring to remain hidden. Young loons, like their parents, can keep very low in the water when they want to, and this they did until the strangers departed and the older birds gave the all-clear signal.

As the young loons grew bigger and less vulnerable, the parents, who seemed to find family life somewhat confining to their freedom-loving and solitary natures, encouraged them to fend for themselves, going off (perhaps for a change of scene as well as to find better fishing waters) for longer and longer stretches of time.

We were returning to camp one evening when my companion broke the even stroke of his paddle. "Listen! What was that?" he asked.

The sun had already set but there were a few bright bars in the western sky. As I listened to the plaintive sound I was suddenly transported back to another night, several years earlier, when we had followed the same sound in the darkness and fog. Now I discovered that it was being made by the young loons, whose parents had gone off somewhere and left them. Darkness was coming on, and, surrounded by enemies, they were lonely and frightened and probably hungry, too, and they were *mewing like kittens*.

One night when their parents seemed to have gone off, we had the first severe thunderstorm of the season and it was a humdinger. The lightning flashed almost continually, illuminating the pond one moment, plunging it into complete darkness the next. It was followed by explosive, earth-shaking crashes of thunder, and the wind came in angry squalls which stirred the little pond into whitecaps. Big trees at opposite ends of the pond were struck with a rending and splintering of wood, as their trunks were blasted into kindling.

The rain fell at last, in such torrents that by morning the water in the pond had risen five inches.

I was distressed when I thought of the young loons out there alone in that tempest. I could imagine that for young animals that had never experienced a storm, and especially for those that had to spend the night unprotected on the water, it must have been terrifying.

It was barely daylight when I went down and stood at the water's edge. There was a peculiar orange glow in the sky and on the fog.

The young loons swam in toward the landing looking like a couple of whipped puppies. It was evident that their fears had been deeply stirred. I spoke to them gently, and with beguiling trust they came in closer than they ever had before. As I talked, they gave me close attention (young loons' eyes are brown, not red), with that wonderful responsiveness all birds, even the wildest, show, and for a few moments, at least, we were fully in tune with each other in one of the memorably happy moments of that summer.

Once it began to rain it didn't seem to know when to stop, and one day, when the pond was hobnailed with rain drops, I was watching the young loons' not very successful efforts at fishing, when my attention was drawn to a wedge-shaped stick poking up out of the water. I had looked at this shoreline so many times that every stub and stick and log was etched on my memory as on a film, and my eyes picked that stick out at once from all the others. I kept staring at it, but not until it submerged and then reappeared did I realize I was seeing the wicked-looking head of a big turtle. . . .

It was midmorning and the young loons were not fishing, just playing around aimlessly as they sometimes did, waiting for their wings to grow strong enough for them to join their parents in flight. The older birds had probably been back earlier to feed them.

They continued to swim toward the turtle which was lurking under the end of the log. I tried throwing sticks in the water, but the young loons only looked surprised at such hostility and hardly changed their course. The turtle was too busy craftily maneuvering and watching the young birds to pay any attention to me. Perhaps he knew he was too far out for me to reach him.

Closer and closer the young loons swam. I hurried along the shore, picking up a couple of stones and throwing them toward the log. I was gratified to see the tip of the turtle's nose disappear. But then, alarmingly, a few seconds later, so did one of the loons. Sometimes, even when they weren't fishing, they would dive under an outjutting log and come up on the other side rather than swim around it. I didn't know, now, whether that was what had happened or whether the turtle had clamped its jaws onto one of its legs and pulled it under.

The other loon changed its course and began swimming out into the middle of the pond, looking back over its shoulder from time to time. I watched and watched with growing anxiety for the reappearance of the first, and when it didn't surface I kept telling myself that it had swum a long way under water and come up beyond the curve in the shoreline. Both young birds had come unscathed through so many dangers, I suppose I had begun to believe them almost invulnerable.

Had it been a lesser breed of bird I'd have given up looking for it sooner than I did. Finally, though, I had sadly to accept the fact that there would be only one young loon this year (if his luck held) to join the fall migration.

Right up until the first week in October I saw one or another of the parents return to see how their remaining offspring was faring. Apparently until they are able to fly (and perhaps for some time afterward) the parents have a feeling of responsibility toward their young. Anyway, when the loonlet followed its parent around and mewed and teased to be fed, the older loons still fed it.

Like all waterfowl that migrate, our young loon grew remarkably fast. It was still brown, and it did not, except for its bill which was growing long and sharp, much resemble a loon. It would not grow its handsome black-and-white plumage until it was at least two years old, and it would lose it again each winter.

Now, when it hung around camp it gave evidence of being almost as hungry for companionship as it was for food. Like all animals, it lived entirely in the present moment and it had no way of knowing it would not be grounded here for the rest of its life. When I called to it, it hunched its shoulders up around its ears and looked back at me almost coyly, rising on the water and flapping its wings in a deliberate, pleased kind of way at being noticed. Was it possible it would survive to return to the pond another year? I asked myself. Or would it succumb to a danger greater than any it had faced so far, once it took to the air? Watching it, I felt the sorrow I often felt for all things tameless and free that live short lives.

Then, one windless morning in late fall, when the air around the pond was spiced with the odor of fallen leaves, wild aster, and ripening cattails and there was a soft, lilac haze on the distant hills, I saw what I think few persons have the luck to see. I was sitting on the shore, regretting that soon, now, we should have to leave the pond, when I saw a true conquest of space as my young loon took to the air for the first time.

For weeks it had been running on the water, as all loons must to take off, fanning the air with its narrow wings, never quite able, or perhaps not daring, to trust itself to the air, yet eager to follow the others. But this morning when it revved its propellers, it found itself suddenly airborne. It was not very high, it is true, but its feet were no longer dragging in the water.

Its uncertain flight took it around and around in a widening circle, back curved, neck drooping, big feet trailing out behind. Each circle took it a little farther above the pond, a little higher in the air, above the woods and water, higher and still higher, all the earth beneath it. It looked like a duck flying. Suddenly, from a full heart, its voice rang out clear and wild and joyous.

When it flew over me I called to it, and it answered in the same triumphant voice, though up until today when it had tried to call like a mature loon it had succeeded only in making what sounded like a shriek of rage, startling even to itself. It wasn't flying easily, but it was making up in intensity for what it lacked in skill. It reminded me of when I learned to skate, how I leaned forward on the wind, skating faster and faster, for fear that if I slowed down I should fall.

It circled the pond around and around, swinging joyously between earth and sky, then it began coming down, not without fear and a sharp cry of distress at the awfulness of having to descend from such a dizzying height on its narrow wings, dropping, plunging, sliding on its breast, until it pulled its feet under it in an awkward, three-point loon landing.

The next day when I looked for it, it was gone, its long journey into the unknown begun—and I and the pond were the lonelier for it.

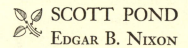

SCOTT POND
Edgar B. Nixon

The Armchair Mountaineer had not seen Scott Pond since his first visit twenty years before. . . . The A. M. had often spoken of this walk to his son (now fourteen), and last August there was finally a day when the boy was willing to climb something other than a "Forty-Sixer" [one of the forty-six peaks in the Adirondacks of four thousand feet and higher]. To avoid the blowdowns, they decided to make both ascent and descent by way of the ravine. This the A. M. found to be as wild and as mysterious as he remembered it from twenty years before. As they began their climb he even thought he remembered individual rocks and cliffs, but he realized this was most unlikely.

The day was warm and there was a threat of thunder storms in the atmosphere; nevertheless, the scramble up the rocks was exhilarating. The boy flung himself at difficult places with more abandon than was wise, but after a few foot-wettings he went more cautiously. His father climbed with care, making sure he had adequate footing. The view of the MacIntyres, framed in the walls of the gorge, was thrilling and impressive, and they were able roughly to gauge their progress up the mountain by their relation to the great ridge.

Absorbed in the climbing and the scenery and in recollections of the former ascent, the A. M. lost track of time, and his first glimpse of the dam, still far up the ravine, was completely unexpected. He suppressed an impulse to call the boy's attention to it and waited to see him discover it for himself. But the boy, similarly engrossed in picking his way back and forth across the stream and up the rocks, did not look up for a long time. When he did, the old dam was there plain enough, a few hundred yards ahead. He laughed with delight and, moving far more rapidly than his father dared, made his way to the head of the ravine and clambered to the top of the dam. Here the wide planked spillway was partly intact.

They had their lunch on the spillway, the rough old planks pleasantly warm and a sudden refreshing breeze for a while turning aside the noontime heat. With mountains all about them and the little blue wilderness lake at their feet, they were silent and content. After they had eaten, they explored the shores of the pond, going counter-clockwise. There was less water in the pond than there had been on the first visit, and with care it was possible to walk on the flat, boggy, sedge-grown banks. The old beaver house was still there, but there was no sign of any inhabitants. The water's edge was closely trodden with the hoof-prints of deer; this must be for them a most secure watering place. Even allowing for prints made by the same animal, the size of the herd was impressive.

The boy wondered if the water was drinkable.

"Of course," said his father, "but you will find it warm and it will have a faintly bitter taste." (He remembered this from the other time.) The boy found that this was so. Water from the little streams that flowed into the pond they found to be somewhat less warm and less tannic in flavor; not exactly unpleasant but not particularly refreshing. On the south side of the pond blueberries grew from the rocky banks to an unbelievable bigness; they had never seen such large ones. They ate until they wanted no more but made no noticeable impression on the huge quantity there. After the blueberry place, the banks became marshy again. Nowhere did they see footprints other than their own; they were (the boy said) Robinson Crusoes on a mountain. Other visitors that summer may have been there, but they saw no sign of them.

At their spillway luncheon place they recovered their packs and then lingered a while, loath to leave the quiet wilderness pond and surrounding forest. The area had an odd feeling of being somehow out of space and time. They decided that some summer they would bring their sleeping bags and spend the night on the spillway; perhaps they would see the evening gathering of the deer. They could also try to find Lost Pond and climb to Wallface Pond.

CABIN VERSUS CITY
Anne LaBastille

My dream had come true. I had spent ten years in a log cabin in the woods, with time away only to do the necessary course work and research for a doctorate, and to carry out occasional short-term consulting and writing assignments for my livelihood.

I had come to know the land, trees, water, and wildlife intimately. Here was my home.

Now I, too, had received a tempting offer. It offered me a highly paid position with a prestigious Washington conservation organization for the winter. Coming so soon after my breakup with Nick, I decided to accept. The change would help me get over my heartache; nevertheless, I faced the move from cabin to city with mixed emotions. This would be the first time since I was born in New York City that I would spend more than a week or two in a metropolis.

On a brisk November day, just before freeze-up, I carried several boxes of books, clothes, files, linens, and kitchen utensils out by boat, loaded them in the truck, and together with Pitzi, started on the 500-mile drive to our nation's capital. Little did I realize that this trip was to introduce the greatest contrast I'd ever known in my life, a culture shock more acute than any experienced in Central or South America, India, or the Caribbean. . . .

Fortunately, I didn't have to stay in Washington more than eight months. One happy day in June, I laid a completed report on my office director's desk, received a letter of commendation, said goodby to my colleagues, and packed up the truck. Then Pitzi and I headed north to where northern lights would be playing softly above the forests, replacing neon lights and their glow over the city. North to cloud-splitting peaks, streams brown as bock beer, sunny beaver meadows, sombre spruce forests, trout-blessed rivers, and fragrant balsam flats.

The cabin never had seemed so beautiful. I found my energy returning, my responses to the environment quickening, my reflexes sharpening, my muscles hardening, and my body slimming again. Packing away my heels, I stretched my toes luxuriously again in moccasins and lumberjack boots. Corns which had appeared in Washington, gradually diminished. My streak of aggressive driving passed. I slept well. How contenting to spend summer mornings again at my desk or on the sun deck, writing, typing, answering correspondence, then dashing into the lake for a swim. How relaxing to rock by the crackling Franklin stove, reading or gazing out the picture windows at an autumn stained-glass sunset. How comforting to burrow into the soft blankets of my sleeping loft on those awesome, frigid winter nights. And how inspiring to wake at dawn to the smell of spring and the trill of peepers.

Yet to be completely honest, my sojourn in the city had been profitable. I came home flushed with success, having done a good job, earned a handsome salary, and made excellent contacts. Although I knew that I could never stand to live in a city again, I also realized that a small connection with it had become necessary to bring a balance into my life. The city (regardless which one it is) *does* provide a certain degree of sophistication and intellectualism. It offers the challenge of professional matters. It throws new and interesting people in one's path. There is a dynamic and an energy in cities which is diametric to the life-forces of the forest.

Still the cabin is the wellspring, the source, the hub of my existence. It gives me tranquility, a closeness to nature and wildlife, good health and fitness, a sense of security, the opportunity for resourcefulness, reflection, and creative thinking. Yet my existence here has not been, and never will be, idyllic. Nature is too demanding for that. It requires a constant response to the environment. I must adapt to its changes—the seasons, the vagaries of weather, wear and tear on house and land, the physical demands on my body, the sensuous pulls on my senses. Despite these demands, I share a feeling of continuity, contentment, and oneness with the natural world, with life itself, in my surroundings of tall pines, clear lakes, flying squirrels, trailless peaks, shy deer, clean air, bullfrogs, black flies, and trilliums.

Sometimes at night when a problem has me turning and twisting in the silent sleeping loft, I get up, wake the dog, and glide onto the lake in my guideboat. Slipping over the star-strewn surface of Black Bear Lake, I'm gradually imbued with the ordered goodness of our earth. Its gentle, implacable push toward balance, regularity, homeostasis. This seeps into my soul as surely as sphagnum moss absorbs water. Surely the entire universe must be operating in this way.

True, some trees get blown over by storms; some stars burn out;

some people encounter crippling misfortunes of health or finances. But the forest remains; the skies keep twinkling; and human beings keep striving.

Drifting about under the night heavens, I think and hope that I can weather the storms which will blow my way. And that these trials will give me depth and stature so that in old age I can be like my big white pines—dignified, lending beauty to the surroundings, and lifting their heads with strength and serenity to both sun and storms, snowflakes and swallows.

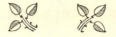

Notes on Writers

The Roman numerals indicate sections of the text; "Obs" stands for the prologue, "Observations."

ABBOTT, HENRY, 1850-1943. An inventor and watchmaker in New York City, he spent his summers for over fifty years at Deerland Lodge on Long Lake and later at his own camp on South Pond. Each year from 1914 to 1932 he wrote a personal narrative of his observations and adventures in the woods with his full-time guide, Bige Smith; printed it privately in a booklet with a cover reproducing a photograph of birch bark and sent copies to his friends as Christmas greetings. These "Birch Bark Books" were exceedingly rare collectors' items till 1980, when Harbor Hill Books of Harrison, N.Y., published a one-volume compilation entitled *The Birch Bark Books of Henry Abbott*, with an introduction by Vincent Engels. Abbott and Bige grew old together as companions of the woods and waters, each becoming quite deaf. A familiar breaking of the sound waves on South Pond was their shouts from separate boats while fishing. "The Purloined Trout" (V) is from the Christmas story of 1919; "Lost Pond" (VI), that of 1915.

ALLEN, ETHAN, 1739-1789. A frontier soldier, he led the Green Mountain Boys, a force of irregulars, in the capture of Fort Ticonderoga from the British. A few months later he was taken prisoner by Crown soldiers. *Narrative of Colonel Ethan Allen's Captivity*, Phila., 1779 (I).

ATHERTON, GERTRUDE, 1857-1948. A popular writer of novels and histories, she was a San Franciscan and world traveler who, widowed at thirty, went to New York to make her independent way. *The Aristocrats*, N.Y., 1901 (VII)—published anonymously "to have some fun with the critics"—is a novel of the Adirondacks in the form of the letters of a titled Englishwoman visitor.

BACHELLER, IRVING, 1859-1950. Journalist, novelist, and after-dinner speaker, he was born on a farm near Canton, N.Y.; the scenes of his early life in the North Country are the settings for many of his novels, short stories, and poems. After making a fortune on *Eben Holden,* with sales of over a million copies, he camped frequently at Big Deer Pond near Cranberry Lake with his favorite guide, Philo (Fide) Scott, the "Him" of "Him an' Me" (III), *Harper's Weekly*, Dec. 10, 1904. Bacheller redeemed the promise in the last line of the poem by sharing with Fide the fee he received from Harper's.

BOARDMAN, WILLIAM H., 1846-1914. Editor and president of the *Railroad Gazette*, he had strong interests in the Adirondacks. He was a member of the Bisby Club and president of the Adirondack League Club. Besides magazine articles on the region, he wrote a series of essays and narratives, *The Lovers of the Woods*, N.Y., 1901 (V).

BRYCE, JAMES, VISCOUNT, 1838-1922. Jurist, historian, politician, educator, he became almost an American institution as British ambassador in Washington from 1907 to 1913. He was a mountain climber and one-time president of the Alpine Club. His *American Commonwealth* was used as a textbook in this country for over thirty years. His impressions on the social relations of the sexes in America and on the Adirondacks in the essay "On Some Peculiarities of Society in America," *Cornhill Magazine,* Dec. 1872 (II), must have been formed on his first visit in 1870. The paragraph on the Adirondacks reappears virtually unchanged in his *American Commonwealth*, N.Y., 1888.

BURROUGHS, JOHN, 1837-1921. Teacher, essayist, and naturalist, he was born on a farm near Roxbury, New York; in later years he settled at West Park on the Hudson, where his cabin Slabsides and his house Riverby became a mecca for nature lovers. The most popular of American nature writers of the late nineteenth and early twentieth centuries, he was called by Henry James "a sort of reduced, but also more humorous, more available, and more sociable Thoreau." He preferred a partly tamed nature to the wilds, but his essay on an 1863 trip to the Adirondacks in *Wake-Robin*, vol. I of his *Works* (X), is charming and evocative.

CADBURY, WARDER H., 1925—. Professor of philosophy at the State University of New York at Albany and Adirondack historian, he grew up as member of the host families at Back Log Camp on Indian Lake in the Adirondacks and has a second home in that vicinity today. His knowledge of Adirondack memorabilia is encyclopedic; he has provided many leads for the compilation of this anthology. He has written many articles on Adirondack subjects. His speech on the land ethic (VIII) was given at St. Lawrence University's Fifth Conference on the Adirondack Park, 1975, and was published as part of the conference series.

CHITTENDEN, LUCIUS EUGENE, 1824-1900. Vermont lawyer, legislator, and Treasury official in Lincoln's administration, he was an ardent camper and hunter in the Adirondacks, describing some of his experiences in *Personal Reminiscences, 1840-1890*, N.Y., 1893 (III).

COLVIN, VERPLANCK, 1847-1920. Comments on this central figure in Adirondack history appear in the introduction to IX. From 1872 to 1900 he was in charge of two overlapping surveys of the wilderness. His speeches and reports drew public attention to the Adirondacks as a reservoir of natural resources and a vacation playground and gave strong support to the movement to establish a state park and forest preserve. His intimate knowledge of the region, his graphic style, and the fact that his writing is not easily accessible to the general reader perhaps justify the length of the selections here, which are from: *Twenty-fourth Annual Report of the New York State Museum of Natural History*, Albany, 1872 ("Seward," IX); *Report of the Topographical Survey of the Adirondack Wilderness . . . for 1873*, Albany, 1874 ("Dix, Nipple-top, Colvin," IX); *Seventh Annual Report of the Topographical Survey . . . to the Year 1879*, Albany, 1880 (Obs and "Gothics," "Seven Years," IX, and "The Elusive Corner," VI); R. M. L. Carson's *Peaks and People of the Adirondacks*, N.Y., 1927, and Glens Falls, 1973 ("Discovery of Lake Tear" [VI], a theretofore unpublished Ms by Colvin).

COOK, MARC, 1854-1882. Newspaper poet, writer of short stories and articles, he went to the Adirondacks in 1879 as a tubercular patient, camping out in the Paul Smiths area in summer and wintering in Saranac. His *Wilderness Cure*, N.Y., 1881 (VIII), appeared first as *Camp Lou* in *Harper's Magazine*.

COOPER, JAMES FENIMORE, 1789-1851. Naval officer, novelist, social critic, and squire of Cooperstown, he gave epic treatment to the wilderness and the frontier in the Leather-Stocking Tales, still widely read the world over. *The Last of the Mohicans*, 1826 (I), is the story of a chase amidst forest and lake scenes in the vicinity of Lake George during the French and Indian Wars. Theodore Roosevelt called Cooper's hero, Natty Bumppo (Hawkeye in the *Mohicans*), "one of the undying men of story."

CURTIS, GEORGE WILLIAM, 1824-1892. Essayist, orator, and editor, he edited *Harper's Weekly* and later *Harper's Magazine*. His wide travel in Europe conditioning his taste, he shows a bias for the "developed" landscape in a book of travel, *Lotos-Eating: A Summer Book*, N.Y., 1852 (IV).

DANA, RICHARD HENRY, JR., 1815-1882. Author, lawyer, he is best known for his *Two Years Before the Mast*. As in that account of a sea voyage in youth, so too in his narrative of getting lost in Indian Pass and stumbling on John Brown's cabin at North Elba, he surrounds the places he visits with a glow of romance: "How We Met John Brown," *Atlantic Monthly*, July, 1871 (VI).

DAWSON, GEORGE, 1813-1883. A journalist of Scottish birth, he came to the States as a child and was educated here. He edited newspapers in Rochester, Detroit, and Albany and was a noted fisherman, often visiting the North Woods. His articles are collected in *Angling Talks* and *Pleasures of Angling*, N.Y., 1876 (II).

DEMING, PHILANDER, 1829-1915. Short story writer and court stenographer, he wrote realistic fiction with poetic touches for the *Atlantic Monthly* when William Dean Howells, who encouraged him, was editor. Many of his stories concern the scenes of his youth in a community on the northern edge of the Adirondacks, where "the spiritual barrenness of the inhabitants" is often contrasted, as A. C. Ravitz says, with "the unparalleled natural beauty and freedom of the physical surroundings." He is all but forgotten today, a fact hardly deserved for some of his character vignettes (VIII) and the autobiographical "An Adirondack Neighborhood," quoted in part in X, from his volume *Adirondack Stories*, Boston, 1880.

DeSORMO, MAITLAND C., 1906—. Adirondack historian, he grew up in the Malone foothills and worked for Mrs. Chase at the Loon Lake House in his teens. After a career as high school teacher of English, speech, and drama, he returned to the North Country he loves and settled in Saranac Lake to launch a second career as lecturer and prolific writer of books and articles on aspects of Adirondack history. "Mrs. Chase" (VIII) appears in his book *The Heydays of the Adirondacks*, Saranac Lake, 1974.

DOCTOROW, E. L., 1931—. Popular novelist, he has been editor-in-chief of Dial Press, writer-in-residence at the University of California, and member of the faculty at Sarah Lawrence College. His novel *Loon Lake* (VII) is the picaresque story of a young hobo of the Depression years who is caught trespassing on a luxury camp in the Adirondacks.

DODGE, HOMER, 1887—. Physicist, educator, president emeritus of Norwich University, he is most widely known as the "Dean of American Canoeing." Born in Ogdensburg on the St. Lawrence, he became the only man in modern times to run successfully that river's Long Sault Rapids in an open canoe before they were stilled by the Seaway development. His protest that at eighty he was "falling apart" exaggerates the facts. Several years later spectators on the banks at the annual Hudson River White-Water Derby were asking one another, "Is the old man running today?" He was.

DONALDSON, ALFRED LEE, 1866-1923. Banker, historian, and poet, he gave up a banking career in New York to come, at twenty-nine, to Saranac Lake for his health. For some years he led an active life as banker and civic leader there. During the last twelve years of his life, in failing health, he devoted his energy to the writing of what is still the standard work in its field, *A History of the Adirondacks*, 2 vols., N.Y., 1921 (V), reprinted in 1963 and now available in the 1977 reprint of Harbor Hill Books, Harrison, N.Y. Although there are factual errors in Donaldson's *History*, it will not soon be superseded in charm of style, vision, and soundness of judgment. In 1924, at the instigation of Russell Carson and the Adirondack Mountain Club, Mount Donaldson in the Seward Range was named for him.

DREISER, THEODORE, 1871-1945. Novelist and social critic, he based his best known novel, *An American Tragedy*, 1925 (IV), on the trial in 1906 of Chester Gillette of Cortland, New York, on the charge of drowning his pregnant sweetheart, Grace Brown, in Big Moose Lake (Big Bittern in the novel). The forest scene selected here does more credit to Dreiser's imagination than to his powers of observation, a reversal of his customary manner.

EMERSON, RALPH WALDO, 1803-1882. Poet, philosopher, essayist, and lecturer, he had celebrated the American forest and frontier before his visit to the Adirondacks in 1858, but he had never seen real wilderness country. The camping trip on Follensby Pond in August of that year deeply impressed him, as is shown in several passages in his journals and letters, his verse portraits of fellow campers, and the long journal-poem "The Adirondacs"

(II, III). See my article "Emerson in the Adirondacks," *New York History*, July, 1958.

❧ EMMONS, EBENEZER, 1800-1863. Professor of natural sciences at Williams College, he was appointed chief geologist of the second district (Adirondacks) of the geological survey of New York in 1836. His reports, especially *Assembly Document No. 200*, 1838, on the mountains of Essex (IX) and *Geology of New-York, Part II*, 1842 (Obs), drew the attention of tourists and developers to the region.

❧ FIELD, KATE, 1838-1896. International journalist, author, lecturer, actress in New York and London for a brief period, and reformer, she was a Betty Friedan of the Victorian age. Living abroad for many years, she was a friend of Walter Savage Landor, the Brownings, George Eliot, and the Trollopes. She wrote for leading American magazines and was London correspondent of the New-York *Herald* and the New-York *Tribune*. In her last years she edited a journal in Washington called *Kate Field's Washington*. Her connection with the Adirondacks was more than casual. Along with friends, she purchased John Brown's farm near Lake Placid in order to preserve his grave. "Murray Vindicated" (II) appeared in the New-York *Daily Tribune*, August 12, 1869; the other selection in II and the one in VIII are from *The Atlantic Almanac for 1870*, an adjunct to the *Atlantic Monthly*.

❧ FISHER, LEWIS, 1899—. A nearly lifelong member of the Jordan Club, a hidden-away summer colony at the mouth of the Jordan River where it enters the Raquette, he has often wintered there as well, shoveling snow off roofs and enjoying the luxury of writing two unpublished novels exactly as he wanted them to be without giving a thought to marketability. His title book *Old Hollywood*, privately printed in 1965, was reissued in 1980 by the St. Lawrence County Historical Association, Canton, N.Y. (IX).

❧ FOSBURGH, HUGH, 1916-1976. Essayist and novelist, he was a member of the North Woods Club at Baker's Clearing, between the Upper Hudson and the Boreas rivers, where he lived year-round. His novels *The Sound of White Water* and *The Drowning-Stone* have Adirondack settings and characters. His best work is *One Man's Pleasure*, N.Y., 1960, a series of concise and vivid essays on man and nature arranged as the journal of an Adirondack year (IV, VI).

FOSBURGH, JAMES, 1910-1978. Painter, lecturer, and art critic, brother of Hugh and Pieter, he taught at the Parsons School of Design and served as chairman of a commission for selecting paintings for the White House, 1961-63. As painter he is represented in the Metropolitan Museum and the Boston Museum of Fine Arts. His essay on Winslow Homer (X) appeared in the quarterly *Portfolio*, Winter 1963 (an earlier version was the introduction to the Adirondack Museum's *Winslow Homer in the Adirondacks*, 1959).

FOSBURGH, PIETER W., 1915-1978. Journalist, editor of the *New York State Conservationist*, he too was a member of the North Woods Club. Speaking of her brothers, James, Pieter, and Hugh, Mrs. Evan Wilson says, "They were three great fellows, each in his own way." "The Goyd" appeared in the NYS *Conservationist* for Oct.-Nov. 1949 under the title "Guides and Guiding."

FOSTER, JEANNE ROBERT, 1884-1970. Poet, literary editor of the *Review of Reviews*, agent of the art collector John Quinn, and artists' model, she was a celebrated beauty in international art and literary circles in the early part of the century. In later life she lived in Schenectady, where she became a civic leader. Her childhood and youth were spent in the Adirondack county of Warren, where her father was a lumberman. *Neighbors of Yesterday*, Boston, 1916; Schenectady 1963, is a volume of poems about real characters she had known in and near Johnsburg, where she was born (VIII).

GILBORN, CRAIG, 1934—. Museum director and critic of the arts and crafts, he has been director of the Adirondack Museum at

Blue Mountain Lake since 1972. His *Durant*, Sylvan Beach, N.Y., 1981, is the story of William West Durant with emphasis on his contributions to the architecture and furnishing of Adirondack private camps (VII).

HALLOCK, CHARLES, 1834-1917. Writer on sports, exploration, and travel, he was a frequent visitor to the Adirondacks from about 1865 to the end of the century. "The Raquette Club" in *Harper's*, Aug., 1870, and a chapter in *The Fishing Tourist*, N.Y., 1873 (VII), deal with the Adirondacks, as well as several articles in *Forest and Stream*, which he founded, edited, and published.

HAMMOND, SAMUEL H., 1809-1878. Editor of the Albany *State Register*, he vacationed frequently in the Adirondacks, where he could think, act, and feel "like a boy again." He was one of the first to propose that the forest be sealed up by the state constitution to conserve resources and provide wilderness recreation—a man thinks more and is better off in the woods than in the settlements, as he quotes a guide. His best work is *Wild Northern Scenes: or Sporting Adventures with the Rifle and the Rod*, N.Y., 1857 (II); his rather stiff and mannered style is often redeemed by enthusiasm.

HEADLEY, JOEL T., 1813-1897. Preacher, journalist, and prolific writer of biographies, histories, and books of travel, he went to the Adirondacks in 1844, 1846, and later dates for health and recreation. His vivid style made him popular. Though Poe called him "the Autocrat of all Quacks," he wrote, as W. C. White says, "the best description of the Adirondack country at midcentury." *The Adirondack; or Life in the Woods*, N.Y., 1849 (VII, VIII), went through several reprintings and editions and was the standard travel guide for twenty years; the second edition of 1864 (III) contains material of a later trip of 1858. *Letters from the Backwoods and the Adirondac*, N.Y., 1850 (II), contains both new and overlapping material.

HENDERSON, DAVID, 1793-1845. A Scottish immigrant with much personal charm and administrative ability, son-in-law and associate of Archibald McIntyre, he was the manager of the Iron Works at Adirondac (later Tahawus) until his death in a shooting accident. The letter quoted in II appears in Arthur H. Masten's *Story of Adirondac*, N.Y., 1923.

HOCHSCHILD, HAROLD K., 1892-1981. Chairman and honorary chairman of Amax (formerly American Metal Climax), chairman of the Temporary Study Commission on the Future of the Adirondack Park, he devoted his years of semi-retirement to research and writing on the history of the central Adirondacks, which he had known since boyhood in Camp Eagle Nest on Eagle Lake. He was president of the Adirondack Historical Association and founder of the Adirondack Museum at Blue Mountain Lake. His monumental local history, *Township 34*, privately printed in 1952 (VII), has been reprinted in part, with revisions, in a series of booklets published by the Adirondack Museum in 1962.

HOFFMAN, CHARLES FENNO, 1806-1884. One-legged traveler (at eleven his right leg was crushed in a ferry-boat landing), frontier news correspondent, editor, poet, and novelist, he was, according to Poe, "chivalric to a fault, enthusiastic, frank without discourtesy, an ardent admirer of the beautful, a gentleman of the best school—a gentleman by birth, by education, and by instinct." He edited the *American Monthly Magazine* and later the weekly *New York Mirror*. In the latter he published a serial account of his trip to the Adirondacks in 1837, later to appear in the first volume of *Wild Scenes in the Forest and Prairie*, 2 vols., London, 1839 (III, X), New York edition, 1843. His book of poems, *The Vigil of Faith*, N.Y., 1842, has several on the Adirondacks. One of the most important and earliest of Adirondack writers, his *Wild Scenes* is a rare collectors' item today.

HOOKER, MILDRED P. STOKES, 1881-1970. Daughter of the New York banker Anson Phelps Stokes, she summered in the Adirondacks from childhood, first in the Stokes camp on an island in Upper St. Regis Lake and later in her own camp in the vicinity. Her little book *Camp Chronicles* (VII), privately printed in 1952 for family and friends, gives an engaging picture of daily life in the family camp of the eighties and after. In 1964 the book was reprinted for general circulation by the Adirondack Museum, with an introduction by Paul Jamieson.

JAMES, WILLIAM, 1842-1910. Philosopher, psychologist, Harvard professor, he was also an excellent writer, whose power of literary expression, John Dewey said, enriched philosophic literature. It also enriched the literature of Keene Valley, which he visited annually for refreshment. His genial temper, his nervous sensitivity, and his love of the woods and mountains are evident in his letters from and about the Adirondacks in *The Letters of William James*, edited by his son Henry James, 2 vols., Boston, 1920 (II, X). See also Josephine Goldmark's "An Adirondack Friendship: Letters of William James," *Atlantic*, Sept., Oct., 1934.

JOGUES, ISAAC, 1607-1646. French Jesuit missionary to the Hurons of Canada, first known white man to see Lake George, Father Jogues was captured by Mohawk Indians in 1642 and escaped after a year of torture and suffering. On a mission to the Mohawks in 1646 he was suspected of sorcery and killed. In 1930 he was pronounced Saint Isaac. His legendary story is told partly in his own words and partly by others in *The Jesuit Relations*, ed. R. G. Thwaites, Cleveland, 1896-1901, vols. 28, 31, 39 (I).

JONES, DICKEY. Writer of "A Summer among the Mountains," in *The Spirit of the Times*, April 2, 1853 (VIII), one of a series of eight articles on a trip through the Adirondacks.

KALINOWSKI, THOMAS, 1951—. A resident of Saranac Lake, he teaches field biology and ecology at Saranac Lake High School.

KAUFFMANN, JOHN M., 1923—. Canoeist, preservationist, writer, he has held positions with the National Park Service and recently served on the Alaska Task Force for the Department of the Interior. He writes for publications of the U.S. Department of the Interior and for *National Geographic Magazine* and is actively involved in river conservation matters. His book *Flow East*, N.Y., 1973 (IX), deals with the wild and scenic rivers of the northern Atlantic states and makes a strong plea for preservation.

LaBastille, Anne, 1938—. Wildlife ecologist, consultant, lecturer, writer, and photographer, she leads wildlife tours in the Caribbean and makes field studies of endangered species and surveys of proposed national parks or wildlife preserves. In 1974 she was awarded the gold medal of the World Wildlife Fund as conservationist of the year. Her permanent home is a cabin in the deep woods of the western Adirondacks. She is a commissioner of the Adirondack Park Agency. The author of many scientific articles and several books, she is most widely known for her autobiography, *Woodswoman*, N.Y., 1976 (X), the story of her life in the Adirondack log cabin.

Longstreth, T. Morris, 1886-1975. Teacher, poet, writer of travel books, histories, biographies, and novels, he lived for ten years at the Lake Placid Club, keeping weather records and writing books. His second book, *The Adirondacks*, N.Y., 1917 (quoted briefly in Obs), is the story of a tour through the Adirondack Park.

MacMullen, John (J. M. M.), 1818-1896. Classicist, teacher, and outdoorsman, he wrote several accounts of walking and boating tours, including "The Adirondacks in 1843," from the New York *Evening Post*, July 23, 1881 (III), reprinted in the *St. Lawrence Plaindealer* of Canton, N.Y., Aug. 24, 1881.

Macready, William Charles, 1793-1873. English Shakespearean actor and manager of Covent Garden Theatre and Drury Lane, he explored Indian Pass in 1844 while on a theatrical tour in America. His letter to his wife in section X, in the collections of the New-York Historical Society of New York City, appeared in print for the first time in a slightly corrupt version in Arthur H. Masten's *Story of Adirondac*, N.Y., 1923; reprinted in 1968, Syracuse.

MARSH, GEORGE PERKINS, 1801-1882. Diplomat, congressman, and author, he played a key role in the conservation movement of the nineteenth century. His book *Man and Nature*, 1864 (Obs), inveighs against the reckless waste and abuse of natural resources. With the Adirondacks in mind, Marsh advocates keeping large areas in their primitive condition.

MARSHALL, GEORGE, 1904—. Mountaineer, conservationist, editor, he grew up in the Adirondacks, summering at the family camp on Lower Saranac Lake, exploring, and mountain climbing. He is a past president of both the Wilderness Society and the Sierra Club and continues to be a member of the former's council, though now living in London. His "Approach to the Mountains" (II) appeared in the *Adirondac*, Mar.-Apr., 1955.

MARSHALL, ROBERT, 1901-1939. Mountaineer, forester, explorer, conservationist, and writer, he acquired in the Adirondacks the enthusiasms of his short but gallant life. With his brother George and their guide Herbert Clark, he climbed in his teens and early twenties all the high peaks of the Adirondacks. He is the author of *Arctic Village* and *The People's Forests;* a third book, *Arctic Wilderness*, 1956, was edited by George Marshall. At the time of his death he was chief of the Division of Recreation and Lands in the United States Forest Service. A great wilderness area was named for him. His articles on the Adirondacks appeared mostly in *High Spots*, including "Fourteen in One," Oct., 1932, and "Herbert Clark," Oct., 1933 (IX). At twenty-one he wrote a booklet entitled *The High Peaks of the Adirondacks*, Albany, 1922, published by the Adirondack Mountain Club (quoted briefly in X).

MATHER, FRED, 1833-1900. Expert on fish culture, writer on outdoor life, sportsman, he was ichthyologist with the Colvin survey and later in charge of the state fish hatchery at Cold Spring Harbor. Much of his writing is technical, but as a member of the editorial staff of *Forest and Stream*, he wrote many essays and narratives of men and sporting activities, often with an Adirondack setting. Some of these are collected in *Men I Have Fished With*, 1897, and *My Angling Friends*, N.Y., 1901 (III, V).

MERRIAM, CLINTON HART, 1855-1942. Naturalist, physician, and writer, he gave up the practice of medicine after six years for his scientific interests. He had started collecting in the Adirondacks at the age of twelve, and at sixteen he was invited to go as naturalist with the Yellowstone Survey. He founded the United States Bureau of Biological Survey and was research associate of the Smithsonian Institution till three years before his death. John Muir, John Burroughs, and Rudyard Kipling were his personal friends. He was president of the American Society of Naturalists, the American Society of Mammologists, and the American Ornithological Union. Though he explored and collected abroad and in every state of the union, he is closely associated with the Adirondack region through his early residence at the foot of its western slope, his years of observation of its wild life, and his popular "biographies" of animals read before the Linnaean Society of New York and published in *The Mammals of the Adirondack Region*, N.Y., 1884 (X).

MURRAY, HON. AMELIA MATILDA, 1795-1884. Writer on education and travel, daughter of Lord George Murray, bishop of St. Davids, she spent much of her youth at the court of George III, where her mother was appointed lady-in-waiting in 1808. She became a good botanist and amateur artist. In 1837 she was appointed maid of honor to Queen Victoria. In 1854-55 she toured North America and the Caribbean, including a journey by boat and foot across the Adirondacks. Returning to England a strong partisan of the abolition of slavery, she was reminded that court officials were not permitted to publish anything savoring of politics. She resigned her position at court to publish *Letters from the United States, Cuba and Canada*, 2 vols., London and New York, 1856 (VII, VIII), but was later reinstated at court as woman of the bedchamber.

MURRAY, WILLIAM HENRY HARRISON, 1840-1904. Writer, clergyman, strong advocate of the outdoor life, flamboyant per-

sonality, he was for seven years minister of the Park Street
Congregational Church in Boston. In the sixties he camped on an
island in Raquette Lake and in 1869 published a book entitled
Adventures in the Wilderness; or Camp-Life in the Adirondacks,
Boston (II, VII), which was an instant success and ran through
many printings. Although the extent of the "Murray Rush" has
been exaggerated (the Adirondacks were popular with tourists a
decade earlier), Murray's book did establish his right to the epithet
"Adirondack Murray." It was written, as Charles Hallock says,
con amore, with vigor and freshness. The first part is reasonably
accurate travel description; the last part, fiction. Adirondack guides
missed the transition from one to the other and, as Stoddard wrote,
"take him literally . . . and have come to the conclusion generally
that if his preaching is not a better guide to heaven than his book
to the Adirondacks, his congregation might manage to worry
through with a cheaper man." His *Adventures* is firmly established
as a classic of regional literature. In reading it, one can understand
the nostalgia of Charles Hallock looking back after thirty years
to the middle sixties: "'Adirondack Murray' had his camp then on
Raquette Lake . . . and his comely wife was with him, attired in
a Tam O'Shanter cap and mountain suit of red and crimson plaid.
How jaunty she looked! How hamadryadic! They kept open house
in those days, with the latch string out, and a halo of welcome
was luminous about the rustic roof. . . . Those were halcyon days
for all of us."

NIXON, EDGAR B., 1902—. Archivist of the Franklin D.
Roosevelt Library, editor of Roosevelt papers on conservation,
scholar, and mountaineer, for several years he edited the *Adirondac*, periodical of the Adirondack Mountain Club, and wrote for
it a series of articles equivocally called "The Armchair Mountaineer." The one on Scott Pond (X) appears in the May-June
issue, 1960.

OATES, JOYCE CAROL, 1938—. Born in Lockport, N.Y., she
has become one of America's leading women of letters, with a
distinguished output of poems, essays, short stories, plays, and

novels. She has held positions as professor of English and writer-in-residence at colleges and universities. She is a member of the American Academy and Institute of Arts and Letters and has received awards for her stories and novels. On the origin of *Bellefleur*, N.Y., 1980 (IV), she writes: "Haunted by a dim ghostly image of a garden . . . I set out originally to create an elaborate, baroque, barbarous metaphor for the unfathomable mysteries of the human imagination, but soon became involved in very literal events . . . [such as] the extraordinary wealth and power belonging to certain American 'aristocrats' (who did, in fact, build castles and immense mansions in what was called the North Country)."

ORTLOFF, GEORGE CHRISTIAN, 1948—. Journalist and civic leader, he served for several years on the Lake Placid Village Board before moving to Plattsburgh in 1981 to become anchorman-producer of WPTZ-TV's nightly news program. He was chief of awards and ceremonies during the 1980 Olympic Winter Games. He is co-author of *Lake Placid: The Olympic Years, 1932-1980*. His article in section II appeared in *Adirondack Life*, Jan.-Feb., 1980.

OSBOURNE, LLOYD, 1868-1947. Stepson of Robert Louis Stevenson, one-time collaborator with him, novelist and short story writer, he was nineteen during the fall and winter the Stevensons spent at Saranac. He writes of that experience in *An Intimate Portrait of R. L. S.* published first in *Scribner's Magazine*, Nov. 1923-Feb. 1924 (IV), and later in book form.

PARKMAN, FRANCIS, 1823-1893. Historian of the American forest, he said of himself that "his thoughts were always in the forest, whose feature possessed his waking and sleeping dreams filling him with vague cravings impossible to satisfy." One of those cravings which he did superbly satisfy was to write the story of the conflict of the English and the French for possession of a continent. This was an aim he set for himself as a sophomore at Harvard. His summer vacations took him to the wilderness of northern New Hampshire and New York as part of his apprentice-ship. He devoted forty years of semi-invalidism to the completion of his history of the French and English in North America. "It is a fortunate thing," wrote Theodore Roosevelt, "when some great historic event, or chain of events, is commemorated by a great historian; and it is a matter for no small congratulation that the greatest historian whom the United States has yet produced should have found ready to his hand the all-important and singularly dramatic struggle which decided whether the destiny of the North American continent should be shared by the French or the English race." The Lake Champlain-Lake George region is of course a major setting of *France and England in North America*. The selections in section I are from vols. 2 and 14 of the *Works of Francis Parkman*, Champlain edition, Boston, 1897.

POWNALL, THOMAS, 1722-1805. British colonial statesman, soldier, and geographer, he was appointed Governor of Massachu-setts in 1757. In 1776 he published his *Topographical Description of North America*. His later revision of this work for a second edition was not finally published until 1949 as *A Topographical Description of the Dominions of the United States of America* (Obs).

RADFORD, HARRY V., 1880-1913. Editor, apostle of "Adi-rondack Murray," he spent many summers in boyhood in the Adirondacks and started at eighteen a quarterly magazine, *Woods and Waters* (the selection in III is from Spring, 1904), devoted mainly to the region. It reached a circulation of twenty thousand before it came to an end in 1906. Radford conducted a campaign to restore moose and elk (unsuccessful) and beaver (successful) to the Adirondacks. He and a companion were murdered by Eskimo guides in a journey along the Mackenzie River in 1913.

REBEN, MARTHA, pseudonym of Martha Ruth Rebentisch, 1911-1964. Writer-naturalist, native of Manhattan, she came to Sar-anac Lake as an invalid—TB patient—at the age of twenty and re-mained till her death at fifty-three. For ten years, from 1931-1941, she camped on Weller Pond under the care of her guide, Fred Rice; in subsequent years she camped at other locations. In her three books—*The Healing Woods*, 1952, *The Way of the Wilderness*, 1955, and *A Sharing of Joy*, 1963 (X)—to a modest degree she "did for Weller Pond what Thoreau did for Walden Pond— enshrined it in literature. . . . She came to the pond in search of health and found there a way of life," as Charles Roseberry remarks in a biographical essay in *Adirondack Life*, Summer 1975.

RIKHOFF, JEAN, 1928—. Writer and professor, she has taught writing at Adirondack Community College in Glens Falls for the last fifteen years. She writes short stories, poems, articles, and novels. In England she started a literary magazine, *Quixote*. Her novel *Buttes Landing*, 1973 (IV), is the chronicle of an Adirondack farm family from pioneer times till after the Civil War.

RONDEAU, NOAH JOHN, 1883-1967. Trouble with the Conservation Department sent him into year-round retreat from civilization. His "Cold River City" consisted of two log huts— Town Hall, his living quarters, and the Hall of Records—and three wigwams, one of which he called the Beauty Parlor, where with female hikers on the Northville-Lake Placid Trail he practiced his old trade of barber by touching up eyebrows. Forced to leave his hermitage in 1950 when the Cold River area was closed after the Big Blow, he spent some time as Santa Claus at the North Pole on Whiteface Mountain. For the fullest account of his life and some of his writings, see Maitland C. DeSormo's *Noah John Rondeau, Adirondack Hermit* and Adolph G. Dittmar's "Rondeau" in *The Adirondack High Peaks*, ed. Grace Hudowalski, Albany, 1970 (VIII).

ROOSEVELT, THEODORE, 1858-1919. Twenty-sixth President of the United States, big game hunter, and prolific writer, he had closer relations to the Adirondacks than any other occupant of the White House (see Edward J. Blankman's "Hail to the Chief," *Adirondack Life*, Winter 1976). He made several trips to the central Adirondacks in youth. In 1877 he was co-author of *Summer*

Birds of the Adirondacks in Franklin County. The account of an early hunting episode in the Paul Smiths area in section X is from *Outdoor Pastimes of an American Hunter*, N.Y., 1905. The climax of his Adirondack adventures came one day in 1901 when he was called down from Mount Marcy with news of McKinley's approaching death. He made the risky midnight ride over rough roads to the railhead at North Creek, becoming President en route (V).

SARGENT, CHARLES SPRAGUE, 1841-1927. Dendrologist, Harvard professor, director of the Arnold Arboretum, he played a leading role in bringing about the preservation of Adirondack and Catskill forest areas. His statement in Obs appeared in an article in the *Nation*, Dec. 6, 1883, two years before the creation of the Forest Preserve.

SCHAEFER, PAUL, 1908—. Architect and contractor in Schenectady, specializing in the building and restoration of Early American period homes, he has made a second career of defending the Forest Preserve. No man in our time has been more vigilant in this capacity. His latest venture is directing the production of Adirondack films. *The Adirondack—the Land Nobody Knows* has won several awards in international amateur film contests. His article in VI appeared in *The Living Wilderness*, Autumn 1965.

SEARS, GEORGE WASHINGTON (NESSMUK), 1821-1890. Shoemaker, woodsman, writer on the outdoors, he made three cruises on Adirondack waterways in lightweight canoes in the early eighties. His accounts of these trips in eighteen letters in *Forest and Stream* have been reprinted in *The Adirondack Letters of George Washington Sears*, introduced by Dan Brenan and published by the Adirondack Museum, Blue Mountain Lake, 1962 (VII, IX). Nessmuk is also the author of a popular manual, *Woodcraft*, 1884, and a book of verse, *Forest Runes*, 1887.

SIMMS, JEPTHA ROOT, 1807-1883. Historian of the frontier in New York State, he left his mark on the methods of historical research of his day. He traveled for several years with horse and carriage through the central counties of the state, interviewing early settlers and old people generally and zealously recording every crumb of fact, tradition, and observation. His own avid pleasure in telling detail is evident throughout his *Trappers of New York*, Albany, 1850 (II), 1871, and 1981 (by Harbor Hill Books).

SMITH, CLYDE H., 1931—. A freelance photographer, writer, and outdoorsman, he lives in Westport on the eastern fringe of the Adirondacks. His photographs have appeared in leading magazines and in his own books, in one of which, *The Adirondacks*, N.Y., 1976, he tells what the Adirondacks have meant to him. Tony Atwill calls him "a man who knows the essence of the Adirondacks" and whose photos "capture the mystical quality" of the region. "Heavy Water" (IX) appeared in the May-June 1981 issue of *Adirondack Life*.

SMITH, MASON, 1936—. Freelance writer, he contributes to *Sports Illustrated*, *Adirondack Life*, and other periodicals, many of his essays having Adirondack settings. His novel, *Everybody Knows and Nobody Cares*, 1971, was widely acclaimed. "Conflict of Interests" (II) appeared in the Jan.-Feb. 1981 issue of *Adirondack Life* under the title of "The Adirondack Council."

STALLKNECHT, F. S., 1820-1874. Immigrant from the island of Viborg, Denmark, in 1834, he studied law at Harvard and, as a New York City lawyer, specialized in admiralty cases. His varied interests included Arctic exploration (he was a member of the Explorers Club), literature, philosophy, and Meissen porcelain. His "Sporting Tour in August, 1858" appeared in *Leslie's Illustrated Weekly Newspaper*, Nov. 13, 20, 1858 (III).

STEVENSON, MARGARET ISABELLA BALFOUR, 1829-1897. Mother of R. L. S., she accompanied him on his travels after the death of her husband. Her letters give more of the detail of daily life in Saranac Lake than his: *From Saranac to the Marquesas and Beyond*, edited by her sister. M. C. Balfour, London, 1903 (IV).

STEVENSON, ROBERT LOUIS, 1850-1894. Poet, essayist, novelist, and traveler, he suffered from chronic lung disease and made frequent journeys in quest of health. One of these took him to the Adirondacks in the fall and winter of 1887-88. The year was a productive and healthful one for him, though he grumbled about the cold and changeable weather. He was a friend and patient of Dr. Trudeau. His writings about the Adirondacks consist of a ballad, "Ticonderoga," based on the legend of Duncan Campbell, the closing scenes of the novel *The Master of Ballantrae*, and his personal letters from Saranac Lake, in *The Letters of Robert Louis Stevenson to His Family and Friends*, London and New York, 1899, vol. 2 (IV). The house the Stevensons lived in in Saranac is now open to the public as a museum.

STILLMAN, WILLIAM JAMES, 1828-1901. Artist, journalist, adventurer, and foreign consul, he spent several summers in the Adirondacks in the 1850s in search of solitude and new subjects to paint. He became an expert woodsman and was the instigator and leader of the camping trip of 1858 on Follensby Pond in which ten notables of the Boston-Cambridge-Concord area took part. The following year he set up another camp for the Adirondack Club of Boston on Ampersand Lake. His writing about the Adirondacks includes letters (see Ida G. Everson, "William J. Stillman: Emerson's 'Gallant Artist,'" in *New England Quarterly*, March, 1958), magazine articles reprinted in *The Old Rome and the New and Other Studies*, London, 1897, and *Autobiography of a Journalist*, vol. 1, Boston, 1901 (II, IV).

STODDARD, SENECA RAY, 1844-1917. Traveler, photographer, editor, author of guidebooks, he founded and edited *Stoddard's Northern Monthly*, 1906-1908, the early issues of which were devoted largely to the Adirondacks. From 1874 to 1913 he brought out annually his popular illustrated guidebook, *The Adirondacks*. The selection in III is from the edition of 1879.

STREET, ALFRED BILLINGS, 1811-1881. Historian, state librarian, poet, he is the writer of two books of travel and description about the Adirondacks. The better of the two, *Woods and Waters; or the Saranac and Racket*, N.Y. 1860 (IV), 1981 (Harbor Hill Books), is the narrative of one or more trips taken, by internal evidence, between 1854 and 1858. *The Indian Pass*, N.Y., 1869, shows enthusiasm but is written in an exclamatory, rhetorical style discouraging to modern readers.

THOREAU, HENRY DAVID, 1817-1862. The foremost of American nature writers knew the Adirondacks only at second hand. His remark in "Observations," quoted from the first part of *The Maine Woods*, first published in 1848, is made to illustrate the point that America in mid-nineteenth century was still an exceedingly new country, with vast areas as yet unexplored and unsettled. If Thoreau had joined his neighbors and friends in the famous Adirondack expedition of 1858, Philosophers' Camp would be an even better story than it is (II). Perhaps a more seemly one too, for he might have restrained the litterbugs among those ten sages. On Emerson's return to Concord, Thoreau wrote in his journal for August 23, 1858, "Emerson says that he and Agassiz and Company broke some dozens of ale-bottles, one after another, with their bullets, in Adirondack country, using them for marks! It sounds rather Cockneyish." So it does, with its dismaying evidence that *slobus americanus* taints even our best and wisest when loose in the woods. For all his practice in marksmanship, the only game Emerson brought down in the Adirondacks, offered as a specimen to Agassiz, was a luckless little "peetweet" (spotted sandpiper), doubtless shot at close range.

THORPE, THOMAS BANGS, 1815-1878. Writer on historical subjects and travel, he had the reputation of a humorist in his day. His "Visit to 'John Brown's Tract,'" *Harper's New Monthly*, July, 1859 (VIII), is of interest historically in spite of its inaccuracy.

TODD, JOHN, 1800-1873. Congregational clergyman, religious leader in western Massachusetts, writer, he published about thirty volumes and was widely read in this country and abroad. One of the least pretentious of his books at the time of publication has kept his name alive, a little travel book called *Long Lake*, Pittsfield, Mass., 1845 (II, VIII), "a blend of Adirondack enthusiasm and pastoral sentimentality of the lachrymose type," as Donaldson calls it. It is invaluable as a picture of pioneer life in the central Adirondacks in the early 1840s. The author was a lover of the woods who came to the Adirondacks every summer for twenty years to hunt and fish. It was probably he whom Longfellow had in mind in lines from *Tales of a Wayside Inn*:

> The wrath of God he preached from year to year,
> And read with fervor Edwards' "On the Will."
> His favorite pastime was to slay the deer,
> In summer, on some Adirondack hill.

TRUDEAU, EDWARD LIVINGSTON, M.D., 1848-1915. Physician, pioneer in the scientific study of tuberculosis in America, he himself developed the disease in 1873 and, with little expectation of a cure, came to the Adirondacks to enjoy what he could of his favorite sports of hunting and fishing. His health improved and he stayed, summering for some years at Paul Smiths, wintering in Saranac, and practicing medicine. His name is intimately associated with Adirondack history. On land given to him, he set up the first sanatorium in America, meeting the yearly deficits by donations of his own and by the solicitation of gifts. "Optimism," he said, "was about my only asset when I built my first little sanatorium cottage on a remote hillside in an uninhabited and inaccessible region." His personal charm, optimism, and love of people won him countless friends and grateful patients. One of the latter, Alfred Donaldson, calls his career "a sheer triumph of personality"; "few men have ever opened for themselves or others so many avenues of victory for the vanquished." He gave Saranac Lake a worldwide reputation as a center of health and medical skill until modern methods of cure were developed. *An Autobiography*, Phila., 1916 (II).

TWICHELL, REV. JOSEPH HOPKINS, 1838-1918. Congregational clergyman in Hartford, Conn., he was an intimate friend of Mark Twain, Charles Dudley Warner, and Noah Porter, president of Yale. After the latter's death he contributed a memoir of Porter's association with the Adirondacks to *Noah Porter*: *A Memorial by Friends*, ed. G. S. Merriam, N.Y., 1893 (X).

VAN DYKE, HENRY, 1852-1933. Author, preacher, educator, diplomat, he was Murray Professor of English Literature at Princeton and a many-sided man of letters, publishing volumes of poems, essays, stories, travel sketches, and literary criticism. His popularity declined along with the vogue of the "genteel tradition," which he represented. His essay on Ampersand Mountain, in *Harper's New Monthly*, July, 1885, reprinted in *Little Rivers*, remains of interest even though, in parts omitted from the selection in IX, it gives some misinformation on forest zones on a mountainside.

VISCOME, LAURA. Journalist and civic leader of Lake Placid, as associate editor of the Lake Place *News* until recently she wrote a weekly column "Odds and Ends" and contributed special articles like the one on the lost climbers of Algonquin (VI).

WACHUSETT. According to a letter from William K. Verner to Kenneth Durant in the Durant collection at the Adirondack Museum, "Wachusett" is probably the pseudonym of one George S. Woods of Boston.

WARNER, CHARLES DUDLEY, 1829-1900. Essayist, novelist, and newspaper editor in Hartford, Conn., he was also a contributor to the *Atlantic* and *Harper's* and editor with his brother of a library of world classics. Though mannered at times, his informal essays on the Adirondacks are a pleasant blend of irony, humor, and enthusiasm. Most of them appear in the volume *In the Wilderness*, Boston, 1878, and numerous other editions and reprintings. The title, a deliberate echo of *Adventures in the Wilderness*, suggests Warner's intention of indulging in a little polite spoofing of "Adirondack" Murray. "How I Killed a Bear" is a classic of Adirondack humor (V), and if Orson Phelps is the best known of Adirondack guides, it is because of Warner's profile of him (III). J. P. Lundy, jealous perhaps of Warner's popularity with readers, says that Warner wrote facetious nonsense for that stronghold of

Boston blue bloods, the *Atlantica Menstrua*. As an Adirondack writer, however, Warner will hold his place for a long time. The problem of an anthologist is which of his essays to choose.

WESTON, HAROLD, 1894-1972. An artist who, unlike Winslow Homer, was articulate enough to write a book on the interrelations of artist and Adirondack landscape, Weston had a lifelong association with the Adirondack Mountain Reserve-Ausable Club. It was his summer playground in youth, hermitage for charting an independent course in art, and year-round home for his family. His *Freedom in the Wilds*, St. Huberts, N.Y., 1971 (V), testifies that wilderness tracts like that magnificent cleft in the mountains where he spent most of his life stir and sustain the wilderness within, from which the creative impulse springs.

WHITE, WILLIAM CHAPMAN, 1903-1955. Traveler, foreign correspondent, columnist, and writer of books, he summered for several years at Lake Colby in the village of Saranac Lake and in 1950 settled there the year-round to become a native, with an active interest in civic affairs. During the last six years of his life he wrote frequently about Adirondack people and places in columns in *The New York Times* and in the New York *Herald Tribune*. Written with the seeing eye of the journalist and the charm of the familiar essayist, these columns "constituted Bill's love letter," writes Roger Tubby, "to the country where he lived his last years and found the greatest happiness." Many of them are collected in *Just About Everything in the Adirondacks*, published by the Adirondack Museum in 1960. "Merry Christmas" appeared originally in the *Herald Tribune*, Dec. 25, 1952 (VIII). White's book *Adirondack Country*, 1954, 1967 (Obs and epigraph in X), is the most comprehensive book on the region since Donaldson's *History*.

WILSON, SLOAN, 1920—. Novelist, autobiographer, lecturer, and writer-in-residence, he has had a long association with the Adirondacks in his family's camp on Lake George, as a graduate of the Florida-Adirondack School, from which he went to Harvard, and as resident of Ticonderoga for several years in the 1970s. His reputation as a fiction writer was established by *The Man in the Gray Flannel Suit*. His novels with an Adirondack setting are *All the Best People* (Lake George) and *Small Town*, N.Y., 1978 (VIII), the absorbing story of a typical eastern Adirondack village in the 1970s.

WOODS, GEORGE A., 1926—. Journalist, editor, he was born and grew up in the Adirondacks. He graduated from Fordham College with a degree in journalism. In 1963 he became children's book editor of *The New York Times Book Review*. His *Vibrations*, N.Y., 1970 (VIII), is a first-person memoir type of novel about growing up in an Adirondack resort community—the long, harsh winters of boredom and the short, full summers when city people return, bringing money, excitement, and glamorous girls.

Index